Unlock the Bible:
Keys to Discovering the People and Places

Other Unlock the Bible Titles

Unlock the Bible: Keys to Understanding the Scripture

Unlock the Bible: Keys to Exploring the Culture and Times

Unlock the Bible

Keys to Discovering the
People and Places

General Editor
Ronald F. Youngblood

General Editor of Original Edition
Herbert Lockyer Sr.

Consulting Editors
F. F. Bruce   R. K. Harrison

THOMAS NELSON
Since 1798

NASHVILLE   DALLAS   MEXICO CITY   RIO DE JANEIRO

Published in Nashville, Tennessee, by Thomas Nelson. Thomas Nelson is a registered trademark of Thomas Nelson, Inc.

Book design and composition by Upper Case Textual Services, Lawrence, Massachusetts.

Thomas Nelson, Inc., titles may be purchased in bulk for educational, business, fund-raising, or sales promotional use. For information, please e-mail SpecialMarkets@ ThomasNelson.com.

The material in this book originally was published in another form in *Nelson's New Illustrated Bible Dictionary*, copyright © 1986, 1995 by Thomas Nelson Publishers, Inc., all rights reserved.

Unless otherwise noted, Scripture quotations are taken from the New King James Version, copyright © 1982 by Thomas Nelson Publishers, Inc., all rights reserved.

Verses marked NASB are taken from the NEW AMERICAN STANDARD BIBLE®. © The Lockman Foundation 1960, 1962, 1963, 1968, 1971, 1972, 1973, 1975, 1977. Used by permission.

Verses marked NIV are taken from the HOLY BIBLE: NEW INTERNATIONAL VERSION®. © 1973, 1978, 1984 by International Bible Society. Used by permission of Zondervan Publishing House. All rights reserved.

Verses marked NRSV are taken from the NEW REVISED STANDARD VERSION of the Bible. © 1989 by the Division of Christian Education of the National Council of the Churches of Christ in the U. S. A. All rights reserved.

Verses marked REB are taken from the REVISED ENGLISH BIBLE, © 1989. The delegates of the Oxford University Press and the Syndics of the Cambridge University Press. Used by Permission.

Verses marked RSV are taken from REVISED STANDARD VERSION of the Bible. © 1946, 1952, 1971, 1973 by the Division of Christian Education of the National Council of the Churches of Christ in the U. S. A. Used by permission.

978-1-4185-4724-0

Printed in the United States of America

11 12 13 QG 6 5 4 3 2 1

Contents

A

B

C

D

E

G

H

I

J

K

L

M

N

O

P

R

S

T

U

V

Z

Contributors

Robert L. Alden
  Conservative Baptist Seminary, Denver, Colorado
Leslie C. Allen
  Fuller Theological Seminary, Pasadena, California
Ronald B. Allen
  Christian Theological Seminary, Indianapolis, Indiana
Timothy R. Ashley
  Acadia Divinity College, Wolfville, Nova Scotia, Canada
David W. Baker
  Ashland Theological Seminary, Ashland, Ohio
John J. Bimson
  Trinity College, Bristol, England
E. M. Blaiklock
  Auckland, New Zealand
Gerald Borchert
  Southern Baptist Theological Seminary, Louisville, Kentucky
Stephen G. Brown
  Shasta Bible College, Redding, California
F. F. Bruce
  University of Manchester, Manchester, England
John A. Burns
  Retired from Criswell Center for Biblical Studies, Dallas, Texas
Newton L. Bush
  Lima, Ohio
G. Lloyd Carr
  Retired from Gordon College, Wenham, Massachusetts
E. Clark Copeland
  Reformed Presbyterian Theological Seminary, Pittsburgh, Pennsylvania

Leonard J. Coppes
  Denver, Colorado

Walter M. Dunnett
  Retired from Northwestern College, St. Paul, Minnesota

Kendell H. Easley
  Mid-America Baptist College, Memphis, Tennessee

Kermit A. Ecklebarger
  Conservative Baptist Seminary, Denver, Colorado

James R. Edwards
  Jamestown College, Jamestown, North Dakota

John M. Elliott
  Aurora, Illinois

Millard J. Erickson
  Bethel Theological Seminary, St. Paul, Minnesota

Harvey E. Finley
  Retired from Nazarene Theological Seminary, Kansas City, Missouri

Royce G. Gruenler
  Gordon-Conwell Theological Seminary, South Hamilton, Massachusetts

Timothy Hadley
  Lubbock Christian University, Lubbock, Texas

Donald A. Hagner
  Fuller Theological Seminary, Pasadena, California

R. K. Harrison
  Wycliffe College, Toronto, Ontario, Canada

Harvey Hartman
  Liberty Baptist College, Lynchburg, Virginia

Robert Hendren
  Donelson, Tennessee

Herschel H. Hobbs
  Oklahoma City, Oklahoma

Harold W. Hoehner
  Dallas Theological Seminary, Dallas, Texas

John J. Hughes
  Whitefish, Montana

Robert Hughes
  Miami Christian College, Miami, Florida

Harry B. Hunt Jr.
  Southwestern Baptist Theological Seminary, Fort Worth, Texas

W. Bingham Hunter
  Trinity Evangelical Divinity School, Deerfield, Illinois

David K. Huttar
    Nyack College, Nyack, New York
William W. Klein
    Conservative Baptist Seminary, Denver, Colorado
Woodrow M. Kroll
    Back to the Bible, Lincoln, Nebraska
Alvin S. Lawhead
    Nazarene Theological Seminary, Kansas City, Missouri
Gordon Lewis
    Conservative Baptist Seminary, Denver, Colorado
Jack P. Lewis
    Harding Graduate School of Religion, Memphis, Tennessee
Walter L. Liefeld
    Trinity Evangelical Divinity School, Deerfield, Illinois
G. Herbert Livingston
    Retired from Asbury Theological Seminary, Wilmore, Kentucky
Tremper Longman, III
    Westminster Theological Seminary, Philadelphia, Pennsylvania
Robert S. MacLennan
    McAlester College, St. Paul, Minnesota
W. Harold Mare
    Covenant Theological Seminary, St. Louis, Missouri
Elmer A. Martens
    Mennonite Brethren Biblical Seminary, Fresno, California
Wayne O. McCready
    University of Calgary, Alberta, Canada
Scot McKnight
    Trinity Evangelical Divinity School, Deerfield, Illinois
Janet McNish
    Nashville, Tennessee
Robert R. Moore
    Asbury College, Wilmore, Kentucky
William Mounce
    Azusa Pacific College, Azusa, California
John Nolland
    Regent College, Vancouver, British Columbia, Canada
Dave O'Brien
    St. Paul Bible College, Bible College, Minnesota
Vernon S. Olson
    St. Bonifacius, Minnesota

Grant R. Osborne
   Trinity Evangelical Divinity School, Deerfield, Illinois

Mildred Ottinger
   Nashville, Tennessee

Arthur G. Patzia
   Fuller Seminary, Pasadena, California

Gary Pratico
   Gordon-Conwell Divinity School, South Hamilton, Massachusetts

Richard A. Purdy
   West Norwalk, Connecticut

Robert V. Rakestraw
   The Criswell College, Dallas, Texas

John Rasko
   Alaska Bible College, Glennallen, Alaska

Richard O. Rigsby
   Talbot Theological Seminary, La Mirada, California

Allen P. Ross
   Dallas Theological Seminary, Dallas, Texas

Glenn E. Schaefer
   Simpson College, San Francisco, California

Stephen R. Schrader
   Liberty Baptist Seminary, Lynchburg, Virginia

Jack B. Scott
   Decatur, Georgia

Martin J. Selman
   Spurgeon's College, London, England

Norman Shepherd
   Minneapolis, Minnesota

Gary V. Smith
   Bethel Theological Seminary, St. Paul, Minnesota

Douglas K. Stuart
   Gordon-Conwell Theological Seminary, South Hamilton, Massachusetts

Robert L. Thomas
   Talbot Theological Seminary, La Mirada, California

Willem A. VanGemeren
   Reformed Theological Seminary, Jackson, Mississippi

Dolores Walker
   Walla Walla, Washington

Larry L. Walker
   Mid-America Baptist Seminary, Memphis, Tennessee

Daniel B. Wallace
  Mukilteo, Washington
Forest Weddle
  Fort Wayne Bible College, Fort Wayne, Indiana
Tom Wells
  Cincinnati, Ohio
Stephen Westerholm
  Toronto, Ontario, Canada
Frederick E. Young
  Central Baptist Seminary, Kansas City, Kansas
Ronald F. Youngblood
  Bethel Theological Seminary, West San Diego, California

AARON [EHR un] — brother of Moses and first high priest of the Hebrew nation. Very little is known about Aaron's early life, other than his marriage to Elisheba, daughter of Amminadab (Ex. 6:23).

When God called Moses to lead the Hebrew people out of slavery in Egypt, Moses protested that he would not be able to speak convincingly to the pharaoh. So Aaron was designated by God as Moses' official spokesman (Ex. 4:14–16). At Moses' instruction, Aaron also performed miracles as signs for the release of the Hebrews. Aaron's rod turned into a serpent that swallowed the rods of the Egyptian magicians (Ex. 7:8–20). Aaron also caused frogs to cover the land by stretching his rod over the lakes and streams of Egypt (Ex. 8:6).

Aaron held an important place of leadership because of his work with his brother, Moses. A central figure in the exodus from Egypt, he also received instructions from God for observing the first Passover (Ex. 12:1). In the wilderness he assisted Moses in keeping order and rendering judgments over the people (Num. 15:33). Both he and Moses were singled out when the people complained about the harsh conditions of these wilderness years (Num. 14:2).

When the priesthood was instituted in the wilderness, Moses consecrated Aaron as the first high priest of Israel (Exodus 28–29; Leviticus 8–9). The priesthood was set within the tribe of Levi, from which Aaron was descended. Aaron's sons (Nadab, Abihu, Eleazar, and Ithamar) inherited the position of high priest from their father (Num. 3:2–3). Aaron was given special robes to wear, signifying his status within the priesthood (Lev. 8:7–9). At his death the robes were transferred to his oldest living son, Eleazar (Num. 20:25–28). The tabernacle, the main sanctuary of worship, was placed under Aaron's supervision (Numbers 4). He received instructions from God on the functions of the priesthood and the tabernacle (Numbers 18). He alone, serving in the capacity of high priest, went into the Holy of Holies once a year to represent the people on the Day of Atonement.

In spite of his responsibility for the spiritual leadership of the nation, Aaron committed a serious sin in the wilderness surrounding Mount Sinai. While Moses was on the mountain praying to God and receiving His commandments, the people demanded that Aaron make one or more gods for them to worship. Aaron made no attempt to stop the people and made a golden calf for them (Ex. 32:1–10). Aaron was saved from God's wrath only because Moses interceded on his behalf (Deut. 9:20).

After all their years of leading the people, neither Moses nor Aaron was permitted to enter the promised land. Apparently this was because they did not make it clear that God would provide for the Hebrews' needs when they believed they would die for lack of water in the wilderness (Num. 20:12). Aaron died at Mount Hor, and Moses died later in Moab.

Upon arriving at Mount Hor from the wilderness of Kadesh, Aaron was accompanied by Moses and his son Eleazar to the top of the mountain. There he was stripped of his high priestly garments, which were transferred to Eleazar. After Aaron's death, the community mourned for 30 days (Num. 20:22–29).

The book of Hebrews contrasts the imperfect priesthood of Aaron with the perfect priesthood of Christ (Heb. 5:2–5; 7:11–12). Christ's priesthood is compared to the order of Melchizedek because it is an eternal office with no beginning and no end. Thus, it replaces the priesthood of Aaron.

ABED-NEGO [uh BED knee goe] (*servant of Nebo*) — the Chaldean name given to Azariah in King Nebuchadnezzar's court when he was chosen as one of the king's servants (Dan. 1:7; 2:49). With Shadrach and Meshach, Abed-Nego was thrown into the fiery furnace for refusing to bow down and worship a golden image. The three men were miraculously protected from the fire (Dan. 3:12–30). Like the three Hebrew men in the fiery furnace, the nation of Israel endured the captivity and were miraculously protected by God.

ABEL [A buhl] (*breath, vapor*) — the name of a person and two places in the Old Testament:

1. The second son of Adam and Eve (Gen. 4:2). His brother Cain, who was a farmer, brought an offering of his produce to the Lord. Abel, a shepherd, brought to the Lord an offering "of the firstlings [the best quality] of his flock." Genesis records: "And the Lord respected Abel and his offering, but he did not respect Cain and his offering" (Gen. 4:4–5). Envious of Abel, Cain killed his brother and was cursed by God for the murder.

In the New Testament, Abel is described as a man of faith, who "offered a more excellent sacrifice than Cain" (Heb. 11:4). Cain murdered his brother Abel, writes John, "because his [Cain's] works were evil and his brother's [Abel's] righteous" (1 John 3:12). Jesus spoke of "the blood of righteous Abel" (Matt. 23:35; Luke 11:51) and implied that Abel, the first righteous martyr, anticipated in symbol His own death on Calvary at the hands of evil men. The blood of the new covenant, however, "speaks better things than that of Abel" (Heb. 12:24). The blood of Abel cried out for vengeance; the blood of Christ speaks of salvation.

2. A large stone in the field of Joshua of Beth Shemesh on which the ark of the covenant was set by the Philistines (1 Sam. 6:18).

3. A fortified city in northern Israel, which Joab besieged after the rebellion of Sheba (2 Sam. 20:14–15, 18). This city, called Abel of Beth Maachah, is probably the same place as Abel Beth Maachah.

ABIATHAR [a BY uh thar] (*father of abundance*) — one of two chief priests in the court of David. Abiathar was the son of Ahimelech of the priestly clan of Eli from Shiloh (1 Sam. 22:20). When the residents of the priestly village of Nob were massacred by Saul for helping David, Abiathar was the only one to escape (1 Sam. 22:6–23). When David eventually became king, he appointed Abiathar, along with Zadok, as priests in the royal court (2 Sam. 8:17; 1 Chr. 18:16).

When David's son Absalom tried to take his throne by force, David was forced to leave Jerusalem. Zadok and Abiathar carried the ark of the covenant out of the capital city but later returned it at the command of David (2 Sam. 15:29). Both priests remained in Jerusalem to inform David of Absalom's plans (2 Sam. 15:34). After Absalom's death, Abiathar and Zadok carried the message of reconciliation to Amasa and the elders of Judah (2 Sam. 19:11–14).

During the struggle over who would succeed as king, Abiathar supported Adonijah. When Solomon emerged as the new ruler, Zadok was appointed priest of the royal court, while Abiathar escaped execution only because of his earlier loyalty to David. He and his family were banished to Anathoth, and his rights and privileges as a Jerusalem priest were taken away (1 Kin. 1:7–25; 2:22–35).

Some scholars believe Abiathar may have written portions of 1 and 2 Samuel, especially the sections describing the royal court life under David.

ABIGAIL [AB ih gale] (*father of joy*) — one or two Old Testament women had this delightful name:

1. Wife of Nabal the Carmelite and, after his death, of David (1 Sam. 25:3, 14–42; 2 Sam. 2:2; 1 Chr. 3:1). Abigail's husband, Nabal, was an ill-tempered, drunken man. When David was hiding from the jealous King Saul, he asked Nabal for food for himself and his men. Nabal blatantly refused. Angered, David threatened to plunder Nabal's possessions and kill Nabal himself. Abigail, in her wisdom, gathered enough food for David's men, rode out to meet David, and bowed before him to show her respect. By agreeing with David that Nabal had acted with great disrespect, she stemmed David's anger. To Abigail's credit, she did not leave her godless husband. When Nabal died, apparently from shock at discovering his near brush with death, David married Abigail and she later bore him a son, Chileab.

2. A sister or half-sister of David and mother of Amasa, whom Absalom made captain of the army instead of Joab (2 Sam. 17:25; Abigal, NRSV, REB; 1 Chr. 2:16–17). She may be the same person as No. 1.

ABIMELECH [uh BIM eh leck] (*my father is king*) — the name of five men in the Old Testament:

1. The king of Gerar in the time of Abraham (Gen. 20:1–18; 21:22–34). Fearing for his own safety, Abraham introduced Sarah, his wife, as his sister when he entered Abimelech's territory. Abimelech claimed Sarah for his harem, only to be warned in a dream that he had taken the wife of another man. Then Abimelech returned Sarah to Abraham. The two men made a covenant with each other, and Abraham asked God to reward the king by giving him many children. Many scholars believe

that the word Abimelech is not a proper name but a royal title of the Philistine kings, just as pharaoh was a title for Egyptian kings.

2. The king of Gerar in the time of Isaac (Gen. 26:1–31).

3. The ruler of the city of Shechem during the period of the judges (Judg. 8:30–10:1; 2 Sam. 11:21). Abimelech was a son of Gideon by a concubine from Shechem. Abimelech tried to become king, and he did reign over Israel for three years (Judg. 9:22). In order to eliminate all who might challenge his authority, he killed all the other sons of Gideon—his brothers and half-brothers—who were potential successors of his father (Judg. 9:5).

Abimelech was killed in a battle at Thebez, a city northeast of Shechem, which he surrounded with his army. When Abimelech ventured too close to the city tower, a woman dropped a millstone on his head, crushing his skull. Abimelech commanded his armorbearer to kill him so it could not be said that he died at the hands of a woman (Judg. 9:50–54; 2 Sam. 11:21).

4. A priest in the time of David (1 Chr. 18:16).

5. A Philistine king whom David met while fleeing from King Saul (Psalm 34, title). Abimelech is apparently the royal title of Achish the king of Gath (1 Sam. 21:10–15).

ABRAHAM [AY bruh ham] (*father of a multitude*); originally Abram (*exalted father*) — the first great Patriarch of ancient Israel and a primary model of faithfulness for Christianity. The accounts about Abraham are found in Genesis 11:26–25:11, with the biblical writer focusing on four important aspects of his life.

The Migration. Abraham's story begins with his migration with the rest of his family from Ur of the Chaldeans in ancient southern Babylonia (Gen. 11:31). He and his family moved north along the trade routes of the ancient world and settled in the flourishing trade center of Haran, several hundred miles to the northwest.

While living in Haran, at the age of 75 Abraham received a call from God to go to a strange, unknown land that God would show him. The Lord promised Abraham that He would make him and his descendants a great nation (Gen. 12:1–3). The promise must have seemed unbelievable to Abraham because his wife Sarah (called Sarai in the early part of the story) was childless (Gen. 11:30–31; 17:15). But Abraham obeyed God with no hint of doubt or disbelief. He took his wife and his nephew, Lot, and went to the land that God would show him.

Abraham moved south along the trade routes from Haran, through Shechem and Bethel in the land of Canaan. Canaan was a populated area at the time, inhabited by the warlike Canaanites; so Abraham's belief that God would ultimately give this land to him and his descendants was an act of faith. The circumstances seemed quite difficult, but Abraham's faith in God's promises allowed him to trust in the Lord.

The Famine and the Separation from Lot. Because of a severe famine in the land of Canaan, Abraham moved to Egypt for a short time (Gen. 12:10–20). During this trip, Abraham introduced Sarah to the Egyptians as his sister rather than as his wife in order to avoid trouble. Pharaoh, the Egyptian ruler, then took Sarah as his wife. It was only because "the Lord plagued Pharaoh and his house with great plagues because of Sarai, Abram's wife" (Gen. 12:17), that Sarah was returned to Abraham.

Upon his return from Egypt, Abraham and his nephew, Lot, quarreled over pasturelands and went separate ways (Gen. 13:8–9). Lot settled in the Jordan River valley, while Abraham moved into Canaan. After this split, God reaffirmed His promise to Abraham: "And I will make your descendants as the dust of the earth; so that if a man could number the dust of the earth, then your descendants also could be numbered" (Gen. 13:16).

Apparently Abraham headed a strong military force by this time as he is called "Abram the Hebrew" (Gen. 14:13). He succeeded in rescuing his nephew Lot from the kings who had captured him while raiding the cities of Sodom and Gomorrah (Gen. 14:14–17).

The Promise Reaffirmed. In Genesis 15 the Lord reaffirmed His promise to Abraham. The relationship between God and Abraham should be understood as a covenant relationship—the most solemn form of arrangement between individuals in the ancient world. According to such an arrangement, individuals or groups agreed to abide by certain conditions that governed their relationship to each other. In this case Abraham agreed to go to the land that God would show him (an act of faith on his part), and God agreed to make Abraham a great nation (Gen. 12:1–3). However, in Genesis 15 Abraham became anxious about the promise of a nation being found in his descendants because of his advanced age. The Lord thus reaffirmed the earlier covenant.

As we know from recent archaeological discoveries, a common practice of that time among heirless families was to adopt a slave who would inherit the master's goods. Therefore, because Abraham was childless, he proposed to make a slave, Eliezer of Damascus, his heir (Gen. 15:2). But God rejected this action and challenged Abraham's faith: "Then he [God] brought him [Abraham] outside and said, 'Look now toward heaven, and count the stars if you are able to number them.' And He said to him, 'So shall your descendants be' " (Gen. 15:5). Abraham's response is the model of believing faith. "And he [Abraham] believed in the Lord, and He [God] accounted it to him for righteousness" (Gen. 15:6).

The rest of chapter 15 consists of a ceremony between Abraham and God that was commonly used in the ancient world to formalize a covenant (Gen. 15:7–21).

According to Genesis 16, Sarah, because she had not borne a child, provided Abraham with a handmaiden. This also appears to be a familiar custom of the ancient world. According to this custom, if the wife had not had a child (preferably a male) by a certain time in the marriage, she was obligated to provide a substitute (usually a slavewoman) to bear a child to her husband and thereby ensure the leadership of the clan. Thus, Hagar, the Egyptian maidservant, had a son by Abraham. The boy was named Ishmael. Although Ishmael was not understood to be the child that would carry on the line promised to Abraham, he was given a favorable blessing (Gen. 16:10–13; 17:20).

The most substantial account of the covenant between Abraham and God is given in Genesis 17—a covenant that extended the promise of the land and descendants to further generations. This covenant required Abraham and the male members of his household to be circumcised as the sign of the agreement (Gen. 17:10–14). In this chapter Abraham and Sarah receive their new names. (Their old names were Abram and Sarai.) The name of the son whom God promises that Sarah will bear is designated as Isaac (Gen. 17:19–21). The practice of circumcision instituted at this time is not unique to the ancient Hebrews, but its emphasis as a religious requirement is a unique feature of God's covenant people. It became a visible symbol of the covenant between Abraham and his descendants and their redeemer God.

After Isaac was born to Sarah (Gen. 21:1–7), Sarah was unhappy with the presence of Hagar and Ishmael. She asked Abraham to cast them out of the family, which he did after the Lord told him they would have His protection. Ishmael does not play an important role in the rest of Abraham's story; he does reenter the picture in Genesis 25:9, accompanying Isaac at Abraham's death.

The Supreme Test. God's command for Abraham to sacrifice his beloved son Isaac was the crucial test of his faith. He was willing to give up his son in obedience to God, although at the last moment the Lord intervened to save Isaac (Gen. 22:1–13). The Lord's promise of descendants as numerous as the stars of the heavens was once again reaffirmed as a result of Abraham's unquestioning obedience (Gen. 22:16–18).

Abraham did not want Isaac to marry a woman from one of the local tribes. Possibly he feared this would introduce Canaanite religious practices into the Hebrew clan. Thus, Abraham sent a senior servant to Haran, the city from which he had migrated, to find a wife for Isaac. This mission was successful, and Isaac eventually married Rebekah, the sister of Laban (Gen. 24:1–67). Sarah had died some time earlier (Gen. 23:1–20); Abraham eventually remarried and fathered several children by Keturah (Gen. 25:1–6). Abraham died at the age of 175 and was buried alongside Sarah in the cave of Machpelah, near Hebron (Gen. 25:7–11).

Summary. Abraham was the father of the Hebrews and the prime example of a righteous man. In spite of impossible odds, Abraham had faith in the promises of God. Therefore, he is presented as a model for human behavior. Hospitable to strangers (Gen. 18:1–8), he was a God-fearing man (Gen. 22:1–18) who was obedient to God's laws (Gen. 26:5). The promises originally given to Abraham were passed on to his son Isaac (Gen. 26:3), and to his grandson Jacob (Gen. 28:13; 35:11–12). In later biblical references, the God of Israel is frequently identified as the God of Abraham (Gen. 26:24), and Israel is often called the people "of the God of Abraham" (Pss. 47:9; 105:6). Abraham was such an important figure in the history of God's people that when they were in trouble, Israel appealed to God to remember the covenant made with Abraham (Ex. 32:13; Deut. 9:27; Ps. 105:9).

In the New Testament, Abraham is presented as the supreme model of vital faith and as the prime example of the faith required for the Christian believer (Rom. 4:11; Gal. 3:6–9; 4:28). He is viewed as the spiritual father for all who share a

similar faith in Christ (Matt. 3:9; Luke 13:16; Rom. 11:1). If anyone deserves to be called God's "friend," it is Abraham (Is. 41:8).

ABSALOM [AB suh lum] (*father of peace*) — the arrogant
and vain son of David who tried to take the kingship from
his father by force.

Absalom was David's third son by Maacah, the daughter of
the king of Geshur (2 Sam. 3:3; 1 Chr. 3:2). Of royal descent
on both sides, Absalom was a potential heir to the throne.
Attractive in appearance and charming in manners, Absalom
was also a popular prince with the people and a favorite of his
father. He was especially noted for his beautiful long hair, in
which he took great pride (2 Sam. 14:25–26).

During the height of Israel's prosperity under David's rule,
another of David's sons, Amnon, raped his half-sister Tamar—
Absalom's sister (2 Sam. 13:1–22). Absalom took it upon himself
to avenge this dishonor, eventually succeeding after two years
in having Amnon murdered by his servants (2 Sam. 13:23–29).
Fearing his father's wrath, Absalom fled into exile. He stayed
with his grandfather Talmai in Geshur for three years (2 Sam.
13:37–38).

Since Absalom was one of David's favorite sons, the king
longed for his return (2 Sam. 13:39) in spite of his crime. Joab,
one of David's advisors, urged that Absalom be allowed to
return to Jerusalem on probation but that he not be allowed to
appear before David.

Absalom did return to Jerusalem, but this turned out to
be an ill-advised move on David's part. Absalom secretly plotted a revolt against the throne. Taking advantage of his natural
appeal and his handsome appearance to win the favor of the
people, he also aroused discontent by implying that he could
rule more justly than his father. When the plot was ready,
Absalom obtained permission to go to Hebron to worship.
Meanwhile, he had sent spies throughout the tribes, inviting

those favorable to him to meet at Hebron (2 Sam. 15:7–11). After gathering these warriors, he then enlisted Ahithophel, a disloyal official of David, as his aide and advisor (2 Sam. 15:12).

When David learned of these rebellious acts, he fled to Mahanaim, beyond the Jordan River (2 Sam. 17:24). Under Ahithophel's advice, Absalom entered Jerusalem and publicly took possession of the wives in his father's harem who had been left in the city. By this act Absalom demonstrated that he would never be reconciled with his father, and even more of the people rallied to his cause.

Absalom then called a council to determine what action to take against David. Present at this meeting was Hushai, a loyal advisor to David who pretended to follow Absalom in order to spy on the proceedings. Ahithophel advised that Absalom move against the retreating king as quickly as possible, but Hushai countered by pointing out that if the attack failed, his revolt would fail. He advised instead that Absalom gather all his forces for one full-scale attack. Absalom heeded Hushai's counsel, giving David time to assemble an army. Absalom was formally anointed king after taking Jerusalem (2 Sam. 19:10). He appointed Amasa as captain of his army, then crossed the Jordan to meet his father's forces. The battle took place in the woods of Ephraim, where Absalom's recruits were no match for David's veterans. Absalom's army was defeated, and 20,000 of his men were killed (2 Sam. 18:6–7).

Absalom tried to flee from the forest on a mule, but his head caught in the thick boughs of a terebinth tree. Joab, the captain of David's army, then killed Absalom in spite of David's request that he not be harmed. Upon hearing the news of his death, David moaned, "O my son Absalom—my son, my son Absalom—if only I had died in your place! O Absalom my son, my son!" (2 Sam. 18:33). These are some of the saddest words in the Bible.

Absalom had many talents and abilities. But he was also spoiled, impatient, and overly ambitious. These, along with his vanity and pride, led to his tragic death. His body was cast into a pit, over which a great heap of stones was piled as a sign of contempt (2 Sam. 18:17). A large mausoleum erroneously called Absalom's Monument, located in the Kidron Valley east of Jerusalem, was built centuries after Absalom's death. It can still be seen today.

ADAM [ADD um] (*red, ground*) — the name of a man and a city in the Old Testament:

1. The first man, created by God on the sixth day of creation, and placed in the garden of Eden (Gen. 2:19–23; 3:8–9, 17, 20–21; 4:1, 25; 5:1–5). He and his wife Eve, created by God from one of Adam's ribs (Gen. 2:21–22), became the ancestors of all people now living on the earth. Adam was unique and distinct from the animals in several ways. His creation is described separately from that of the animals and the rest of God's creative acts (Gen. 1:3–25; 1:26–27; 2:7).

God breathed into Adam's body of "dust" the divine "breath of life; and man became a living being" (Gen. 2:7). God also made man in his own image and likeness. The exact words are "Let Us make man in Our image, according to Our likeness" (Gen. 1:26). The apostle Paul interprets this to mean that God created man with spiritual, rational, emotional, and moral qualities (Eph. 4:24–32; Col. 3:8–10).

God placed Adam in the garden of Eden where he was to work the ground (Gen. 2:5, 15) and take care of the animals (Gen. 1:26–28; 2:19–20). God made Eve as a "helper comparable to" Adam (Gen. 2:20), creating her out of one of Adam's ribs so they were "one flesh" (Gen. 2:24).

God told the human pair, "Be fruitful and multiply; fill the earth" (Gen. 1:28). As a consequence, they had a number of children: Cain, Abel, Seth, and a number of other sons and daughters (Gen. 4:1–2; 5:3–4). Created in innocence, they did not know sin (Gen. 2:25).

Genesis 3 tells how Adam failed to keep God's command not to eat of the Tree of Knowledge of Good and Evil. The consequence of this disobedience was death (Gen. 2:17), both physical (Gen. 5:5) and spiritual (Eph. 2:1). Eve disobeyed first, lured by pride and the desire for pleasure (Gen. 3:5–6; 1 Tim. 2:14). Then Adam, with full knowledge of the consequences, joined Eve in rebellion against God (Gen. 3:6).

The consequences of disobedience were: (1) loss of innocence (Gen. 3:7); (2) continued enmity between the seed of the woman [Christ] (Gen. 3:15; Gal. 3:16) and the seed of the serpent [Satan and his followers] (John 8:44); (3) the cursing of the ground and the resultant hard labor for man (Gen. 3:17–19); (4) the hard labor of childbirth (Gen. 3:16); (5) the submission of woman to her husband (Gen. 3:16; Eph. 5:22–23); and (6) separation from God (Gen. 3:23–24; 2 Thess. 1:9). Adam lived 930 years (Gen. 5:5).

The New Testament emphasizes the oneness of Adam and Eve (Matt. 19:3–9), showing that Adam represented man in bringing the human race into sin and death (Rom. 5:12–19; 1 Cor. 15:22). In contrast, Christ, the "last Adam," represented His redeemed people in bringing justification and eternal life to them (Rom. 5:15–21).

2. A city located "beside Zaretan" (Josh. 3:16), near the junction of the Jabbok River and the Jordan River, about 30 kilometers (18 miles) north of Jericho.

ADONIJAH [add oh NYE juh] (*the Lord is my Lord*) — the name of three men in the Old Testament:

1. The fourth of the six sons born to David while he was at Hebron (2 Sam. 3:4). Adonijah's mother was Haggith. With the exception of Absalom, David apparently favored Adonijah over his other five sons. When David was old, Adonijah attempted

to seize the throne, although he probably knew that his father intended Solomon to succeed him (1 Kin. 1:13).

Adonijah won two important people to his cause—Joab, the captain of the army, and Abiathar, the priest. At an open-air feast at the stone of Zoheleth beside En Rogel, he had himself proclaimed king. But Adonijah had not won over Zadok the priest, Benaiah the commander of the royal bodyguard, or Nathan the prophet. Bathsheba, Solomon's mother, and Nathan told David of Adonijah's activities; David immediately ordered Solomon, who had been divinely chosen as David's successor, to be proclaimed king. When Adonijah sought sanctuary at the altar (1 Kin. 1:5–50), Solomon forgave him.

Adonijah, however, foolishly made another attempt to become king—this time after David's death. He asked that the beautiful Abishag, who had taken care of David during his final days, be given to him in marriage. According to the custom of the day, claiming a king's wife or concubine amounted to the same thing as claiming his throne. This time Solomon ordered that Adonijah be killed (1 Kin. 2:13, 25).

2. One of the Levites sent by Jehoshaphat to instruct the people of Judah in the law (2 Chr. 17:8).

3. A chieftain who, with Nehemiah, sealed the covenant (Neh. 10:14–16); he is also called Adonikam (Ezra 2:13).

A HAB [A hab] (*father is brother*) — the name of two men in the Old Testament:

1. The son of Omri and the seventh king of Israel (1 Kin. 16:30). Under the influence of Jezebel, his wife, Ahab gave Baal equal place with God. Ahab also built a temple to Baal in which he erected a "wooden image" of the Canaanite goddess Asherah (1 Kin. 16:33). At Jezebel's urging, Ahab opposed the worship of the Lord, destroyed His altars, and killed His prophets. He reigned over Israel in Samaria for 22 years (873–852 B.C.) (1 Kin. 16:29).

Ahab strengthened the friendly relations with Phoenicia that David had begun when he was king of the united kingdom. He sealed the friendship between the two nations with a political marriage to Jezebel, the notoriously wicked daughter of Ethbaal, king of the Sidonians (1 Kin. 16:31). Ahab may have been the first king of Israel to establish peaceful relations with Judah.

False religion soon led to immoral civil acts. Because Jezebel had neither religious scruples nor regard for Hebrew civil laws (Lev. 25:23–34), she had Naboth tried unjustly and killed so that Ahab could take over his property (1 Kin. 21:1–16).

Throughout Ahab's reign, the prophet Elijah stood in open opposition to Ahab and the worship of Baal. Ahab also had frequent conflicts with Ben-Hadad, king of Syria, who once besieged Ahab's capital city, Samaria, but was driven off (1 Kin. 20:1–21).

Later, Ahab defeated Ben-Hadad in a battle at Aphek (1 Kin. 20:22–34); but Ahab was lenient with him, perhaps in view of a greater threat, Shalmaneser III of Assyria. In 853 B.C., Ahab and Ben-Hadad joined in a coalition to stop Shalmaneser's army at Qarqar on the Orontes River in Syria. Ahab contributed 2,000 chariots and 10,000 soldiers to this coalition. Still later, Ahab fought Ben-Hadad again. In spite of his precautions, Ahab was killed at Ramoth Gilead (1 Kin. 22:1–38).

Ahab was a capable leader and an avid builder. He completed and adorned the capital city of Samaria, which his father Omri had begun. Archaeological discoveries show that Ahab's "ivory house" (1 Kin. 22:39; Amos 3:15) was faced with white stone, which gave it the appearance of ivory. It also was decorated with ivory inlays. The ivory fragments that have been found show similarities with Phoenician ivories of the period. These findings illustrate the close political and social ties that existed between Israel and Phoenicia. Archaeology has also shown that

Ahab refortified the cities of Megiddo and Hazor, probably in defense against growing threats from Syria and Assyria.

Ahab's story is particularly sad because of his great potential. His tragedy was forming an alliance with Jezebel and turning from God to serve idols.

2. The son of Kolaiah and one of two false prophets denounced by Jeremiah (Jer. 29:21–23). Because Ahab prophesied falsely in God's name, Jeremiah declared that he would die at the hand of Nebuchadnezzar, king of Babylon, and would be cursed by all Babylonian captives from Judah.

AHASUERUS [ah has you EH rus] (*mighty man*) — the name of two kings in the Old Testament:

1. A king of Persia and the husband of the Jew Esther. Scholars generally agree that Ahasuerus is the same person as Xerxes I (485–464 B.C.).

The picture of Ahasuerus presented in the book of Esther— the vastness of his empire (1:1), his riches (1:4), his sensuality and feasting (1:5–12), and his cruelty and lack of foresight (1:13–22)—is consistent with the description of Xerxes provided by the Greek historian Herodotus. Ahasuerus succeeded his father, Darius Hystaspis, in 485 B.C. The book of Esther tells the story of how Ahasuerus banished his queen, Vashti, because of her refusal to parade herself before the drunken merrymakers at one of his feasts. Following a two-year search for Vashti's replacement, Ahasuerus chose Esther as his queen. Esther and her people, the Jews, were in Persia as a consequence of the fall of Jerusalem (in 586 B.C.) and the scattering of the Jews into captivity in foreign lands.

Ahasuerus's advisor, Haman, hated the Jews; he prevailed upon Ahasuerus to order them to be wiped out—an order that the king gave with little concern for its consequences. During a sleepless night, Ahasuerus sent for his royal records and read of how the Jew Mordecai, Esther's guardian, had uncovered a plot to kill the king and thus had saved his life. Ahasuerus's discovery led to Mordecai's being raised to a position of honor in the kingdom. Haman's treachery soon led to his own fall, and he and his ten sons were hanged on the gallows he had previously prepared for Mordecai. In 464 B.C. a courtier murdered Ahasuerus, and his son, Artaxerxes Longimanus, succeeded him. In Ezra 4:6, the reign of Ahasuerus is mentioned chronologically between Cyrus (v. 5) and Artaxerxes (v. 7).

2. A king of the Medes and the father of Darius (Dan. 9:1).

A HAZ [A haz] — the name of two men in the Old Testament: 1. A son of Jotham and the 11th king of Judah (2 Kin. 15:38; 16:1–20; Achaz, KJV). He was an ungodly king who promoted the worship of Molech, with its pagan rites of human sacrifice (2 Chr. 28:1–4).

The reign of Ahaz probably overlapped the reign of his father Jotham and possibly the reign of his own son Hezekiah. His age when he became king was 20 and he reigned for 16 years, beginning about 735 B.C. Early in his reign Ahaz adopted policies that favored Assyria. When he refused to join the anti-Assyrian alliance of Pekah of Israel and Rezin of Syria, they invaded Judah and besieged Jerusalem, threatening to dethrone Ahaz and replace him with a puppet king (Is. 7:1–6). Pekah and Rezin killed 120,000 people and took 200,000 captives. However, through the intervention of Oded the prophet, the captives were released immediately (2 Chr. 28:5–15).

In view of his precarious circumstances, Ahaz requested help from Tiglath-Pileser III, king of Assyria, offering him silver and gold. At first the plan worked, and Assyria invaded Israel and Syria (2 Kin. 15:29). Ultimately, however, Assyria "distressed" Ahaz, demanding excessive tribute (2 Chr. 28:20–21).

Spiritually, Ahaz stopped following in the ways of the four relatively good kings who had preceded him (Joash, Amaziah, Azariah, and Jotham). He made images of Baal, offered infant sacrifices in the Valley of Hinnom, and sacrificed on the high places (2 Chr. 28:1–4). He came under further pagan influence at Damascus where he had gone to meet Tiglath-Pileser III. Seeing a pagan altar there, he commanded Uriah the priest at Jerusalem to build a copy of it. He then installed it next to the bronze altar in the Jerusalem temple.

It was to King Ahaz that Isaiah's announcement of the promised Immanuel was made (Is. 7:10–17). The prophet Isaiah sent a message to the terrified Ahaz, but Ahaz would not turn to God and trust Him for deliverance. Instead, he plunged deeper into idolatry and self-destruction. Ahaz's conduct brought divine judgment to Judah in the form of military defeats. Edom revolted and took captives from Judah. The Philistines invaded Judah, capturing several cities. Rezin of Damascus seized control of Elath, Judah's port on the Gulf of Aqaba (2 Kin. 16:5–6).

At his death, Ahaz was buried without honor in Jerusalem. He was not deemed worthy of a burial in the royal tombs (2 Chr. 28:27).

2. A Benjamite and descendant of King Saul. Ahaz was a son of Micah and the father of Jehoaddah (1 Chr. 8:35–36; 9:42).

AHAZIAH [a huh ZIE uh] (*the Lord sustains*) — the name of two kings in the Old Testament:

1. The son and successor of Ahab and the ninth king of Israel (1 Kin. 22:40, 49, 51). Ahaziah reigned from 853 to 852 B.C. The son of Jezebel, Ahaziah followed policies that showed evidence of his mother's pagan influence. After reigning only two years, he "fell through the lattice of his upper room in Samaria" (2 Kin. 1:2) and was seriously injured. Sending his messengers to ask Baal-Zebub, the god of Ekron, about his recovery, Ahaziah was frustrated when the prophet Elijah interrupted their mission and prophesied Ahaziah's death. Enraged by Elijah's predictions, Ahaziah tried to seize him, but the men sent to capture

the prophet were destroyed by fire from heaven and Elijah's prophecy was quickly fulfilled (2 Kin. 1:9–17).

At the time of Ahaziah's ascent to the throne, Mesha, the king of Moab, rebelled because of the tribute imposed on him by Omri, Ahaziah's grandfather (2 Kin. 1:1; 3:4–5). Ahaziah formed an alliance with Jehoshaphat, king of Judah, to build ships and trade with other nations. God judged this effort and it failed (1 Kin. 22:49).

2. The son and successor of Joram and the nephew of Ahaziah No. 1 (2 Kin. 8:24–26). Ahaziah is also called Jehoahaz (2 Chr. 21:17; 25:23) and Azariah (2 Chr. 22:6). The sixth king of Judah, Ahaziah reigned for only one year (841 B.C.).

Ahaziah became king at age 22 (2 Kin. 8:26; 2 Chr. 22:1). His wicked reign was heavily influenced by his mother Athaliah, who was the evil power behind his throne: "He walked in the way of the house of Ahab" (2 Kin. 8:27).

Ahaziah cultivated relations with Israel and joined with his uncle, King Jehoram (2 Kin. 1:17; 9:24; 2 Chr. 22:5–7), in a military expedition at Ramoth Gilead against Hazael, king of Syria. Jehoram was wounded and returned to Jezreel, near Mount Gilboa, to convalesce. While visiting his uncle Jehoram, Ahaziah was killed by Jehu, Israel's captain, who had been ordered by God to exterminate the house of Ahab (2 Kin. 9:4–10).

AHIJAH [a HIGH juh] (*my brother is the Lord*) — the name of nine men in the Old Testament:

1. The performer of High Priestly functions at Gibeah during part of Saul's reign (1 Sam. 14:3, 18). Many scholars identify him with Ahimelech, the priest at Nob who is also identified as a son of Ahitub (1 Sam. 22:9). Ahijah's name is usually spelled Ahiah, a variant of Ahijah.

2. A secretary or scribe in Solomon's reign and a son of Shisha (1 Kin. 4:3); also spelled Ahiah.

3. The prophet from Shiloh who prophesied Israel's division into two kingdoms because of its idolatries (1 Kin. 11:29–39). While Solomon was king, Jeroboam rebelled against him. Ahijah tore his own garment into 12 pieces and instructed Jeroboam to take ten of them. This symbolic action indicated that Jeroboam would be king over the ten tribes that would be known as the northern kingdom of Israel. Ahijah stood up for the people in the face of their oppression under Solomon and Rehoboam.

Later, King Jeroboam disguised his queen and sent her to the aging and nearly blind prophet to ask whether their sick child would recover. Ahijah prophesied that because of Jeroboam's wickedness the child would die (1 Kin. 14:1–18). His prophecies were also put into writing (2 Chr. 9:29).

4. The father of Baasha, who killed Jeroboam's son Nadab. He then reigned over Israel in his stead (1 Kin. 15:27).

5. A man of the tribe of Judah and a son of Jerahmeel (1 Chr. 2:25).

6. A Benjamite who helped carry off the inhabitants of Geba (1 Chr. 8:7).

7. One of David's mighty men (1 Chr. 11:36).

8. A Levite during David's reign (1 Chr. 26:20) who kept the temple treasury.

9. One of the priests who, with Nehemiah, sealed the covenant (Neh. 10:26).

AI [A eye] (*the ruin*) — the name of two cities in the Old Testament:

1. A Canaanite city (Josh. 10:1) located east of Bethel (Gen. 12:8), "beside Beth Aven" (Josh. 7:2), and north of Michmash (Isa. 10:28). Many years before Joshua's time, Abraham pitched his tent at Ai before journeying to Egypt (Gen. 12:8).

Ai figures prominently in the story of Israel's conquest of Canaan. After Joshua conquered Jericho, he sent men to spy out

Ai and the surrounding countryside. Because Ai was small, the spies assured Joshua that he could take Ai with only a handful of soldiers. Joshua dispatched about 3,000 soldiers to attack Ai. This army was soundly defeated, due to Achan's sin of taking spoils from Jericho contrary to God's commandment. When God singled out Achan and his family, the people stoned them to death. Joshua then sent 30,000 soldiers against Ai and captured the city by a clever military tactic—an ambush (Joshua 7–8).

Although Ai has been identified with modern et-Tell, situated southeast of Bethel, recent archaeological discoveries conflict with this placement and make this identification uncertain. Nearby Khirbet Nisya is another possible location for Ai. Ai is also called Aiath (Is. 10:28, KJV), Aija (Neh. 11:31, KJV), and Hai (Gen. 12:8; 13:3, KJV).

2. An Ammonite city in Moab (Jer. 49:3).

AMMON [AM muhn] (*kinsman* or *people*) — the land of Ammon, settled by those who were descended from Ben-Ammi, Lot's son. Ben-Ammi was born in a cave near Zoar (Gen. 19:30–38), a city near the southern end of the Dead Sea. The land of the Ammonites generally was located in the area north and east of Moab, a region between the river Arnon and the river Jabbok. Its capital city was Rabbah (Deut. 3:11; 2 Sam. 11:1). Amman, the name of the capital of the modern Hashemite kingdom of Jordan, is a continuing use of this ancient name.

AMON [A mun] — the name of three men in the Old Testament:

1. A governor of Samaria (1 Kin. 22:26; 2 Chr. 18:25). When the prophet Micaiah prophesied that Ahab, king of Israel, would be killed in battle, he was sent to Amon as a prisoner.

2. A son of Manasseh and a king of Judah (2 Kin. 21:18–26; 2 Chr. 33:20–25). Amon became king at the age of 22 and

reigned for only two years. His reign was characterized by idolatry. His wicked father may have deliberately named him after the Egyptian god Amun.

Finally, Amon's own servants conspired to kill him, possibly because his corruption and idolatry had made him a weak king and they hoped to claim the throne for themselves. However, after Amon was assassinated, the people of Judah killed the conspirators and set Amon's eight-year-old son, Josiah, on the throne. Amon is mentioned in the New Testament as an ancestor of Jesus (Matt. 1:10).

3. The head of a captive family that returned to Israel from Babylon (Neh. 7:59). He was a descendant of one of Solomon's servants. He is also called Ami (Ezra 2:57).

AMOS [AIM us] (*burden bearer*) — the famous shepherd-prophet of the Old Testament who denounced the people of the northern kingdom of Israel for their idol worship, graft and corruption, and oppression of the poor. He was probably the earliest of the writing prophets. His prophecies and the few facts known about his life are found in the book of Amos.

Although he prophesied to the Northern Kingdom, Amos was a native of Judah, Israel's sister nation to the south. He came from the village of Tekoa (Amos 1:1), situated about 16 kilometers (10 miles) south of Jerusalem.

On one occasion, Amos's authority in Israel was questioned by a priest who served in the court of King Jeroboam II, and Amos admitted he was not descended from a line of prophets or other religious officials. By vocation, he claimed to be nothing but "a herdsman and a tender of sycamore fruit" (Amos 7:14), but he pointed out that his right to speak came from the highest authority of all: "The Lord took me as I followed the flock, and the Lord said to me, 'Go, prophesy to My people Israel' " (Amos 7:15).

Amos spoke because the Lord had called him to deliver His message of judgment. This is one of the clearest statements of the compulsion of the divine call to be found in the Bible. The theme of Amos's message was that Israel had rejected the one true God in order to worship false gods. He also condemned the wealthy class of the nation for cheating the poor through oppressive taxes (Amos 5:11) and the use of false weights and measures (Amos 8:5). He urged the people to turn from their sinful ways, to acknowledge God as their Maker and Redeemer, and to restore justice and righteousness in their dealings with others.

Amaziah the priest, who served in the court of King Jeroboam, made a report to the king about Amos and his message (Amos 7:10–13). This probably indicates that the prophet's stern warning created quite a stir throughout the land. But there is no record that the nation changed its ways as a result of Amos's message. About 40 years after his prophecies, Israel collapsed when the Assyrians overran their capital city, Samaria, and carried away the leading citizens as captives.

After preaching in Israel, Amos probably returned to his home in Tekoa. No facts are known about his later life or death. He will always serve as an example of courage and faithfulness.

ANANIAS [an uh NYE us] (*the Lord is gracious*) — the name of three New Testament men:

1. A Christian in the early church at Jerusalem (Acts 5:1–11). With the knowledge of his wife, Sapphira, Ananias sold a piece of property and brought only a portion of the proceeds from its sale to Peter, claiming this represented the total amount realized from the sale. When Peter rebuked him for lying about the amount, Ananias immediately fell down and died. Sapphira later repeated the same falsehood, and she also fell down and died. Apparently, their pretense to be something they were not caused God to strike Ananias and Sapphira dead.

2. A Christian disciple living in Damascus at the time of Paul's conversion (Acts 9:10–18; 22:12–16). In a vision the Lord told Ananias of Paul's conversion and directed him to go to Paul and welcome him into the church. Aware of Paul's reputation as a persecutor of Christians, Ananias reacted with alarm. When the Lord informed him that Paul was "a chosen vessel of Mine" (Acts 9:15), Ananias went to Paul and laid his hands upon him. Paul's sight was restored immediately, and he was baptized (Acts 9:18).

3. The Jewish high priest before whom Paul appeared after his arrest in Jerusalem following his third missionary journey, about A.D. 58 (Acts 23:2). Ananias was also one of those who spoke against Paul before the Roman governor Felix (Acts 24:1). Ananias was appointed high priest about A.D. 48 by Herod. In A.D. 52 the governor of Syria sent Ananias to Rome to be tried for the Jews' violent treatment of the Samaritans. Ananias was acquitted of the charges through Agrippa's influence, and he was returned to his office in Jerusalem. About A.D. 59 Ananias was deposed by Agrippa. Known to the Jews as a Roman collaborator, Ananias was murdered by a Jewish mob at the beginning of the Jewish–Roman War of A.D. 66–73.

ANATHOTH [AN uh thoth] — the name of two men and one city in the Old Testament:

1. A city in the tribe of Benjamin given to the Levites (1 Kin. 2:26). Anathoth was the birthplace of the prophet Jeremiah (Jer. 1:1; 29:27). During a time of siege, the Lord instructed Jeremiah to purchase a field in Anathoth. This was to serve as a sign of God's promised redemption of Israel (Jer. 32:7–9). Anathoth was located about 5 kilometers (3 miles) northeast of Jerusalem.

2. A son of Becher (1 Chr. 7:8).

3. A leader of the people who placed his seal on the covenant, along with Nehemiah (Neh. 10:19).

ANDREW [AN droo] (*manly*) — brother of Simon Peter and one of Jesus' first disciples. Both Andrew and Peter were fishermen (Matt. 4:18; Mark 1:16–18) from Bethsaida (John 1:44), on the northwest coast of the Sea of Galilee. They also had a house at Capernaum in this vicinity (Mark 1:29).

According to the gospel of John, Andrew and an unnamed friend were among the followers of John the Baptist (John 1:35–40). When John the Baptist identified Jesus as the Lamb of God, both he and Andrew followed Jesus (John 1:41). Andrew then brought his brother Simon to meet the Messiah (John 1:43–51)—an action that continues to be a model for all who bring others to Christ.

At the feeding of the five thousand, Andrew called Jesus' attention to the boy with five barley loaves and two fish (John 6:5–9). Later Philip and Andrew decided to bring to Jesus the request of certain Greeks for an audience with Him (John 12:20–22). Andrew is mentioned a final time in the Gospels, when he asked Jesus a question concerning last things in the company of Peter, James, and John (Mark 13:3–4).

All lists of the disciples name Andrew among the first four (Matt. 10:2–4; Mark 3:16–19; Luke 6:14–16; Acts 1:13). According to tradition, Andrew was martyred at Patrae in Achaia by crucifixion on an X-shaped cross. According to Eusebius, Andrew's field of labor was Scythia, the region north of the Black Sea. For this reason he became the patron saint of Russia. He is also considered the patron saint of Scotland.

ANNAS [AN us] (*grace of the Lord*) — one of the high priests at Jerusalem, along with Caiaphas, when John the Baptist began his ministry, about A.D. 26 (Luke 3:2). Quirinius, governor of Syria, appointed Annas as high priest about A.D. 6 or 7. Although Annas was deposed by Valerius Gratus, the Procurator of Judea, about A.D. 15, he was still the most influential of the priests and continued to carry the title of high priest (Luke 3:2; Acts 4:6).

After his removal, Annas was officially succeeded by each of his five sons, one grandson, and his son-in-law Caiaphas, the high priest who presided at the trial of Jesus (Matt. 26:3, 57; John 18:13–14). During His trial, Jesus was first taken to Annas, who then sent Jesus to Caiaphas (John 18:13, 24). Both Annas and Caiaphas were among the principal examiners when Peter and John were arrested (Acts 4:6).

ANTIOCH OF PISIDIA [AN tih ock, pih SID ih uh] —

a city of southern Asia Minor in Phrygia, situated just north of the territory of Pisidia. Antioch was an important first-century commercial center and an important center for the spread of the gospel. Founded by Seleucus I Nicator (about 300 B.C.) and named for his father Antiochus, it became a great center for commerce and was inhabited by many Jews.

The apostle Paul preached in this city's synagogue and founded a church there during his first missionary journey (Acts 13:14–49). Just as Antioch exerted great cultural and political influence over the surrounding area, so also it became a strong base from which to launch the church's evangelistic outreach (Acts 13:42–49). In reaction to Paul's success, the Jews at Antioch caused some influential women to turn against the gospel and had Paul driven out of the city (Acts 13:50).

ANTIOCH OF SYRIA [AN tih ock, SIHR ih uh] — the

capital of the Roman province of Syria that played an important part in the first-century expansion of the church. Antioch was situated on the east bank of the Orontes River, about 27 kilometers (16.5 miles) from the Mediterranean Sea and 485 kilometers (300 miles) north of Jerusalem. The city was founded about 300 B.C. by Seleucus I Nicator, one of the three successors to Alexander the Great, and named for his father Antiochus.

The early history of the church is closely connected with Antioch of Syria. One of the first seven "deacons," Nicolas, was a "proselyte from Antioch" (Acts 6:5). After the stoning of Stephen (Acts 7:54–60), great persecution caused certain disciples to flee from Jerusalem to Antioch where they preached the gospel to the Jews (Acts 8:1; 11:19). Others arrived later and had success preaching to the Gentiles (Acts 11:20–21).

When the church leaders at Jerusalem heard of this success in Antioch, they sent Barnabas to visit the church there (Acts 11:25–26).

Apparently, Paul and Barnabas used Antioch as the base for their missionary journeys into Asia Minor (Acts 13:1–3; 15:36–41; 18:22–23). Following the first missionary journey, Antioch became the scene of an important dispute. Certain men from Judea taught that Gentile converts must be circumcised and follow other rules for converts to Judaism before becoming Christians (Acts 15:1–2). This theological disagreement led to a church council at Jerusalem. Paul and Barnabas were sent here to report how God had given them success in bringing the gospel to the Gentiles. The council decided that Gentile converts did not have to be circumcised. Antioch is now known as Antakya, in modern-day Turkey.

APOLLOS [a POL lus] (*destroyer*) — a learned and eloquent Jew from Alexandria in Egypt and an influential leader in the early church. Well-versed in the Old Testament, Apollos was a disciple of John the Baptist and "taught accurately the things of the Lord" (Acts 18:25). However, while Apollos knew some of Jesus' teaching, "he knew only the baptism of John" (Acts 18:25). When Priscilla and Aquila, two other leaders in the early church, arrived in Ephesus, they instructed Apollos more accurately in the way of God (Acts 18:26).

In Corinth, Apollos publicly contended with the Jewish leaders and refuted their objections to Christian teaching. He was apparently quite popular in Corinth, for in 1 Corinthians 1:12 Paul wrote of four parties into which the church at Corinth had become divided: one "following" Apollos, one Paul, one Cephas [Peter], and one Christ. In dealing with this division, Paul compared himself to the one who planted and Apollos to the one who watered what was already planted (1 Cor. 3:6).

AQUILA [A kwil uh] (*eagle*) — a Jewish Christian living in Corinth with his wife Priscilla at the time of Paul's arrival from Athens (Acts 18:2). Aquila was born in Pontus (located in Asia Minor) but lived in Rome until Claudius commanded that all Jews leave the city. He and Priscilla moved to Corinth, where Aquila took up his trade, tentmaking.

When Paul left Corinth, Aquila and Priscilla traveled with him as far as Ephesus (1 Cor. 16:19), where they met Apollos and instructed him more thoroughly in the Christian faith (Acts 18:24–26). Apparently, they returned to Rome, because Paul sent them greetings in his letter to the Romans (Rom. 16:3).

ARABAH [AIR ah bah] (*plain, desert*) — a major region of the land of Israel, referring usually to the entire valley region between Mount Hermon in the north to the Red Sea in the south (Num. 22:1; Deut. 1:7). The Arabah is more than 390 kilometers (240 miles) long, varying in width from 10 to 40 kilometers (6 to 25 miles).

The Arabah includes the Sea of Galilee, the Jordan River valley, the Dead Sea, and the area between the Dead Sea and the Red Sea. Much of this region lies below sea level, and the Dead Sea, which lies at approximately 394 meters (1,292 feet) below sea level, is the lowest spot on the earth's surface. The NKJV refers several times to the "Sea of the Arabah," meaning the Salt Sea or the Dead Sea (Deut. 3:17; Josh. 3:16; 2 Kin. 14:25).

Before their entry into the promised land, the people of Israel camped in the Arabah, in an area called "the plains of Moab" (Num. 22:1), just north of the Dead Sea. While the Israelites were camped there, God turned Balaam's curses to blessings (Num. 22:1–24:25), Israel committed idolatry and immorality (Numbers 25), Moses renewed the covenant, and Joshua sent out spies to prepare for the invasion of Canaan (Josh. 1:1–3:17).

ARARAT [AIR uh rat] — the mountainous region between the Black Sea and the Caspian Sea where Noah's ark rested when the Flood subsided (Gen. 8:4). From this region streams converge to form the Tigris and the Euphrates Rivers. Originally called Urartu, Ararat referred to the whole mountainous area; its use, however has gradually come to be restricted to the huge volcanic mountain at the borders of Turkey, Iran, and Azerbaijan.

This volcanic mountain includes two peaks, 5,600 meters (17,000 feet) and 4,200 meters (13,000 feet) above sea level. The taller peak rises 920 meters (3,000 feet) above the line of perpetual snow. Some people believe that Noah's ark still rests on Mount Ararat, and occasional expeditions have been launched to find it. However, shifting glaciers, avalanches, hidden crevices, and sudden storms make the mountain so difficult to climb that it is referred to by the native inhabitants of that region as "the Painful Mountain."

ASHDOD [ASH dahd] — one of the five principal Philistine cities (1 Sam. 6:17), situated 5 kilometers (3 miles) from the Mediterranean coast and 32 kilometers (20 miles) north of Gaza. The city's military and economic significance was enhanced by its location on the main highway between Egypt and Syria.

Joshua and the Israelites drove the Canaanites out of the hill country of Judah, but the Anakim—a group of

Canaanites—remained in Ashdod, Gaza, and Gath (Josh. 11:22). During the time of Eli and Samuel, the ark of the covenant accompanied Israel's army (1 Sam. 4:3). When the Philistines defeated Israel, they took the ark to the temple of Dagon in Ashdod (1 Sam. 5:1–7).

Uzziah, the powerful king of Judah, captured Ashdod (2 Chr. 26:6). The prophet Amos predicted the destruction of the city because of its inhumane treatment of Israelites (Amos 1:8; 3:9). When Sargon II, king of Assyria, destroyed Ashdod in 711 B.C., he fulfilled this prophecy (Is. 20:1).

In New Testament times, Ashdod was renamed Azotus. Philip the evangelist preached in all the cities from Azotus to Caesarea (Acts 8:40).

ASHKELON [ASH kuh lon] — one of the five principal cities of the Philistines (Josh. 13:3). Situated on the seacoast 19 kilometers (12 miles) north of Gaza, Ashkelon and her sister cities (Ashdod, Gath, Gaza, and Ekron) posed a serious threat to the Israelites during the period of the Judges. Shortly after Joshua's death, Ashkelon was captured and was briefly controlled by the tribe of Judah (Judg. 1:18). A few years later Samson killed 30 men from this city (Judg. 14:19). During most of the Old Testament era, however, Ashkelon remained politically and militarily independent of Israel.

In the eighth century B.C. Ashkelon was denounced by the prophet Amos (Amos 1:8). Shortly before the Babylonian captivity, Zephaniah prophesied that the Jews would return from Babylonia and occupy the ruins of Ashkelon (Zeph. 2:4, 7). Zechariah also prophesied the destruction of Ashkelon (Zech. 9:5).

ATHALIAH [ath ah LIE ah] (*the Lord is strong*) — the name of one woman and two men in the Old Testament:

1. The queen of Judah for six years (2 Kin. 11:1–3). Athaliah was the daughter of King Ahab of Israel. Presumably, Jezebel was her mother.

Athaliah married Jehoram (or Joram), son of Jehoshaphat, king of Judah. Jehoram reigned only eight years and was succeeded by his son Ahaziah, who died after reigning only one year. Desiring the throne for herself, Athaliah ruthlessly killed all her grandsons—except the infant Joash, who was hidden by his aunt (2 Kin. 11:2).

Athaliah apparently inherited Jezebel's ruthlessness. She was a tyrant whose every whim had to be obeyed. As her mother had done in Israel, Athaliah introduced Baal worship in Judah and in so doing destroyed part of the temple. Joash was hidden in the house of the Lord for six years (2 Kin. 11:3), while Athaliah reigned over the land (841–835 B.C.). In the seventh year, the high priest Jehoiada declared Joash the lawful king of Judah. Guards removed Athaliah from the temple before killing her, to avoid defiling the temple with her blood (2 Kin. 11:13–16; 2 Chr. 23:12–15).

Athaliah reaped what she sowed. She gained the throne through murder and lost her life in the same way. She also failed to thwart God's promise, because she did not destroy the Davidic line, through which the Messiah was to be born.

2. A son of Jeroham, a Benjamite (1 Chr. 8:26).

3. The father of Jeshaiah (Ezra 8:7).

ATHENS [ATH ins] — the capital city of the ancient Greek state of Attica and the modern capital of Greece. It was the center of Greek art, architecture, literature, and politics during the golden age of Greek history (the fifth century B.C.) and was visited by the apostle Paul on his second missionary journey (Acts 17:15–18:1).

B

BAASHA [BAY uh shah] — the son of Ahijah, of the tribe of Issachar, and the third king of the northern kingdom of Israel. Baasha succeeded Nadab, the son of Jeroboam I, as king by assassinating him. Then he murdered every member of the royal house, removing all who might claim his throne (1 Kin. 15:27–29).

Baasha's 24-year reign (909–885 B.C.) was characterized by war with Asa, king of Judah (1 Kin. 15:32; Jer. 41:9). He fortified Ramah (2 Chr. 16:1), six kilometers (four miles) north of Jerusalem, to control traffic from the north to Jerusalem during a time of spiritual awakening under Asa (2 Chr. 15:1–10). When the Syrian king, Ben-Hadad, invaded Israel, Baasha withdrew to defend his cities (1 Kin. 15:16–21).

Baasha's dynasty ended as it began; his son Elah was murdered by a servant, and the royal household of Baasha came to an end (1 Kin. 16:8–11).

BABEL, TOWER OF [BAY buhl] — an ancient tower symbolizing human pride and rebellion. It was built during the period after the Flood.

The narrative of the Tower of Babel appears in Genesis 11:1–9 as the climax to the account of early mankind found in Genesis

1–11. The geographical setting is a plain in the land of Shinar (Gen. 11:2). In the light of information contained in Genesis 10:10, Shinar probably refers to Babylonia.

The tower was constructed of brick, because there was no stone in southern Mesopotamia. It corresponds in general to a notable feature of Babylonian religion, the Ziggurat or temple tower. The one built at Ur in southern Mesopotamia about 2100 B.C. was a pyramid consisting of three terraces of diminishing size as the building ascended, topped by a temple. Converging stairways on one side led up to the temple. Its surviving lower two terraces were about 21 meters (70 feet) high. The outside of the structure was built of fired bricks and bituminous mortar, just like the tower described in Genesis 11:3.

The narrative in Genesis 11 is told with irony and with a negative attitude toward the people involved. Human beings delight in bricks, but the narrator and readers know that these are an inferior substitute for stone (Is. 9:10). To people the tower is a skyscraper (Deut. 1:28), but to God it is so small that He must come down from heaven to catch a glimpse of this tiny effort. The construction of the tower and city is described as an act of self-glorification by the builders (Gen. 11:4). People seek for their own security in community life and culture, independent of God. This is human initiative apart from God (Ps. 127:1). As such, the activity is evil and sinful.

The account moves from a description of the sin to a narration of the punishment. God has to step in to prevent mankind from seizing yet more power for themselves and going beyond the limits of their creaturehood (Gen. 3:22; 11:5–8). Their communication with one another to advance their efforts is frustrated because they begin to speak different languages. Finally, they abandon the building of the city and go their own way, becoming scattered over the earth.

The climax of the story occurs when the city is identified with *Babel*, the Hebrew name for Babylonia. This nation's sophisticated culture and power deliberately excluded God. Just as the Old Testament prophets foresaw the future downfall of Babylonia in spite of its glory (Is. 13:19; Rev. 18), this downfall is anticipated in Genesis 11: The end corresponds to the beginning. *Babel* derives ultimately from an Akkadian word that means "gateway to God." A similar Hebrew word, *balal,* means "confuse" and provides the author with a useful wordplay that stresses God's confusing of the builders' languages and His scattering of them throughout the earth (Gen. 11:9).

God's rejection of the nations symbolized by the Tower of Babel is reversed in Genesis 12:1–3 by the call of Abraham, through whom all nations would be blessed. Ultimately the sinful and rejected condition of mankind, which is clearly shown by the diversity of human language and territory described in this account, needed Pentecost as its answer. On this day the Holy Spirit was poured out on all people so they understood one another, although they spoke different languages (Acts 2:1–11; Eph. 2:14–18). The barriers that divide people and nations were thus removed.

BABYLON, CITY OF [BAB uh lon] — ancient walled city between the Tigris and Euphrates Rivers and capital of the Babylonian Empire. The leading citizens of the nation of Judah were carried to this city as captives in 586 B.C. after Jerusalem fell to the invading Babylonians. Biblical writers often portrayed this ancient capital of the Babylonian people as the model of paganism and idolatry (Jer. 51:44; Dan. 4:30).

Babylon was situated along the Euphrates River about 485 kilometers (300 miles) northwest of the Persian Gulf and about 49 kilometers (30 miles) southwest of modern Baghdad in Iraq. Its origins are unknown. According to Babylonian tradition, it was built by the god Marduk. The city must have been built some time before 2300 B.C., because it was destroyed about that time by an invading enemy king. This makes Babylon one of the oldest cities of the ancient world. Genesis 10:10 mentions Babel (the Hebrew spelling of Babylon) as part of the empire of Nimrod.

Sometime during its early history, the city of Babylon became a small independent kingdom. Its most famous king was Hammurapi (about 1792–1750 B.C.), who conquered southern Mesopotamia and territory to the north as far as Mari. He was known for his revision of a code of law that showed concern for the welfare of the people under his rule. But the dynasty he established declined under his successors. It came to an end with the conquest of Babylon by the Hittite king Murshilish I about 1595 B.C. Then the Kassites took over for a period, ruling southern Mesopotamia from the city of Babylon as their capital. The Assyrians attacked and plundered Babylon about 1250 B.C., but it recovered and flourished for another century until the Assyrians succeeded in taking over the city with their superior forces about 1100 B.C. After Tiglath-Pileser I of Assyria arrived on the scene, the city of Babylon became subject to Assyria by treaty or conquest. Tiglath-Pileser III (745–727 B.C.) declared himself king of Babylon with the name Pulu (Pul, 2 Kin. 15:19), deporting a number of its citizens to the subdued territory of the northern kingdom of Israel (2 Kin. 17:24).

In 721 B.C. a Chaldean prince, Marduk-apal-iddina, (Hebrew, Merodach-Baladan), seized control of Babylon and became a thorn in Assyria's side for a number of years. He apparently planned a large-scale rebellion of eastern and western parts of the Assyrian Empire (2 Kin. 20:12). In retaliation against this rebellion, Sennacherib of Assyria (704–681 B.C.) attacked Babylon in 689 B.C., totally destroying it, although it was rebuilt by his successor Esarhaddon (680–669 B.C.). After this, Assyrian power gradually weakened, so the city and kingdom of Babylonia grew stronger once again.

In 626 B.C. Nabopolassar seized the throne of Babylon. He was succeeded by Nebuchadnezzar II (605–562 B.C.), the greatest king of Babylon, who enlarged the capital city to an area of six square miles and beautified it with magnificent buildings. This period of the city's development has been the focal point of all archaeological research done in ancient Babylon. The city's massive double walls spanned both sides of the Euphrates River. Set into these walls were eight major gates. One of the numerous pagan temples in the city was that of the patron god Marduk, flanked by a Ziggurat or temple-tower. To this temple a sacred processional way led from the main gate, the Ishtar Gate. Both the gate and the walls facing the way were decorated with colored enameled bricks picturing lions, dragons, and bulls.

The city of Babylon also contained a palace complex, or residence for the king. On the northwest side of this palace area, the famous terraced "hanging gardens" may have been situated. They were one of the Seven Wonders of the ancient world. According to tradition, Nebuchadnezzar built these gardens for one of his foreign wives to remind her of the scenery of her homeland. Babylon's glory reflected the king's imperial power. Captured kings were brought to his court at Babylon. These included Jehoiachin (2 Kin. 24:15) and Zedekiah (2 Kin. 25:7), kings of Judah. During the reign of Nabonidus (555–539 B.C.), while Belshazzar was co-regent (Daniel 5), the city surrendered to the Persians without opposition.

Eventually the balance of power passed from the Persians to Alexander the Great, to whom Babylon willingly submitted in 331 B.C. Alexander planned to refurbish and expand the city and make it his capital, but he died before accomplishing these plans. The city later fell into insignificance because one of Alexander's successors founded a new capital at Seleucia, a short distance away.

The books of Isaiah and Jeremiah predicted the downfall of Babylon. This would happen as God's punishment of the Babylonians because of their destruction of Jerusalem and their deportation of the citizens of Judah (Is. 14:22; 21:9; 43:14; Jer. 50:9; 51:37). Today, the ruins of this city stand as an eloquent testimony to the passing of proud empires and to the providential hand of God.

BALAAM [BAY lum] — a magician or soothsayer (Josh. 13:22) who was summoned by the Moabite king Balak to curse the Israelites before they entered Canaan (Num. 22:5–24:25; Deut. 23:4–5). Recently, a plaster inscription concerning Balaam that dates to the 8th century B.C. has been found at Tell Deir Alla in Jordan.

Balaam lived in Aram in the town of Pethor on the Euphrates River. A curious mixture of good and evil, Balaam wavered when he was asked by Balak to curse the Israelites. But he finally agreed to go when the Lord specifically instructed him to go to Balak (Num. 22:20).

The exact meaning of the account of Balaam's "stubborn" donkey is not clear. After telling Balaam it was all right to go, God either tried to forbid him from going or wanted to impress upon him that he should speak only what he was told to say. When the angel of the Lord blocked their way, the donkey balked three times and was beaten by Balaam, who had not seen the angel. Finally, after the third beating, the donkey spoke, reproving Balaam. When the angel told Balaam, "Your way is perverse before Me" (Num. 22:32), Balaam offered to return home. The angel told him to go on, however, and reminded him to speak only the words God gave him to speak.

Balaam and Balak met at the river Arnon and traveled to "the high places of Baal" (Num. 22:41). From there they could see part of the Israelite encampment at Acacia Grove (Num. 25:1). After sacrificing on seven altars, Balaam went off alone. When he heard the word of God, he returned to Balak and blessed the people whom Balak wanted him to curse.

The New Testament mentions Balaam in three passages. Peter speaks of false teachers who "have forsaken the right way and gone astray, following the way of Balaam" (2 Pet. 2:15). Jude speaks of backsliders who "have run greedily in the error of Balaam for profit" (Jude 11). Balaam's error was greed or covetousness; he was well paid to bring a curse upon the people of Israel.

The nature of Balaam's curse is made clear by John in the book of Revelation. It refers to some members of the church in Pergamos who held "the doctrine of Balaam, who taught Balak to put a stumbling block before the children of Israel" (Rev. 2:14).

Before leaving Balak, Balaam apparently told the Moabite leader that Israel could be defeated if its people were seduced to worship Baal, "to eat things sacrificed to idols and to commit sexual immorality" (Rev. 2:14). Indeed, this was exactly what happened: "The people [of Israel] began to commit harlotry with the women of Moab. They invited the people to the sacrifice of their gods, and the people ate and bowed down to their gods. So Israel was joined to Baal of Peor, and the anger of the Lord was aroused against Israel" (Num. 25:1–3).

In condemning "the way of Balaam," the New Testament condemns the greed of all who are well paid to tempt God's people to compromise their moral standards.

BARAK [BAR ack] (*lightning*) — a son of Abinoam of the city of Kedesh. Barak was summoned by Deborah, a prophetess who was judging Israel at that time. Deborah told Barak to raise a militia of 10,000 men to fight Jabin, king of Canaan, who had oppressed Israel for 20 years. The commander-in-chief of Jabin's army was Sisera.

Apparently during the battle, the Lord sent a great thunderstorm. The rain swelled the Kishon River and the plain surrounding the battle area, making Sisera's 900 iron chariots useless (Judg. 5:21). The Israelites routed the Canaanites. The victory is described twice: in prose (Judges 4) and in poetry, the beautiful "Song of Deborah" (Judges 5). Barak is listed in the New Testament among the heroes of faith (Heb. 11:32).

BARNABAS [BAR nuh bus] (*son of encouragement*) — an apostle in the early church (Acts 4:36–37; 11:19–26) and Paul's companion on his first missionary journey (Acts 13:1– 15:41). A Levite from the island of Cyprus, Barnabas's given name was Joseph, or Joses (Acts 4:36). When he became a Christian, he sold his land and gave the money to the Jerusalem apostles (Acts 4:36–37).

Early in the history of the church, Barnabas went to Antioch to check on the growth of this early group of Christians. Then he journeyed to Tarsus and brought Saul (as Paul was still called) back to minister with him to the Christians in Antioch (Acts 11:25). At this point Barnabas apparently was the leader of the church at Antioch, because his name is repeatedly mentioned before Paul's in the book of Acts. But after Saul's name was changed to Paul, Barnabas's name is always mentioned after Paul's (Acts 13:43).

Because of his good reputation, Barnabas was able to calm the fear of Saul among the Christians in Jerusalem (Acts 9:27). He and Saul also brought money from Antioch to the Jerusalem church when it was suffering a great famine (Acts 11:27–30). Shortly thereafter, the Holy Spirit led the Antioch church to commission Barnabas and Paul, along with John Mark, Barnabas's cousin (Col. 4:10), to make a missionary journey (Acts 13:1–3) to Cyprus and the provinces of Asia Minor.

A rift eventually developed between Barnabas and Paul over John Mark (Col. 4:10). Barnabas wanted to take John Mark on their second missionary journey. Paul, however, felt John Mark should stay behind because he had left the first mission at Cyprus (Acts 13:13). Paul and Barnabas went their separate ways, and Barnabas took John Mark with him on a second mission to Cyprus (Acts 15:36–39). A pseudepigraphic epistle named after Barnabas is falsely attributed to him.

BARTHOLOMEW [bar THOL oh mew] (*son of Tolmai*) — one of the twelve apostles of Jesus, according to the four lists given in the New Testament (Matt. 10:3; Mark 3:18; Luke 6:14; Acts 1:13). Many scholars equate Bartholomew with Nathanael (John 1:45–49), but no proof of this identification exists, except by inference. According to church tradition, Bartholomew was a missionary to various countries, such as Armenia and India. He is reported to have preached the gospel along with Philip and Thomas. According to another tradition, he was crucified upside down after being flayed alive.

BARUCH [bah RUKE] (*blessed*) — the name of three or four men in the Old Testament:

1. A son of Zabbai. Baruch helped Nehemiah repair the walls of Jerusalem (Neh. 3:20).

2. A man who sealed the covenant with Nehemiah (Neh. 10:6). He may be the same person as No. 1.

3. A son of Col-Hozeh and a returned captive of the tribe of Judah (Neh. 11:5).

4. The scribe or secretary of Jeremiah the prophet (Jer. 32:12–16; 36:1–32; 45:1–5). A son of Neriah, Baruch was a member of a prominent Jewish family. In the fourth year of the reign of Jehoiakim, king of Judah (605 B.C.), Baruch wrote Jeremiah's prophecies of destruction from the prophet's dictation (Jer. 36:1–8). Baruch read Jeremiah's words publicly on a day of fasting, then read them to the officials of the king's court. A clay seal inscribed "Baruch son of Neriah the scribe," dating from Jeremiah's time and clearly belonging to his secretary (see Jer. 36:32), was recently discovered in a burnt archive in Israel.

BASHAN [BAY shan] — the territory east of the Jordan River and the Sea of Galilee.

At the time of the Exodus, King Og ruled Bashan. His kingdom included 60 cities (Num. 21:33; Deut. 3:4; 29:7). His capital was at Ashtaroth. When Og was defeated at Edrei (Deut. 3:1–3), the territory was given to the half-tribe of Manasseh (Deut. 3:13), except for the cities of Golan and Be Eshterah, which were given to the Levites (Josh. 21:27). In the days of Jehu, the region was captured by the Aramean king, Hazael (2 Kin. 10:32–33).

A rich, fertile tableland about 490 to 700 meters (1600 to 2300 feet) above sea level, with abundant rainfall and volcanic soil, Bashan became the "breadbasket" of the region. Wheat fields and livestock were abundant. But in the Old Testament, the prosperity of Bashan became a symbol of selfish indulgence and arrogant pride. Evil persons who attacked the righteous were compared to "strong bulls of Bashan" (Ps. 22:12). The pampered, pleasure-seeking women of Samaria were called "cows of Bashan" (Amos 4:1).

BATHSHEBA [bath SHE buh] (*daughter of oath*) — a wife of Uriah the Hittite and of King David (2 Sam. 11; 12:24). Standing on the flat roof of his palace in Jerusalem one evening, David saw the beautiful Bathsheba bathing on the roof of a nearby house. With his passion aroused, David committed adultery with Bathsheba. Out of that union Bathsheba conceived a child.

When David discovered her pregnancy, he hurriedly sent for Uriah, who was in battle with the Ammonites. But Uriah refused to engage in marital relations with his wife while his companions were involved in battle. When David's attempt to trick Uriah failed, he sent him back into battle. This time, David ordered that Uriah be placed at the front of the battle and that his fellow soldiers retreat from him, so that he might be killed. After a period of mourning, Bathsheba became David's wife (2 Sam. 11:27). But the child conceived in adultery died.

When Nathan the prophet confronted David with the enormity of his sin, David repented (2 Sam. 12:13). God blessed them with four more children—Shammua (or Shimea), Shobab, Nathan, and Solomon (1 Chr. 3:5). The New Testament mentions Bathsheba indirectly in the genealogy of Jesus (Matt. 1:6). Bathsheba is also called Bathshua (1 Chr. 3:5).

BEERSHEBA [BEE ur SHE buh] (*well of the seven* or *well of the oath*) — the chief city of the Negev. Beersheba was situated in the territory of Simeon (Josh. 19:1–2) and was "at the limits of the tribe of the children of Judah, toward the border of Edom in the South" (Josh. 15:21, 28). Midway between the Mediterranean Sea and the southern end of the Dead Sea, Beersheba was considered the southern extremity of the promised land, giving rise to the often-used expression, "from Dan [in the north] to Beersheba" (Judg. 20:1) or "from Beersheba to Dan" (1 Chr. 21:2).

In Beersheba Abraham and Abimelech, king of Gerar (in Philistia), made a covenant and swore an oath of mutual assistance (Gen. 21:31). Abraham pledged to Abimelech seven ewe lambs to bear witness to the sincerity of his oath; from this transaction came the name Beersheba. It was in the Wilderness of Beersheba that Hagar wandered as she fled from Sarah (Gen. 21:33). Abraham dug a well and also planted a tamarisk tree here (Gen. 21:33), and he returned to Beersheba after God prevented him from offering Isaac as a sacrifice on Mount Moriah (Gen. 22:19).

At Beersheba a number of important encounters took place between God and various people. Here God appeared to Hagar (Gen. 21:17), Isaac (Gen. 26:23–33), and Jacob (Gen. 46:1–5). Ancient Beersheba has been identified with a large tract known as Tell es-Saba, situated about 3 kilometers (2 miles) east of the modern city.

BENJAMIN [BEN juh mun] (*son of the right hand* or *son of the south*) — the name of three or four men in the Old Testament:

1. Jacob's youngest son, born to his favorite wife, Rachel (Gen. 35:18, 24). After giving birth to Benjamin, the dying Rachel named him Ben-Oni (Gen. 35:18), which means "son of my pain." But Jacob renamed him Benjamin. When Jacob lost his beloved son Joseph, he became very attached to Benjamin because Benjamin was the only surviving son of Rachel. When his sons went to Egypt in search of food to relieve a famine, Jacob was reluctant to let Benjamin go with them (Gen. 43:1–17).

It is apparent that Joseph also loved Benjamin, his only full brother (Gen. 43:29–34). During this trip Joseph ordered that his silver cup be planted in Benjamin's sack. The reaction of Jacob and Benjamin's brothers shows the great love they had for Benjamin (Gen. 44). Benjamin had five sons and two grand-sons, and he became the founder of the tribe that carried his name (Gen. 46:21; Num. 26:38–41; 1 Chr. 7:6–12; 8:1–40).

2. A son of Bilhan, a Benjamite (1 Chr. 7:10).

3. A son of Harim who lived in Jerusalem following the return from the captivity. Benjamin divorced his pagan wife at Ezra's urging (Ezra 10:31–32).

4. A priest during the time of Nehemiah (Neh. 12:34) who helped repair and dedicate the wall of Jerusalem (Neh. 3:23). He may be the same person as No. 3.

BETHANY [BETH ah nih] — the name of two villages in the New Testament:

1. A village on the southeastern slopes of the Mount of Olives about 3 kilometers (2 miles) east of Jerusalem near the road to Jericho (Mark 11:1). Bethany was the scene of some of the most

important events of Jesus' life. It was the home of Martha, Mary, and Lazarus and the place where Jesus raised Lazarus from the dead (John 11). During Jesus' final week, He spent at least one night in Bethany (Matt. 21:17). At Bethany Jesus was anointed by Mary in the home of Simon the leper (Matt. 26:6–13). From a site near Bethany, He ascended into heaven (Luke 24:50).

2. A village in Transjordan where John the Baptist was baptizing (John 1:28, NIV; Bethabara, KJV, NKJV).

BETHEL [BETH uhl] (*house of God*) — the name of two cities in the Old Testament:

1. A city of Canaan about 19 kilometers (12 miles) north of Jerusalem. Bethel is mentioned more often in the Bible than any other city except Jerusalem. It is first mentioned in connection with Abraham, who "pitched his tent with Bethel on the west and . . . built an altar to the LORD" (Gen. 12:8; 13:3). The region around Bethel is still suitable for grazing by livestock.

Jacob, Abraham's grandson, had a life-changing experience at this site. He had a vision of a staircase reaching into the heavens with the angels of God "ascending and descending on it" (Gen. 28:12). Jacob called the name of that place Bethel, "the house of God" (Gen. 28:19). He erected a pillar at Bethel to mark the spot of his vision (Gen. 28:22; 31:13). Jacob later built an altar at Bethel, where he worshiped the Lord (Gen. 35:1–16).

During Israel's war with the Benjamites in later years (Judg. 20), the children of Israel suffered two disastrous defeats (Judg. 20:21, 25). They went to Bethel (the house of God, NKJV) to inquire of the Lord, for the ark of the covenant was located there (Judg. 20:26–27). At Bethel they built an altar and offered burnt offerings and peace offerings before the Lord. The third battle ended in disaster for the Benjamites. At the end of the war the Israelites returned to Bethel (the house of God, NKJV), built an altar, and again offered burnt offerings and peace offerings (Judg. 21:1–4).

After the death of Solomon and the division of his kingdom, Jeroboam, the king of Israel (the Northern Kingdom), set up two calves of gold, one in Bethel and one in Dan (1 Kin. 12:29, 32–33). Thus, Bethel became a great center of idolatry (1 Kin. 13:1–32; 2 Kin. 10:29) and the chief sanctuary of Israel (Amos 7:13), rivaling the temple in Jerusalem.

The prophets Jeremiah and Amos denounced Bethel for its idolatries (Jer. 48:13; Amos 5:5–6). Hosea, deploring its great wickedness (Hos. 10:5, 15), called it Beth Aven ("house of idols"), because of the golden calf set up there. Bethel, the house of God, had deteriorated into Beth Aven, the house of idols.

In a religious reformation that sought to restore the true worship of God, King Josiah broke down the altar at Bethel (2 Kin. 23:15). Still later in Israel's history, Bethel was occupied by Jewish people who returned from the captivity in Babylon with Zerubbabel (Ezra 2:28; Neh. 7:32). The place again reverted to the Benjamites (Neh. 11:31). The city was destroyed about 540 B.C. by a great fire. This destruction may have been the work of Nabonidus of Babylon or of the Persians in the period just before Darius. Today the site of Bethel is occupied by a small village called Beitin.

The New Testament does not refer to Bethel, but Jesus must have gone through this area on His trips. The city was situated on the main road from Shechem to Jerusalem.

2. A city in the territory of Simeon (1 Sam. 30:27). Scholars believe this Bethel is a variant reading for Bethul (Josh. 19:4) or Bethuel (1 Chr. 4:30).

BETHESDA [buh THEZ duh] (*house of grace*) — a pool in the northeastern part of Jerusalem, near the Sheep Gate. At this pool Jesus healed the man "who had an infirmity thirty-eight years" (John 5:5). Archaeologists have discovered two pools in this vicinity, 16 1/2 and 19 1/2 meters (55 and 65 feet) long respectively. The shorter pool had five arches over it with a porch beneath each arch, corresponding to the description given in John 5:2. The Crusaders later built a church on this site to commemorate the healing miracle that took place.

The man who had been lame for 38 years came to the pool hoping to be cured by its miraculous waters; instead he was healed by the word of Jesus (John 5:1–15).

BETHLEHEM [BETH luh hem] (*house of bread* or *house of* [the god] *Lahmu*) — the name of two cities and possibly one man in the Bible:

1. The birthplace of Jesus Christ. Bethlehem was situated about 8 kilometers (5 miles) south of Jerusalem in the district known as Ephrathah in Judah (Mic. 5:2), a region known for its fertile hills and valleys.

Bethlehem was the burial place of Rachel, the wife of Jacob (Gen. 35:19). The original home of Naomi and her family, it was also the setting for much of the book of Ruth. Bethlehem also was the ancestral home of David (1 Sam. 17:12) and was rebuilt and fortified by King Rehoboam (2 Chr. 11:6).

The most important Old Testament figure associated with Bethlehem was David, Israel's great king. At Bethlehem Samuel anointed David as Saul's successor (1 Sam. 16:1, 13). Although David made Jerusalem his capital city, he never lost his love for Bethlehem. Second Samuel 23:14–17 is a warm story about David's longing for a drink of water from the well of Bethlehem, which was a Philistine garrison at the time. But when three of David's mighty men broke through the Philistine lines to draw a drink of water, David refused to drink it because it symbolized "the blood of the men who went in jeopardy of their lives" (2 Sam. 23:17).

The prophet Micah predicted that Bethlehem would be the birthplace of the Messiah (Mic. 5:2), a prophecy quoted in Matthew 2:6. It is significant that the King of kings, who was of the house of David, was born in David's ancestral home. According to Luke 2:11, Jesus was born in "the city of David," Bethlehem. Christ, who is the Bread of Life, was cradled in a town whose name means "house of bread."

The Church of the Nativity, which marks the birthplace of the Savior, is one of the best authenticated sites in the Holy Land. The present structure, built over the cave area that served as a stable for the inn, goes back to the time of the Roman emperor Justinian (sixth century A.D.). This church replaces an earlier building, built in A.D. 330 by Helena, the mother of the Roman emperor Constantine.

2. A town in the land of Zebulun (Josh. 19:15).

3. A son of Salma, a descendant of Caleb (1 Chr. 2:51). As the "father" of Bethlehem, Salma may have been the founder of Bethlehem rather than being the father of a son named "Bethlehem."

BETHSAIDA [beth SAY ih duh] (*house of fishing*) — the name of one or possibly two cities in the New Testament:

1. Bethsaida, which was later called Julias, was situated 3 kilometers (2 miles) north of the Sea of Galilee and east of the Jordan River. The name Julias was given to it by the tetrarch Philip (Luke 3:1), after Julia, the daughter of Caesar Augustus. In the wilderness near Bethsaida, Jesus fed the 5,000 and healed the multitudes (Luke 9:10–17). It was also in Bethsaida that He restored sight to a blind man (Mark 8:22).

2. The Gospels of Mark, Luke, and John seem to speak of another Bethsaida, which was the home of Philip, Andrew, and Peter (John 1:44) and perhaps of James and John (Luke 5:10). This city was situated northwest of the Sea of Galilee in the fertile plain of Gennesaret (Mark 6:45, 53) near Capernaum (John 6:17) in the province of Galilee (John 12:21).

Some scholars argue that there was only one city called Bethsaida. The Jewish historian Josephus identified the

Bethsaida developed by Philip as being near the Jordan in "Lower Gaulanitis." Yet, the Gospels seem to indicate that there was another Bethsaida west of the Jordan River (for example, see Mark 6:45, 53). Philip, Peter, and Andrew were from "Bethsaida of Galilee" (John 12:21). Bethsaida-Julias could not be considered to be "of Galilee." The close connection of Bethsaida with Chorazin (Matt. 11:21) and Capernaum (Matt. 11:23) as the center of Jesus' ministry in Galilee is strong evidence for another Bethsaida situated closer to them.

BOAZ [BOE az] (*in him is strength*) — the name of a prominent man and an object in the temple:

1. A wealthy and honorable man of Bethlehem from the tribe of Judah. He was a kinsman of Elimelech, Naomi's husband, and he became the husband of Ruth, Naomi's widowed daughter-in-law (Ruth 2–4). Through their son Obed, Boaz and Ruth became ancestors of King David and of the Lord Jesus Christ (Matt. 1:5; Booz, KJV).

2. One of the two bronze pillars that stood in front of King Solomon's magnificent temple (2 Chr. 3:17). The name of the other was Jachin.

CAESAREA [sess uh REE uh] (*pertaining to Caesar*) — an important biblical seaport located south of modern Haifa. Built at enormous expense by Herod the Great between 25 and 13 B.C., and named in honor of Caesar Augustus, the city was sometimes called Caesarea of Palestine to distinguish it from Caesarea Philippi.

Herod spent 12 years building his seaport jewel on the site of an ancient Phoenician city named Strato's Tower. He constructed a huge breakwater. The enormous stones he used in this project were 15.25 meters (50 feet) long, 5.5 meters (18 feet) wide, and 2.75 meters (9 feet) deep. Some of them still can be seen extending 45.75 meters (150 feet) from the shore. Caesarea frequently was the scene of disturbances as cities of mixed Jewish–Gentile population tended to be. When Pilate was prefect (governor) of Judea, he lived in the governor's residence at Caesarea. In 1961, a stone inscribed with his name was found in the ruins of an ancient amphitheater there. Philip the evangelist preached there (Acts 8:40), and Peter was sent there to minister to the Roman centurion Cornelius (Acts 10:1, 24; 11:11). Herod Agrippa I died at Caesarea, being "eaten of worms" (Acts 12:19–23).

Caesarea was prominent in the ministry of the apostle Paul as well. After Paul's conversion, some brethren brought him to the port at Caesarea to escape the Hellenists and sail to his hometown of Tarsus (Acts 9:30). Paul made Caesarea his port of call after both his second and third missionary journeys (Acts 18:22; 21:8). Felix sent Paul to Caesarea for trial (Acts 23:23, 33) and the apostle spent two years in prison before making his celebrated defense before Festus and Agrippa (Acts 26). Paul sailed from the harbor in chains to appeal his case before the emperor in Rome (Acts 25:11; 26:1–13).

CAESAREA PHILIPPI [sess uh REE uh FILL uh pie] (*Caesar's city of Philip*) — a city on the southwestern slope of Mount Hermon and at the northernmost extent of Jesus' ministry (Matt. 16:13; Mark 8:27). In New Testament times the city was known as Paneas, although Philip the tetrarch renamed the city Caesarea Philippi, in honor of the Roman emperor Augustus Caesar. Agrippa II later changed its name to Neronias, in honor of Nero. The present-day village of Baniyas is built on the same site. It was near Caesarea Philippi that Jesus asked His disciples who He was and received the inspired answer from Simon Peter: "You are the Christ, the Son of the living God" (Matt. 16:16).

CAIAPHAS [KY uh fuhs] — the high priest of Israel appointed about A.D. 18 by the Roman procurator, Valerius Gratus. Caiaphas and his father-in-law, Annas, were high priests when John the Baptist began his preaching (Matt. 26:3, 57; Luke 3:2). Caiaphas also was a member of the Sadducees.

After Jesus raised Lazarus from the dead, the Jewish leaders became alarmed at Jesus' increasing popularity. The Sanhedrin quickly called a meeting, during which Caiaphas called for Jesus' death. As High Priest, Caiaphas's words carried great authority, and his counsel was followed (John 11:49–53). Subsequently,

Caiaphas plotted the arrest of Jesus (Matt. 26:3–4) and was a participant in the illegal trial of Jesus (Matt. 26:57–68).

The final appearance of Caiaphas in the New Testament was at the trial of Peter and John. He was one of the leaders who questioned the two disciples about the miraculous healing of the lame man "at the gate of the temple which is called Beautiful", Acts 4:6–7). In 1990, an ornate ossuary bearing the name of Caiaphas and containing the bones of a sixty-year-old man was found outside of Jerusalem. The bones may be those of Caiaphas himself.

CAIN [kane] (*metalworker*) — the name of a person and a city in the Old Testament:

1. The oldest son of Adam and Eve and the brother of Abel (Gen. 4:1–25). Cain was the first murderer. A farmer by occupation, Cain brought fruits of the ground as a sacrifice to God. His brother Abel, a shepherd, sacrificed a lamb from his flock. The Lord accepted Abel's offering but rejected Cain's (Gen. 4:7). The proof of Cain's wrong standing before God is seen in his impulse to kill his own brother Abel when his own offering was rejected (Gen. 4:8). Cain was the ancestor of a clan of metalworkers (Gen. 4:18–19, 22).

The New Testament refers to Cain in three places. Abel's offering to God was "a more excellent sacrifice" than Cain's because Abel was "righteous." His heart was right with God, and Cain's was not (Heb. 11:4). John calls Cain "the wicked one" and asks why he murdered his brother; the answer was "Because his works were evil, and his brother's righteous" (1 John 3:12). Jude warns his readers to beware of those who have "gone in the way of Cain" (Jude 11).

2. A town in the mountains of southern Judah, also spelled Kain (Josh. 15:57).

CALEB [KAY lubb] (*dog*) — the name of two men in the Old Testament:

1. One of the 12 spies sent by Moses to investigate the land of Canaan (Num. 13:6, 30; 14:6, 24, 30, 38). Ten of the 12 spies frightened the Israelites with reports of fortified cities and gigantic peoples. Compared to the giants in the land, they saw themselves as "grasshoppers" (Num. 13:33).

Joshua and Caleb also saw the fortified cities in the land, but they reacted in faith rather than fear. They advised Moses and Aaron and the Israelites to attack Canaan immediately (Num. 13:30). The Israelites listened to the spies rather than the two, and the Lord viewed their fear as a lack of faith and judged them for their spiritual timidity. Of all the adults alive at that time, only Caleb and Joshua would live to possess the land (Josh. 14:6–15).

Caleb was also part of the group selected by Moses to help divide the land among the tribes. He was 85 years old when Canaan was finally conquered. Hebron was given to Caleb as a divine inheritance.

2. A son of Hezron of the family of Perez of the tribe of Judah (1 Chr. 2:18–19, 42). Descended from this Caleb were Aaron's associate Hur and Hur's grandson Bezaleel, a skilled craftsman. An alternate spelling of the name is Chelubai (1 Chr. 2:9).

CALVARY [KAL vuh rih] (from the Latin word *calvaria*, "the skull") — the name used in the KJV and NKJV for the place outside Jerusalem where the Lord Jesus was crucified (Luke 23:33; the Skull, NIV). No one knows for sure why this place was called "the skull." The most likely reason is that the site was a place of execution; the skull is a widely recognized symbol for death. The site may have been associated with a cemetery, although its location near Jerusalem makes it improbable that skulls could be viewed there. Perhaps the area was an outcropping of rock that in some way resembled a skull.

Mark 15:40 and Luke 23:49 indicate that some people viewed Jesus' crucifixion from a distance. John 19:20 says the place was "near the city" of Jerusalem; and Hebrews 13:12 reports that our Lord "suffered outside the gate," which means outside the city walls. From Matthew's reference to "those who passed by" (27:39), it seems the site was close to a well-traveled road. It also is reasonable to think that Joseph's tomb (John 19:41) was quite close. But the Bible does not clearly indicate exactly where Jesus died.

Sites of the crucifixion have been proposed on every side of Jerusalem. One factor that makes it difficult to pinpoint the site is that Jerusalem was destroyed in A.D. 70 by the Romans, and another Jewish revolt was crushed in a similar manner in A.D. 135. Many geographical features and the location of the city walls were greatly changed because of these and a series of conflicts that continued for centuries.

Except in areas that have been excavated, Jerusalem's present walls date from more recent times. The presence of modern buildings prevents digging to find where the walls were located during New Testament times. Some groups claim to have found the very place where Jesus died, but these complicating factors make it unlikely. At present, Christian opinion is divided over two possible sites for Calvary. One is on the grounds of the Church of the Holy Sepulcher. The other, called "Gordon's Calvary," is about 229 meters (250 yards) northeast of the Damascus Gate in the old city wall. A tradition going back to the fourth century says that a search was initiated by the Christian historian Eusebius and that the site was found by Bishop Macarius. Later the Roman emperor Constantine built a church on the site. Previously the place was the location of a temple to Aphrodite. Tradition also has it that while looking for Jesus' tomb, Constantine's mother, Helena, found part of "the true cross" on which Jesus died. These traditions are very old, but their historical value is uncertain. The Church of the Holy

Sepulcher is now inside what is called "the old city," but supporters claim the location was outside the walls of the city in New Testament times. Following an earlier lead, a British general, Charles Gordon, in 1885 strongly advocated the other major site, which is outside the present existing city walls. The place is a grass-covered rocky knoll that, due to excavations (perhaps mining) some time during the past three centuries, now looks something like a skull when viewed from one direction. Beside the hill is what has been called "Jeremiah's Grotto," where an ancient tomb has been recently landscaped to produce a garden setting. This area is sometimes called the "Garden Tomb." The site known as "Gordon's Calvary" has commended itself especially to some Protestant groups, while the location at the Church of the Holy Sepulcher is highly regarded by the Roman Catholic and Orthodox churches. For Christians, it is the fact of our Lord's self-sacrifice—"that Christ died for our sins according to the Scriptures, and that He was buried, and that He rose again" (1 Cor. 15:3–4)—not the location, that should concern us. At "Calvary," Golgotha's cross—"the emblem of suffering and shame"—became the symbol of love, blessing, and hope.

The Aramaic name for the place where Jesus was crucified is Golgotha (Matt. 27:33; Mark 15:22; John 19:17), which, like Calvary, also means "the skull."

CANAAN [KANE un] (*land of purple*) — the name of a man and a land or region in the Old Testament:

1. The fourth son of Ham and the grandson of Noah (Gen. 9:18–27; 10:6, 15). Ham's descendants were dispersed into several distinctive tribes, such as the Jebusites and the Zemarites. These people became known collectively in later years as the Canaanites, pagan inhabitants of the land that God promised to Abraham and his descendants. Under the leadership of Joshua, the people of Israel occupied the land of Canaan and divided it among the twelve tribes.

2. The region along the Mediterranean Sea occupied by the Canaanites before it was taken and settled by the Israelite people (Gen. 11:31; Josh. 5:12). The land of Canaan stretched from the Jordan River on the east to the Mediterranean Sea on the west. From south to north, it covered the territory between the Sinai Peninsula and the ancient coastal nation of Phoenicia. Much of this territory was dry, mountainous, and rocky, unfit for cultivation. But it also contained many fertile farmlands, particularly in the river valleys and the coastal plains along the sea. While leading the people of Israel toward the land of Canaan, Moses sent scouts, or spies, into the territory on a fact-finding mission. They returned with grapes, pomegranates, and figs to verify the fertility of the land (Num. 13:2, 17, 23).

The land of Canaan was ideally situated on the trade routes that stretched from Egypt in the south to Syria and Phoenicia in the north and the ancient Babylonian Empire to the east. This location gave the small region a strategic position in the ancient world. After the Israelites captured the land of Canaan, they developed a thriving commercial system by trading goods with other nations along these routes. The finest royal purple dye was manufactured in Canaan, giving the territory is name.

CAPERNAUM [kuh PURR nay uhm] (*village of Nahum*) — the most important city on the northern shore of the Sea of Galilee in New Testament times and the center of much of Jesus' ministry. Capernaum is not mentioned in the Old Testament, and the Nahum after whom it was named is probably not the prophet Nahum. In all likelihood, Capernaum was founded sometime after the Jews returned from captivity.

By the New Testament era, Capernaum was large enough that it always was called a "city" (Matt. 9:1; Mark 1:33). It had its own synagogue, in which Jesus frequently taught (Mark 1:21; Luke 4:31–38; John 6:59). Apparently the synagogue was built by the Roman soldiers garrisoned in Capernaum (Matt. 8:8;

Luke 7:1–10). The synagogue was a center for the Roman system of taxation; for it had a permanent office of taxation (Matt. 9:9; Mark 2:14; Luke 5:27), and itinerant tax collectors operated in the city (Matt. 17:24). Ruins of a later synagogue cover those of the one where Jesus worshiped, although sections of the latter can still be seen today.

After being rejected in His hometown, Nazareth, Jesus made Capernaum the center of His ministry in Galilee. He performed many miracles here, including the healing of the centurion's paralyzed servant (Matt. 8:5–13), a paralytic carried by four friends (Mark 2:1–12), Peter's mother-in-law (Matt. 8:14–15; Mark 1:29–31), and the nobleman's son (John 4:46–54).

As Jesus walked by the Sea of Galilee near Capernaum, He called the fishermen Simon, Andrew, James, and John to be his disciples (Mark 1:16–21, 29). It was also in "His own city" (Capernaum) that Jesus called the tax collector Matthew (Matt. 9:1, 9; Mark 2:13–14). Immediately following the feeding of the five thousand, Jesus delivered His discourse on the Bread of Life near this city (John 6:32).

Although Jesus centered His ministry in Capernaum, the people of that city did not follow him. Jesus pronounced a curse on the city for its unbelief (Matt. 11:23–24), predicting its ruin (Luke 10:15). So strikingly did this prophecy come true that only recently has Tell Hum been identified confidently as ancient Capernaum.

CARMEL [KAHR muhl] (*garden/orchard of God*) — the name of a mountain range and a town in the Old Testament:

1. A town in the hill country of Judah (Josh. 15:55; 1 Sam. 25:2, 5, 7, 40). It has been identified as present-day Khirbet el-Kermel, about 13 kilometers (8 miles) southeast of Hebron. Carmel, near Maon, was the home of a very rich and very foolish man named Nabal. This man was a stubborn, churlish fellow who insulted David by refusing to show hospitality to

David's servants. The Lord struck Nabal so that "his heart died within him, and he became like a stone" (1 Sam. 25:37). After Nabal's death, David sent for Abigail the Carmelitess, widow of Nabal, to take her as his wife. Abigail, "a woman of good understanding and beautiful appearance" (1 Sam. 25:3), became one of David's wives. Hezrai (2 Sam. 23:35), or Hezro (1 Chr. 11:37), one of David's mighty men, also came from Carmel.

2. A mountain range stretching about 21 kilometers (13 miles) from the Mediterranean coast southeast to the Plain of Dothan. At the Bay of Accho (Acre), near the modern city of Haifa, this mountain range juts out into the Mediterranean Sea in a promontory named Mount Carmel. It rises sharply from the seacoast to a height of 143 meters (470 feet) near Haifa. The mountain range as a whole averages over 1,000 feet above sea level, with 530 meters (1,742 feet) being the summit.

The Canaanites built sanctuaries to pagan deities on this mountain. Thus, Carmel was an appropriate site for a confrontation between Elijah, the prophet of the Lord, and the "prophets of Baal" (1 Kin. 18:19–20), the idolatrous Canaanite priests. It was also from the top of Mount Carmel that Elijah saw a sign of the coming storm: "a cloud, as small as a man's hand, rising out of the sea" (1 Kin. 18:44), a cloud that signaled the end of a prolonged drought. The prophet Elisha also visited Mount Carmel (2 Kin. 2:25; 4:25).

CHALDEA [kal DEE uh] — originally, the lower Tigris and Euphrates valley, or the southern portion of Babylonia. Later, beginning with the reign of Nebuchadnezzar II (king of Babylonia from 605 to 562 B.C.), the term "Chaldea" came to include practically all of Babylonia and was virtually synonymous with the Neo-Babylonian Empire.

In the NKJV the term "Chaldea" is found only in the books of Jeremiah and Ezekiel. Jeremiah prophesied the fall of Babylon by saying, "Chaldea shall become plunder" (Jer. 50:10) and "I will repay Babylon, and all the inhabitants of Chaldea for all the evil they have done" (Jer. 51:24). In a vision, the Spirit of God took Ezekiel into Chaldea to his fellow Jews in captivity (Ezek. 11:24). Ezekiel later referred to "the Babylonians of Chaldea" (Ezek. 16:29; 23:15–16).

CHEDORLAOMER [ked awr LAY oh muhr] (*servant of [the Elamite God] Lagamar*) — a king of Elam, a country east of Babylonia, in Abraham's day (Gen. 14:1, 4–5, 9, 17; Kedorlaomer, NIV). Allied with three other Mesopotamian kings—Amraphel of Shinar, Arioch of Ellasar, and Tidal of "nations"—Chedorlaomer led a campaign against southern Canaan and defeated the inhabitants in the Valley of Siddim near the Dead Sea. The conquered people served Chedorlaomer for 12 years, but in the 13th year they rebelled (Gen. 14:4).

Chedorlaomer came again with his allies and conquered the region east of the Jordan River from Bashan southward to the Red Sea as well as the plain around the Dead Sea, thus gaining control of the lucrative caravan routes from Arabia and Egypt through Canaan. In making this conquest, Chedorlaomer captured Lot, Abraham's nephew. Aided by his allies and numerous servants, Abraham launched a night attack on Chedorlaomer at Dan, defeating him and recovering Lot and the spoils. Although Chedorlaomer has not been identified in references outside the Old Testament, the elements of his name are typically Elamite.

CHINNERETH, CHINNEROTH, CINNEROTH [CHIN uh reth, CHIN uh roth, SIN uh roth] (*lute, harp*) — the name of a lake, a region, and a city in the Bible:

1. The early name of the Sea of Galilee (Num. 34:11; Josh. 12:3; 13:27; Kinnereth, NIV). It was also called the "Lake of Gennesaret" (Luke 5:1) and the "Sea of Tiberias" (John 6:1; 21:1). The lake is shaped like the outline of a harp.

2. A fortified city of Naphtali on the northwest shore of the Sea of Galilee (Deut. 3:17; Josh. 19:35).

3. A region in or near the territory of Naphtali commonly identified with the Plain of Gennesaret (1 Kin. 15:20).

CITIES OF THE PLAIN — a term used for five cities located near the Dead Sea (Gen. 14:2, 8). Because of their great wickedness, four of these cities—Sodom, Gomorrah, Admah, and Zeboiim (Gen. 19:28–29)—were completely destroyed. Only Zoar escaped destruction (Gen. 19:21–22).

Prior to its destruction, this area was well watered and productive; it was compared to the garden of Eden and the rich Nile Delta of Egypt (Gen. 13:10). Today this area is totally barren and supports no life—an eloquent testimony of God's judgment upon the sin of these ancient peoples. Genesis 19 describes the complete destruction of the area; even today earthquakes are common.

Recent archaeological evidence locates the cities of the plain near the entrance to the Lisan, the tongue of land that juts out into the Dead Sea from its eastern shore.

CITY OF DAVID — the name of two cities in the Bible:
1. The stronghold of Zion, the fortified city of the Jebusites, later known as Jerusalem. King David and his men captured it (2 Sam. 5:7, 9). The Jebusite fortress of Zion was situated on a hill overlooking the pool of Siloam, at the junction of the Kidron and Tyropoeon valleys (later in southeastern Jerusalem). The account of the capture of Zion implies that David's army entered the fortress by surprise (2 Sam. 5:8). The "water shaft" mentioned in this passage was apparently a tunnel leading from the underground spring of Gihon into the citadel. Joab was the one who went up the shaft first (1 Chr. 11:6); true to his promise, David made him the commander, or "chief," of the armies of Israel.

After the capture of Zion, "David dwelt in the stronghold, and called it the City of David" (2 Sam. 5:9). Not only did David establish his residence here, but he also strengthened the city's fortifications (1 Chr. 11:8). Solomon further strengthened the defenses of the city (1 Kin. 11:27). The site of Solomon's temple was on the neighboring Mount Moriah, part of the same strong rock outcropping as Mount Zion.

2. Bethlehem, the birthplace or home of David (1 Sam. 16:1, 13; Luke 2:4, 11; John 7:42) and of Jesus, David's greatest descendant.

COLOSSE — a city in the Roman province of Asia (western Turkey), situated in the Lycus River Valley about 160 kilometers (100 miles) east of Ephesus. The apostle Paul wrote a letter to the church at Colosse (Col. 1:2; Colossae, NASB, REB, NRSV). The Christian community at Colosse apparently grew up under the leadership of Epaphras (Col. 1:7; 4:12) and Archippus (Col. 4:17; Philem. v. 2). Philemon and Onesimus lived at Colosse (Col. 4:9).

Colosse formed a triangle with two other cities of the Lycus Valley, Hierapolis and Laodicea, both of which are mentioned in the New Testament. As early as the fifth century B.C., Colosse was known as a prosperous city; but by the beginning of the Christian era it was eclipsed by its two neighbors. Thereafter its reputation declined to that of a small town.

Shortly after the apostle Paul sent his epistle to Colosse, the cities of the Lycus Valley suffered a devastating earthquake in A.D. 61. They were soon rebuilt, even Laodicea, which had suffered the greatest damage. Although Colosse was increasingly overshadowed by Laodicea and Hierapolis, it retained considerable importance into the second and third centuries A.D. Later, the population of Colosse moved to Chonai (modern Honaz), 3 miles to the south. The mound that marks the site of Colosse remains uninhabited today.

CORINTH [KAWR inth] — ancient Greece's most important trade city (Acts 18:1; 19:1; 1 Cor. 1:2; 2 Cor. 1:1, 23; 2 Tim. 4:20). Ideally situated on the Isthmus of Corinth between the Ionian Sea and the Aegean Sea, Corinth was the connecting link between Rome, the capital of the world, and the East. At Corinth the apostle Paul established a flourishing church, made up of a cross section of the worldly minded people who had flocked to Corinth to participate in the gambling, legalized temple prostitution, business adventures, and amusements available in a first-century navy town (1 Cor. 6:9–11).

Although the apostle Paul did not establish the church in Corinth until about A.D. 51 (Acts 18:1–18), the city's history dates back to prehistoric times, when ancient tribesmen first settled the site. Always a commercial and trade center, Corinth was already prosperous and famous for its bronze, pottery, and shipbuilding more than 800 years before Christ. The Greek poet Homer mentioned "wealthy Corinth" in 850 B.C. In the following centuries Corinth competed for power with Athens, its stronger neighbor across the isthmus to the north. And in 146 B.C. invading Roman armies destroyed Corinth, killing the men and enslaving the women and children. Only a token settlement remained until 44 B.C., when Julius Caesar ordered the city rebuilt. Not only did he restore it as the capital city of the Roman province of Achaia; he also repopulated it with freed Italians and slaves from every nation. Soon the merchants flocked back to Corinth, too.

The city soon became a melting pot for the approximately 500,000 people who lived there at the time of Paul's arrival. Merchants and sailors, eager to work the docks, migrated to Corinth. Professional gamblers and athletes, betting on the Isthmian games, took up residence. Slaves, sometimes freed but with no place to go, roamed the streets day and night. And prostitutes (both male and female) were abundant. People from Rome, the rest of Greece, Egypt, Asia Minor—indeed, all of the Mediterranean world—relished the lack of standards and freedom of thought that prevailed in the city. These were the people who eventually made up the Corinthian church. They had to learn to live together in harmony, although their national, social, economic, and religious backgrounds were very different. Perched on a narrow strip of land connecting the Peloponnesus, a peninsula of southern Greece, with central Greece and the rest of Europe, Corinth enjoyed a steady flow of trade. The city had two splendid harbor cities—Cenchreae, the eastern port on the Saronic Gulf; and Lechaeum, the western port on the Corinthian Gulf. In the outlying areas around Corinth, farmers tended their grain fields, vineyards, and olive groves. But the pulse of Corinth was the city itself, enclosed by walls 10 kilometers (6 miles) in circumference. Most of the daily business was conducted in the marble-paved agora, or marketplace, in the central part of the city. Although only 1 percent of the ancient city has been excavated by archaeologists, some interesting discoveries give ideas of what the city was like when Paul arrived. A marble lintel or crosspiece of a door was found near the residential section of Corinth. It bore part of the inscription "Synagogue of the Hebrews." This may have been on the same site of the earlier synagogue in which Paul first proclaimed the gospel message to Corinth, accompanied by his newfound Jewish friends, Aquila and Priscilla (Acts 18:2).

Not far from the synagogue excavation site was the magnificent judgment seat, covered with ornate blue and white marble. There, the Roman proconsul of Achaia, Gallio, dismissed Paul's case (Acts 18:12–17). In the pavement of an amphitheater is inscribed the name Erastus, perhaps the official of Corinth mentioned in Romans 16:23 and 2 Timothy 4:20.

South of the marketplace were the butcher stalls (shambles, KJV; meat market, NKJV, NASB, NIV, REB, NRSV) that Paul mentioned in 1 Corinthians 10:25. Corinthians purchased their meat from these stalls. The meat was often dedicated to pagan idols before being sold. This presented a cultural problem for the Christians in Corinth (1 Corinthians 8).

Today the temple of Apollo, partially in ruins, towers above the ancient marketplace. Each fluted Doric column, about 7 meters (almost 24 feet) tall, was cut from a single piece of stone in one of several quarries outside Corinth's walls. Rising 457 meters (1,500 feet) above the city itself and to the south is the Acrocorinth, the acropolis or citadel. From there, the acropolis at Athens, about 73 kilometers (45 miles) away, can be seen. Also, the infamous temple of Aphrodite (or Venus) was located on top of this fortified hill. This pagan temple and its 1,000 "religious" prostitutes poisoned the city's culture and morals. For this reason, the apostle Paul sometimes had to deal harshly with the converts in the Corinthian church. Most of the Corinthians had lived in this godless society all their lives, and the idea of tolerating even incest had not seemed so terrible to them (1 Corinthians 5).

In spite of Corinth's notorious reputation, God used the apostle Paul to establish a vigorous church in the city about A.D. 51 (Acts 18:1–18). Later, Paul wrote at least two letters to the church at Corinth. Both deal with divisions in the church, as well as immorality and the abuse of Christian freedom.

The Corinth that Paul knew was partially destroyed by an earthquake in A.D. 521, then totally devastated by another in 1858. Modern Corinth, rebuilt about 4 kilometers (2.5 miles) from the ancient site, is little more than a town. It is certainly not a thriving trade center, but the inhabitants only need to look at the ancient ruins to recall the former glory of their city. The success of the gospel at Corinth—bittersweet though it was—illustrates that the grace of God comes not so much to the noble as to the needy (1 Cor. 1:26–31).

CORNELIUS [kor NEEL yus] — a Roman soldier stationed in Caesarea who was the first recorded Gentile convert to Christianity (Acts 10:1–33).

Cornelius was a God-fearing man strongly attracted to the Jewish teaching of monotheism (the belief in one God), as opposed to pagan idolatry and immorality, and to the concern expressed in the law of Moses concerning helping the poor and needy (Acts 10:2). He is introduced in the book of Acts as a representative of thousands in the Gentile world who were weary of paganism and who were hungry for the coming of the Messiah—the Christ who would deliver them from their sins and lead them into an abundant, Spirit-filled life.

God sent a heavenly vision both to Cornelius and to Simon Peter. Obeying his vision, Cornelius sent some of his men to Joppa, about 58 kilometers (36 miles) south of Caesarea, to find Peter. Peter, in turn, obeyed his own vision (which he interpreted to mean that Gentiles were to be included in Christ's message) and went to Cornelius. While Peter was still preaching to Cornelius and his household, "the Holy Spirit fell upon all those who heard the word" (Acts 10:44). And Peter commanded them to be baptized in the name of the Lord.

This incident marked the expansion of the early church to include Gentiles as well as Jews (Acts 10:34–35; 11:18). Peter alluded to Cornelius's conversion at the Jerusalem Council (Acts 15:7–11).

CUSH [kush] — the name of two men and two lands in the Old Testament:

1. A land that bordered the Gihon River, one of the four rivers of the garden of Eden (Gen. 2:10–14). Since the Tigris (Hiddekel) and Euphrates are mentioned, this land must have been in or near Mesopotamia. It was named after No. 2.

2. A son of Ham and grandson of Noah. His brothers settled in Egypt and Canaan, and his famous son Nimrod lived in Mesopotamia (Gen. 10:6–12; 1 Chr. 1:8–10; also Mic. 5:6).

3. A man from the tribe of Benjamin who was an enemy of David (see the title of Psalm 7).

4. The land south of Egypt, also called Nubia, which includes part of Sudan. Cush began just beyond Syene (modern Aswan; Ezek. 29:10). The Persian Empire of Ahasuerus (Xerxes, 486–465 B.C.) extended to this point, "from India to Ethiopia" (Esth. 1:1; 8:9). Precious stones came from Cush, "the topaz of Ethiopia" (Job 28:19), and the people were tall with smooth skin (Isa. 18:2, 7) that could not be changed (Jer. 13:23). The prophets predicted that the distant land of Cush would be judged by God (Is. 18:1–6; Zeph. 2:12). Other texts indicate, however, that some from Cush will bring gifts to God and worship Him as their king (Ps. 68:31; Is. 11:11; 18:7). Its ancient Greek name was Ethiopia, not to be confused with the modern nation of Ethiopia (Abyssinia).

DAMASCUS [duh MASS cuss] — the oldest continually inhabited city in the world and capital of Syria (Is. 7:8), located northeast of the Sea of Galilee.

Damascus was situated on the border of the desert at the intersection of some of the most important highways in the ancient Near Eastern world. Three major caravan routes passed through Damascus. Major roads extended from the city to the southwest into Canaan and Egypt, straight south to Edom and the Red Sea, and east to Babylonia. Because of its ideal location, the city became a trade center. Its major exports (Ezek. 27:18) included a patterned cloth called "damask." Egypt, Arabia, and Mesopotamia, as well as Canaan, were some of the trade neighbors that made Damascus the "heart of Syria."

Damascus owed its prosperity to two rivers, the Abana and the Pharpar (2 Kin. 5:12). These rivers provided an abundant source of water for agriculture. The Syrian people were so proud of these streams that Naaman the Syrian leper almost passed up his opportunity to be healed when the prophet Elisha asked him to dip himself in the waters of the Jordan River in Israel. He thought of the Jordan as an inferior stream in comparison with these majestic rivers in his homeland (2 Kin. 5:9–14).

History. The Bible first mentions the city as the hometown of Eliezer, Abraham's faithful servant.

Early Egyptian texts refer to Egypt's control over Damascus, but this influence did not last long. By the time of David's reign, Syria (Aram) was a powerful state with Damascus as its capital. David defeated the Syrians and stationed his own troops in Damascus (2 Sam. 8:5–6; 1 Chr. 18:5–6). During Solomon's reign, however, God allowed Rezon (1 Kin. 11:23–25), Solomon's enemy, to take Syria from Israel's control because of Solomon's sins. Rezon founded a powerful dynasty based in Damascus that lasted more than 200 years.

Shortly after Solomon's death, the king of Damascus formed a powerful league with other Aramean states. This alliance resulted in many years of conflict between Israel and Damascus. First, Ben-Hadad I of Damascus defeated King Baasha of Israel (1 Kin. 15:16–20; 2 Chr. 16:1–4). Later, God miraculously delivered King Ahab of Israel and his small army from the superior Syrian forces (1 Kin. 20:1–30).

Even after this miraculous deliverance, Ahab made a covenant with Ben-Hadad II against God's will (1 Kin. 20:31–43). Ahab was killed a few years later in a battle with Syria (1 Kin. 22:29–38).

In the midst of these wars, the prophet Elijah was instructed by God to anoint Hazael as the new king of Damascus (1 Kin. 19:15). King Joram of Israel successfully opposed Hazael for a time (2 Kin. 13:4–5), but the situation was eventually reversed. Hazael severely oppressed both Israel and Judah during later years (2 Kin. 13:3, 22).

Much later, God sent Rezin, king of Syria, and Pekah, king of Israel, against wicked King Ahaz of Judah (2 Kin. 16:1–6). Ahaz called on the Assyrians, who had become a powerful military force, for help (2 Kin. 16:7). The Assyrian king Tiglath-Pileser responded by conquering Syria, overthrowing the Aramean dynasty, killing Rezin, and destroying Damascus (732 B.C.), just as the prophets Amos and Isaiah had prophesied (Is. 17:1; Amos 1:4–5). This marked the end of Syria as an independent nation. The city of Damascus was also reduced to a fraction of its former glory.

The exact date of the reconstruction of Damascus is unknown, but such an excellent location could not long remain weak and insignificant. Damascus was the residence of Assyrian and Persian governors for five centuries after its conquest by Tiglath-Pileser. Still later, the city was conquered by Alexander the Great, who made it a provincial capital. In 64 B.C. the Romans invaded Syria, making it a province with Damascus as the seat of government.

All references to Damascus in the New Testament are associated with the apostle Paul's conversion and ministry. During this time, the city was part of the kingdom of Aretas (2 Cor. 11:32), an Arabian prince who held his kingdom under the Romans. The New Testament reports that Paul was converted while traveling to Damascus to persecute early Christians who lived in the city (Acts 9:1–8). After his dramatic conversion, Paul went to the house of Judas, where God sent Ananias, a Christian who lived in Damascus, to heal Paul of his blindness (Acts 9:10–22).

Paul preached boldly in the Jewish synagogues in Damascus, but eventually he was forced to flee the city because of the wrath of those to whom he preached. The governor of Damascus tried to capture Paul, but the apostle escaped in a large basket through an opening in the city wall (Acts 9:25; 2 Cor. 11:32–33).

DAN [dan] (*a judge*) — the name of a man and a city in Israel named after him:

1. The fifth son of Jacob and the first born to Rachel's handmaid Bilhah (Gen. 30:1–6). Dan had one son—Hushim (Gen. 46:23), or Shuham (Num. 26:42). Jacob's blessing of Dan predicted:

"Dan shall judge his people as one of the tribes of Israel. Dan shall be a serpent by the way / A viper by the path / That bites the horse's heels / So that its rider shall fall backward" (Gen. 49:16–17).

Nothing else is known of Dan himself.

2. A city in the northern territory of the tribe of Dan, identified as the modern ruin or archaeological site known as Tell el-Qadi. This city was located farther north than any other village in Israel during much of the Old Testament period. This explains the phrase "from Dan to Beersheba" (Judg. 20:1), used to describe the entire territory of the Israelites from north to south.

Archaeologists excavating at Dan have uncovered remains that include an intact Middle Bronze Age mud-brick, triple-arch gateway as well as pagan altars dated to the period of Israel's divided monarchy (see 1 Kin. 12:28–30).

DANIEL [DAN yuhl] (*God is my judge*) — the name of three or four men in the Bible:

1. A son of David and Abigail (1 Chr. 3:1). He is also called Chileab (2 Sam. 3:3).

2. A priest of the family of Ithamar who returned with Ezra from the captivity (Ezra 8:2). Daniel sealed the covenant in the days of Nehemiah (Neh. 10:6).

3. A wise (Ezek. 28:3) and righteous man (perhaps non-Israelite), mentioned together with Noah and Job (Ezek. 14:14, 20), to be identified with an ancient Canaanite worthy named Daniel or equated with No. 4.

4. A prophet during the period of the captivity of God's covenant people in Babylon and Persia (Dan. 1:6–12:9; Matt. 24:15). Daniel also wrote the book in the Old Testament that bears his name.

Daniel was a teenager when he was taken from Jerusalem into captivity by the Babylonians in 605 B.C. He was in his 80s when he received the vision of the prophecy of the 70 weeks (Daniel 9). In more than 60 years of his life in Babylon, Daniel faced many challenges. But in all those years, he grew stronger in his commitment to God.

We know very little about Daniel's personal life. His family history is not mentioned, but he was probably from an upper-class family in Jerusalem. It seems unlikely that Nebuchadnezzar, the king of Babylon, would have selected a trainee for his court from the lower classes. Neither do we know whether Daniel married or had a family. As a servant in Nebuchadnezzar's court, he may have been castrated and made into a eunuch, as was common in those days. But the text does not specify that this happened. It does indicate that Daniel was a person of extraordinary abilities.

We tend to think of Daniel as a prophet because of the prophetic dimension of his book. But he also served as an advisor in the courts of foreign kings. Daniel remained in governmental service through the reigns of the kings of Babylon and into the reign of Cyrus of Persia after the Persians became the dominant world power (Dan. 1:21; 10:1).

Daniel was also a person of deep piety. His book is characterized not only by prophecies of the distant future but also by a sense of wonder at the presence of God. From his youth Daniel was determined to live by God's law in a distant land (see Daniel 1). In moments of crisis, Daniel turned first to God in prayer before turning to the affairs of state (2:14–23). His enemies even used his regularity at prayer to trap him and turn the king against him. But the grace of God protected Daniel (chap. 6).

After one of his stunning prophecies (chap. 9), Daniel prayed a noble prayer of confession for his own sins and the sins of his people. This prayer was based on Daniel's study of the book of Jeremiah (Dan. 9:2). He was a man of true devotion to God.

So the book of Daniel is more than a treasure of prophetic literature. It also paints a beautiful picture of a man of God who lived out his commitment in very troubled times. We should never get so caught up in the meanings of horns and beasts that we forget the human dimension of the book—the intriguing person whose name means "God Is My Judge."

DAVID [DAY vid] (*beloved*) — second king of the united kingdom of Israel, ancestor of Jesus Christ, and writer of numerous psalms. The record of David's life is found in 1 Samuel 16–31; 2 Samuel 1–24; 1 Kings 1–2; and 1 Chronicles 10–29. An Aramaic inscription including the words *house [dynasty] of David* was found in 1993 in the ruins of the city of Dan. It dates to the 9th century B.C. and is the only known mention of David in ancient contemporary writings outside of the Old Testament itself.

David as a Youth. David's youth was spent in Bethlehem. The youngest of eight brothers (1 Sam. 16:10–11; 17:12–14), he was the son of Jesse, a respected citizen of the city. His mother was tenderly remembered for her godliness (Ps. 86:16). As the youngest son, David was the keeper of his father's sheep. In this job he showed courage and faithfulness by killing both a lion and a bear that attacked the flock.

As a lad, he displayed outstanding musical talent with the harp, a fact that figured prominently in his life. When Saul was rejected by God as king, the prophet Samuel went to Bethlehem to anoint David as the future king of Israel. Apparently, there was no public announcement of this event, although David and his father surely must have been aware of it.

David's Service under Saul. King Saul, forsaken by God and troubled by an evil spirit, was subject to moods of depression and insanity. His attendants advised him to secure a harpist, whose music might soothe his spirit. David was recommended for this task. As harpist for Saul, David was exposed to governmental affairs, a situation that prepared him for his later service as king of Israel. Apparently, David did not remain with Saul all the time, since the Bible indicates he returned to Bethlehem to continue caring for his father's sheep.

During one of these visits to his home, the Philistines invaded the country and camped 24 kilometers (15 miles) west of Bethlehem. Saul led the army of Israel to meet the enemy. Three of David's brothers were in Saul's army, and Jesse sent David to the battle area to inquire about their welfare. While on this expedition, David encountered the Philistine giant Goliath.

David as Warrior. Goliath's challenge for an Israelite to do battle with him stirred David's spirit. Weighted with heavy armor, Goliath was equipped to engage in close-range combat. David's strategy was to fight him at a distance. Taking five smooth stones from a brook, David faced Goliath with only a sling and his unflinching faith in God. Goliath fell, struck by a stone from David's sling. For this feat, he became a hero in the eyes of the nation. But it aroused jealousy and animosity in the heart of Saul. Saul's son, Jonathan, however, admired David because of his bravery, and they soon became good friends. This friendship lasted until Jonathan's death, in spite of Saul's hostility toward David.

Saul had promised to make the victor in the battle with Goliath his son-in-law, presenting one of his daughters as his wife. He also promised to free the victor's family from taxation. But after the battle, David was no longer allowed to return occasionally to his father's house. He remained at Saul's palace continually. Perhaps Saul realized that Samuel's prediction that the kingdom would be taken from him could reach fulfillment in David. On two occasions, he tried to kill David with a spear; he also gave his daughter, whom he had promised as David's wife, to another man. As David's popularity grew, Saul's fear increased until he could no longer hide his desire to kill him. David was forced to flee with Saul in pursuit.

David as Fugitive Hero. David gathered a handful of fugitives as his followers and fled from Saul. On at least two occasions, David could have killed Saul while the king slept, but he refused to do so. Perhaps David hesitated to kill Saul because he realized that he would be king one day, and he wanted the office to be treated with respect. If he had killed Saul, David also would have entered the office of king through his own personal violence. Perhaps this was a situation he wanted to avoid.

When the Philistines battled Saul and his army at Gilboa, they were victorious, killing Saul and his son, Jonathan, whom David loved as a dear friend. When David heard this news, he mourned their fate (2 Samuel 1).

David as King of Judah. At Saul's death the tribe of Judah, to whom David belonged, elected him as king of Judah and placed him on the throne in Hebron. The rest of the tribes of Israel set up Ishbosheth, Saul's son, as king at Mahanaim. For the next two years civil war raged between these two factions. It ended in the assassination of Ishbosheth, an event that saddened David.

David as King of All Israel. On the death of Ishbosheth, David was elected king over all the people of Israel. He immediately began work to establish a united kingdom. One of his first acts as king was to attack the fortified city of Jebus. Although the inhabitants thought it was safe from capture, David and his army took it. He then made it the capital city of his kingdom and erected his palace there. Also known as Jerusalem, the new capital stood on the border of the southern tribe of Judah and the other tribal territories to the north. This location tended to calm the jealousies between the north and the south, contributing greatly to the unity of the kingdom.

After establishing his new political capital, David proceeded to reestablish and strengthen the worship of God. He moved the ark of the covenant from Kirjath Jearim (Josh. 15:9) and placed it within a tabernacle that he pitched in Jerusalem.

Next, he organized worship on a magnificent scale and began plans to build a house of worship. But God brought a halt to his plans, informing David that the building of the temple would be entrusted to his successor.

Although David was a righteous king, he was subject to sin, just like other human beings. On one occasion when his army went to battle, David stayed home. This led to his great sin with Bathsheba. While Uriah, the Hittite, Bathsheba's husband, was away in battle, David committed adultery with her. Then in an effort to cover his sin, he finally had Uriah killed in battle. David was confronted by the prophet Nathan, who courageously exposed his wrongdoing. Faced with his sin, David repented and asked for God's forgiveness. His prayer for forgiveness is recorded in Psalm 51.

Although God forgave David of this act of adultery, the consequences of the sin continued to plague him. The child born to David and Bathsheba died. The example he set as a father was a bad influence on his sons. One son, Amnon, raped and humiliated his half-sister. Another son, Absalom, rebelled against David and tried to take away his kingdom by force.

One of David's deep desires was to build a temple in Jerusalem. But he was prevented from doing so. The prophet Nathan informed David that he would not build the temple because he had been a warrior. David did not build the temple, but he did gather material for the temple to be built later. It was Solomon, David's son and successor, who finally erected the first temple in Jerusalem. David died when he was 71 years old, having been king for a total of over 40 years, including both his reign in Hebron and his kingship over the united kingdom.

DEBORAH [DEB uh rah] (*bee*) — the name of two women in the Old Testament:

1. A nurse to Rebekah, Isaac's wife (Gen. 24:59; 35:8). Deborah accompanied Rebekah when she left her home in Mesopotamia

to become Isaac's wife and lived with Isaac and Rebekah. She probably spent her years caring for their sons, Jacob and Esau. Deborah died at an advanced age. She was buried below Bethel under a tree that Jacob called Allon Bachuth (literally "oak of weeping")—a fitting name for the burial place of one who had served so long and so faithfully (Gen. 35:8).

2. The fifth judge of Israel, a prophetess and the only female judge (Judg. 4–5). The Bible tells us nothing about her family except that she was the wife of Lapidoth. Deborah's home was in the hill country of Ephraim between Bethel and Ramah. The palm tree under which she sat and judged Israel was a landmark; it became known as "the palm tree of Deborah" (Judg. 4:5).

Deborah summoned Barak (Judg. 4; 5:1; Heb. 11:32) and told him it was God's will that he lead her forces against the mighty warrior, Sisera. Sisera was the commander of the army of Jabin, king of Canaan, who had terrorized Israel for 20 years. Barak accepted on one condition: Deborah must accompany him. Deborah and Barak's army consisted of only 10,000, while Sisera had a multitude of fighters and 900 chariots of iron.

God was on Israel's side, however. When the battle ended, not a single man of Sisera's army survived, except Sisera himself, who fled on foot. When Sisera took refuge in the tent of Heber the Kenite, Jael (the wife of Heber) drove a tent peg through his temple (Judg. 4:21), killing him.

The "Song of Deborah" (Judges 5) is one of the finest and earliest examples of Hebrew poetry.

DELILAH [dih LIE lah] — the woman loved by Samson, the mightiest of Israel's judges. She was probably a Philistine. She betrayed Samson to the lords of the Philistines for 1,100 pieces of silver (Judg. 16:5). Deluding Samson into believing she loved him, Delilah persuaded him to tell her the secret of his strength—his long hair, which was the symbol of his Nazirite vow. While Samson slept at her home in the Valley of Sorek, the Philistines entered and cut his hair. With his strength gone, Samson was easily captured and imprisoned, then blinded.

No biblical evidence supports the popular belief that Delilah was deeply repentant over her actions. She even may have been one of the 3,000 Philistines buried beneath the temple of Dagon Samson destroyed when his God-given strength returned (Judg. 16:27-30).

EDEN [EE den] (*delight*) — the name of a garden, a man, and a region in the Old Testament:

1. The first home of Adam and Eve, the first man and woman. The concept "Garden of Delight" fits perfectly the setting of Genesis 2–3, a place of God's blessing and prosperity.

Suggestions offered as to the location of Eden include Babylonia (in Mesopotamia), Armenia (north of Mesopotamia), and an island in the Indian Ocean. The statement in Genesis 2:10 that four "riverheads" divided from the river that flowed out of the garden of Eden (Gen. 2:10–14) supports a location somewhere in Mesopotamia.

Two of the rivers are clearly identified: the Tigris, which ran along the east side of Asshur (Assyria), and the Euphrates. The Pishon ("Spouter") and Gihon ("Gusher") rivers are hard to identify. The Gihon may have been in Mesopotamia, since Genesis 2:13 says it encompassed the whole land of "Cush" (possibly southeast Mesopotamia). Some think Pishon and Gihon represent the Indus and the Nile, respectively, suggesting that Eden included the whole of the Fertile Crescent from India to Egypt.

The garden of Eden included many kinds of beautiful and fruitbearing trees, including "the tree of life" and "the tree of the knowledge of good and evil" (Gen. 2:9). Man was to tend and keep the garden (Gen. 2:15), which, in addition to trees, could have contained other vegetation such as grain crops and vegetables (Gen. 1:11–12). The garden was also filled with all kinds of birds and land animals (Gen. 2:19–20), probably including many of the animals created on the sixth day of creation (Gen. 1:24–25). It was well-watered (Gen. 2:10), ensuring lush vegetation and pasture.

After Adam and Eve sinned against God (Gen. 3:1–19), the Lord banished them from the garden. Cain, the son of Adam and Eve, is said to have lived "east of Eden" (Gen. 4:16).

In several Old Testament passages Eden is used as a symbol of beauty and fruitfulness, the place blessed by God (Is. 51:3). Revelation 22:1–2 alludes to the garden of Eden by picturing a "river of water of life" and "the tree of life" in the heavenly Jerusalem.

2. A Levite who lived during the reign of King Hezekiah of Judah. He assisted in the religious reformation under Hezekiah, helping cleanse the temple (2 Chr. 29:12) and overseeing the distribution of the freewill offerings (2 Chr. 31:15).

3. A region or city in Mesopotamia that supplied Tyre with choice items such as beautiful and luxurious clothing (Ezek. 27:23–24). Called Bit-Adini on the Assyrian monuments, the place probably was near Damascus (Beth Eden, Amos 1:5; house of Eden, KJV).

EDOM [EE dum] (*red*) — the name of a person and a region in the Old Testament:

1. An alternate name for Esau, who traded his birthright to his brother Jacob for a meal, which consisted of a red stew (Gen. 25:29–34).

2. The land inhabited by the descendants of Edom, or Esau (Gen. 32:3; 36:8). Ancient Edom included the region beginning in the north at the river Zered, a natural boundary also

for southern Moab, and extending southward to the Gulf of Aqabah. At times it included mountain ranges and fertile plateaus on the east and west of the Arabah, the desert valley south of the Dead Sea.

The most significant area of ancient Edom was the mountain-encircled plain on the east of the Arabah. Mount Seir, the highest of this range, rises to an elevation of nearly 1,200 meters (3,500 feet) above the Arabah. Edom's capital during the days of Israel's monarchy was Sela, situated at the southern end of a secluded valley that became the location of the city of Petra in later times. Other important Edomite cities were Bozrah and Teman (Is. 34:6; Amos 1:12). In New Testament times, Edom was known as Idumea.

From the Conquest until the Division. In dividing the land of Canaan after the conquest, Joshua established Judah's border to the west of the Dead Sea and to the border of Edom (Josh. 15:1, 21). During the reign of Saul, Israel fought against Edom (1 Sam. 14:47). But Edomites at times served in Saul's army (1 Sam. 21:7; 22:9). David conquered Edom, along with a number of other adjacent countries, and stationed troops in the land (2 Sam. 8:13–14). In later years, Solomon promoted the building of a port on the northern coast of the Red Sea in Edomite territory (1 Kin. 9:26–27).

After the Division. During the time of the divided kingdom, a number of hostile encounters occurred between the nations of Judah or Israel and Edom. During Jehoshaphat's reign, Edomites raided Judah but were turned back (2 Chr. 20:1, 8). An attempt to reopen the port at Ezion Geber failed (1 Kin. 22:48), and the Edomites joined forces with those of Judah in Jehoshaphat's move to put down the rebellion of Mesha of Moab (2 Kin. 3:4–5). During the reign of Joram, Edom freed herself from Judah's control (2 Kin. 8:20–22), but again became subject to Judah when Amaziah assaulted and captured Sela, their capital city. Edom became a vassal state of Assyria, beginning about

736 B.C. So antagonistic were relationships between Israel and Edom that Edom is pictured as Israel's representative enemy (Is. 34:5–17). The entire book of Obadiah is a prophecy against Edom.

The Place of the Nabateans. After the downfall of Judah in 586 B.C., Edom rejoiced (Ps. 137:7). Edomites settled in southern Judah as far north as Hebron. Nabateans occupied old Edom beginning in the third century B.C., continuing their civilization well into the first century A.D. Judas Maccabeus subdued the Edomites and John Hyrcanus forced them to be circumcised and then made them a part of the Jewish people. The Herod family of New Testament times was of Idumean (Edomite) stock.

Knowledge of the Edomites comes mainly from the Bible, archaeological excavations of their ancient cities, and references to Edom in Egyptian, Assyrian, and Babylonian sources.

EGLON [EGG lahn] (*young bull*) — the name of a city and a king in the Old Testament:

1. An Amorite city in the western Shephelah (lowlands). Eglon was one of five allied cities that attacked Gibeon but were conquered by Joshua (Josh. 10:3).

2. An overweight Moabite king who reigned during the period of the judges (Judg. 3:12–25). Allied with the Ammonites and the Amalekites, Eglon invaded the land of Israel. His army captured Jericho, and he exacted tribute from the Israelites.

After 18 years of Eglon's rule, the Lord raised up Ehud the Benjamite, a left-handed man, to deliver Israel. Ehud stabbed Eglon in the belly with a dagger. Because Eglon was a very fat man, "even the hilt went in after the blade, and the fat closed over the blade, for [Ehud] did not draw the dagger out of his belly" (Judg. 3:22).

EGYPT [EE jipt] — the country in the northeast corner of Africa that extended from the Mediterranean Sea on the north to the first waterfall on the Nile River in the south—a distance of about 880 kilometers (540 miles). The Israelites spent 430 years in this land (Ex. 12:40) between the time of Joseph and Moses. Jesus lived temporarily in Egypt during His infancy (Matt. 2:13–15).

The Egyptians called their country Tawy, "the two lands"—referring to Upper and Lower Egypt—or Kemyt, "the black land," which distinguished the fertile Nile Valley from the red desert sand. In the Bible the word for Egypt is Mizraim, which means "Two Egypts" and is the name of one of the sons of Ham who founded the country (Gen. 10:6; 1 Chr. 1:8).

EKRON [ECK ron] — the northernmost of the five chief cities of the Philistines, near the Mediterranean Sea and about 66 kilometers (35 miles) west of Jerusalem (1 Sam. 6:16–17). Ekron was apportioned first to the tribe of Judah (Josh. 15:45–46), then given to the tribe of Dan (Josh. 19:40–43). After David killed Goliath, the Israelites pursued the Philistines to the very gates of Ekron, their fortified stronghold (1 Sam. 17:52).

The prophets pronounced God's judgment upon Ekron, along with her sister cities (Amos 1:8).

ELEAZAR [el e A zur] (*God is helper*) — the name of seven men in the Bible:

1. Aaron's third son by his wife, Elisheba (Ex. 6:23). Eleazar was the father of Phinehas (Ex. 6:25). Consecrated a priest, he was made chief of the Levites after his elder brothers, Nadab and Abihu, were killed for offering unholy fire (Lev. 10:1–7). Before Aaron died, Eleazar ascended Mount Hor with him and was invested with Aaron's high priestly garments (Num. 20:25–28). Eleazar served as high priest during the remainder of Moses' life and throughout Joshua's leadership. He helped in

the allotment of Canaan among the twelve tribes of Israel (Josh. 14:1), and was buried "in a hill that belonged to Phinehas his son ... in the mountains of Ephraim" (Josh. 24:33). Phinehas succeeded him as high priest (Judg. 20:28).

2. The son of Abinadab who was charged with keeping watch over the ark while it stayed in Abinadab's house in Kirjath Jearim (1 Sam. 7:1).

3. The son of Dodo the Ahohite (1 Chr. 11:12). He was one of David's three mighty men (2 Sam. 23:9).

4. A man from the tribe of Levi, the family of Merari, and the house of Mahli (1 Chr. 23:21–22).

5. The Levite son of Phinehas (Ezra 8:33). He assisted the high priest.

6. A priest who acted as a musician when the rebuilt walls of Jerusalem were dedicated (Neh. 12:27, 42).

7. Eliud's son and one of the ancestors of Jesus (Matt. 1:15).

ELI [EE lie] (*the Lord is high*) — a judge and high priest with whom the prophet Samuel lived during his childhood (1 Sam. 1–4; 14:3).

The first mention of Eli occurs when the childless Hannah poured out to him her unhappiness over her barren condition. Later, her prayers for a son were answered when Samuel was born. True to her word, she brought her son to the tabernacle and dedicated him to God. There the future prophet lived with the high priest Eli. Eli was a deeply pious man whose service to the Lord was unblemished. However, he was a lax father who had no control over his two sons. Phinehas and Hophni took meat from sacrificial animals before they were dedicated to God. They also "lay with the women that assembled at the door of the tabernacle" (1 Sam. 2:22). God pronounced judgment on Eli because of his failure to discipline his sons.

God's judgment was carried out through the Philistines. Hophni and Phinehas carried the ark of the covenant into battle to help the Israelites. Both were killed, and the ark was captured. When Eli, 98 years old and nearly blind, heard the news, he fell backward and broke his neck. God's final judgment against Eli and his descendants occurred when Solomon removed Abiathar, Eli's descendant, and put Zadok in his place as high priest of the nation (1 Kin. 2:35).

ELIJAH [ee LIE juh] (*the Lord is my God*) — the name of three or four men in the Old Testament:

1. A Benjamite, the son of Jeroham (1 Chr. 8:27).

2. An influential prophet who lived in the ninth century B.C. during the reigns of Ahab and Ahaziah in the northern kingdom of Israel. Elijah shaped the history of his day and dominated Israelite thinking for centuries afterward.

Elijah's prophetic activities emphasized the unconditional loyalty to God required of the nation of Israel. His strange dress and appearance (2 Kin. 1:8), his fleetness of foot (1 Kin. 18:46), his rugged constitution that resisted famine (1 Kin. 19:8), and his cave-dwelling habits (1 Kin. 17:3; 19:9) all suggest that he was a robust, outdoors-type person.

Elijah was opposed to the accepted standards of his day, when belief in many gods was normal. He appears in the role of God's instrument of judgment upon a wayward Israel because of the nation's widespread idolatry. The miracles that Elijah performed occurred during the period when a life-or-death struggle took place between the religion of the Lord and Baal worship.

Elijah's views were in conflict with those of King Ahab, who had attempted to cultivate economic ties with Israel's neighbors, especially Tyre. One of the consequences was that he had married Jezebel, a daughter of Ethbaal, king of Tyre. Ahab saw no harm in participating in the religion of his neighbors, particularly the religion of his wife. Therefore, he established a center of Baal worship at Samaria. Influenced by Jezebel, Ahab gave himself to the worship of Baal. Suddenly Elijah appeared on the scene.

Contest on Mount Carmel. After the drought had lasted three years, the Lord instructed Elijah to present himself before Ahab with the message that the Lord would provide rain. Elijah then challenged the 850 prophets of Baal and Asherah to a contest on Mount Carmel (1 Kin. 18:21). Each side would offer sacrifices to their God without building a fire. The ignition of the fire was left to the strongest god, who would thereby reveal himself as the true God.

The best efforts of the pagan prophets through the better part of a day failed to evoke a response from Baal. Elijah poured water over his sacrifice to remove any possibility of fraud or misunderstanding about the offering. After Elijah prayed briefly to the Lord, his sacrifice was consumed by fire from heaven. The people of Israel responded strongly in favor of God (1 Kin. 18:39). Then the prophets of Baal were slaughtered at Elijah's command (1 Kin. 18:40), and God sent rain to end the drought (1 Kin. 18:41–46).

Flight from Jezebel. Queen Jezebel was furious over the fate of her prophets. She vowed that she would take revenge on Elijah. He was forced to flee to Mount Horeb—the mountain where Moses had received the Ten Commandments. Like Moses, Elijah was sustained for 40 days and nights in the wilderness.

While Elijah was at Mount Horeb, the Lord revealed Himself in a low, murmuring sound. The prophet received a revelation of the coming doom on Ahab and Israel (1 Kin. 19:14). Then Elijah was given a threefold charge: He was instructed to anoint Hazael as king of Syria, Jehu as the future king of Israel, and Elisha as the prophet who would take his place (1 Kin. 19:16). These changes would bring to power those who would reform Israel in the coming years.

Naboth's Vineyard and the Challenge of Ahaziah. In the years of war that followed between Ahab and Ben-Hadad of Syria, Elijah did not appear (1 Kings 20). But he did appear after Jezebel acquired a family-owned vineyard for Ahab by having its owner, Naboth, falsely accused and executed (1 Kin. 21:1–29). Elijah met the king in the vineyard and rebuked him for the act (1 Kin. 21:1–24). Ahab repented, and Elijah brought him word from the Lord that the prophesied ruin on his house would not come during his lifetime, but would occur in the days of his son.

Shortly after Ahaziah, the son of Ahab, took the throne from his father, he was involved in a serious accident. He sent messengers to inquire of Baal-Zebub ("Lord of Flies"), the god of Ekron, whether he would recover. Elijah intercepted the messengers and predicted his death because of his belief in other gods (2 Kin. 1:1–17). This event would also be a fulfillment of the doom pronounced earlier upon Ahab's house.

Twice King Ahaziah sent a detachment of soldiers to capture Elijah. But both times they were consumed by fire from heaven. The third group sent by the king begged for mercy, and an angel of God directed Elijah to go with the commander to see the king. Elijah repeated his message of doom to Ahaziah, who soon died (2 Kin. 1:9–17). Elijah's prophecy that Jezebel would meet a violent death was also fulfilled (2 Kin. 9:36).

Ascension to Heaven. The prophet Elijah did not die. He was carried bodily to heaven in a whirlwind (2 Kin. 2:1–11). This was an honor previously bestowed only upon Enoch (Gen. 5:24). Elisha, the only witness to this event, picked up Elijah's mantle, which fell from him as he ascended. He carried it during his ministry as a token of his continuation of Elijah's ministry (2 Kin. 2:13–14).

Elijah's influence continued even after he ascended into heaven. King Jehoram of Israel received a letter from the prophet seven years after his ascension, indicating that the king would be punished severely for his sins (2 Chr. 21:12–15).

Elijah's Contribution. The prophet Elijah understood that the nation of Israel had a mission to preserve its religious system—the worship of the one true God—in a pure form without any mixture with idol worship. Elijah was strongly opposed to the worship of pagan gods such as Baal and Asherah. This uncompromising stand often endangered his life by bringing him into conflict with those in positions of power, especially Queen Jezebel and her followers.

Elijah's impact on the prophetic movement among the Hebrew people was extensive. He stands as the transitional figure between Samuel (the adviser and anointer of kings) and the later writing prophets. Like the prophets who followed him, Elijah emphasized Israel's responsibility for total commitment to their God and the covenant responsibilities that God and His people had sworn to each other. Both ideas are more fully developed in later prophets, such as Amos and Hosea. In later Jewish thought, the messianic age was frequently associated with Elijah's return. The Old Testament spoke of the reappearance of Elijah. The prophet Malachi prophesied that the Lord would send Elijah before the day of the Lord arrived. This prophecy was fulfilled in the coming of John the Baptist (Matt. 11:4; 17:10–13; Luke 1:17). John the Baptist was similar to Elijah in his preaching as well as his dress and physical appearance (Matt. 11:7–8; Luke 7:24–28). During Jesus' earthly ministry, some identified him with Elijah (Matt. 16:14; Luke 9:8).

The New Testament also mentions the reappearance of Elijah in person. Along with Moses, he appeared with Jesus on the Mount of Transfiguration (Matt. 17:3).

3. A son of Harim (Ezra 10:21). Elijah divorced his foreign wife following the captivity in Babylon.

4. An Israelite who divorced his foreign wife (Ezra 10:26). He may be the same as No. 3.

ELISHA [ee LIE shuh] (*my God saves*) — an early Hebrew prophet who succeeded the prophet Elijah when Elijah's time on earth was finished (1 Kin. 19:16). Elisha ministered for about 50 years in the northern kingdom of Israel, serving God during the reigns of Jehoram, Jehu, Jehoahaz, and Joash. The period of his ministry dates from about 850–800 B.C. Elisha's work consisted of presenting the Word of God through prophecy, advising kings, anointing kings, helping the needy, and performing several miracles.

Elisha was the son of Shaphat of Abel Meholah, a town on the western side of the Jordan River. Elijah found Elisha plowing with a team of oxen. As Elijah walked past Elisha, he threw his mantle over the younger man's shoulders. Elisha "arose and followed Elijah, and became his servant" (1 Kin. 19:21), but Elisha is not mentioned again until 2 Kings 2:1, shortly before Elijah ascended to heaven in a chariot of fire. Before taking his leave, Elijah fulfilled the final request of Elisha by providing him with a double portion of his prophetic spirit (2 Kin. 2:9–10), making him his spiritual firstborn. Upon receiving Elijah's mantle, Elisha demonstrated this gift by parting the waters of the Jordan River, allowing him to cross on dry land (2 Kin. 2:14). In this way, Elisha demonstrated that he had received God's blessings on his ministry as Elijah's successor.

Elisha cultivated a different image from his predecessor. Instead of following Elijah's example as a loner and an outsider, Elisha chose to work within the established system. He assumed his rightful place as the head of the "official" prophetic order in Israel, where his counsel and advice were sought out by kings. In contrast to Elijah's strained relationship with the king and his officials, Elisha enjoyed the harmonious role of trusted advisor. This is not to say that Elisha never had a word of criticism for the government, as for example in the part he played in the overthrow of Jezebel and the dynasty of Ahab (2 Kin. 9:1–3).

Elisha's appearance was much more typical and average than Elijah's. He was bald (2 Kin. 2:23), while Elijah had been an extremely hairy man (2 Kin. 1:8). Elisha did not wander as extensively as Elijah. Instead, he had a house in Samaria (2 Kin. 6:32). Much tension had existed between Elijah and his audience. Elisha's ministry provided a strong contrast as he was welcomed into virtually all levels of society.

In perhaps the most important part of his ministry, however, Elisha followed in Elijah's footsteps. This consisted of his performance of miracles, which answered a wide variety of needs in every level of society. He had a reputation for sympathizing with the poor and the oppressed. Elisha's activities and miracles as a prophet were often focused on those who were abused by officials in positions of power. One of Elisha's "community service" miracles was his purification of an unhealthy spring near Jericho. After learning that the spring was bad, Elisha threw a bowl of salt into it, making it pure (2 Kin. 2:19–21). The Bible reports that "the water remains healed to this day" (2 Kin. 2:22).

In another miracle, Elisha helped the widow of one of the sons of the prophets. To help her pay off creditors who intended to take the widow's two sons, Elisha multiplied the amount of oil in one jar to fill all available containers. This brought in enough money to pay off the debts and provided a surplus on which the widow and her sons could live (2 Kin. 4:1–7).

Elisha became a friend of a wealthy family in Shunem. The Shunammite woman displayed hospitality toward the prophet by regularly feeding him and building a room onto her home where he could lodge. Elisha repaid the childless couple by promising them a son (2 Kin. 4:8–17). Later, when tragedy struck the child, Elisha raised him from the dead (2 Kin. 4:18–37). When Elisha learned that a famine would strike Israel, he warned the family to flee the land. When the family returned seven years later, the king restored their property because of their relationship with Elisha (2 Kin. 8:1–6).

Elisha also advised kings and performed miracles for them. He helped Jehoram, king of Israel, and Jehoshaphat, king of Judah. He also helped the king of Edom defeat Mesha, king of Moab (2 Kin. 3:1–19).

Elisha ministered to all people, regardless of their nationalities. He cured Naaman, the commander of the Syrian army (2 Kin. 5:1–14), of leprosy, but he also advised the king of Israel of the plans (2 Kin. 6:8–10) of their Assyrian enemies. Even the bones of the dead Elisha had miraculous powers. When a corpse was hidden in Elisha's tomb, it came back to life as it touched the prophet's bones (2 Kin. 13:21).

ELIZABETH [ee LIZ uh buth] (*God is my oath*) — the mother of John the Baptist (Luke 1). Of the priestly line of Aaron, Elizabeth was the wife of the priest Zacharias. Although both "were ... righteous before God, they had no child, because Elizabeth was barren" (Luke 1:6–7). But God performed a miracle, and Elizabeth conceived the child who was to be the forerunner of the Messiah.

Elizabeth was privileged in another way. When her cousin Mary visited her, Elizabeth, six months pregnant, felt the child move as if to welcome the child whom Mary was carrying. Elizabeth recognized the significance of this action and acknowledged the Messiah before He had been born.

EMMAUS [em MAY us] (*warm wells*) — a village in Judea where Jesus revealed Himself to two disciples after His resurrection. The disciples, Cleopas and an unidentified companion, encountered Jesus on the road to Emmaus, but they did not recognize Him. Jesus accompanied them to Emmaus, and they invited Him to stay there with them. As He blessed and broke bread at the evening meal, the disciples' "eyes were opened and they knew Him" (Luke 24:31). The modern location of ancient Emmaus is uncertain. Luke reported the village was

11 kilometers (7 miles) from Jerusalem, but he did not specify in which direction.

EPHESUS [EFF uh sus] — a large and important city on the west coast of Asia Minor where the apostle Paul founded a church. A number of factors contributed to the prominence that Ephesus enjoyed.

The first factor was economics. Situated at the mouth of the river Cayster, Ephesus was the most favorable seaport in the province of Asia and the most important trade center west of Tarsus. Today, because of silting from the river, the ruins of the city lie in a swamp 8 to 11 kilometers (5 to 7 miles) inland. Another factor was size. Although Pergamum was the capital of the province of Asia in Roman times, Ephesus was the largest city in the province, having a population of perhaps 300,000 people. A third factor was culture. Ephesus contained a theater that seated an estimated 25,000 people. A main thoroughfare, some 35 meters (105 feet) wide, ran from the theater to the harbor, at each end of which stood an impressive gate. The thoroughfare was flanked on each side by rows of columns 15 meters (50 feet) deep. Behind these columns were baths, gymnasiums, and impressive buildings. The fourth, and perhaps most significant, reason for the prominence of Ephesus was religion. The temple of Artemis (or Diana, according to her Roman name) at Ephesus ranked as one of the Seven Wonders of the Ancient World. As the twin sister of Apollo and the daughter of Zeus, Artemis was known variously as the moon goddess, the goddess of hunting, and the patroness of young girls. The temple at Ephesus housed the image of Artemis that was reputed to have come directly from Zeus (Acts 19:35).

The temple of Artemis in Paul's day was supported by 127 columns, each of them 60 meters (197 feet) high. The Ephesians took great pride in this grand edifice. During the Roman period, they promoted the worship of Artemis by minting coins with the inscription "Diana of Ephesus." The history of Christianity at Ephesus began about A.D. 50, perhaps as a result of the efforts of Priscilla and Aquila (Acts 18:18). Paul came to Ephesus in about A.D. 52, establishing a resident ministry for the better part of three years (Acts 20:31). During his Ephesian ministry, Paul wrote 1 Corinthians (1 Cor. 16:8).

The book of Acts reports that "all who dwelt in Asia heard the word of the Lord Jesus" (Acts 19:10), while Paul taught during the hot midday hours in the lecture hall of Tyrannus (Acts 19:9). Influence from his ministry undoubtedly resulted in the founding of churches in the Lycus River valley at Laodicea, Hierapolis, and Colossae.

So influential, in fact, was Paul's ministry at Ephesus that the silversmiths' league, which fashioned souvenirs of the temple, feared that the preaching of the gospel would undermine the great temple of Artemis (Acts 19:27). As a result, one of the silversmiths, a man named Demetrius, stirred up a riot against Paul.

During his stay in Ephesus, Paul encountered both great opportunities and great dangers. He baptized believers who apparently came to know the gospel through disciples of John the Baptist (Acts 19:1–5), and he countered the strong influence of magic in Ephesus (Acts 19:11–20).

After Paul departed from Ephesus, Timothy remained to combat false teaching (1 Tim. 1:3; 2 Tim. 4:3; Acts 20:29). Many traditions testify that the apostle John lived in Ephesus toward the end of the first century. In his vision from the island of Patmos off the coast of Asia Minor, John described the church of Ephesus as flourishing, although it was troubled with false teachers and had lost its first love (Rev. 2:1–7).

EPHRAIM [EE freh em] (*doubly fruitful*) — the second son of Joseph by Asenath.

When Ephraim was born to Joseph in Egypt, he gave him his name meaning "fruitful" because "God has caused me to be fruitful in the land of my affliction" (Gen. 41:52). Even though Joseph was a foreigner (a Hebrew) in Egypt, he had been blessed by God as he rose to a high position in the Egyptian government and fathered two sons. Later this same theme of fruitfulness and blessing was echoed by Joseph's father, Jacob, as he accepted Ephraim as his grandson (Gen. 48:5). Eventually Ephraim's thousands of descendants settled in the land of Canaan as one of the most numerous of the tribes of Israel (Gen. 48:19; Num. 1:10).

ESAU [EE saw] — a son of Isaac and Rebekah and the twin brother of Jacob. Also known as Edom, Esau was the ancestor of the Edomites (Gen. 25:24–28; Deut. 2:4–8).

Most of the biblical narratives about Esau draw a great contrast between him and his brother, Jacob. Esau was a hunter and outdoorsman who was favored by his father, while Jacob was not an outdoors type and was favored by Rebekah (Gen. 25:27–28).

Even though he was a twin, Esau was considered the oldest son because he was born first. By Old Testament custom, he would have inherited most of his father's property and the right to succeed him as family patriarch. But in a foolish, impulsive moment, he sold his birthright to Jacob in exchange for a meal (Gen. 25:29–34). This determined that Jacob would carry on the family name in a direct line of descent from Abraham and Isaac, his grandfather and father.

The loss of Esau's rights as firstborn is further revealed in Genesis 27. Jacob deceived his blind father by disguising himself as Esau in order to receive his father's highest blessing. Esau was therefore the recipient of a lesser blessing (Gen. 27:25–29, 38–40; Heb. 11:20). He was so enraged by Jacob's actions that he determined to kill him once his father died. But Jacob fled to his uncle Laban in Haran and remained there for 20 years. Upon Jacob's return to Canaan, Esau forgave him and set aside their old feuds (Gen. 32:1–33:17). Years later, the two brothers together buried their father in the cave at Machpelah without a trace of their old hostilities (Gen. 35:29).

Esau in many ways was more honest and dependable than his scheming brother, Jacob. But he sinned greatly by treating his birthright so casually and selling it for a meal (Heb. 12:16–17). To the ancient Hebrews, one's birthright actually represented a high spiritual value. But Esau did not have the faith and farsightedness to accept his privileges and responsibilities. Thus, the right passed to his younger brother.

ESTHER [ESS ter] (*star*) — the Jewish queen of the Persian king Ahasuerus (Xerxes). Esther saved her people, the Jews, from a plot to eliminate them. A daughter of Abihail (Esth. 2:15; 9:29) and a cousin of Mordecai (Esth. 2:7, 15), Esther was raised by Mordecai as his own daughter after her mother and father died. Esther was a member of a family carried into captivity in Babylon that later chose to stay in Persia rather than return to Jerusalem. Her Jewish name was Hadassah, which means "myrtle" (Esth. 2:7).

The story of Esther's rise from an unknown Jewish girl to become the queen of a mighty empire illustrates how God used events and people as instruments to fulfill His promise to His chosen people. Following several days of revelry, the drunken king Ahasuerus—identified with Xerxes I (reigned 486–465 B.C.)—asked his queen, Vashti, to display herself to his guests. When Vashti courageously refused, she was banished from the palace. Ahasuerus then had "all the beautiful young virgins" (Esth. 2:3) of his kingdom brought to his palace in order to choose from among them Vashti's replacement.

Scripture records that "the young woman [Esther] was lovely and beautiful" (Esth. 2:7). The king loved Esther more than all the other women. He appointed her queen to replace Vashti (Esth. 2:17).

At the time, Haman was Ahasuerus's most trusted advisor. An egotistical and ambitious man, Haman demanded that people bow to him as he passed—something that Mordecai, a devout Jew, could not do in good conscience. In rage, Haman sought revenge not only on Mordecai but also on the entire Jewish population of the empire. He persuaded the king to issue an edict permitting him to kill all the Jews and seize their property.

With great tact and skill, Esther exposed Haman's plot and true character to the king. As a result, Ahasuerus granted the Jews the right to defend themselves and to destroy their enemies. With ironic justice, "they hanged Haman on the gallows that he had prepared for Mordecai (Esth. 7:10).

Even today Jews celebrate their deliverance from Ahasuerus's edict at the Feast of Purim (Esth. 9:26–32), celebrated on the 14th and 15th days of the month of Adar.

ETHIOPIAN EUNUCH [YOU nuck] — a person baptized by Philip who held a responsible position as the royal treasurer in the court of Candace, queen of Ethiopia (Acts 8:26–40). The word *eunuch* refers to an emasculated servant who could rise to positions of power and influence in ancient times. The Ethiopian eunuch had apparently been a convert to Judaism. A keen student of the Bible, he was probably a proselyte who had come to Jerusalem to participate in worship at the temple. On his return to his own country, he encountered Philip. On Philip's explanation of Isaiah 53, he confessed his faith in Christ and was baptized.

EUPHRATES [you FRAY tease] — the longest river of Western Asia and one of two major rivers in Mesopotamia. The river begins in the mountains of Armenia in modern-day

Turkey. It then heads west toward the Mediterranean Sea, turns to the south, swings in a wide bow through Syria, and then flows some 1,000 miles southeast to join the Tigris River before it empties into the Persian Gulf.

The Euphrates is about 2,890 kilometers (1,780 miles) long and is navigable for smaller vessels for about 1,950 kilometers (1,200 miles). The ruins of many ancient cities are located along the river in Iraq. Among them are Babylon, Eridu, Kish, Larsa, Nippur, Sippar, and Ur. In the Bible the Euphrates is referred to as "the River Euphrates," "the great river, the River Euphrates," or simply as "the River." It was one of the four rivers that flowed from the garden of Eden (Gen. 2:14). The Euphrates formed the northern boundary of the territories promised by God to Israel (Gen. 15:18; Josh. 1:4).

The biblical writer declared that the fathers of Israel had lived on "the other side of the River" (Josh. 1:2–3, 14–15; "beside the Euphrates," REB), where they served other gods. But God took Abraham "from the other side of the River" (v. 3) and brought him to the land of Canaan. David attempted to expand the boundaries of his kingdom to this river (2 Sam. 8:3). The Euphrates also was the site of the great battle at Carchemish (605 B.C.) that led to the death of King Josiah (2 Chr. 35:20–24). "The great river Euphrates" is also mentioned in Revelation 9:14 and 16:12.

EVE [eev] (*life-giving*) — the first woman (Gen. 3:20; 4:1), created from one of Adam's ribs to be "a helper comparable to him" (Gen. 2:18–22).

Adam and Eve lived together in innocence and happiness, enjoying sexual union ("one flesh") without guilt and sin (Gen. 2:25). However, the serpent tempted Eve to eat the forbidden fruit (Gen. 2:17).

Eve succumbed to the serpent's temptation and ate the fruit. Then "she also gave to her husband with her, and he ate" (Gen.

3:6). The result of this disobedience was losing innocence and receiving the disturbing knowledge of sin and evil. "Then the eyes of both of them were opened, and they knew that they were naked; and they sewed fig leaves together and made themselves coverings" (Gen. 3:7) to conceal their shame.

In falling into temptation (Gen. 3:6), Eve learned about sin and death (Gen. 2:17). She and her descendants experienced the animosity between Satan and Christ—the "offspring of the serpent" and "the seed of the woman" (Gen. 3:15). Her pain in childbirth and Adam's authority over her were other results of her sin (Gen. 3:16).

The apostle Paul referred to Eve twice. By saying "the serpent deceived Eve by his craftiness," Paul gave an example of how easily a person can be led into temptation and sin, with disastrous consequences (2 Cor. 11:3; 1 Tim. 2:12–14).

EZEKIEL [ih ZEEK e uhl] (*God will strengthen*) — a prophet of a priestly family carried captive to Babylon in 597 B.C. when he was about 25 years old. His call to the prophetic ministry came five years later. Ezekiel prophesied to the captives who dwelled by the river Chebar at Tel Abib. He is the author of the book of Ezekiel.

In his book, Ezekiel identifies himself as a priest, the son of Buzi (1:3). He was married to a woman who was "the desire of his eyes" (24:16). One of the saddest events of his life was the death of his wife. The prophet was told that on the very day he received this revelation, his wife would die as the armies of Babylon laid siege against the holy city of Jerusalem. Ezekiel's sadness at the death of his wife was to match the grief of the people at the destruction of Jerusalem. Ezekiel was commanded not to grieve her death; he was to steel himself for this tragedy even as God's people were to prepare themselves for the death of their beloved city (24:15–22). Perhaps no other event in the lives of the Old Testament prophets is as touching as this.

Ezekiel shows us just how ugly and serious our sin is. Perhaps this is why God acted so dramatically in dealing with the human condition—by sending His Son Jesus to die in our place and set us free from the bondage of sin.

EZRA [EZ ruh] ([God is]*a help*) — the name of three men in the Old Testament:

1. A descendant of Judah (1 Chr. 4:17; Ezrah, NIV, NRSV; perhaps Ezer, 1 Chr. 4:4).

2. A scribe and priest who led the returned captives in Jerusalem to make a new commitment to God's law. A descendant of Aaron through Eleazar, Ezra was trained in the knowledge of the law while living in captivity in Babylon with other citizens of the nation of Judah. Ezra gained favor during the reign of Artaxerxes, king of Persia. This king commissioned him to return to Jerusalem about 458 B.C. to bring order among the people of the new community. Artaxerxes even gave Ezra a royal letter (Ezra 7:11–16), granting him civil as well as religious authority, along with the finances to furnish the temple, which had been rebuilt by the returned captives.

Ezra was a skilled scribe and teacher with extensive training in the Books of the Law (Genesis, Exodus, Leviticus, Numbers, and Deuteronomy). After his return to Jerusalem, he apparently did a lot of work on the Hebrew Bible of that time, modernizing the language, correcting irregularities in the transmitted text, and updating and standardizing expressions in certain passages. References to this work by Ezra are found in 2 Esdras, one of the apocryphal books of the Old Testament. He also refers to himself in his own book as a skilled scribe (Ezra 7:6, 12), whose task was to copy, interpret, and transmit the Books of the Law.

When he arrived in Jerusalem, Ezra discovered that many of the Hebrew men had married foreign wives from the surrounding nations (Ezra 9:1, 2). After a period of fasting and prayer (Ezra 9:3, 15), he insisted that these men divorce their wives (Ezra 10:1, 17). He feared that intermarriage with pagans would lead to worship of pagan gods in the restored community of Judah.

In addition to these marriage reforms, Ezra also led his countrymen to give attention to the reading of the law. Several priests helped Ezra read the law, translating and interpreting it for the people's clear understanding in their new language (Aramaic). This reading process went on for seven days as the people focused on God's commands (Neh. 7:73–8:18).

During this period, they also celebrated one of their great religious festivals, the Feast of Tabernacles, to commemorate their sustenance by God in the wilderness following their miraculous escape from Egyptian bondage (Nehemiah 8). The result of this week of concentration on their heritage was a religious revival. The people confessed their sins and renewed their covenant with God (Nehemiah 9–10).

Ezra must have been a competent scribe and priest, since he found favor with the ruling Persians. But he was also devoted to his God and the high standards of holiness and righteousness that the Lord demanded of His people. As he communicated God's requirements to the captives in Jerusalem, Ezra also proved he was a capable leader who could point out shortcomings while leading the people to a higher commitment to God's law at the same time. Through it all, Ezra worked with a keen sense of divine guidance, "according to the good hand of his God upon him" (Ezra 7:9).

3. One of the priests who returned from the captivity with Zerubbabel (Neh. 12:1, 13).

GAD [gad] (*good fortune*) — the name of the founder of a tribe in Israel, a prophet, and a pagan god:

1. The seventh of Jacob's twelve sons. Gad was the firstborn of Zilpah (Leah's maid) and a brother of Asher (Gen. 30:11). Moses praised Gad for his bravery and faithfulness to duty (Deut. 33:20–21). With the possible exception of Ezbon, Gad's seven sons all founded tribal families (Num. 26:15–18).

2. A prophet described as David's "seer" (1 Chr. 21:9). Gad commanded David to buy the threshing floor of Araunah the Jebusite, which became the site of the temple. Gad the prophet also helped arrange the tabernacle music (2 Chr. 29:25) and is credited with writing an account of David's reign (1 Chr. 29:29).

3. The name of a pagan god (Is. 65:11, NKJV; Fortune, NIV). The name "Gad" appears in compound names, such as Baal Gad (Josh. 11:17) and Migdal Gad (Josh. 15:37).

GALATIA [guh LAY shih uh] — a region in central Asia Minor (modern Turkey) bounded on the east by Cappadocia, on the west by Asia, on the south by Pamphylia and Cilicia, and on the north by Bithynia and Pontus. The northern part of the region was settled in the third century B.C. by Celtic tribes that had been driven out of Gaul (France). From these tribes, the region derived its name, Galatia.

In 64 B.C. the Roman general Pompey defeated the king of Pontus, Mithradates VI, and established a foothold for Rome in the region. When the last Galatian king, Amyntas, died in 25 B.C., the Romans inherited the kingdom. Caesar Augustus then created the Roman province of Galatia, making Ancyra the capital and annexing a number of districts to the south and west, including Pisidia, Isauria, Phrygia, and Lycaonia. The term "Galatia," consequently, is somewhat ambiguous. It may refer to the older ethnic region in north-central Asia Minor (north Galatia), or to the later and larger Roman province (including south Galatia).

On his first missionary journey (about A.D. 46–48), the apostle Paul and Barnabas evangelized the Galatian cities of Pisidian Antioch, Iconium, Lystra, and Derbe (Acts 13–14). Paul revisited the area on his second and third missionary journeys.

Although the point is debated, it appears that Paul's Epistle to the Galatians (Gal. 1:2; 3:1) was addressed to the churches founded by him in the southern part of the province of Galatia (south Galatian theory). No evidence exists to show that Paul visited the region of Galatia in north-central Asia Minor. Although Acts 16:6 and 18:23 are sometimes thought to refer to this more remote northern region, the context of these passages seems to point to southern Galatia (Acts 13–14).

GALILEE [GAL ih lee] (*circle* or *circuit*) — a Roman province of Palestine during the time of Jesus. Measuring roughly 80 kilometers (50 miles) north to south and about 58 kilometers (30 miles) east to west, Galilee was the most northerly of the three provinces of Palestine—Galilee, Samaria, and Judea. Covering more than a third of Palestine's territory, Galilee extended from the base of Mount Hermon in the north to the Carmel and Gilboa ranges in the south. The Mediterranean Sea and the Jordan River valley were its western and eastern borders, respectively.

Originally a district in the hill country of Naphtali (2 Kin. 15:29; 1 Chr. 6:76), Galilee was inhabited by a "mixed race" of Jews and heathen. The Canaanites continued to dominate Galilee for many years after Joshua's invasion (Judg. 1:30–33; 4:2). It was historically known among the Jews as "Galilee of the Gentiles" (Is. 9:1; Matt. 4:15).

Galilee had such a mixed population that Solomon could award unashamedly to Hiram, king of Tyre, 20 of its cities in payment for timber from Lebanon (1 Kin. 9:11). After conquest by TiglathiPileser, king of Assyria (about 732 B.C.), Galilee was repopulated by a colony of heathen immigrants (2 Kin. 15:29; 17:24). Thus the Galilean accent and dialect were very distinct (Matt. 26:69, 73). For this and other reasons, the pure-blooded Jews of Judea, who were more orthodox in tradition, despised the Galileans (John 7:52). Rather contemptuously Nathanael asked, "Can anything good come out of Nazareth?" (John 1:46).

Galilee consisted essentially of an upland area of forests and farmlands. An imaginary line from the plain of Acco (Acre) to the north end of the Sea of Galilee divided the country into Upper and Lower Galilee. Since this area was actually the foothills of the Lebanon mountains, Upper and Lower Galilee had two different elevations. The higher of the elevations, Upper Galilee, was more than 1,000 meters (3,000 feet) above sea level; and in the days of the New Testament it was densely forested and thinly inhabited. The lower elevation, Lower Galilee, averaged between 500 to 700 meters (1,500 to 2,000 feet) above sea level; it was less hilly and enjoyed a milder climate than Upper Galilee. This area included the rich plain of Esdraelon and was a "pleasant" land (Gen. 49:15). Chief exports of the region were olive oil, grains, and fish.

Galilee was the boyhood home of Jesus Christ. He was a lad of Nazareth, as it was prophesied: "He shall be called a

Nazarene" (Matt. 2:23). Here He attempted to begin His public ministry, but was rejected by His own people (Luke 4:16–30).

All the disciples of Jesus, with the exception of Judas Iscariot, came from Galilee (Matt. 4:18; John 1:43–44; Acts 1:11; 2:7). In Cana of Galilee He performed His first miracle (John 2:11); in fact, most of His 33 great miracles were performed in Galilee. Capernaum in Galilee became the headquarters of His ministry (Matt. 4:13; 9:1). Of His 32 parables, 19 were spoken in Galilee. The first three Gospels concern themselves largely with Christ's Galilean ministry. Most of the events of our Lord's life and ministry are set against the backdrop of the Galilean hills.

When Herod the Great died in 4 B.C., Galilee fell to the authority of Herod Antipas, who governed until A.D. 39. He built his capital city at Tiberias on the Sea of Galilee and was succeeded by Herod I who took the title of "king." After Agrippa's death in A.D. 44 (Acts 12:23), Galilee became a Zealot stronghold until the Romans crushed Jewish resistance in Palestine between A.D. 66 and 73.

G ALILEE, SEA OF — a freshwater lake, fed by the Jordan River, which was closely connected with the earthly ministry of Jesus. This "sea" is called by four different names in the Bible: the "Sea of Chinnereth" [or "Chinneroth"] (the Hebrew word for "harp-shaped," the general outline of the lake; Num. 34:11; Josh. 12:3; 13:27); the "Lake of Gennesaret" (Luke 5:1), taking the name from the fertile Plain of Gennesaret that lies on the northwest (Matt. 14:34); the "Sea of Tiberias" (John 6:1; 21:1), because of its association with the capital of Herod Antipas; and the "Sea of Galilee" (Matt. 4:18; Mark 1:16).

Situated some 98 kilometers (60 miles) north of Jerusalem, the Sea of Galilee contains fresh water since it is fed by the Jordan. The lake itself is the deepest part of the northern Jordan Rift and thus the water collects there before it flows on its way. The surface of Galilee is about 230 meters (700 feet) below the

Mediterranean Sea. The floor of the lake is another 25 to 50 meters (80 to 160 feet) lower. The lake itself is nearly 21 kilometers (13 miles) long and 13 kilometers (8 miles) wide at Magdala, the point of its greatest width. The lake is surrounded, except on the southern side, by steep cliffs and sharply rising mountains. On the east these mountains rise to the fertile Golan Heights as high as 900 meters (2,700 feet). As a result of this formation, cool winds frequently rush down these slopes and unexpectedly stir up violent storms on the warm surface of the lake. Waves such as these were easily calmed at the command of Jesus (Mark 4:35–41).

A fishing industry thrived on the Sea of Galilee. Jesus called His first disciples—Peter, Andrew, James, and John—from that industry (1:16–20). In spite of the steep hillsides around the lake, nine cities of 15,000 population or more thrived in the first century as part of an almost continuous belt of settlements around the lake. Of these cities, Bethsaida, Tiberias, and Capernaum were the most important. On and around the Sea of Galilee Jesus performed most of His 33 recorded miracles and issued most of His teachings to His disciples and the multitudes that followed Him.

GAMALIEL [guh MAY lih el] (*God is my recompense*) — the name of two men in the Bible:

1. A leader of the tribe of Manasseh chosen to help take the census during Israel's wandering in the wilderness (Num. 1:10).

2. A famous member of the Jewish Sanhedrin and a teacher of the law. Gamaliel, who had taught the apostle Paul (Acts 22:3), advised the Sanhedrin to treat the apostles of the young Christian church with moderation. Gamaliel's argument was simple. If Jesus was a false prophet, as many others had been, the movement would soon fade into obscurity. If, however, the work was "of God," he pointed out, "you cannot overthrow it" (Acts 5:39).

GATH [gath] (*wine press*) — one of the five chief cities of the Philistines (Judg. 3:3). Although Gath is frequently used as a prefix in combination with a proper name to refer to other cities—for example, Gath Hepher (Josh. 19:13) and Gath Rimmon (Josh. 19:45)—when it appears alone it refers to the great Philistine city.

Gath was known as the residence of the Anakim, men of great stature (Josh. 11:22). Goliath and other giants belonged to this race and the city of Gath (1 Sam. 17:4). David captured Gath during his reign (1 Chr. 13:1). The residents of Gath, known as Gittites, were still subject to Israel during Solomon's reign, although they still had their own king (1 Kin. 2:39, 42).

Solomon's son, Rehoboam, later fortified Gath (2 Chr. 11:8), but the city returned to the hands of the Philistines. Later, it was recaptured by Hazael (2 Kin. 12:17), and Uzziah broke down its walls (2 Chr. 26:6).

GAZA [GAY zuh] (*stronghold*) — one of the five principal cities of the Philistines. The southernmost city of Canaan, Gaza was situated on the great caravan route between Mesopotamia and Egypt, at the junction of the trade route from Arabia. This location made Gaza an ideal rest stop and a commercial center for merchants and travelers.

Gaza was originally inhabited by the Avvim, a people who were replaced by the Caphtorim (Deut. 2:23). Gaza was allotted to the tribe of Judah by Joshua (Josh. 15:47), but it was not immediately occupied (Judg. 1:18), because the Anakim were still present in the city (Josh. 11:22; 13:3). Soon afterward the Philistines recovered Gaza (Judg. 13:1). Here the mighty Samson was humiliated by being forced to grind grain as a blinded prisoner (Judg. 16:21). In a final victorious performance, Samson brought down the house of the pagan god Dagon, destroying many Philistines (Judg. 16:23–31).

Although Solomon ruled over Gaza, not until the reign of Hezekiah, king of Judah, was the decisive blow dealt to the Philistines (2 Kin. 18:8). Through the prophet Amos, God threatened Gaza with destruction by fire for its sins (Amos 1:6–7). This prophecy was fulfilled by the army of Alexander the Great in 332 B.C., when Gaza was destroyed and her inhabitants massacred (Zeph. 2:4; Zech. 9:5).

In the New Testament the evangelist Philip was directed by God to preach the gospel along the road from Jerusalem to Gaza (Acts 8:26). On this road the Ethiopian eunuch professed faith in Jesus and was baptized.

GEBAL [GHEE buhl] (*mountain*) — the name of a city and a region:

1. A mountainous region between Petra and the southern end of the Dead Sea. Inhabited by the Edomites, Gebal was one of the areas allied against Israel (Ps. 83:7).

2. An ancient and thriving seaport situated on a bluff in the foothills of Lebanon that overlooked the Mediterranean Sea. Gebal was about 32 kilometers (20 miles) north of Beirut between Sidon and Tripoli (Ezek. 27:9). One of the most important seaports of Phoenicia, Gebal imported so much papyrus from Egypt that its Greek name, *Byblos,* ultimately gave rise to words like "Bible" and "bibliography."

GEDALIAH [gad uh LIE ah] (*The Lord is great*) — the name of five Old Testament men:

1. A person of high birth appointed governor of Judah by Nebuchadnezzar (2 Kin. 25:22–25). Gedaliah governed Judah from Mizpah, where after ruling for only two or three months he was assassinated by Jewish nationalists led by Ishmael. Gedaliah's father had protected the prophet Jeremiah, and Gedaliah probably did the same.

2. A Levite musician of David's time. Gedaliah was one of the six sons of Jeduthun (1 Chr. 25:3, 9).

3. A priest who divorced his pagan wife after the captivity (Ezra 10:18).

4. A son of Pashhur who called for the death of the prophet Jeremiah (Jer. 38:1, 4).

5. An ancestor of the prophet Zephaniah (Zeph. 1:1).

GERIZIM [GEH ruh zim] — a mountain in the district of Samaria. Mount Gerizim is located southwest of Mount Ebal. The main north–south road through central Palestine ran between these two mountains. Thus, Gerizim was of strategic military importance.

When the Hebrew people reached the promised land, Moses directed them to climb Mount Gerizim and Mount Ebal. Six tribes stood on each mountain (Deut. 27:11–14). Then Moses pronounced the blessings for keeping the law from Mount Gerizim and the curses for not keeping it from Mount Ebal (Deut. 11:29; 27:4–26). A ledge halfway to the top of Gerizim is called "Jotham's pulpit" (see Judg. 9:7). The characteristics of the two mountains make it possible to speak from either mountain and be heard easily in the valley below.

When the Israelites returned from their years of captivity in Babylon, they refused to allow the Samaritans, the residents of this mountain region, to assist in rebuilding Jerusalem (Ezra 4:1–4; Neh. 2:19–20; 13:28). In the days of Alexander the Great, a Samaritan temple was built on Mount Gerizim. Although it was destroyed by the Hasmonean king John Hyrcanus in 128 B.C., the Samaritans still worshiped on Mount Gerizim in Jesus' day (John 4:20–21). The small Samaritan community in Israel continues to celebrate the Passover on Mount Gerizim to this day.

Jacob's Well is situated at the foot of Mount Gerizim, today called Jebel et-Tor. This is the well where Jesus met the woman of Samaria, discussed Samaritan worship practices on Mount Gerizim, and told her of Himself—"a fountain of water springing up into everlasting life" (John 4:14).

GERSHON [GUR shun] — the oldest of the three sons of Levi; his brothers were Kohath and Merari (Gen. 46:11; Num. 3:17). He is also called Gershom (1 Chr. 15:7). Gershon was founder of the family called the Gershonites (Num. 26:57), one of three main divisions of the Levitical priesthood. Gershon was apparently born to Levi before Jacob's family moved to Egypt to escape a famine (Ex. 6:16). Although Gershon was the oldest of Levi's sons, it was through the line of Gershon's younger brother, Kohath, that the priestly line of Aaron sprang years later after the Exodus of the Hebrew people from Egypt.

GETHSEMANE [geth SEMM uh nee] (*olive press*) — the garden where Jesus often went alone or with His disciples for prayer, rest, or fellowship, and the site where He was betrayed by Judas on the night before His crucifixion (Luke 21:37; John 18:1–2).

Gethsemane was situated on the Mount of Olives just east of Jerusalem, across the Kidron Valley and opposite the temple (Mark 13:3; John 18:1). From its name scholars conclude that the garden was situated in an olive grove that contained an olive press. Attempts to locate the exact site of the garden have been unsuccessful. Many Christians have agreed on one site—the place that Constantine's mother Helena designated about A.D. 325. But at least two other sites are also defended by tradition and have their supporters. The gospel accounts do not provide enough details to show the exact site of the garden.

The four gospel writers focus special attention on Jesus' final visit to Gethsemane just before His arrest and crucifixion. After the Last Supper, Jesus returned there with His disciples for final instructions and a period of soul-searching prayer. All the disciples were instructed; but only Peter, James, and John went to Gethsemane with Jesus to pray (Mark 14:26–32). Jesus urged them to stand watch while He prayed. Then He pleaded with God to deliver Him from the coming events (Mark 14:32–42). But His prayer was not an arrogant attempt to resist God's will or even to change God's plan. His pleas clearly acknowledged His obedience to the will of the Father: "O My Father, if this cup cannot pass away from Me unless I drink it, Your will be done" (Matt. 26:42).

GIBEAH, GIBEATH [GIB ee ah, GIB ee ath] (*hill*) — the name of three or four different places in the Old Testament:

1. Gibeath-Haaraloth, "the hill of the foreskins" (Josh. 5:3), a place in Canaan where male Israelites were circumcised.

2. A small, unidentified city in the territory of Judah (Josh. 15:57).

3. A city belonging to Benjamin (Judg. 19:14). Scholars disagree over whether this is the same city called Gibeath in Joshua 18:28. Gibeah has been excavated at the modern site of Tell el-Ful, 5 kilometers (3 miles) north of Jerusalem. This city figured prominently in two separate periods of Old Testament history. It first appeared in Judges 19–20 as the site of a crime of lewdness and obscenity. All the children of Israel came together to punish Gibeah for its crimes. After a prolonged and mostly unsuccessful war against the Benjamites, the Israelites completely destroyed Gibeah (Judg. 20:40). The Tel el-Ful excavations have uncovered the remains of a village completely destroyed by fire.

Gibeah was apparently rebuilt after the fire. The birthplace of Saul, it became the capital of his kingdom (1 Sam. 14:16; 15:34). In many passages, it is even called "Gibeah of Saul" (1 Sam. 11:4; Is. 10:29). At Tell el-Ful, the remains of Saul's fortress, built around 1015 B.C., have been found. The fortress walls, 2.5 to 3.5 meters (8 to 10 feet) thick, enclosed an area of 52 x 47 meters

(170 x 155 feet). The stronghold was made up of two stories joined by a stone staircase.

4. The KJV uses "Gibeah" instead of "hill" in some passages, such as "the house of Abinadab that was in Gibeah" (2 Sam. 6:4).

GIBEON [GIBB eh un] (*pertaining to a hill*) — a city in the territory of Benjamin about 10 kilometers (6 miles) northwest of Jerusalem. It was the chief city of the Hivites.

The first reference to Gibeon in the Bible is Joshua 9:3. After the Israelites destroyed the cities of Jericho and Ai (Joshua 6–8), Gibeon's inhabitants, fearing the same fate, made a covenant with the Israelites. Although they established the treaty by deceit and thus were made slaves by the Israelites, the Gibeonites were still protected from the alliance of five Amorite kings. In a battle over Gibeon between Joshua and the Amorite alliance (Josh. 10:1–11), the sun stood still for a day and hailstones rained down on the fleeing Amorites.

Gibeon does not appear again in Scripture until about 1000 B.C. Then, in a gruesome contest of strength, 12 of David's men and 12 of the men of Ishbosheth (Saul's son) killed one another with their swords. The place was named "the Field of the Sharp Swords" (2 Sam. 2:16) because of this event. There followed a great battle in which David's forces were victorious (2 Sam. 2:12–17).

The prophet Jeremiah mentioned a "great pool that is in Gibeon" (Jer. 41:12). This pool was discovered in an excavation of the site, beginning in 1956. Archaeologists discovered a large open pit about 11 meters (35 feet) deep that had been dug into the solid rock. A large stone stairway descended into the pit, then continued another 11 meters down to a water chamber. Gibeon was the center of a winemaking industry during the seventh century B.C. The lower chamber of the "great pool" provided water for the wine and also served as the city's main water supply.

GIDEON [GIDD ee un] — a military hero and spiritual leader who delivered Israel from the oppression of the Midianites.

As a young lad, Gideon had seen the land oppressed by the Midianites and Amalekites for seven years (Judg. 6:1). Like invading locusts, the roving bands camped on the land of the Israelites. At harvest time, they destroyed the crops and animals and plundered the farmers' houses. Israel's misfortune was apparently caused by their spiritual relapse into Baal worship (Judg. 6:1).

As young Gideon was threshing wheat, the angel of the Lord appeared with strong words of encouragement: "The Lord is with you, you mighty man of valor.... Surely, I will be with you, and you shall defeat the Midianites as one man" (Judg. 6:12, 16).

Gideon then asked the messenger for a sign that God had selected him for divine service. He prepared an offering and placed it on an altar. The angel touched the offering with his staff, and fire consumed it (6:19–21). Gideon then recognized his personal call to serve God.

Gideon's first assignment was to destroy his father's altar of Baal in the family's backyard (Judg. 6:25). This act required great courage, for Gideon feared his father's house and the men of the city who must have worshiped at the altar. For this reason, Gideon and ten servants destroyed the altar of Baal and a wood idol by night and erected an altar to the Lord. Gideon immediately presented an offering to the Lord on the altar (6:27–28). When Gideon's fellow citizens discovered that the altar to Baal had been destroyed, they were outraged. When it was learned that "Gideon the son of Joash has done this thing" (6:29), Joash was called to account for his son's behavior. To his credit, Joash defended Gideon by implying that an authentic god should require no defense. "If he [Baal] is a god, let him plead for himself" (6:31). So that day Gideon was called Jerubbaal, meaning "Let Baal plead" (6:25–32).

As the oppression of the Midianites intensified, Gideon sent out messengers to all Manasseh and the surrounding tribes to rally volunteers to Israel's cause (Judg. 6:35). When Gideon's volunteers assembled, about 32,000 citizen soldiers stood in the ranks (Judg. 7:1). Although there were 135,000 Midianites camped in a nearby valley, God directed Gideon to thin out the ranks. After dismissing the fearful and afraid, only 10,000 remained. Gideon's band was now outnumbered about 13 to 1.

"There are still too many," God told Gideon. "Bring them down to the water, and I will test them for you there" (7:4). Those who scooped up the water with their hands, never taking their eyes from the horizon, were retained in Gideon's army; those who got down on their knees to drink, forgetting to keep watch for the enemy, were dismissed. Now only 300 soldiers remained (Judg. 7:5–7). The Midianites outnumbered Gideon's band 450 to 1. But God and Gideon had a secret plan.

Gideon divided the army into three companies. Then he gave each man a trumpet, a pitcher, and a torch. At the appointed time, 300 trumpets blasted the air, 300 hands raised their pitchers and smashed them to bits, 300 burning torches pierced the darkness, and 300 warriors cried, "The sword of the LORD and of Gideon" (Judg. 7:19–21).

The Midianites were thrown into panic. In the confusion, some committed suicide or killed their comrades. The remaining soldiers fled. The enemies of Israel were completely routed, and Israel's homeland was secure (Judg. 7:22; 8:10). It was a glorious victory for God and for Gideon, who became an instant hero (8:22).

Gideon and his men pursued the fleeing enemy. Many of them were killed or captured by Gideon's allies. Two Midianite kings, Zebah and Zalmunna, were captured and killed for their murderous deeds (Judges 8).

As a conquering warrior, Gideon was invited to become king (Judg. 8:22), but he declined. Modest and devout, he was careful not to grasp at the power and glory that belonged to God. After he retired to his home, Israel was blessed with 40 years of peace (Judg. 8:28).

Through the life and exploits of Gideon, God reveals much about Himself and the preparation that His leaders need for divine service. Gideon shows that God calls leaders from unlikely situations. Gideon was a poor farmer's son who worked with his hands, and his father was an idol worshiper (Judg. 6:15, 25). Still, Gideon was an effective leader in God's service.

The story of Gideon also reminds us that God prefers a few dedicated and disciplined disciples to throngs of uncommitted workers. God can win victories with a fully committed minority (Judg. 7:2, 4, 7).

Another leadership lesson from Gideon's life is that a leader's spiritual life is sustained by regular worship. Devout Gideon appears to have worshiped frequently—in times of personal crisis as well as celebration (Judg. 6:18–21; 7:15).

GIHON [GIH hon] (*gusher*) — the name of a river and a spring in the Old Testament:

1. One of the four rivers of the garden of Eden (Gen. 2:13). Some scholars believe the name refers to the Nile River. Others, however, believe it refers to a smaller river in the Euphrates Valley system—perhaps a major irrigation ditch or canal.

2. A spring outside the walls of Jerusalem where the city obtained part of its water supply (2 Chr. 32:30). The Canaanite inhabitants of ancient Jerusalem, or Jebus, had used and protected the spring in their fortifications, too. When David and his soldiers conquered Jebus, they entered it through the water

shaft that led from the spring into the city (2 Sam. 5:8). Israel continued to use Gihon and its water channel. King Hezekiah channeled the water more elaborately when he constructed the famous Siloam tunnel in 701 B.C. as part of the city's preparation against the siege of the Assyrians (2 Kin. 20:20).

Gihon was the site where Solomon was anointed and proclaimed king (1 Kin. 1:33, 38, 45). Some scholars believe it later became customary for the new king to drink from the waters of Gihon during his coronation ceremony (Ps. 110:7).

GILEAD [GILL ee ad] — the name of three men, two mountains, and one city in the Old Testament:

1. A son of Machir and grandson of Manasseh (Josh. 17:1). He founded a tribal family, the Gileadites.

2. A mountain region east of the Jordan River 915 meters (3,000 feet) above sea level. Extending about 97 kilometers (60 miles) from near the south end of the Sea of Galilee to the north end of the Dead Sea, Gilead is about 32 kilometers (20 miles) wide. It is bounded on the west by the Jordan River, on the south by the land of Moab, on the north by the Yarmuk River, and on the east by the desert.

The Jabbok River divides Gilead into two parts: northern Gilead, the land between the Jabbok and the Yarmuk, and southern Gilead, the land between the Jabbok and the Arnon (Josh. 12:2). The term "Gilead," however, came to be applied to the entire region of Israelite Transjordan (Deut. 34:1).

This lush region receives an annual rainfall of from 71 to 81 centimeters (28 to 32 inches). Thus, much of it is thickly wooded today, as it was in Absalom's day (2 Sam. 18:6–9). Many fugitives fled to this region for safety. Jacob fled to Gilead from Laban, his father-in-law (Gen. 31:21). The Israelites who feared the Philistines in King Saul's day fled here (1 Sam. 13:7), as did Ishbosheth (2 Sam. 2:8–9) and David (2 Sam. 17:22, 26) during

Absalom's revolt. Gilead also contains rich grazing land (1 Chr. 5:9–10).

The Balm of Gilead, an aromatic resin used for medical purposes (Jer. 8:22), was exported to Tyre and elsewhere (Ezek. 27:17). The Ishmaelites who carried Joseph into Egyptian bondage also traded in Gilead's balm (Gen. 37:25).

When Canaan was being allocated to the Israelite tribes, Gilead fell to the Reubenites and Gadites because of its suitability for grazing cattle (Deut. 3:12–17). The half-tribe of Manasseh also shared in the land of Gilead.

3. A mountain on the edge of the Jezreel Valley (Judg. 7:3). Gideon and his men were camped here when Gideon ordered a reduction in his troops before he fought the Midianites.

4. The father of Jephthah, a judge of Israel (Judg. 11:1–12:7).

5. A chief of the family of Gad (1 Chr. 5:14).

6. A city in the region of Gilead condemned by the prophet Hosea (Hos. 6:8). The name Gilead in this passage is probably a poetic shortening of Ramoth Gilead or Jabesh Gilead, two of the cities of Gilead.

GILGAL [GILL gal] (circle) — the name of a campsite and two cities in the Old Testament:

1. A village from which the prophet Elijah ascended into heaven (2 Kin. 2:1). Gilgal was perhaps in the hill country of Ephraim, about 13 kilometers (8 miles) northwest of Bethel.

2. The first campsite of the people of Israel after they crossed the Jordan River and entered the promised land (Josh. 4:19–20). They took stones from the Jordan and set them up at Gilgal as a memorial to God's deliverance. Many important events in Israel's history are associated with this city. The first Passover in Canaan was held at Gilgal (Josh. 5:9–10). It also became the base of military operations for Israel during the conquest of Canaan. From Gilgal Joshua led Israel against the city of Jericho (Josh. 6:11, 14) and conducted his southern campaign

(Joshua 10). It was there that he began allotting the promised land to the tribes.

In later years, Gilgal was the site of King Saul's coronation as well as his rejection by God as king (1 Sam. 11:15; 13:4–12; 15:12–33). After Absalom's revolt, the people of Judah gathered at Gilgal to welcome David back as their king (2 Sam. 19:15, 40). But during the days of later kings, Gilgal became a center of idolatry. Like Bethel, it was condemned by the prophets (Hos. 4:15; Amos 5:5). The presumed site of Gilgal is about 2 kilometers (1 mile) northeast of Old Testament Jericho (Josh. 4:19).

3. A town between Dor and Tirzah (Josh. 12:23), probably Jiljulieh, a little town north of the brook Kanah and 8 kilometers (5 miles) northeast of Antipatris.

GOG [gog] — the name of two men in the Bible:

1. A descendant of Joel, of the tribe of Reuben (1 Chr. 5:4).

2. The leader of a confederacy of armies that attacked the land of Israel. Described as "the prince of Rosh, Meshech, and Tubal," Gog is also depicted as being "of the land of Magog" (Ezek. 38:2–3), a "place out of the far north" of Israel. Ezekiel prophetically describes Gog and his allies striking at Israel with a fierce and sudden invasion (Ezekiel 38–39). According to Ezekiel's prophecy, Gog will be crushed on the mountains of Israel in a slaughter so great it will take seven months to bury the dead (Ezek. 39:12).

In the book of Revelation, Gog and Magog reappear as symbols of the nations of the world that will march against God's people in the end times (Rev. 20:7–8).

GOLIATH [goe LIE ahth] — a Philistine giant whom David felled with a stone from his sling (1 Sam. 17:4–51). Goliath, who lived in the Philistine city of Gath, was probably a descendant of a tribe of giants known as the Anakim, or descendants of Anak (Num. 13:33). These giants probably served in a capacity similar to that of a foreign mercenary or soldier of fortune.

Based on the figures in the Bible (1 Sam. 17:4), Goliath was over 9 feet tall. The magnificence of Goliath's armor and weapons—his bronze coat of mail, bronze greaves, bronze javelin, spear with an iron spearhead, and huge sword—must have made him appear invincible.

For 40 days this enormous man challenged Saul's army to find one man willing to engage in hand-to-hand combat. The winner of that one battle would determine the outcome of the war. The young David, chosen by God as Israel's next king, accepted the challenge, felling Goliath with a single stone to the forehead from his sling. When David beheaded the fallen giant, the Philistines fled in panic.

GOMER [GOAM ur] — the name of a man, a people, and a woman:

1. The oldest son of Japheth (Gen. 10:2–3).

2. The people descended from Gomer, son of Japheth. Apparently they lived to the far north, beyond the Black Sea (Ezek. 38:6). They were probably the Cimmerians of classical history.

3. A prostitute who became the wife of the prophet Hosea (Hos. 1:1–11). When Gomer left Hosea and became the slave of one of her lovers, Hosea bought her back at God's command for the price of a slave. Gomer's unfaithfulness and Hosea's forgiveness symbolized God's forgiving love for unfaithful Israel.

GOMORRAH [guh MOR ruh] (*submersion*) — one of the five "cities of the plain" located in the Valley of Siddim (Salt Sea or Dead Sea). The other cities were Sodom, Admah, Zeboiim, and Zoar (Gen. 14:2–3). Gomorrah is associated closely with its twin city, Sodom. Because these cities became the site of intolerable wickedness, they were destroyed by fire

(Gen. 19:24, 28). The destruction of Sodom and Gomorrah is often referred to in the Bible as a clear example of divine judgment against the vilest of sinners (Is. 13:19; Jer. 49:18; Amos 4:11; Matt. 10:15; 2 Pet. 2:6; Jude 7).

The exact location of the "cities of the plain" has been a subject of much debate. The current consensus, however, places them near Bab edh-Dhra, the entrance to the "tongue" (Lisan) of land that juts out into the Dead Sea on its eastern shore.

GOSHEN [GOE shun] — the name of two areas and one city in the Old Testament:

1. The northeastern territory of the Nile Delta in Egypt, known today as the area of the Wadi Tumilat. Jacob and his family were granted permission to settle in this fertile section during Joseph's rule as prime minister of Egypt (Gen. 46:28).

During the time of the Exodus, Goshen was protected from the plagues of flies (Ex. 8:22) and hail (Ex. 9:26) that engulfed the rest of Egypt. The district was not large, containing perhaps 900 square miles, and it had two principal cities: Rameses and Pithom.

2. A district of southern Palestine between Gaza and Gibeon and the hill country and the Negeb (Josh. 10:41).

3. A town in the mountains of southwest Judah (Josh. 15:51).

HABAKKUK [huh BAK uhk] — a courageous Old
Testament prophet and author of the book of Habakkuk.
The Scriptures say nothing of his ancestry or place of birth. A
man of deep emotional strength, Habakkuk was both a poet
and a prophet. His hatred of sin compelled him to cry out to
God for judgment (Hab. 1:2–4). His sense of justice also led
him to challenge God's plan to judge the nation of Judah by the
pagan Babylonians (Hab. 1:12–2:1). His deep faith led him to
write a beautiful poem of praise in response to the mysterious
ways of God (Habakkuk 3).

HAGAR [HAY gahr] — the Egyptian bondwoman of Sarah
who bore a son, Ishmael, to Abraham (Gen. 16:1–16). After
waiting ten years for God to fulfill his promise to give them a
son, Sarah presented Hagar to Abraham so he could father a
child by her, according to the custom of the day. Sarah's plan
and Abraham's compliance demonstrated a lack of faith in God.

When Hagar became pregnant, she mocked Sarah, who
dealt with her harshly. Hagar then fled into the wilderness,
where, at a well on the way to Shur, she encountered an angel
of the Lord. The angel revealed Ishmael's future to Hagar—
that his descendants would be a great multitude. Tradition

has it that Hagar is the ancestress of all the Arab peoples and of the prophet Muhammad. Hagar called the well Beer Lahai Roi, "The well of the Living One who sees me." When Hagar returned to Abraham's camp, Ishmael was born and accepted by Abraham as his son. But when Ishmael was 14, Isaac, the promised son, was born. The next year Ishmael mocked Isaac at the festival of Isaac's weaning. At Sarah's insistence and with Abraham's approval, Hagar and Ishmael were expelled from Abraham's family. Abraham grieved for Ishmael, but God comforted him by revealing that a great nation would come out of Ishmael. Hagar and Ishmael wandered in the wilderness until their water was gone. When Hagar laid her son under the shade of a bush to die, the angel of the Lord appeared to Hagar and showed her a well. This is a beautiful picture of God's concern for the outcast and helpless. In Paul's allegory in Galatians 4, Hagar stands for Mount Sinai and corresponds to the earthly Jerusalem, while Isaac stands for the children of promise who are free in Christ.

HAGGAI [HAG eye] (*festive*) — an Old Testament prophet and author of the book of Haggai. As God's spokesman, he encouraged the captives who had returned to Jerusalem to complete the reconstruction of the temple. This work had started shortly after the first exiles returned from Babylon in 538 B.C. But the building activity was soon abandoned because of discouragement and oppression. Beginning in 520 B.C., Haggai and his fellow prophet, Zechariah, urged the people to resume the task. The temple was completed five years later, about 515 B.C. (Ezra 5:1).

HAM [hamm] — the name of a person and two places in the Old Testament:

1. The youngest of Noah's three sons (Gen. 9:18, 24). Ham, along with the rest of Noah's household, was saved from the

great Flood by entering the ark (Gen. 7:7). After the waters went down and Noah's household left the ark, Ham found his father, naked and drunk, asleep in his tent. Ham told his brothers, Shem and Japheth, who covered their father without looking on his nakedness. Noah was furious because Ham had seen him naked, and he placed a prophetic curse on Canaan, the son of Ham (Gen. 9:18, 25). The Canaanites were to serve the descendants of Shem and Japheth (Gen. 9:26–27; Josh. 9:16–27).

Ham had four sons: Cush, Mizraim, Put, and Canaan (Gen. 10:6). The tribe of Mizraim settled in Egypt, while the tribes of Cush and Put settled in other parts of Africa. The tribe of Canaan populated Phoenicia and Palestine.

2. A city east of the Jordan River during the time of Abraham. It was attacked by Chedorlaomer and other allied kings (Gen. 14:5). The modern city of Ham lies 6 kilometers (4 miles) south of Irbid.

3. Another name for Egypt, used in poetry (Ps. 78:51; 105:23, 27).

HAMAN [HAY mun] — the evil and scheming prime minister of Ahasuerus (Xerxes I), king of Persia (485–464 B.C.). When Mordecai refused to bow to Haman, Haman plotted to destroy Mordecai and his family, as well as all of the Jews in the Persian Empire. But Esther intervened and saved her people. Haman was hanged on the very gallows he had constructed for Mordecai (Esth. 3:1–9:25). This shows that God is always in control of events, even when wickedness and evil seem to be winning out.

HARAN [HAIR uhn] (*crossroads*) — a city of northern Mesopotamia. Abraham and his father Terah lived there for a time (Gen. 11:31–32; 12:4–5). The family of Abraham's brother Nahor also lived in this city for a time, as did Jacob and his wife Rachel (Gen. 28:10; 29:4–5). The city was on the Balikh, a tributary of the Euphrates River, 386 kilometers (240 miles) northwest of Nineveh and 450 kilometers (280 miles) northeast of Damascus. Haran lay on one of the main trade routes between Babylonia and the Mediterranean Sea. Like the inhabitants of Ur of the Chaldeans, Haran's inhabitants worshiped Sin, the moon-god. Second Kings 19:12 records that the city was captured by the Assyrians. Today Haran is a small Arab village, Harran, a spelling that preserves the two *r*'s of the original place name and helps to distinguish it from the personal name Haran (see above). The city name is also spelled Charran (Acts 7:2, 4; KJV).

HAZOR [HAH zohr] (*enclosure*) — the name of three cities and one district in the Bible:

1. An ancient Canaanite fortress city in northern Palestine, situated about 16 kilometers (10 miles) northwest of the Sea of Galilee. When Joshua and the Israelites invaded Palestine, Hazor was one of the most important fortresses in the land (Josh. 11:10). This was due to its enormous size, its large population, and its strategic location on the main road between Egypt and Mesopotamia.

When the Israelites approached Palestine, Jabin, the king of Hazor, and several other kings formed an alliance against them. Through God's power the Israelites defeated these armies, killed all the people of Hazor, and burned the city (Josh. 11:1–14). The city regained its strength during the time of the Judges. Because of Israel's sinfulness, God allowed the armies of Hazor to oppress the Israelites for 20 years (Judg. 4:1–3). Sisera, the captain of the armies of Hazor, and his 900 chariots were miraculously defeated by God through the efforts of Deborah and Barak (Judg. 4:4–24). Solomon later chose Hazor as one of his military outposts (1 Kin. 9:15). The rebuilt city continued to play an important part in the northern defenses of Israel until it was destroyed by the Assyrian king Tiglath-Pileser (2 Kin. 15:29), about ten years before the collapse of the Northern Kingdom in 722 B.C.

2. A city in the southern desert of Judah (Josh. 15:23).

3. Hazor-Hadattah ("New Hazor") and Kerioth-Hazor ("City of Hazor"), which may be identical sites in southern Judea (Josh. 15:25).

4. A nomadic district or kingdom of villages in the Arabian desert (Jer. 49:28).

HEBRON [HEE bruhn] (*alliance*) — the name of two cities and two men in the Bible:

1. A city situated 31 kilometers (19 miles) southwest of Jerusalem on the road to Beersheba. Although it lies in a slight valley, the city is 927 meters (3,040 feet) above sea level, which makes it the highest town in Palestine. Originally Hebron was called Kirjath Arba (Gen. 23:2). Numbers 13:22 speaks of Hebron being built seven years before Zoan in Egypt. This probably refers to the rebuilding of the city by the Hyksos rulers of Egypt. The 12 Hebrew spies viewed Hebron on their mission to explore the promised land.

The area surrounding Hebron is rich in biblical history. Abram spent much of his time in Mamre in the area of Hebron (Gen. 13:18). He was living in Mamre when the confederacy of kings overthrew the cities of the plain and captured Lot (Gen. 14:1–13). Here, too, Abram's name was changed to Abraham (Gen. 17:5). At Hebron the angels revealed to Abraham that he would have a son who would be called Isaac (Gen. 18:1–15). Later, Sarah died at Hebron (Gen. 23:2); Abraham bought the cave of Machpelah as her burial place (Gen. 23:9). The present mosque built over the cave is called Haran el-Khalil, "the sacred precinct of the friend (of God)," reminiscent of a title given to Abraham in 2 Chr. 20:7; Is. 41:8; Jas. 2:23.

During the period of the conquest of the land of Canaan, Joshua killed the king of Hebron (Josh. 10:3–27). Later, Caleb drove out the Anakim and claimed Hebron for his inheritance (Josh. 14:12–15). Hebron was also designated as one of the cities of refuge (Josh. 20:7). David ruled from Hebron the first seven years of his reign (2 Sam. 2:11), after which he established Jerusalem as his capital.

When Absalom rebelled against his father, David, he made Hebron his headquarters (2 Sam. 15:7–12). King Rehoboam fortified the city to protect his southern border (2 Chr. 11:10–12). The discovery of 5 jar handles stamped with the royal seal dating from the eighth century B.C. testifies that Hebron was a key storage city, perhaps for rations of Uzziah's army (2 Chr. 26:10).

2. The third son of Kohath, the son of Levi (Ex. 6:18). Hebron was an uncle of Moses, Aaron, and Miriam. His descendants were called Hebronites (Num. 3:27).

3. A descendant of Caleb (1 Chr. 2:42–43).

4. A town in Asher (Josh. 19:28, KJV; Ebron, NRSV, NKJV). This may be the same town as Abdon (Josh. 21:30).

HERMON [HUR mon] (*sacred place*) — the northern boundary of the land east of the Jordan River that Israel took from the Amorites (Deut. 3:8; Josh. 12:1). The mountain is the southern end of the Anti-Lebanon range and is about 32 kilometers (20 miles) long. It has three peaks (Ps. 42:6), two of which rise over 2,750 meters (9,000 feet) above sea level.

Hermon was regarded as a sacred place by the Canaanites who inhabited the land before the Israelites (Judg. 3:3). Snow covers the mountain during most of the year. Patches of snow remain even through the summer in shaded ravines. The beautiful snow-covered peaks of Mount Hermon can be seen from the region of the Dead Sea, over 196 kilometers (120 miles) distant. The glaciers of Mount Hermon are a major source of the Jordan River, and water from its slopes ultimately flows into the Dead Sea.

The psalmist speaks of the "dew of Hermon" (Ps. 133:3). The snow condenses to vapor during the summer, so that a heavy dew descends on the mountain while the areas surrounding Hermon are parched.

Mount Hermon probably was the site of our Lord's transfiguration (Matt. 17:1–9; Mark 9:2–9; Luke 9:28–37). Jesus traveled with His disciples from Bethsaida, on the Sea of Galilee, to the area of Caesarea Philippi to the north and from there to a "high mountain." There, in the presence of His disciples, Jesus was transfigured. A late tradition identifies the "high mountain" as Mount Tabor, but Mount Hermon is nearer Caesarea Philippi.

HEROD [HEHR ud] — the name of several Roman rulers in the Palestine region during Jesus' earthly ministry and the periods shortly before His birth and after His resurrection.

The Herodian dynasty made its way into Palestine through Antipater, an Idumean by descent. The Idumeans were of Edomite stock as descendants of Esau. Antipater was installed as procurator of Judea by Julius Caesar, the emperor of Rome, in 47 B.C. He appointed two of his sons to ruling positions. One of these was Herod, known as "Herod the Great," who was appointed governor of Judea.

Herod the Great (37–4 B.C.). The title "Herod the Great" refers not so much to Herod's greatness as to the fact that he was the eldest son of Antipater. Nevertheless, Herod did show some unusual abilities. He was a ruthless fighter, a cunning negotiator, and a subtle diplomat. The Romans appreciated the way he subdued opposition and maintained order among the Jewish people. These qualities, combined with an intense loyalty to the emperor, made him an important figure in the life of Rome and the Jews of Palestine.

After Herod became governor of Galilee, he quickly established himself in the entire region. For 33 years he remained a loyal friend and ally of Rome. He was appointed king of

Judea, where he was in direct control of the Jewish people. This required careful diplomacy because he was always suspect by the Jews as an outsider (Idumean) and thus a threat to their national right to rule. At first Herod was conscious of Jewish national and religious feelings. He moved slowly on such issues as taxation, Hellenism, and religion. He did much to improve his relationship with the Jews when he prevented the temple in Jerusalem from being raided and defiled by invading Romans.

Herod the Great established his authority and influence through a centralized bureaucracy, well-built fortresses, and foreign soldiers. To assure his continued rule, he slaughtered all male infants who could possibly be considered legal heirs to the throne. His wife, Mariamne, also became a victim. The territories under Herod's rule experienced economic and cultural growth. His business and organizational ability led to the erection of many important buildings. Hellenistic (Greek) ideas were introduced into Palestine through literature, art, and athletic contests. His major building project was the temple complex in Jerusalem, which, according to John 2:20, had taken 46 years to build up to that time. From the Jewish perspective, this was his greatest achievement.

At times Herod implemented his policies with force and cruelty. His increasing fear of Jewish revolt led to suppression of any opposition. His personal problems also increased, and by 14 B.C. his kingdom began to decline. This decline was brought on mainly by his personal and domestic problems.

Herod's murder of his wife, Mariamne, apparently haunted him. This was compounded when his two sons from that marriage, Alexander and Aristobulus, realized that their father was responsible for their mother's death. By 7 B.C., Herod had both of these sons put to death. Of Herod it was said, "It is better to be Herod's pig (*hys*) than to be his son (*huios*)."

As Herod became increasingly ill, an intense struggle for succession to his throne emerged within the family. His

10 marriages and 15 children virtually guaranteed such a struggle. One son, Antipater, poisoned Herod's mind against two other eligible sons, Archelaus and Philip. This resulted in his initial choice of a younger son, Antipas, as sole successor. However, he later changed his will and made Archelaus king. Antipas and Philip received lesser positions as Tetrarchs, or rulers, over small territories.

After Herod died, his will was contested in Rome. Finally Archelaus was made ethnarch over Idumea, Judea, and Samaria—with a promise to be appointed king if he proved himself as a leader. Antipas became tetrarch over Galilee and Perea. Philip was made tetrarch over Gaulanitis, Trachonitis, Batanea, and Paneas in the northern regions. Jesus was born in Bethlehem during the reign of Herod the Great. The wise men came asking, "Where is he that is born King of the Jews?" This aroused Herod's jealous spirit. According to Matthew's account, Herod tried to eliminate Jesus by having all the male infants of the Bethlehem region put to death (Matt. 2:13–16). But this despicable act failed. Joseph and Mary were warned by God in a dream to take their child and flee to Egypt. Here they hid safely until Herod died (Matt. 2:13–15).

Herod Archelaus (4 B.C.–A.D. 6). Archelaus inherited his father Herod's vices without his abilities. He was responsible for much bloodshed in Judea and Samaria. Jewish revolts, particularly those led by the Zealots, were brutally crushed. Antipas and Philip did not approve of Archelaus's methods; so they complained to Rome. Their complaints were followed by a Jewish delegation that finally succeeded in having Archelaus stripped of power and banished to Rome.

The only biblical reference to Archelaus occurs in Matthew 2:22. Matthew recorded the fear that Mary and Joseph had about going through Judea on their way from Egypt to Galilee because Archelaus was the ruler.

Herod Antipas (4 B.C.–A.D. 39). Antipas, another of Herod the Great's sons, began as tetrarch over Galilee and Perea. He was the ruling Herod during Jesus' life and ministry. Herod Antipas was first married to the daughter of Aretas, a Nabatean king. But he became infatuated with Herodias, the wife of his half-brother, Philip I. The two eloped, although both were married at the time. This scandalous affair was condemned severely by John the Baptist (Matt. 14:4; Mark 6:17–18; Luke 3:19).

Although Antipas apparently had some respect for John the Baptist, he had John arrested and imprisoned for his outspokenness. Later, at a royal birthday party, Antipas granted Salome, the daughter of Herod Philip, a wish. Probably at the prodding of Herodias (Mark 6:19), Salome requested the head of John the Baptist (Matt. 14:6–12; Mark 6:21–29). Since he was under oath and did not want to lose face before his guests, Herod ordered John's execution.

Antipas's contacts with Jesus occurred at the same time as the ministry of John the Baptist. Because of Jesus' popularity and miraculous powers, Antipas may have been haunted by the possibility that Jesus was John the Baptist come back to life. The New Testament record shows that the relationship between Jesus and Antipas must have been strained. Jesus' popularity and teachings may have threatened Antipas, who, according to the Pharisees, sought to kill Him (Luke 13:31). By calling Herod a fox ("Go, tell that fox," Luke 13:32), Jesus showed His disapproval of his cunning and deceitful ways.

The next encounter between Antipas and Jesus occurred at the trial of Jesus (Luke 23:6–12). Luke indicated that Herod could not find anything in the charges against Jesus that deserved death, so he sent Jesus back to Pilate for a final decision.

During this time of his rule, Antipas was experiencing political problems of his own. Aretas, the Nabatean king whose daughter had been Antipas's wife before he became involved with Herodias, returned to avenge this insult. Antipas's troops were defeated. This, together with some other problems, led to his political downfall. Antipas was finally banished by the Roman emperor to an obscure section of France.

Herod Agrippa I (A.D. 37–44). Agrippa took over Antipas's territory after Antipas fell from favor. Agrippa's power and responsibilities extended far beyond his ability. As a young person growing up in the imperial court, he developed an undisciplined and extravagant lifestyle. But Agrippa had enough charm and intelligence to stay on the good side of Rome.

After the Roman Emperor Caligula was murdered, Agrippa helped Claudius gain the throne. His loyalty was rewarded. Claudius confirmed Agrippa in his present position and added the territories of Judea and Samaria. This made Agrippa ruler of a kingdom as large as that of his grandfather, Herod the Great. Very little about Agrippa I is recorded in Scripture. From the comments in Acts 12:1–23, we know that Agrippa sought to win the favor of his Jewish subjects by opposing the early Christian church and its leaders. The record of his death as recorded in Acts 12:20–23 shows the humiliating way he died. After his death, Palestine struggled through a number of chaotic years before Rome was able to establish order.

Herod Agrippa II (A.D. 50–100). Agrippa II was judged to be too young to assume leadership over all the territory of his father, Agrippa I. Thus, Emperor Claudius appointed Cuspius Fadus procurator of Palestine. But in A.D. 53, Agrippa II was appointed as the legitimate ruler over part of this territory.

The only reference to Agrippa II in the New Testament occurs in Acts 25:13–26:32, which deals with Paul's imprisonment in Caesarea. Agrippa listened to Paul's defense, but the apostle appealed to Rome. Agrippa had no power to set him free.

Agrippa was caught in the Jewish revolts that preceded the destruction of Jerusalem in A.D. 70 under the Roman Emperor Titus. He continued to rule by appointment of Vespasian until his death in A.D. 100. His death marked the end of the Herodian dynasty in the affairs of the Jewish people in Palestine.

HERODIAS [heh ROE dee uhs] — the queen who demanded John the Baptist's head on a platter (Matt. 14:1–12). The granddaughter of Herod the Great, Herodias first married her father's brother, Herod Philip I. One child was born to this union. Philip's half-brother, the tetrarch Herod Antipas, wanted Herodias for his own wife, so he divorced his wife and married Herodias while Philip was still living.

When John the Baptist denounced their immorality, Herodias plotted John's death. She had her daughter Salome gain Herod's favor by dancing seductively for him at a banquet. As a result, Herod promised her anything she wanted. Following her mother's wishes, Salome asked for the head of John the Baptist.

HEZEKIAH [hez uh KIGH uh] (*the Lord is my strength*) — the name of three or four men in the Old Testament:

1. The thirteenth king of Judah. Born the son of Ahaz by Abi, daughter of Zechariah, Hezekiah became known as one of Judah's godly kings. That an ungodly man like Ahaz could have such a godly son can only be attributed to the grace of God. Hezekiah's father had given the kingdom over to idolatry; but upon his accession to the throne, Hezekiah decisively and courageously initiated religious reforms (2 Kin. 18:4).

In the first month of his reign, Hezekiah reopened the temple doors that his father had closed. He also assembled the priests and Levites and commissioned them to sanctify themselves for service and to cleanse the temple. Appropriate sacrifices were then offered with much rejoicing (2 Chr. 29:3–36).

Hezekiah faced a golden opportunity to reunite the tribes spiritually. In the north Israel had fallen to Assyria in 722 B.C. Hezekiah invited the remnant of the people to come to Jerusalem to participate in the celebration of the Passover. Although some northern tribes scorned the invitation, most responded favorably (2 Chr. 30:1–27).

Hezekiah's reformation reached beyond Jerusalem to include the cleansing of the land, extending even to the tribes of Benjamin, Ephraim, and Manasseh. High places, images, and pagan altars were destroyed. The bronze serpent that Moses had made in the wilderness centuries earlier (Num. 21:5–9) had been preserved, and people were worshiping it. Hezekiah had it destroyed also (2 Kin. 18:4; 2 Chr. 31:1). The land had never undergone such a thorough reform.

When Hezekiah experienced a serious illness, the prophet Isaiah informed the king that he would die. In response to Hezekiah's prayer for recovery, God promised him 15 additional years of life. God also provided a sign for Hezekiah as evidence that the promise would be fulfilled. The sign, one of the most remarkable miracles of the Old Testament, consisted of the sun's shadow moving backward ten degrees on the sundial of Ahaz (Is. 38:1–8).

Shortly after he recovered from his illness (Is. 39:1), Hezekiah received visitors from the Babylonian king Merodach-Baladan (2 Kin. 20:12). They came with letters to congratulate Hezekiah on his recovery and to inquire about the sign (2 Chr. 32:31) in the land. But their real reason for visiting may have been to gain an ally in their revolt against Assyria. When they lavished gifts upon Hezekiah, he in turn showed them his wealth—an action that brought stiff rebuke from Isaiah (2 Kin. 20:13–18).

There is no evidence to indicate that Hezekiah formed an alliance with Babylon. Neither is there any indication that he joined the rebellion in 711 B.C. led by Ashdod, the leading Philistine city. However, Scripture does reveal that he finally did rebel. Sargon II had died in 705 B.C., and his successor, Sennacherib, was preoccupied with trying to consolidate the kingdom when Hezekiah rebelled. With that accomplished, however, Sennacherib was ready to crush Hezekiah's revolt.

Anticipating the Assyrian aggression, Hezekiah made extensive military preparations. He strengthened the fortifications of Jerusalem, produced weapons and shields for his army, and organized his fighting forces under trained combat commanders. Realizing the importance of an adequate water supply, Hezekiah constructed a tunnel that channeled water from the Spring of Gihon outside the city walls to the Pool of Siloam inside the walls (2 Kin. 20:20). This waterway (now known as Hezekiah's Tunnel) was cut through solid rock, extending more than 520 meters (1,700 feet).

As Sennacherib captured the fortified cities of Judah, Hezekiah realized that his revolt was a lost cause and he attempted to appease the Assyrian king. To send an apology and tribute, he emptied the palace treasuries and the temple, even stripping the gold from the doors and pillars. But this failed to appease Sennacherib's anger. At the height of the Assyrian siege, the angel of the Lord struck the Assyrian camp, leaving 185,000 dead (2 Kin. 19:35). In humiliation and defeat, Sennacherib withdrew to his capital city of Nineveh.

Little more is said about Hezekiah's remaining years as king, but his achievements are recorded in 2 Chronicles 32:27–30. When he died, after reigning for 29 years, the people of Jerusalem "buried him in the upper tombs of the sons of David" (2 Chr. 32:33), a place of honor.

2. A descendant of David's royal line, a son of Neariah (1 Chr. 3:23).

3. A head of a family who returned from the captivity in Babylon (Neh. 7:21).

4. The great-great-grandfather of the prophet Zephaniah (Zeph. 1:1; Hizkiah, KJV, perhaps the same as No. 1).

HILKIAH [**hill KYE ah**] (*the Lord is my portion*) — the name of seven or eight Old Testament men:

1. The father of Eliakim (2 Kin. 18:18, 26, 37).

2. A high priest during the reign of King Josiah of Judah (2 Kin. 22:4–14). Hilkiah assisted Josiah in reforming Judah's backslidden people.

3. A Levite and a son of Amzi (1 Chr. 6:45–46).

4. A son of Hosah (1 Chr. 26:11) and a tabernacle gatekeeper.

5. A priest who helped Ezra read the book of the Law to the people (Neh. 8:4; 11:11). He may be the same person as No. 6.

6. A chief priest who returned from the captivity with Zerubbabel (Neh. 12:7).

7. Father of Jeremiah the prophet (Jer. 1:1).

8. Father of Gemariah, a contemporary of Jeremiah (Jer. 29:3).

HINNOM, VALLEY OF [**HIN nahm**] — a deep, narrow ravine west and south of Jerusalem. At the high places of Baal in the Valley of Hinnom, parents sacrificed their children as a burnt offering to Molech (2 Kin. 23:10). Ahaz and Manasseh, kings of Judah, were both guilty of this awful wickedness (2 Chr. 28:3; 33:6). But good King Josiah destroyed the pagan altars to remove this temptation from the people of Judah.

The prophet Jeremiah foretold that God would judge this awful abomination of human sacrifice and would cause such a destruction that "the Valley of the Son of Hinnom" would become known as "the Valley of Slaughter" (Jer. 7:31–32; 19:2, 6; 32:35). The place was also called "Tophet."

Apparently, the Valley of Hinnom was used as the garbage dump for the city of Jerusalem. Refuse, waste materials, and dead animals were burned here. Fires continually smoldered, and smoke from the burning debris rose day and night. Hinnom thus became a graphic symbol of woe and judgment and of the place of eternal punishment called hell.

Translated into Greek, the Hebrew "Valley of Hinnom" becomes *gehenna,* which is used 12 times in the New Testament (11 times by Jesus and once by James), each time translated as "hell" (Matt. 5:22; Mark 9:43, 45, 47; Luke 12:5; James 3:6).

HOPHNI [HOFF nigh] (*tadpole*) — a son of Eli the high priest who, along with his brother Phinehas, proved unworthy of priestly duties (1 Sam. 1:3; 2:34; 4:4–17). Their behavior was characterized by greed (1 Sam. 2:13–16) and lust (1 Sam. 2:22). Eli made only a halfhearted attempt to control his sons' scandalous behavior. Consequently, God's judgment was pronounced upon Eli and his household. Hophni and Phinehas were killed in a battle, and the ark of the covenant was captured by the Philistines (1 Sam. 4:1–11). When Eli heard the news, he fell backward and died of a broken neck (1 Sam. 4:12–18).

HOR, MOUNT [hoer] — the name of two mountains in the Old Testament:

1. The mountain on the border of the Edomites where Aaron died and was buried (Num. 20:22–29; Deut. 32:50). Numbers 20:23 indicates that Mount Hor was situated by the border of the land of Edom. This was the place where the Hebrew people stopped after they left Kadesh (Num. 20:22; 33:37).

Early tradition established Jebel Harun, meaning "Aaron's Mountain," as the site of Mount Hor. It is a conspicuous mountain about 1,440 meters (4,800 feet) high on the eastern side of the Arabah, midway between the southern tip of the Dead Sea and the northern end of the Gulf of Aqaba. However, this peak is far from Kadesh. In recent years Jebel Madurah northeast of Kadesh on the northwest border of Edom has been suggested as the more likely site for Mount Hor.

2. A mountain in northern Palestine between the Mediterranean Sea and the approach to Hamath (Num. 34:7–8).

The barren mountain traditionally identified as Mount Hor, the place where Aaron was buried along the border of ancient Edom (Num. 20:22–29).

HOSEA [hoe ZAY uh] (*deliverance*) — an Old Testament prophet and author of the book of Hosea. The son of Beeri (Hos. 1:1), Hosea ministered in the northern kingdom of Israel during the chaotic period just before the fall of this nation in 722 B.C. The literary features within Hosea's book suggest he was a member of the upper class. The tone and contents of the book also show he was a man of deep compassion, strong loyalty, and keen awareness of the political events taking place in the world at that time. As a prophet, he was also deeply committed to God and His will as it was being revealed to His covenant people.

Hosea is one of the most unusual prophets of the Old Testament, since he was commanded by God to marry a prostitute (Hos. 1:2–9). His wife, Gomer, eventually returned to her life of sin, but Hosea bought her back from the slave market and restored her as his wife (Hos. 3:1–5). His unhappy family experience was an object lesson of the sin or "harlotry" of the nation of Israel in rejecting the one true God and serving pagan gods. Although the people deserved to be rejected because they had turned their backs on God, Hosea emphasized that God would continue to love them and use them as His special people.

In his unquestioning obedience of God, Hosea demonstrated he was a prophet who would follow his Lord's will, no matter what the cost. He was a sensitive, compassionate spokesman for righteousness whose own life echoed the message that God is love.

I

ISAAC [EYE zik] ([God]*laughs*) — the only son of Abraham by his wife Sarah; father of Jacob and Esau. God promised to make Abraham's descendants a great nation that would become God's chosen people. But the promised son was a long time in coming. Isaac was born when Abraham was 100 years old and Sarah was 90 (Gen. 17:17; 21:5). Both Abraham and Sarah laughed when they heard they would have a son in their old age (Gen. 17:17–19; 18:9–15). This partially explains why they named their son Isaac.

On the eighth day after his birth, Isaac was circumcised (Gen. 21:4). As he grew, his presence as Abraham's rightful heir brought him into conflict with Ishmael, Abraham's son by Sarah's handmaid Hagar. The strained relationship caused Sarah to send away Hagar and Ishmael (Gen. 21:9–21). God comforted Abraham by telling him that Ishmael would also become the father of a great nation (Gen. 21:13).

Birthright. Isaac's birthright was an important part of his life. The blessings that God gave to Abraham were also given to his descendants. Thus, to inherit this covenant with God was of far greater value than to inherit property or material goods.

Isaac's life gave evidence of God's favor. His circumcision was a sign of the covenant with God. God's favor toward him was also evident in Ishmael's disinheritance. The dismissal of the sons of Abraham's concubines to the "country of the east" is associated with the statement that Isaac inherited all that Abraham had, including God's blessing. Isaac was in a unique position historically because he would carry on the covenant. When Isaac was a young man, God tested Abraham's faith by commanding him to sacrifice Isaac as an offering. But when Abraham placed Isaac upon the altar, an angel appeared and stopped the sacrifice, providing a ram instead (Genesis 22). This showed clearly that Isaac was God's choice to carry on the covenant.

Marriage. Isaac married Rebekah when he was 40 years old. She became Isaac's wife when God directed one of Abraham's servants to her. The Bible reveals that Isaac loved Rebekah and that she was a comfort to him after his mother Sarah's death (Gen. 24:67). Isaac and Rebekah had twin sons, Jacob and Esau, who were born when Isaac was 60 years old (Gen. 25:20–26).

Famine prompted the family to move to Gerar, where God appeared to Isaac and reaffirmed the covenant. Moving through the Valley of Gerar, where he reopened the wells that Abraham had dug (Gen. 26:23; 28:10), Isaac made a camp at Beersheba. This place became his permanent home. There he built an altar just as his father had done (Gen. 26:24–25).

Jacob and Esau. The older twin, Esau, was Isaac's favorite son, although God had declared that the older should serve the younger (Gen. 25:23). Jacob was Rebekah's favorite. Disagreement arose over which of the twins would receive the birthright and carry on the covenant that God had made with Abraham. Rebekah conspired with Jacob to trick the aging, blind Isaac into giving his blessing to Jacob rather than Esau.

Shortly thereafter, Isaac sent Jacob to Laban in Padan Aram to find a wife and to escape Esau's wrath. Esau soon left his father's household. Many years passed before the two brothers were at peace with each other. But they were united at last in paying last respects to their father after his death. Isaac lived to be 180 years old. He was buried alongside Abraham, Sarah, and Rebekah in the cave of Machpelah (Gen. 35:28–29; 49:30–31).

ISAIAH [eye ZAY uh] (*the Lord has saved*) — a famous Old Testament prophet who predicted the coming of the Messiah; the author of the book of Isaiah. Isaiah was probably born in Jerusalem of a family that was related to the royal house of Judah. He recorded the events of the reign of King Uzziah of Judah (2 Chr. 26:22). When Uzziah died (740 B.C.), Isaiah received his prophetic calling from God in a stirring vision of God in the temple (Isaiah 6). The king of Judah had died; now Isaiah had seen the everlasting King in whose service he would spend the rest of his life.

Isaiah was married to a woman described as "the prophetess" (Is. 8:3). They had two sons whom they named Shear-Jashub, "A Remnant Shall Return" (Is. 7:3), and Maher-Shalal-Hash-Baz, "Speed the Spoil, Hasten the Booty" (Is. 8:3). These strange names portray two basic themes of the book of Isaiah: God is about to bring judgment upon His people, hence Maher-Shalal-Hash-Baz, but after that there will be an outpouring of God's mercy and grace to the remnant of people who will remain faithful to God, hence Shear-Jashub.

After God called Isaiah to proclaim His message, He told Isaiah that most of his work would be a ministry of judgment. Even though the prophet would speak the truth, the people would reject his words (6:10). Jesus found in these words of Isaiah's call a prediction of the rejection of his message by many of the people (Matt. 13:14–15).

Isaiah's response to this revelation from the Lord was a lament: "Lord, how long?" (Isaiah 6:11). The Lord answered that Isaiah's ministry would prepare the people for judgment, but one day God's promises would be realized. Judah was to experience utter devastation, to be fulfilled with the destruction of the city of Jerusalem by the Babylonians in 586 B.C. (Is. 6:11). This destruction would be followed by the deportation of the people to Babylon (Is. 6:12). But although the tree of the house of David would be cut down, there would still be life in the stump (Is. 6:13). Out of the lineage of David would come a Messiah who would establish His eternal rule among His people.

Isaiah was a writer of considerable literary skill. The poetry of his book is magnificent in its sweep. A person of strong emotion and deep feelings, Isaiah also was a man of steadfast devotion to the Lord. His vision of God and His holiness in the temple influenced his messages during his long ministry. Isaiah's ministry extended from about 740 B.C. until at least 701 B.C. (Isaiah 37–39). His 40 years of preaching doom and promise did not turn the nation of Judah from its headlong rush toward destruction. But he faithfully preached the message God gave him until the very end.

According to a popular Jewish tradition, Isaiah met his death by being sawn in half during the reign of the evil king Manasseh of Judah. This tradition seems to be supported by the writer of Hebrews (Heb. 11:37). Certainly Isaiah is one of the heroes of the faith "of whom the world was not worthy" (Heb. 11:38).

ISHBOSHETH [ihsh BOE sheth] (*man of shame*) — a son of Saul whom Abner proclaimed king after Saul's death (2 Sam. 2:8–10). The tribe of Judah proclaimed David king after the death of Saul and Jonathan at Gilboa, but the 11 other tribes remained loyal to Saul's family. Ishbosheth reigned two turbulent years from Mahanaim, east of the Jordan River, while David ruled Judah from Hebron. Throughout the period, each side attempted unsuccessfully to gain control of the entire kingdom (2 Sam. 2:12–3:1).

Ishbosheth made a grave error in charging Abner with having relations with Saul's concubine, Rizpah. In anger, Abner changed his allegiance to David (2 Sam. 3:6–21). When Joab murdered Abner in Hebron (2 Sam. 3:27), Ishbosheth became discouraged (2 Sam. 4:1). Two captains of his guard, Baanah and Rechab, assassinated Ishbosheth as he lay napping. They carried Ishbosheth's severed head to David, who ordered it buried in the tomb of Abner in Hebron. Then David put the assassins to death (2 Sam. 4:5–12). Saul's dynasty ended with Ishbosheth's death.

ISHMAEL [IHSH may ell] (*God hears*) — the name of six men in the Old Testament:

1. The first son of Abraham, by his wife's Egyptian maid-servant, Hagar. Although God had promised Abraham an heir (Gen. 15:4), Abraham's wife Sarah had been unable to bear a child. When Abraham was 85, Sarah offered her maid to him in order to help fulfill God's promise (Gen. 16:1–2).

After Hagar learned that she was pregnant, she grew proud and began to despise Sarah. Sarah complained to Abraham, who allowed her to discipline Hagar. Sarah's harsh treatment of Hagar caused her to flee into the wilderness. There she met the angel of God, who told her to return to Sarah and submit to her authority. As an encouragement, the angel promised Hagar that her son, who would be named Ishmael, would have uncounted descendants. Hagar then returned to Abraham and Sarah and bore her son (Gen. 16:4–15).

When Ishmael was 13, God appeared to Abraham to tell him that Ishmael was not the promised heir. God made a covenant with Abraham that was to be passed down to the descendants of Isaac—a son who would be conceived by Sarah the following year. Because Abraham loved Ishmael, God promised to bless Ishmael and make him a great nation (Gen. 17:19–20).

At the customary feast to celebrate Isaac's weaning, Sarah saw 16-year-old Ishmael making fun of Isaac. She was furious and demanded that Abraham disown Ishmael and his mother so Ishmael could not share Isaac's inheritance. Abraham was reluctant to cast out Ishmael and Hagar, but he did so when instructed by God (Gen. 21:8–13).

Hagar and Ishmael wandered in the wilderness of Beersheba. When their water was gone and Ishmael grew weary, Hagar placed him under a shrub to await death. The angel of God again contacted Hagar and showed her a well. After drawing water, she returned to Ishmael. Ishmael grew up in the wilderness of Paran and gained fame as an archer. Hagar arranged his marriage to an Egyptian wife (Gen. 21:14–21).

When Abraham died, Ishmael returned from exile to help Isaac with the burial (Gen. 25:9). As God promised, Ishmael became the father of 12 princes (Gen. 25:16), as well as a daughter, Mahalath, who later married Esau, son of Isaac (Gen. 28:9). Ishmael died at the age of 137 (Gen. 25:17).

Ishmael was the father of the Ishmaelites, a nomadic nation that lived in northern Arabia. Modern-day Arabs claim descent from Ishmael.

2. The son of Nethaniah and a member of the house of David. After the Babylonian conquest of Judah, King Nebuchadnezzar appointed a Jewish captive, Gedaliah, as governor. Gedaliah promised to welcome all Jews who came under his protection. Ishmael and several others accepted Gedaliah's offer with the intent of killing him (2 Kin. 25:22–24). Gedaliah was warned that Ishmael was allied with the Ammonite king in plotting to kill him, but he refused to believe it (Jer. 40:14–16). When Gedaliah invited Ishmael and ten others to a banquet, they murdered everyone in attendance. The killers fled toward the Ammonite country with several hostages, but they were overtaken by pursuers in Gibeon. The hostages were rescued, but Ishmael and eight men escaped to the Ammonites (Jer. 41:1–15).

3. A descendant of Jonathan, son of Saul (1 Chr. 8:38; 9:44).

4. The father of Zebadiah, ruler of the house of Judah and the highest civil authority under King Jehoshaphat (2 Chr. 19:11).

5. A son of Jehohanan. Ishmael was one of five army officers recruited by Jehoiada to help overthrow Queen Athaliah of Judah in favor of the rightful heir, Joash (2 Chr. 23:1).

6. A priest of the clan of Pashhur who divorced his foreign wife after the Babylonian captivity (Ezra 10:22).

ISRAEL [IS ray ell] (*he strives with God*) — the name given to Jacob after his great struggle with God at Peniel near the brook Jabbok (Gen. 32:28; 35:10). The name Israel has been interpreted by different scholars as "prince with God," "he strives with God," "let God rule," or "God strives." The name was later applied to the descendants of Jacob. The twelve tribes were called "Israelites," "children of Israel," and "house of Israel," identifying them as the descendants of Israel through his sons and grandsons.

ISSACHAR [IHZ ah car] (*there is hire* or *reward*) — the name of two men in the Old Testament:

1. The ninth son of Jacob; the fifth by his wife Leah (Gen. 30:17–18; 35:23). He fathered four sons: Tola, Puvah or Puah, Job or Jashub, and Shimron. He and his sons went with their father, Jacob, to Egypt to escape the famine (Gen. 46:13; Ex. 1:3; Num. 26:23–24; 1 Chr. 2:1; 7:1). Before his death, Jacob described Issachar as "a strong donkey lying down between two burdens" (Gen. 49:15). In other words, Jacob saw that Issachar could be a strong fighter but that his love of comfort could also cause him to settle for the easy way out.

2. A Levite gatekeeper in David's time (1 Chr. 26:5).

J

JABESH GILEAD [JAY besh GIL ih add] (*Jabesh of Gilead*) — a town of Gilead (1 Sam. 31:11; 2 Sam. 2:4), situated about 16 kilometers (10 miles) southeast of Beth Shan and about 3 kilometers (2 miles) east of the Jordan River. It was within the territory assigned to the half-tribe of Manasseh (Num. 32:29, 40).

Jabesh Gilead refused to join in the punishment of the Benjamites (Judg. 21:8–14), an offense for which every man was put to the sword. Four hundred young virgins of Jabesh were given to the Benjamites as wives.

During King Saul's reign, the king of Ammon besieged the city of Jabesh. He promised to spare the lives of those who lived in Jabesh if each of the men would submit to having his right eye put out. A seven-day truce was called and appeal was made to Saul, who mustered an army and defeated the Ammonites (1 Samuel 11).

The people of Jabesh Gilead never forgot this act of Saul. When Saul and his sons were slain at Gilboa, the men of Jabesh Gilead rescued their bodies, cremated them, and buried the ashes near Jabesh (1 Sam. 31:1–13).

Jabesh (1 Chr. 10:12) is the abbreviated name of Jabesh Gilead.

JACOB [JAY cub] (*he supplants*) — one of the twin sons of Isaac and Rebekah. The brother of Esau, he was known also as Israel (Gen. 32:28).

Jacob was born in answer to his father's prayer (Gen. 25:21), but he became the favorite son of his mother (25:28). He was named Jacob because, at the birth of the twins, "his hand took hold of Esau's heel" (25:26). According to the accounts in Genesis, Jacob continued to "take hold of" the possessions of others—his brother's birthright (25:29–34), his father's blessing (27:1–29), and his father-in-law's flocks and herds (30:25–43; 31:1).

The pattern of Jacob's life is found in his journeys, much like the travels of his grandfather Abraham. Leaving his home in Beersheba, he traveled to Bethel (28:10–22); later he returned to Shechem (33:18–20), Bethel (35:6–7), and Hebron (35:27). At Shechem and Bethel he built altars, as Abraham had done (12:6–7, 8). Near the end of his life Jacob migrated to Egypt; he died there at an advanced age (Genesis 46–49).

The most dramatic moments in Jacob's life occurred at Bethel (Gen. 28:10–22), at the ford of the river Jabbok (32:22–32), and on his deathbed (49:1–33).

The experience at Bethel occurred when he left the family home at Beersheba to travel to Haran (a city in Mesopotamia), the residence of his uncle Laban (28:10). On the way, as he stopped for the night at Bethel, he had a dream of a staircase reaching from earth to heaven with angels upon it and the Lord above it. He was impressed by the words of the Lord, promising Jacob inheritance of the land, descendants "as the dust of the earth" in number, and His divine presence. Jacob dedicated the site as a place of worship, calling it Bethel (literally, "house of God"). More than 20 years later, Jacob returned to this spot, built an altar, called the place El Bethel (literally, "God of the house of God"), and received the divine blessing (35:6–15).

The experience at the ford of the river Jabbok occurred as Jacob returned from his long stay at Haran. While preparing for a reunion with his brother, Esau, of whom he was still afraid (32:7), he had a profound experience that left him changed in both body and spirit.

At the ford of the Jabbok, "Jacob was left alone" (32:24). It was night, and he found himself suddenly engaged in a wrestling match in the darkness. This match lasted until the breaking of the dawn. The socket of Jacob's hip was put out of joint as he struggled with this mysterious stranger, but he refused to release his grip until he was given a blessing. For the first time in the narrative of Genesis, Jacob had been unable to defeat an opponent. When asked to identify himself in the darkness, he confessed he was Jacob—the "heel-grabber."

But Jacob's struggling earned him a new name. For his struggle "with God and with men" in which he had prevailed, his name was changed to Israel (literally, "he struggles with God") [see Hos. 12:3]. In return, he gave a name to the spot that marked the change; it would be called Peniel—"For I have seen God face to face, and my life is preserved" (32:30).

In these first two instances, a deep spiritual sensitivity is evident in Jacob. He appears outwardly brash and grasping, always enriching himself and securing his future. Yet he responded readily to these night experiences—the dream and the wrestling contest—because he apparently sensed "the presence of the holy" in each of them. He also proved to be a man of his word in his dealings with Laban (Gen. 31:6), and in the fulfillment of his vow to return to Bethel (35:1–3).

At the end of his life, Jacob—now an aged man (47:28)—gathered his 12 sons about his bed to tell them what should befall them "in the last days" (49:1).

The harshest language came against Reuben, the firstborn, who was rejected by his father for his sin (49:3–4), and Simeon and Levi, who were cursed for their anger and cruelty

(49:5–7). The loftiest language was applied to Judah, who would be praised by his brothers and whose tribe would be the source of royalty, even the ruler of the people (49:8–12).

Words of warning were addressed to Dan, called "a serpent" and "a viper," a life that would be marked by violence (49:16–17). The two longest speeches were addressed to Judah and to Joseph, Jacob's favorite son (49:22–26).

Following this scene, Jacob died and was embalmed by the physicians (Gen. 49:33; 50:2). By his own request Jacob was carried back to the land of Canaan and was buried in the family burial ground in the cave of the field of Machpelah (Gen. 49:29–32; 50:13).

JAMES — five men in the New Testament:
    1. James, the son of Zebedee, one of Jesus' twelve apostles. James's father was a fisherman; his mother, Salome, often cared for Jesus' daily needs (Matt. 27:56; Mark 15:40–41). In lists of the twelve apostles, James and his brother John always form a group of four with two other brothers, Peter and Andrew. The four were fishermen on the Sea of Galilee. Their call to follow Jesus is the first recorded event after the beginning of Jesus' public ministry (Matt. 4:18–22; Mark 1:16–20).

James is never mentioned apart from his brother John in the New Testament, even at his death (Acts 12:2). When the brothers are mentioned, James is always mentioned first, probably because he was the older. After the resurrection, however, John became the more prominent, probably because of his association with Peter (Acts 3:1; 8:14). James was killed by Herod Agrippa I, the grandson of Herod the Great, sometime between A.D. 42–44. He was the first of the twelve apostles to be put to death and the only one whose martyrdom is mentioned in the New Testament (Acts 12:2).

James and John must have contributed a spirited and headstrong element to Jesus' band of followers, because Jesus nicknamed them "Sons of Thunder" (Mark 3:17). On one occasion (Luke 9:51–56), when a Samaritan village refused to accept Jesus, the two asked Jesus to call down fire in revenge, as Elijah had done (2 Kin. 1:10, 12). On another occasion, they earned the anger of their fellow disciples by asking if they could sit on Jesus' right and left hands in glory (Matt. 20:20–28; Mark 10:35–45).

James was one of three disciples—Peter, James, and John—whom Jesus took along privately on three special occasions. The three accompanied Him when He healed the daughter of Jairus (Mark 5:37; Luke 8:51); they witnessed His transfiguration (Matt. 17:1; Mark 9:2; Luke 9:28); and they were also with Him in His agony in Gethsemane (Matt. 26:37; Mark 14:33).

2. James, the son of Alphaeus. This James was also one of the twelve apostles. In each list of the apostles he is mentioned in ninth position (Matt. 10:3; Mark 3:18; Luke 6:15; Acts 1:13).

3. James the Less. This James is called the son of Mary (not the mother of Jesus), and the brother of Joses (Matt. 27:56; Mark 16:1; Luke 24:10). Mark 15:40 refers to him as "James the Less." The Greek word *mikros* can mean either "small" or "less." It could, therefore, mean James the smaller (in size), or younger (NIV), or James the less (well-known).

4. James, the father of Judas. Two passages in the New Testament refer to a James, the father of Judas (Luke 6:16; Acts 1:13). Judas was one of the twelve apostles; he was the last to be listed before his more infamous namesake, Judas Iscariot.

5. James, the brother of Jesus. James is first mentioned as the oldest of Jesus' four younger brothers (Matt. 13:55; Mark 6:3).

In the third and fourth centuries A.D., when the idea of the perpetual virginity of Mary gained ground, a number of church fathers argued that James was either a stepbrother to Jesus (by a former marriage of Joseph) or a cousin. But both options are forced. The New Testament seems to indicate that Mary and Joseph bore children after Jesus (Matt. 1:25; 12:47; Luke

2:7; John 2:12; Acts 1:14), and that the second oldest was James (Matt. 13:55–56; Mark 6:3). The Gospels reveal that Jesus' family adopted a skeptical attitude toward His ministry (Matt. 12:46–50; Mark 3:31–35; Luke 8:19–21; John 7:5). James apparently held the same attitude, because his name appears in no lists of the apostles, nor is he mentioned elsewhere in the Gospels.

After Jesus' crucifixion, however, James became a believer. Paul indicated that James was a witness to the resurrection of Jesus (1 Cor. 15:7). He called James an apostle (Gal. 1:19), though, like himself, not one of the original Twelve (1 Cor. 15:5, 7).

In the book of Acts, James emerges as the leader of the church in Jerusalem. His brothers also became believers and undertook missionary travels (1 Cor. 9:5). But James considered it his calling to oversee the church in Jerusalem (Gal. 2:9). He advocated respect for the Jewish law (Acts 21:18–25), but he did not use it as a weapon against Gentiles. Paul indicated that James endorsed his ministry to the Gentiles (Gal. 2:1–10).

The decree of the Council of Jerusalem (Acts 15:12–21) cleared the way for Christianity to become a universal religion. Gentiles were asked only "to abstain from things polluted by idols, from sexual immorality, from things strangled, and from blood" (Acts 15:20). The intent of this decree was practical rather than theological. It asked the Gentiles to observe certain practices that otherwise would offend their Jewish brothers in the Lord and jeopardize Christian fellowship with them.

Both Paul and Acts portray a James who was personally devoted to Jewish tradition but flexible enough to modify it to admit non-Jews into Christian fellowship. This James is probably the author of the Epistle of James in the New Testament.

JANNES AND JAMBRES [JAN iz, jam BREZ] — two men who, according to the apostle Paul, "resisted Moses" (2 Tim. 3:8). Although Jannes and Jambres are not named in the Old Testament, they are common figures in late Jewish tradition.

According to legend, they were two Egyptian magicians who opposed Moses' demand that the Israelites be freed. They sought to duplicate the miracles of Moses in an attempt to discredit him before pharaoh "so the magicians of Egypt, they also did in like manner with their enhancement" (Ex. 7:11–12, 22).

JEHOIACHIN [juh HOI uh kin] (*the Lord establishes*) — the son and successor of Jehoiakim as king of Judah, about 598 or 597 B.C. (2 Chr. 36:8–9; Ezek. 1:2). Jehoiachin did evil in the sight of the Lord, like his father. But he had little opportunity to influence affairs of state, since he reigned only three months. His brief reign ended when the armies of Nebuchadnezzar of Babylon besieged Jerusalem. When the city surrendered, Jehoiachin was exiled to Babylonia (2 Kin. 24:6–15).

Nebuchadnezzar then made Mattaniah, Jehoiachin's uncle, king in his place and changed Mattaniah's name to Zedekiah (v. 17). Zedekiah was destined to rule over a powerless land containing only poor farmers and laborers, while Jehoiachin was held a prisoner in Babylon.

In the 37th year of his captivity, Jehoiachin was finally released by a new Babylonian king, Evil-Merodach (Amel-Marduk). He must have been awarded a place of prominence in the king's court, since he ate his meals regularly in the presence of the king himself (2 Kin. 25:27–30).

Jehoiachin is also called Jeconiah (1 Chr. 3:16–17) and Coniah (Jer. 22:24). In the New Testament he is listed by Matthew as an ancestor of Jesus (Matt. 1:11–12).

JEHOIAKIM [juh HOI uh kim] (*the Lord raises up*) — an evil king of Judah whose downfall was predicted by the prophet Jeremiah.

A son of the good king Josiah, Jehoiakim was 25 years old when he succeeded to the throne. He reigned 11 years in Jerusalem, from 609 B.C. to 598 B.C. During his reign Pharaoh

Necho of Egypt exacted heavy tribute from the people of Judah (2 Chr. 36:3, 5). Jehoiakim was forced to levy a burdensome tax upon his people to pay this tribute.

The prophet Jeremiah described the arrogance of Jehoiakim in great detail (Jer. 1:3; 24:1; 27:1, 20; 37:1; 52:2). He censured Jehoiakim for exploiting the people to build his own splendid house with expensive furnishings (Jer. 22:13–23). Unlike his father Josiah, Jehoiakim ignored justice and righteousness. Jehoiakim had no intention of obeying the Lord; he "did evil in the sight of the Lord" (2 Kin. 23:37). His 11-year reign was filled with abominable acts against God (2 Chr. 36:8). Because of this evil, Jeremiah predicted that no one would lament the death of Jehoiakim.

Jeremiah also told of Jehoiakim's execution of Urijah, a prophet of the Lord (Jer. 26:20–23). Perhaps Jehoiakim's most cynical act was his burning of Jeremiah's prophecies (Jer. 36:22–23). Jeremiah wrote a scroll of judgment against the king, but as this scroll was read, Jehoiakim sliced it into pieces and threw them into the fire.

Jehoiakim could burn the Word of God, but he could not destroy its power. Neither could he avoid Jeremiah's prophecy of his approaching destruction. Recognizing the power of the Babylonians, he made an agreement with Nebuchadnezzar to serve as his vassal king on the throne of Judah. After three years of subjection, he led a foolish rebellion to regain his nation's independence. The rebellion failed and Jerusalem was destroyed by the Babylonians. Jehoiakim was bound and carried away as a captive (2 Chr. 36:6).

JEHOSHAPHAT [juh HAH shuh fat] (*the Lord is judge*) — the name of five men in the Old Testament:

1. An official under David and Solomon (2 Sam. 8:16).

2. A son of Paruah and an official responsible for supplying food for King Solomon's table (1 Kin. 4:17).

3. A son of Asa who succeeded his father as king of Judah (1 Kin. 15:24). Jehoshaphat was 35 years old when he became king, and he reigned 25 years in Jerusalem (2 Chr. 20:31), from about 873 B.C. to about 848 B.C. Jehoshaphat received an excellent heritage from his father, Asa, who in the earlier years of his reign showed a reforming spirit in seeking God (2 Chr. 15:1–19). Jehoshaphat's faith in God led him to "delight in the ways of the LORD" (2 Chr. 17:6). He attacked pagan idolatry and he sent teachers to the people to teach them more about God (2 Chr. 17:6–9). In affairs of state, Jehoshaphat also showed a willingness to rely on the Lord. In a time of danger he prayed for God's help (2 Chr. 20:6–12).

Jehoshaphat showed a high regard for justice in his dealings (2 Chr. 19:4–11). He reminded the judges whom he appointed that their ultimate loyalty was to God. His attitude toward impartial justice is reflected in these words: "Behave courageously, and the LORD will be with the good" (2 Chr. 19:11).

But in his dealings with Ahab, king of Israel, Jehoshaphat made some serious mistakes. Through the marriage of his son, Jehoram, to Ahab's daughter, Jehoshaphat allied himself with Ahab (2 Chr. 21:5–6). This alliance led to even further dealings with the wicked king of Israel (2 Chr. 18:1–34), which the prophet Jehu rebuked (2 Chr. 19:1–3).

Jehoshaphat and his father, Asa, are bright lights against the dark paganism that existed during their time. Both father and son had certain weaknesses, but their faith in the Lord brought good to themselves as well as God's people during their reigns.

4. A son of Nimshi and father of Jehu, king of Israel (2 Kin. 9:2, 14).

5. A priest who helped move the ark of the covenant from the house of Obed-Edom to Jerusalem (1 Chr. 15:24; Joshaphat, NIV, NRSV).

JEHU [JEE hyoo] (*the Lord is He*) — the name of five men in the Old Testament:

1. A prophet who announced a message of doom against Baasha, king of Israel (1 Kin. 16:12). Jehu also rebuked Jehoshaphat, king of Judah (2 Chr. 19:2).

2. The eleventh king of Israel (2 Chr. 22:7–9). Jehu was anointed by Elisha the prophet as king; he later overthrew Joram (Jehoram), King Ahab's son and successor, and reigned for 28 years (841–813 B.C.). His corrupt leadership weakened the nation. He is known for his violence against all members of the "house of Ahab" as he established his rule throughout the nation.

At Jehu's command, Jezebel, the notorious wife of Ahab, was thrown out of the window of the palace to her death, as prophesied by Elijah (1 Kin. 21:23). Ahab's murder of Naboth and the subversion of the religion of Israel had brought terrible vengeance, but more blood was to be shed by Jehu. Next to feel the new king's wrath were the 70 sons of Ahab who lived in Samaria (2 Kings 10). Jehu ordered them killed by the elders of Samaria. Jehu's zeal extended even further, commanding the death of Ahab's advisors and close acquaintances. This excessive violence led the prophet Hosea to denounce Jehu's bloodthirstiness (Hos. 1:4).

Jehu continued his slaughter against the family of Ahaziah, king of Judah (2 Kin. 10:12–14). Then he made an alliance with Jehonadab, the chief of the Rechabites, to destroy the followers of Baal. Jehu and Jehonadab plotted to conduct a massive assembly in honor of Baal. After assuring the Baal worshipers of their sincerity and gathering them into the temple of Baal, Jehu had them all killed (2 Kin. 10:18–28). So complete was this destruction that Baalism was wiped out in Israel, and the temple of Baal was torn down and made into a garbage dump.

Although Jehu proclaimed his zeal for the Lord (2 Kin. 10:16), he failed to follow the Lord's will completely (2 Kin.

10:31). He did not completely eliminate worship of the golden calves at Dan and Bethel, and his disobedience led to the conquest of many parts of Israel by the Syrians (2 Kin. 10:32–33).

3. A son of Obed and a descendant of Hezron (1 Chr. 2:38). Jehu was descended from the family of Jerahmeel and the tribe of Judah.

4. A son of Joshibiah, of the tribe of Simeon (1 Chr. 4:35).

5. A Benjamite of Anathoth (1 Chr. 12:3) who joined David's army at Ziklag.

JEREMIAH [jer uh MIGH uh] (*the Lord hurls*) — the name of nine men in the Old Testament:

1. The father of Hamutal (Jer. 52:1).

2. The head of a family of the tribe of Manasseh (1 Chr. 5:23–24).

3. A Benjamite who joined David at Ziklag (1 Chr. 12:4).

4. A Gadite who joined David at Ziklag (1 Chr. 12:10).

5. Another Gadite who joined David at Ziklag (1 Chr. 12:13).

6. A priest who sealed Nehemiah's covenant after the captivity (Neh. 10:2).

7. A priest who returned from the captivity with Zerubbabel (Neh. 12:1, 12, 34).

8. A son of Habazziniah and father of Jaazaniah, of the house of the Rechabites (Jer. 35:3).

9. The major prophet during the decline and fall of the southern kingdom of Judah and author of the book of Jeremiah. He prophesied during the reigns of the last five kings of Judah. Jeremiah was born in Anathoth, situated north of Jerusalem in the territory of Benjamin (Jer. 1:1–2). He was called to the prophetic ministry in the 13th year of Josiah's reign, about 627 B.C. He must have been a young man at the time, since his ministry lasted for about 40 years—through the very last days of the nation of Judah when the capital city of Jerusalem was destroyed in 586 B.C. Jeremiah's call is one of the most instructive

passages in his book. God declared that he had sanctioned him as a prophet even before he was born (Jer. 1:5). But the young man responded with words of inadequacy: "Ah, Lord GOD!" (Jer. 1:6). These words actually mean "No, Lord GOD!" Jeremiah pleaded that he was a youth and that he lacked the ability to speak. But God replied that he was being called not because of age or ability but because God had chosen him.

Immediately Jeremiah saw the hand of God reaching out and touching his mouth. "Behold, I have put My words in your mouth," God declared (Jer. 1:9). From that moment, the words of the prophet were to be the words of God. And his ministry was to consist of tearing down and rebuilding, uprooting and replanting: "See, I have this day set you over the kingdoms, to root out and to pull down, to destroy and to throw down, to build and to plant" (Jer. 1:10).

Because of the negative nature of Jeremiah's ministry, judgmental texts abound in his book. Jeremiah was destined from the very beginning to be a prophet of doom. He was even forbidden to marry so he could devote himself fully to the task of preaching God's judgment (Jer. 16:1–13). A prophet of doom cannot be a happy man. All of Jeremiah's life was wrapped up in the knowledge that God was about to bring an end to the holy city and cast off His covenant people.

Jeremiah is often called "the weeping prophet" because he wept openly about the sins of his nation (Jer. 9:1). He was also depressed at times about the futility of his message. As the years passed and his words of judgment went unheeded, he lamented his unfortunate state: "O LORD, You induced me, and I was persuaded; You are stronger than I, and have prevailed. I am in derision daily; everyone mocks me" (Jer. 20:7).

At times Jeremiah tried to hold back from his prophetic proclamation. But he found that the word of the Lord was "like a burning fire shut up in my bones" (Jer. 20:9). He had no choice but to proclaim the harsh message of God's judgment.

Jeremiah did not weep and lament because of weakness, nor did he proclaim evil because of a dark and gloomy personality. He cried out because of his love for his people and his God. This characteristic of the prophet is actually a tribute to his sensitivity and deep concern. Jeremiah's laments remind us of the weeping of the Savior (Matt. 23:37–39).

As Jeremiah predicted, the nation of Judah was eventually punished by God because of its sin and disobedience. In 586 B.C. Jerusalem was destroyed and the leading citizens were deported to Babylonia. Jeremiah remained in Jerusalem with a group of his fellow citizens under the authority of a ruling governor appointed by the Babylonians. But he was forced to seek safety in Egypt after the people of Jerusalem revolted against Babylonian rule. He continued his preaching in Egypt (Jeremiah 43–44). This is the last we hear of Jeremiah. There is no record of what happened to the prophet during these years of his ministry.

In the New Testament (KJV) Jeremiah was referred to as Jeremy (Matt. 2:17; 27:9) and Jeremias (Matt. 16:14).

JERICHO [JEHR ih coe] — one of the oldest inhabited cities in the world. Situated in the wide plain of the Jordan Valley (Deut. 34:1, 3) at the foot of the ascent to the Judean mountains, Jericho lies about 13 kilometers (8 miles) northwest of the site where the Jordan River flows into the Dead Sea, some 8 kilometers (5 miles) west of the Jordan.

Since it is approximately 244 meters (800 feet) below sea level, Jericho has a climate that is tropical and at times is very hot. Only a few inches of rainfall are recorded at Jericho each year, but the city is a wonderful oasis, known as "the city of palm trees" (Deut. 34:3) or "the city of palms" (Judg. 3:13). Jericho flourishes with date palms, banana trees, balsams, sycamores, and henna (Song 1:14; Luke 19:4).

There have been three different Jerichos throughout its long history. Old Testament Jericho is identified with the mound of Tell es-Sultan, about 2 kilometers (a little more than a mile) from the village of er-Riha. This village is modern Jericho, located about 27 kilometers (17 miles) northeast of Jerusalem. New Testament Jericho is identified with the mounds of Tulul Abu el-'Alayiq, about 2 kilometers west of modern Jericho and south of Old Testament Jericho. By far the most imposing site of the three is Old Testament Jericho, a pear-shaped mound about 366 meters (400 yards) long, north to south, 183 meters (200 yards) wide at the north end, and some 67 meters (70 yards) high. It has been the site of numerous archaeological diggings and is a favorite stop for Holy Land tourists.

Old Testament Jericho. Jericho first appears in the biblical record when the Israelites encamped at Shittim on the east side of the Jordan River (Num. 22:1; 26:3). Joshua sent spies to examine the city (Josh. 2:1–24) and later took the city by perhaps the most unorthodox method in the history of warfare (Joshua 6). Joshua placed a curse on anyone who would attempt to rebuild Jericho (Josh. 6:26).

As the Israelites settled into the land, Jericho was awarded to the tribe of Benjamin, although it was on the border between Ephraim and Benjamin (Josh. 16:1, 7). Jericho is only incidentally mentioned in the reign of David (2 Sam. 10:5) and does not figure prominently again in Old Testament history until the reign of King Ahab (about 850 B.C.; 1 Kin. 16:34), when Hiel the Bethelite attempted to fortify the city and Joshua's curse was realized. During the days of Elijah and Elisha, Jericho was a community of the prophets (2 Kin. 2:5) and was mentioned on other occasions as well (Ezra 2:34; Neh. 3:2; Jer. 39:5).

New Testament Jericho. In the early years of Herod the Great, the Romans plundered Jericho. But Herod later beautified the city and ultimately died there. Jesus passed through Jericho on numerous occasions. Near there He was baptized

in the Jordan River (Matt. 3:13–17), and on the adjacent mountain range He was tempted (Matt. 4:1–11). At Jericho Jesus
healed blind Bartimaeus (Mark 10:46–52). Here too Zacchaeus
was converted (Luke 19:1–10). And Jesus' parable of the good
Samaritan has the road from Jerusalem to Jericho as its setting
(Luke 10:30–37).

JEROBOAM [jehr uh BOE ahm] (*let the kinsman plead*) —
the name of two kings of the northern kingdom of Israel:
  1. Jeroboam I, the first king of Israel (the ten northern tribes,
or the Northern Kingdom), a state established after the death
of Solomon (1 Kin. 11:26–14:20). The son of Nebat and Zeruah,
Jeroboam reigned over Israel for 22 years (1 Kin. 14:20), from
931/30 to 910/09 B.C. Jeroboam I first appears in the biblical
record as Solomon's servant: "the officer over all the labor force
of the house of Joseph" (1 Kin. 11:28). One day as Jeroboam went
out of Jerusalem, the prophet Ahijah the Shilonite met him on
the road and confronted him with an enacted parable. Ahijah,
who was wearing a new garment, took hold of the garment and
tore it into 12 pieces. He then said to Jeroboam, "Take for yourself ten pieces, for thus says the Lord, the God of Israel: 'Behold,
I will tear the kingdom out of the hand of Solomon and will
give ten tribes to you' " (1 Kin. 11:31).
  When Solomon learned of Ahijah's words, he sought to kill
Jeroboam. But Jeroboam fled to Egypt, where he was granted
political asylum by Shishak I, the king of Egypt. Only after the
death of Solomon did Jeroboam risk returning to his native
Palestine (1 Kin. 11:40; 12:2–3).
  Solomon's kingdom was outwardly rich, prosperous, and
thriving. But the great building projects he undertook were
accomplished by forced labor, high taxes, and other oppressive
measures. Discontent and unrest existed throughout Solomon's
kingdom. When the great king died, the kingdom was like a
powder keg awaiting a spark. The occasion for the explosion,

the tearing of the ten northern tribes from Solomon's successor, came because of the foolish insensitivity of Solomon's son Rehoboam. Rehoboam had gone to Shechem to be anointed as the new king. A delegation led by Jeroboam, who had returned from Egypt following Solomon's death, said to Rehoboam, "Your father made our yoke heavy; now therefore, lighten the burdensome service of your father, and his heavy yoke which he put on us, and we will serve" (1 Kin. 12:4).

But Rehoboam followed the advice of his inexperienced companions and replied, "Whereas my father laid a heavy yoke on you, I will add to your yoke; my father chastised you with whips, but I will chastise you with scourges!" (1 Kin. 12:11). After this show of Rehoboam's foolishness, the ten northern tribes revolted against Rehoboam and appointed Jeroboam as their king (1 Kin. 12:16–20).

Jeroboam was concerned that the people of Israel might return to the house of David if they continued to journey to Jerusalem for the festivals and observances at the temple of Solomon. So he proposed an alternative form of worship that was idolatrous. He made two calves of gold that bore a close resemblance to the mounts of the Canaanite pagan god Baal. The king told his countrymen: "It is too much for you to go up to Jerusalem. Here are your gods, O Israel, which brought you up from the land of Egypt!" (1 Kin. 12:28). One calf was erected in Bethel and one in Dan.

Once committed to this sinful direction, Jeroboam's progress was downhill. He next appointed priests from tribes other than Levi. He offered sacrifices to these images and gradually polluted the worship of Israel. The Lord confronted Jeroboam by sending him an unnamed prophet who predicted God's judgment on the king and the nation. Although outwardly he appeared to be repentant, Jeroboam would not change his disastrous idolatry. His rebellious, arrogant attitude set the pattern for rulers of Israel for generations to come. Eighteen kings sat on the throne of Israel after his death, but not one of them gave up his pagan worship.

2. Jeroboam II, the fourteenth king of Israel, who reigned for 41 years (793–753 B.C.). Jeroboam was the son and successor of Joash (or Jehoash); he was the grandson of Jehoahaz and the great-grandson of Jehu (2 Kin. 13:1, 13; 1 Chr. 5:17). The Bible declares that Jeroboam "did evil in the sight of the LORD" (2 Kin. 14:24).

Jeroboam was successful in his military adventures. His aggressive campaigns "recaptured for Israel, from Damascus and Hamath, what had belonged to Judah" (2 Kin. 14:28). The boundaries of Israel expanded to their greatest extent since the days of David and Solomon: "He restored the territory of Israel from the entrance of Hamath to the Sea of the Arabah" (2 Kin. 14:25).

Jeroboam II was king during the prosperous interval between the economic reverses of other rulers. Hosea, Amos, and Jonah lived during his reign (2 Kin. 14:25; Hos. 1:1; Amos 1:1–2). During this time of superficial prosperity, the prophet Amos especially spoke out against the many social abuses in Israel. A severe oppression of the poor had been instituted by the newly prosperous class. Justice was in the hands of lawless judges, dishonest merchants falsified the balances by deceit, and worship was little more than a pious smokescreen that covered the terrible abuses of the poor. Amos prophesied that the destructive fury of God would fall upon the house of Jeroboam (Amos 7:9).

After Jeroboam's death, his son Zechariah succeeded him on the throne of Israel (2 Kin. 14:29). Zechariah reigned in Samaria only six months before he was assassinated by Shallum (2 Kin. 15:10).

JERUSALEM [jeh ROO sah lem] (*city of peace*) — sacred city and well-known capital of Palestine during Bible times. The earliest known name for Jerusalem was Urushalem. Salem, of which Melchizedek was king (Gen. 14:18), was a natural abbreviation for Jerusalem. Thus, Jerusalem appears in the Bible as early as the time of Abraham, although the city had probably been inhabited for centuries before that time.

The city of Jerusalem is mentioned directly in the Bible for the first time during the struggle of Joshua and the Israelites to take the land of Canaan (Josh. 10:1–4). Their efforts to take the city were unsuccessful, although the areas surrounding it were taken and the land was given to the tribe of Judah. Still remaining in the fortress of the city itself were the Jebusites. Thus, the city was called Jebus.

Jerusalem under David. After the death of Saul, the first king of the united kingdom of the Hebrew people, David was named the new king of Israel. One of his first efforts was to unite the tribes of the north and south by capturing Jerusalem from the Jebusites, making the city the political and religious capital of the kingdom (1 Chr. 11:4–9). Because it was captured during his reign, Jerusalem also came to be known as the "City of David." The city is often referred to by this title in the Bible.

David built a palace in the section of Jerusalem that served previously as the Jebusite stronghold. This section, situated in the highest part of the city, frequently is referred to as Mount Zion. The location was probably selected because it was easily defended from invaders. Jerusalem has little to recommend it as a capital city, when compared to other major cities of the ancient world. It was an inland city not situated near a seaport. Moreover, it was not near the major trade routes used during that time. Why, then, did David select Jerusalem as the capital of his nation? The reasons are twofold. First, Jerusalem was centrally located between the northern and southern tribes. Thus, it was geographically convenient for the nation. The central location of the capital city tended to unite the people into one kingdom. Second, the topography of the city made it easy to defend. Jerusalem was situated on a hill. The eastern and western sides of the city consisted of valleys that made invasion by opposing forces difficult. The southern portion consisted of ravines that made an attack from this position unwise. The best point from which to attack Jerusalem was the north, which had the highest elevation of any portion of the city. It was from this position that attacks on the city were made in the centuries following the establishment of Jerusalem as the capital. David also made Jerusalem the religious capital of the nation. He moved the ark of the covenant, which had been kept at Kirjath-jearim (Josh. 15:9), to Jerusalem. One of his desires was to build a temple in the capital city, but he was prevented from completing this task. The prophet Nathan instructed him that God did not want him to build the temple because his hands had been involved in so much bloodshed (1 Chronicles 17). David did make preparation for the building of the temple, however, leaving the actual building task to Solomon, his son and successor.

During the reign of David, Jerusalem was firmly established politically and religiously as the capital city of the Israelite nation. The selection of this site resulted in the unification of the nation as David had hoped. But the selection of Jerusalem as the capital was more than a choice by a human king. Divine providence was also involved. Jerusalem was referred to as "the place which the Lord your God shall choose out of all your tribes to put his name there" (Deut. 12:5, 11, 14, 18, 21).

Jerusalem under Solomon. The glory of Jerusalem, begun under David, reached its greatest heights under Solomon. Solomon proceeded to construct the temple about which David had dreamed (2 Chronicles 3; 4). He also extended the borders of the city to new limits. Because surrounding nations were engaged in internal strife, Jerusalem was spared from invasions from opposing forces during Solomon's administration.

After completing the temple, Solomon built the palace complex, a series of five structures. These other buildings were the "house of the Forest of Lebanon," an assembly hall and a storage place for arms; an anteroom for the throne, where distinguished guests were received; the throne room, an ornately carved enclosure that contained the throne, which was made of carved ivory inlaid with gold; the king's palace, which was very large so as to hold the king's family; and the residence for Solomon's Egyptian wives, which adjoined the king's palace. Solomon also planted vineyards, orchards, and gardens that contained all types of trees and shrubs. These were watered by streams and pools that flowed through the complex. Unfortunately, this splendor came to an end with the death of Solomon about 931 B.C. The division of the kingdom into two separate nations after Solomon's reign resulted in the relapse of Jerusalem to the status of a minor city.

Jerusalem under Siege. After the death of Solomon, the division that occurred in the kingdom resulted in the ten northern tribes establishing their own capital, first at Shechem and later at Samaria. The southern tribes, consisting of Judah and Benjamin, retained Jerusalem as the capital. Although separated politically from Jerusalem, the northern tribes continued their allegiance to the "holy city" by occasionally coming there for worship.

In 722 B.C., the northern tribes were conquered by the Assyrians. Many of the citizens of the northern kingdom of Israel were deported to the Assyrian nation, never to return to the "promised land." But the Southern Kingdom, with Jerusalem as its capital, continued to exist as an independent nation. Although occasionally threatened and plundered by surrounding nations, Jerusalem remained intact until 586 B.C. At that time, Nebuchadnezzar, king of Babylonia, ravaged the city and carried the inhabitants into captivity. During the siege of the city, Jerusalem's beautiful temple was destroyed and the walls around the city were torn down. While a few inhabitants remained in the city, the glory of Jerusalem was gone.

The memory of Jerusalem among the Jewish people, however, would not die. They continued to grieve and to remember the City of David with affection. Psalm 137 is a good example of their expression of grief: "By the rivers of Babylon, there we sat down, yea, we wept, when we remembered Zion. We hanged our harps upon the willows in the midst thereof. For there they that carried us away captive required of us a song; and they that wasted us required of us mirth, saying, Sing us one of the songs of Zion. How shall we sing the LORD's song in a strange land? If I forget thee, O Jerusalem, let my right hand forget her cunning. If I do not remember thee, let my tongue cleave to the roof of my mouth; if I prefer not Jerusalem above my chief joy."

The Restoration. For more than half a century the Jews remained captives in Babylonia, and their beloved Jerusalem lay in ruins. But this changed when Cyrus, king of Persia, defeated the Babylonians. He allowed the Jewish captives to return to Jerusalem to restore the city. Zerubbabel was the leader of a group that left Babylon in 538 B.C. to return to Jerusalem to rebuild the temple. After a period of over 20 years, the temple was restored, although it was not as lavish as Solomon's original temple had been.

Under the leadership of Nehemiah, a second group of Jewish exiles returned to the holy city to restore the wall around the city. Through a masterful strategy of organization and determination, "the wall was finished on the twenty-fifth day of the month of Elul, in fifty-two days" (Neh. 6:15).

During the succeeding years of domination by the Persian Empire, Jerusalem apparently enjoyed peace and prosperity. When Alexander the Great conquered Persia, the Jews were reluctant to pledge loyalty to the Greek ruler, preferring instead to remain under Persian rule. Only by tactful concessions of religious privileges was Alexander able to win the loyalty of the Jews.

Jerusalem during the Period between the Testaments. The years that followed the death of Alexander brought many contending armies into conflict in the territory that surrounded Jerusalem. But the greatest threat to the Jews was the onslaught of Greek or Hellenistic culture, which threatened to erode the Jewish way of life. When the Jews resisted Greek cultural influence, the Greek leader Antiochus IV Epiphanes attacked the city and destroyed the temple. Many of the inhabitants fled the city, taking refuge in the surrounding hills.

Led by Judas, these inhabitants later recaptured Jerusalem and restored the temple. The successors to Judas Maccabeus were able to gain independence and to set up Jerusalem as the capital of a newly independent Judea—a position the city had not enjoyed since its defeat by the Babylonians four centuries before. This situation prevailed until the Roman Empire conquered Judea and reduced Jerusalem to a city-state under Roman domination. This was the situation that prevailed during New Testament times.

Jerusalem in the New Testament. The wise men who sought Jesus after His birth came to Jerusalem because this was considered the city of the king (Matt. 2:1–2). Although Jesus was born in Bethlehem, Jerusalem played a significant role in His life and ministry. It was to Jerusalem that He went when He was 12 years old. Here He amazed the temple leaders with His knowledge and wisdom (Luke 2:47). In Jerusalem He cleansed the temple, chasing away the moneychangers who desecrated the holy place with their selfish practices. And, finally, it was outside Jerusalem where He was crucified, buried, and resurrected.

The record of the New Testament church indicates that Jerusalem continued to play a significant role in the early spread of Christianity. After the martyrdom of Stephen, the early believers scattered from Jerusalem to various parts of the Mediterranean world (Acts 8:1). But Jerusalem always was the place to which they returned for significant events. For example, Acts 15 records that when the early church leaders sought to reconcile their differences about the acceptance of Gentile believers, they met in Jerusalem. Thus, the city became a holy city for Christians as well as Jews.

The Jerusalem of New Testament times contained a temple that had been built by Herod, the Roman leader. Although the main portion of the temple was completed in 18 months, other areas of this building were still under construction during Jesus' ministry. In fact, the temple was not completed until A.D. 67—only three years before it was finally destroyed by the Roman leader, Titus, and the Roman army.

As Jesus had prophesied in Matthew 24, the city of Jerusalem was completely destroyed in A.D. 70. The temple was destroyed, and the high priesthood and the Sanhedrin were abolished. Eventually, a Roman city was erected on the site, and Jerusalem was regarded as forbidden ground for the Jews.

Topography. Unlike many other ancient cities, Jerusalem is neither a harbor city nor a city situated on trade routes. It sits about 800 meters (2,500 feet) above sea level in mountainous country about 60 kilometers (37 miles) from the Mediterranean Sea and 23 kilometers (14 miles) from the northern end of the Dead Sea. The site seems unattractive because it lacks an adequate supply of water, is surrounded by relatively infertile land, and is hemmed in by deep valleys and difficult roads.

But these disadvantages were probably the major factors that led to its establishment as a capital city. Its location made the city a fortress that could be easily defended against attack—a very important consideration in Old Testament times. Topographically, Jerusalem was built on two triangle-shaped ridges that converge to the south. On the east lay the ravine known as the Kidron Valley. On the west lay the deep gorge known as the Valley of Hinnom. At the southern border of the city, the two valleys converged. Only on the northern border was the city vulnerable to attack.

The lack of a water supply was solved by using a natural spring that flowed from the Kidron Valley. During the reign of Hezekiah in the Old Testament period, this spring was diverted underground so that it flowed into the city. Thus, the inhabitants of the city had water, while invading armies did not. According to 2 Chronicles 32:30, "Hezekiah ... stopped the upper watercourse of Gihon, and brought it straight down to the west side of the City of David." Hezekiah's new water supply helped save the city when it was attacked by the Assyrians a short time later (701 B.C.).

Jerusalem is considered a holy city not only by Jews and Christians but also by Muslims. The book of Revelation speaks of a "new Jerusalem" (Rev. 21:2), a heavenly city fashioned by God Himself for those who are known as His people.

JESSE [JES ee] (meaning unknown) — the father of King David (1 Sam. 16:18–19) and an ancestor of Jesus. Jesse was the father of eight sons—Eliab, Abinadab, Shimea (Shammah), Nethanel, Raddai, Ozem, Elihu, and David—and two daughters, Zeruiah and Abigail (1 Chr. 2:13–16). He is called a "Bethlehemite" (1 Sam. 16:1, 18).

On instructions from the Lord, the prophet Samuel went to Bethlehem to select a new king from among Jesse's eight sons. After the first seven were rejected, David was anointed by Samuel to replace Saul as king of Israel (1 Sam. 16:1–13). Later King Saul asked Jesse to allow David to visit his court and play soothing music on the harp. Jesse gave his permission and sent Saul a present (1 Sam. 16:20).

The title "son of Jesse" soon became attached to David. It was sometimes used in a spirit of insult and ridicule, mocking David's humble origins (1 Sam. 20:27; 1 Kin. 12:16). But the prophet Isaiah spoke of "a Rod from the stem of Jesse" (11:1) and of "a Root of Jesse" (11:10)—prophecies of the Messiah to come. For the apostle Paul, the "root of Jesse" (Rom. 15:12) was a prophecy fulfilled in Jesus Christ.

JESUS [GEE zus] (*the Lord is salvation*) — the name of five men in the Bible:

1. Jesus Barabbas, a prisoner released by the Roman governor Pontius Pilate before Jesus was crucified (Matt. 27:16–17, REB; some manuscripts omit the word *Jesus* and have simply *Barabbas*).

2. An ancestor of Christ (Luke 3:29; Jose, KJV, NKJV; Joshua, NASB, REB, NIV).

3. The KJV rendering of Joshua, the son of Nun, in the New Testament (Acts 7:45; Heb. 4:8).

4. Jesus Justus, a Jewish Christian who, with the apostle Paul, sent greetings to the Colossians (Col. 4:11).

5. Jesus, the son of Mary.

JESUS CHRIST — the human-divine Son of God born of the Virgin Mary; the great High Priest who intercedes for His people at the right hand of God; founder of the Christian church and central figure of the human race.

To understand who Jesus was and what He accomplished, students of the New Testament must study: (1) His life, (2) His teachings, (3) His person, and (4) His work.

The Life of Jesus. The twofold designation Jesus Christ combines the personal name "Jesus" and the title "Christ," meaning "anointed" or "Messiah." The significance of this title became clear during the scope of His life and ministry.

Birth and Upbringing — Jesus was born in Bethlehem, a town about 10 kilometers (6 miles) south of Jerusalem, toward the end of Herod the Great's reign as king of the Jews (37–4 B.C.). Early in His life He was taken to Nazareth, a town of Galilee. There He was brought up by His mother, Mary, and her husband, Joseph, a carpenter by trade. Hence He was known as

"Jesus of Nazareth" or, more fully, "Jesus of Nazareth, the son of Joseph" (John 1:45).

Jesus was His mother's firstborn child; He had four brothers (James, Joses, Judas, and Simon) and an unspecified number of sisters (Mark 6:3). Joseph apparently died before Jesus began His public ministry. Mary, with the rest of the family, lived on and became a member of the church of Jerusalem after Jesus' death and resurrection.

The only incident preserved from Jesus' first 30 years (after his infancy) was His trip to Jerusalem with Joseph and Mary when He was 12 years old (Luke 2:41–52). Since He was known in Nazareth as "the carpenter" (Mark 6:3), He may have taken Joseph's place as the family breadwinner at an early age.

The little village of Nazareth overlooked the main highway linking Damascus to the Mediterranean coast and Egypt. News of the world outside Galilee probably reached Nazareth quickly. During His boyhood Jesus probably heard of the revolt led by Judas the Galilean against the Roman authorities. This happened when Judea, to the south, became a Roman province in A.D. 6 and its inhabitants had to pay tribute to Caesar. Jews probably heard also of the severity with which the revolt was crushed.

Galilee, the province in which Jesus lived, was ruled by Herod Antipas, youngest son of Herod the Great. So the area where He lived was not directly involved in this revolt. But the sympathies of many Galileans were probably stirred. No doubt the boys of Nazareth discussed this issue, which they heard their elders debating. There is no indication of what Jesus thought about this event at the time. But we do know what he said about it in Jerusalem 24 years later (Mark 12:13–17).

Sepphoris, about 6 kilometers (4 miles) northwest of Nazareth, had been the center of an anti-Roman revolt during Jesus' infancy. The village was destroyed by the Romans, but it was soon rebuilt by Herod Antipas. Antipas lived there as tetrarch of Galilee and Perea until he founded a new capital for his principality at Tiberias, on the western shore of the Lake of Galilee (A.D. 22). Reports of happenings at his court, while he lived in Sepphoris, were probably carried to Nazareth. A royal court formed the setting for several of Jesus' parables.

Scenes from Israel's history could be seen from the rising ground above Nazareth. To the south stretched the Valley of Jezreel, where great battles had been fought in earlier days. Beyond the Valley of Jezreel was Mount Gilboa, where King Saul fell in battle with the Philistines. To the east Mount Tabor rose to 562 meters (1,843 feet), the highest elevation in that part of the country. A growing boy would readily find his mind moving back and forth between the stirring events of former days and the realities of the contemporary situation: the all-pervasive presence of the Romans.

Beginnings of Jesus' Ministry — Jesus began His public ministry when He sought baptism at the hands of John the Baptist. John preached between A.D. 27 and 28 in the lower Jordan Valley and baptized those who wished to give expression to their repentance (Matt. 3:13–17; Mark 1:9–11; Luke 3:21–22; John 1:29–34). The descent of the dove as Jesus came up out of the water was a sign that He was the One anointed by the Spirit of God as the Servant-Messiah of His people (Is. 11:2; 42:1; 61:1).

A voice from heaven declared, "You are My beloved Son; in You I am well pleased" (Luke 3:22). This indicated that He was Israel's anointed King, destined to fulfill His kingship as the Servant of the Lord described centuries earlier by the prophet Isaiah (Is. 42:1; 52:13).

In the Gospels of Matthew, Mark, and Luke, Jesus' baptism is followed immediately by His temptation in the wilderness (Matt. 4:1–11; Mark 1:12–13; Luke 4:1–13). This testing confirmed His understanding of the heavenly voice and His acceptance of the path that it marked out for Him. He refused to use His power as God's Son to fulfill His personal desires, to amaze the people, or to dominate the world by political and military force.

Apparently, Jesus ministered for a short time in southern and central Palestine, while John the Baptist was still preaching (John 3:22–4:42). But the main phase of Jesus' ministry began in Galilee after John's imprisonment by Herod Antipas. This was the signal, according to Mark 1:14–15, for Jesus to proclaim God's good news in Galilee: "The time is fulfilled, and the kingdom of God is at hand. Repent, and believe in the gospel." What is the character of this kingdom? How was it to be established?

A popular view was that the kingdom of God meant throwing off the oppressive yoke of Rome and establishing an independent state of Israel. Judas and his brothers and followers had won independence for the Jewish people in the second century B.C. by guerrilla warfare and diplomatic skill. Many of the Jewish people believed that with God's help, the same thing could happen again. Other efforts had failed, but the spirit of revolt remained. If Jesus had consented to become the military leader, which the people wanted, many would gladly have followed Him. But in spite of His temptation, Jesus resisted taking this path.

Jesus' proclamation of the kingdom of God was accompanied by works of mercy and power, including the healing of the sick, particularly those who were demon-possessed. These works also proclaimed the arrival of the kingdom of God. The demons that caused such distress to men and women were signs of the kingdom of Satan. When they were cast out, this proved the superior strength of the kingdom of God. For a time, Jesus' healing aroused great popular enthusiasm throughout Galilee. But the religious leaders and teachers found much of Jesus' activity disturbing. He refused to be bound by their religious ideas. He befriended social outcasts. He insisted on understanding and applying the law of God in the light of its original intention, not according to the popular interpretation of the religious establishment. He insisted on healing sick people on the Sabbath day. He believed that healing people did not profane the Sabbath but honored it, because it was established by God for the rest and relief of human beings (Luke 6:6–11).

This attitude brought Jesus into conflict with the scribes, the official teachers of the law. Because of their influence, He was soon barred from preaching in the synagogues. But this was no great inconvenience. He simply gathered larger congregations to listen to Him on the hillside or by the lakeshore. He regularly illustrated the main themes of His preaching by parables. These were simple stories from daily life that would drive home some special point and make it stick in the hearer's understanding.

The Mission of the Twelve and Its Sequel — From among the large number of His followers, Jesus selected 12 men to remain in His company for training that would enable them to share His preaching and healing ministry. When He judged the time to be ripe, Jesus sent them out two by two to proclaim the kingdom of God throughout the Jewish districts of Galilee. In many places, they found an enthusiastic hearing.

Probably some who heard these disciples misunderstood the nature of the kingdom they proclaimed. Perhaps the disciples themselves used language that could be interpreted as stirring political unrest. News of their activity reached Herod Antipas, ruler of Galilee, arousing His suspicion. He had recently murdered John the Baptist. Now he began to wonder if he faced another serious problem in Jesus. On the return of His 12 apostles, they withdrew under Jesus' leadership from the publicity that surrounded them in Galilee to the quieter territory east of the Lake of Galilee. This territory was ruled by Antipas' brother Philip—"Philip the tetrarch"—who had only a few Jews among his subjects. Philip was not as likely to be troubled by Messianic excitement. But even here Jesus and His disciples found themselves pursued by enthusiastic crowds from Galilee. He recognized them for what they were, "sheep without a shepherd," aimless people who were in danger of being led to disaster under the wrong kind of leadership. Jesus gave these people further teaching, feeding them also with loaves and fishes. But this only stimulated them to try to compel Him to be the king for whom they were looking. He would not be the kind of king they wanted, and they had no use for the only kind of king He was prepared to be. From then on, His popularity in Galilee began to decline. Many of His disciples no longer followed Him. He took the Twelve further north, into Gentile territory. Here He gave them special training to prepare them for the crisis they would have to meet shortly in Jerusalem. He knew the time was approaching when He would present His challenging message to the people of the capital and to the Jewish leaders. At the city of Caesarea Philippi, Jesus decided the time was ripe to encourage the Twelve to state their convictions about His identity and His mission. When Peter declared that He was the Messiah, this showed that He and the other apostles had given up most of the traditional ideas about the kind of person the Messiah would be. But the thought that Jesus would have to suffer and die was something they could not accept. Jesus recognized that He could now make a beginning with the creation of a new community. In this new community of God's people, the ideals of the kingdom He proclaimed would be realized. These ideals that Jesus taught were more revolutionary in many ways than the insurgent spirit that survived the overthrow of Judas the Galilean. The Jewish rebels against the rule of Rome developed into a party known as the Zealots. They had no better policy than to counter force with force, which, in Jesus' view, was like invoking Satan to drive out Satan. The way of nonresistance that He urged upon the people seemed impractical. But it eventually proved to be more effective against the might of Rome than armed rebellion.

Jerusalem: The Last Phase — At the Feast of Tabernacles in the fall of A.D. 29, Jesus went to Jerusalem with the Twelve. He apparently spent the next six months in the southern part of Palestine. Jerusalem, like Galilee, needed to hear the message of the kingdom. But Jerusalem was more resistant to it even than Galilee. The spirit of revolt was in the air; Jesus' way of peace was not accepted. This is why He wept over the city. He realized the way that so many of its citizens preferred was bound to lead to their destruction. Even the magnificent temple, so recently rebuilt by Herod the Great, would be involved in the general overthrow.

During the week before Passover in A.D. 30, Jesus taught each day in the temple area, debating with other teachers of differing beliefs. He was invited to state His opinion on a number of issues, including the question of paying taxes to the Roman emperor. This was a test question with the Zealots. In their eyes, to acknowledge the rule of a pagan king was high treason against God, Israel's true King.

Jesus replied that the coinage in which these taxes had to be paid belonged to the Roman emperor because his face and name were stamped on it. Let the emperor have what so obviously belonged to him, Jesus declared; it was more important to make sure that God received what was due Him. This answer disappointed those patriots who followed the Zealot line. Neither did it make Jesus popular with the priestly authorities. They were terrified by the rebellious spirit in the land. Their favored position depended on maintaining good relations with the ruling Romans. If revolt broke out, the Romans would hold them responsible for not keeping the people under control. They were afraid that Jesus might provoke an outburst that would bring the heavy hand of Rome upon the city. The enthusiasm of the people when Jesus entered Jerusalem on a donkey alarmed the religious leaders. So did his show of authority when he cleared the temple of traders and moneychangers. This was a "prophetic action" in the tradition of the great prophets of Israel. Its message to the priestly establishment came through loud and clear. The prophets' vision of the temple—"My house shall be called a house of prayer for all nations" (Is. 56:7)—was a fine ideal. But any attempt to make it measure up to reality would be a threat to the priestly privileges. Jesus' action was as disturbing as Jeremiah's speech foretelling the destruction of Solomon's temple had been to the religious leaders six centuries earlier (Jer. 26:1–6).

To block the possibility of an uprising among the people, the priestly party decided to arrest Jesus as soon as possible. The opportunity came earlier than they expected when one of the Twelve, Judas Iscariot, offered to deliver Jesus into their power without the risk of a public disturbance. Arrested on Passover Eve, Jesus was brought first before a Jewish court of inquiry, over which the high priest Caiaphas presided. The Jewish leaders attempted first to convict Him of being a threat to the temple. Protection of the sanctity of the temple was the one area in which the Romans still allowed the Jewish authorities to exercise authority. But this attempt failed. Then Jesus accepted their charge that He claimed to be the Messiah. This gave the religious leaders an occasion to hand Him over to Pilate on a charge of treason and sedition. While "Messiah" was primarily a religious title, it could be translated into political terms as "king of the Jews." Anyone who claimed to be king of the Jews, as Jesus admitted He did, presented a challenge to the Roman emperor's rule in Judea. On this charge Pilate, the Roman governor, finally convicted Jesus. This was the charge spelled out in the inscription fixed above His head on the cross. Death by crucifixion was the penalty for sedition by one who was not a Roman citizen. With the death and burial of Jesus, the narrative of His earthly career came to an end. But with His resurrection on the third day, He lives and works forever as the exalted Lord. His appearances to His disciples after His resurrection assured them He was "alive after His suffering" (Acts 1:3). These appearances also enabled them to make the transition in their experience from the form in which they had known Him earlier to the new way in which they would be related to Him by the Holy Spirit.

The Teachings of Jesus. Just as Jesus' life was unique, so His teachings are known for their fresh and new approach. Jesus taught several distinctive spiritual truths that set Him apart from any other religious leader who ever lived.

The Kingdom of God — The message Jesus began to proclaim in Galilee after John the Baptist's imprisonment was the good news of the kingdom of God. When He appeared to His disciples after the resurrection, He continued "speaking of the things pertaining to the kingdom of God" (Acts 1:3). What did Jesus mean by the kingdom of God?

When Jesus announced that the kingdom of God was drawing near, many of His hearers must have recognized an echo of those visions recorded in the book of Daniel. These prophecies declared that one day "the God of heaven will set up a kingdom which shall never be destroyed" (Dan. 2:44). Jesus' announcement indicated the time had come when the authority of this kingdom would be exercised.

The nature of this kingdom is determined by the character of the God whose kingdom it is. The revelation of God lay at the heart of Jesus' teaching. Jesus called Him "Father" and taught His disciples to do the same. But the term that He used when He called God "Father" was *Abba* (Mark 14:36), the term of affection that children used when they addressed their father at home or spoke about him to others. It was not unusual for God to be addressed in prayer as "my Father" or "our Father." But it was most unusual for Him to be called *Abba*. By using this term, Jesus expressed His sense of nearness to God and His total trust in Him. He taught His followers to look to God with the trust that children show when they expect their earthly fathers to provide them with food, clothes, and shelter.

This attitude is especially expressed in the Lord's Prayer, which may be regarded as a brief summary of Jesus' teaching. In this prayer the disciples were taught to pray for the fulfillment of God's eternal purpose (the coming of His kingdom) and to ask Him for daily bread, forgiveness of sins, and deliverance from temptation. In Jesus' healing of the sick and proclamation of good news to the poor, the kingdom of God was visibly present, although it was not yet fully realized. Otherwise, it would not have been necessary for Him to tell His disciples to pray, "Your kingdom come" (Matt. 6:10). One day, He taught, it would come "with power" (Mark 9:1), and some of them would live to see that day.

In the kingdom of God the way to honor is the way of service. In this respect, Jesus set a worthy example, choosing to give service instead of receive it. The death and resurrection of Jesus unleashed the kingdom of God in full power. Through proclamation of the kingdom, liberation and blessing were brought to many more than could be touched by Jesus' brief ministry in Galilee and Judea.

The Way of the Kingdom — The ethical teaching of Jesus was part of His proclamation of the kingdom of God. Only by His death and resurrection could the divine rule be established. But even while the kingdom of God was in the process of inauguration during His ministry, its principles could be translated into action in the lives of His followers. The most familiar presentation of these principles is found in the Sermon on the Mount (Matthew 5–7), which was addressed to His disciples. These principles showed how those who were already children of the kingdom ought to live.

Jesus and the Law of Moses — The people whom Jesus taught already had a large body of ethical teaching in the Old Testament law. But a further body of oral interpretation and application had grown up around the law of Moses over the centuries. Jesus declared that He had come to fulfill the law, not to destroy it (Matt. 5:17). But He emphasized its ethical quality by summarizing it in terms of what He called the two great commandments: "You shall love the Lord your God" (Deut. 6:5) and "You shall love your neighbor as yourself" (Lev. 19:18). "On these two commandments," He said, "hang all the Law and the Prophets" (Matt. 22:40).

Jesus did not claim uniqueness or originality for His ethical teaching. One of His purposes was to explain the ancient law of God. Yet there was a distinctiveness and freshness about His teaching, as He declared His authority: "You have heard that it was said ... But I say to you" (Matt. 5:21-22). Only in listening to His words and doing them could people build a secure foundation for their lives (Matt. 7:24-27; Luke 6:46-49).

In His interpretation of specific commandments, Jesus did not use the methods of the Jewish rabbis. He dared to criticize their rulings, which had been handed down by word of mouth through successive generations of scribes. He even declared that these interpretations sometimes obscured the original purpose of the commandments. In appealing to that original purpose, He declared that a commandment was most faithfully obeyed when God's purpose in giving it was fulfilled. His treatment of the Sabbath law is an example of this approach. In a similar way, Jesus settled the question of divorce by an appeal to the original marriage ordinance (Gen. 1:26-27; 2:24-25). Since husband and wife were made one by the Creator's decree, Jesus pointed out, divorce was an attempt to undo the work of God. If the law later allowed for divorce in certain situations (Deut. 24:1-4), that was a concession to people's inability to keep the commandment. But it was not so in the beginning, He declared, and it should not be so for those who belong to the kingdom of God.

Jesus actually injected new life into the ethical principles of the law of Moses. But He did not impose a new set of laws that could be enforced by external sanctions; He prescribed a way of life for His followers. The act of murder, forbidden in the sixth commandment, was punishable by death. Conduct or language likely to provoke a breach of the peace could also bring on legal penalties. No human law can detect or punish the angry thought; yet it is here, Jesus taught, that the process that leads to murder begins. Therefore, "whoever is angry with his brother … shall be in danger of the judgment" (Matt. 5:22). But He was careful to point out that the judgment is God's, not man's.

The law could also punish a person for breaking the seventh commandment, which forbade adultery. But Jesus maintained that the act itself was the outcome of a person's internal thought. Therefore, "whoever looks at a woman to lust for her has already committed adultery with her in his heart" (Matt. 5:28).

Jesus' attitude and teaching also made many laws about property irrelevant for His followers. They should be known as people who give, not as people who get. If someone demands your cloak (outer garment), Jesus said, give it to him, and give him your tunic (undergarment) as well (Luke 6:29). There is more to life than abundance of possessions (Luke 12:15); in fact, He pointed out, material wealth is a hindrance to one's spiritual life. The wise man therefore will get rid of it: "It is easier for a camel to go through the eye of a needle than for a rich man to enter the kingdom of God" (Mark 10:25). In no area have Jesus' followers struggled more to avoid the uncompromising rigor of his words than in His teaching about the danger of possessions.

Jesus insisted that more is expected of His followers than the ordinary morality of decent people. Their ethical behavior should exceed "the righteousness of the scribes and Pharisees" (Matt. 5:20). "If you love [only] those who love you," He asked, "what credit is that to you? For even sinners love those who love them" (Luke 6:32). The higher standard of the kingdom of God called for acts of love to enemies and words of blessing and goodwill to persecutors. The children of the kingdom should not insist on their legal rights but cheerfully give them up in response to the supreme law of love.

The Way of Nonviolence — The principle of nonviolence is deeply ingrained in Jesus' teaching. In His references to the "men of violence" who tried to bring in the kingdom of God by force, Jesus gave no sign that He approved of their ideals or methods. The course He called for was the way of peace and submission. He urged His hearers not to strike back against injustice or oppression but to turn the other cheek, to go a second mile when their services were demanded for one mile, and to take the initiative in returning good for evil.

But the way of nonviolence did not appeal to the people. The crowd chose the militant Barabbas when they were given the opportunity to have either Jesus or Barabbas set free. But the attitude expressed in the shout, "Not this man, but Barabbas!" (Matt. 27:15–26) was the spirit that would one day level Jerusalem and bring misery and suffering to the Jewish nation.

The Supreme Example — In the teaching of Jesus, the highest of all incentives is the example of God. This was no new principle. The central section of Leviticus is called "the law of holiness" because of its recurring theme: "I am the Lord your God.... Be holy; for I am holy" (Lev. 11:44). This bears a close resemblance to Jesus' words in Luke 6:36, "Be merciful, just as your Father also is merciful." The children of God should reproduce their Father's character. He does not discriminate between the good and the evil in bestowing rain and sunshine; likewise, His followers should not discriminate in showing kindness to all. He delights in forgiving sinners; His children should also be marked by a forgiving spirit.

The example of the heavenly Father and the example shown by Jesus on earth are one and the same, since Jesus came to reveal the Father. Jesus' life was the practical demonstration of His ethical teaching. To His disciples He declared, "I have given you an example, that you should do as I have done to you" (John 13:15).

This theme of the imitation of Christ pervades the New Testament letters. It is especially evident in the writings of Paul, who was not personally acquainted with Jesus before he met Him on the Damascus Road. Paul instructed his converts to follow "the meekness and gentleness of Christ" (2 Cor. 10:1). He also encouraged them to imitate him as he himself imitated Christ (1 Cor. 11:1). When he recommended to them the practice of all the Christian graces, he declared, "Put on the Lord Jesus Christ" (Rom. 13:14). Throughout the New Testament, Jesus is presented as the One who left us an example, that we should follow in His steps (1 Pet. 2:21).

The Person of Christ. The doctrine of the person of Christ, or christology, is one of the most important concerns of Christian theology. The various aspects of the person of Christ are best seen by reviewing the titles that are applied to Him in the Bible.

Son of Man — The title "Son of Man" was Jesus' favorite way of referring to Himself. He may have done this because this was not a recognized title already known by the people and associated with popular ideas. This title means essentially "The Man." But as Jesus used it, it took on new significance.

Jesus applied this title to Himself in three distinct ways: First, He used the title in a general way, almost as a substitute for the pronoun "I." A good example of this usage occurred in the saying where Jesus contrasted John the Baptist, who "came neither eating bread nor drinking wine," with the Son of Man, who "has come eating and drinking" (Luke 7:33–34). Another probable example is the statement that "the Son of Man has nowhere to lay His head" (Luke 9:58). In this instance He warned a would-be disciple that those who wanted to follow Him must expect to share His homeless existence.

Second, Jesus used the title to emphasize that "the Son of Man must suffer" (Mark 8:31). The word *must* implies that His suffering was foretold by the prophets. It was, indeed, "written concerning the Son of Man, that He must suffer many things and be treated with contempt" (Mark 9:12). So when Jesus announced the presence of the betrayer at the Last Supper, He declared, "The Son of Man indeed goes just as it is written of Him" (Mark 14:21). Later the same evening He submitted to His captors with the words "The Scriptures must be fulfilled" (Mark 14:49).

Finally, Jesus used the title "Son of Man" to refer to Himself as the one who exercised exceptional authority—authority delegated to Him by God. "The Son of Man has power [authority] on earth to forgive sins" (Mark 2:10), He declared. He exercised this authority in a way that made some people criticize Him for acting with the authority of God: "The Son of Man is also Lord of the Sabbath" (Mark 2:28).

The Son of Man appeared to speak and act in these cases as the representative human being. If God had given people dominion over all the works of His hands, then He who was the Son of Man in this special representative sense was in a position to exercise that dominion. Near the end of His ministry, Jesus spoke of His authority as the Son of Man at the end of time. Men and women "will see the Son of Man coming in the clouds with great power and glory," He declared (Mark 13:26). He also stated to the high priest and other members of the supreme court of Israel: "You will see the Son of Man sitting at the right hand of Power, and coming with the clouds of heaven" (Mark 14:62). He seemed deserted and humiliated as He stood there awaiting their verdict. But the tables would be turned when they saw Him vindicated by God as Ruler and Judge of all the world.

Only once was Jesus referred to as the Son of Man by anyone other than Himself. This occurred when Stephen, condemned by the Jewish Sanhedrin, saw "the Son of Man standing at the right hand of God" (Acts 7:56). In Stephen's vision the Son of

Man stood as his heavenly advocate, in fulfillment of Jesus' words: "Whoever confesses Me before men, him the Son of Man also will confess before the angels of God" (Luke 12:8).

Messiah — When Jesus made His declaration before the high priest and His colleagues, He did so in response to the question: "Are You the Christ, the Son of the Blessed?" (Mark 14:61). He replied, "I am" (Mark 14:62). "It is as you said" (Matt. 26:64).

The Christ was the Messiah, the Son of David—a member of the royal family of David. For centuries the Jewish people had expected a Messiah who would restore the fortunes of Israel, liberating the nation from foreign oppression and extending His rule over Gentile nations.

Jesus belonged to the family of David. He was proclaimed as the Messiah of David's line, both before His birth and after His resurrection. But He Himself was slow to make messianic claims. The reason for this is that the ideas associated with the Messiah in the minds of the Jewish people were quite different from the character and purpose of His ministry. Thus, He refused to give them any encouragement. When, at Caesarea Philippi, Peter confessed Jesus to be the Messiah, Jesus directed him and his fellow disciples to tell no one that He was the Christ. After His death and resurrection, however, the concept of messiahship among His followers was transformed by what He was and did. Then He could safely be proclaimed as Messiah, God's Anointed King, resurrected in glory to occupy the throne of the universe.

Son of God — Jesus was acclaimed as the Son of God at His baptism (Mark 1:11). But He was also given this title by the angel Gabriel at the annunciation: "That Holy One who is to be born will be called the Son of God" (Luke 1:35). The gospel of John especially makes it clear that the Father-Son relationship belongs to eternity—that the Son is supremely qualified to reveal the Father because He has His eternal being "in the bosom of the Father" (John 1:18).

At one level the title "Son of God" belonged officially to the Messiah, who personified the nation of Israel. "Israel is My son, My firstborn," said God to pharaoh (Ex. 4:22). Of the promised prince of the house of David, God declared, "I will make him My firstborn" (Ps. 89:27).

But there was nothing merely official about Jesus' consciousness of being the Son of God. He taught His disciples to think of God and to speak to Him as their Father. But He did not link them with Himself in this relationship and speak to them of "our Father"—yours and mine. The truth expressed in His words in John 20:17 is implied throughout His teaching: "My Father and your Father ... My God and your God."

As the Son of God in a special sense, Jesus made Himself known to the apostle Paul on the Damascus Road. Paul said, "It pleased God ... to reveal His Son in me" (Gal. 1:15–16). The proclamation of Jesus as the Son of God was central to Paul's preaching (Acts 9:20; 2 Cor. 1:19).

When Jesus is presented as the Son of God in the New Testament, two aspects of His person are emphasized: His eternal relation to God as His Father and His perfect revelation of the Father to the human race.

Word and Wisdom — Jesus' perfect revelation of the Father is also expressed when He is described as the Word (*logos*) of God (John 1:1–18). The Word is the self-expression of God; that self-expression has personal status, existing eternally with God. The Word by which God created the world (Ps. 33:6) and by which He spoke through the prophets "became flesh" in the fullness of time (John 1:14), living among men and women as Jesus of Nazareth.

Much that is said in the Old Testament about the Word of God is paralleled by what is said of the Wisdom of God: "The Lord by wisdom founded the earth" (Prov. 3:19). In the New

Testament Christ is portrayed as the personal Wisdom of God (1 Cor. 1:24, 30)—the one through whom all things were created (1 Cor. 8:6; Col. 1:16; Heb. 1:2).

The Holy One of God — This title was given to Jesus by Peter (John 6:69, NIV, NRSV) and, remarkably, by a demon-possessed man (Mark 1:24). In their preaching, the apostles called Jesus "the Holy One and the Just" (Acts 3:14). This was a name belonging to Him as the Messiah, indicating He was especially set apart for God. This title also emphasized His positive goodness and His complete dedication to the doing of His Father's will. Mere "sinlessness," in the sense of the absence of any fault, is a pale quality in comparison to the unsurpassed power for righteousness that filled His life and teaching.

The Lord — "Jesus is Lord" is the ultimate Christian creed. "No one can say that Jesus is Lord except by the Holy Spirit" (1 Cor. 12:3). A Christian, therefore, is a person who confesses Jesus as Lord.

Several words denoting lordship were used of Jesus in the New Testament. The most frequent, and the most important in relation to the doctrine of His person, was the Greek word *kyrios*. It was frequently given to Him as a polite term of address, meaning "Sir." Sometimes the title was used of Him in the third person, when the disciples and others spoke of Him as "The Lord" or "The Master."

After His resurrection and exaltation, however, Jesus was given the title "Lord" in its full, christological sense. Peter, concluding his address to the crowd in Jerusalem on the Day of Pentecost, declared, "Let all the house of Israel know assuredly that God has made this Jesus, whom you crucified, both Lord and Christ" (Acts 2:36).

The title "Lord" in the christological sense must have been given to Jesus before the church moved out into the Gentile world. The evidence for this is the invocation "Maranatha" (KJV) or "O Lord, come!" (1 Cor. 16:22). The apostle Paul, writing to a Gentile church in the Greek-speaking world, assumed that its members were familiar with this Aramaic phrase. It was an early Christian title for Jesus that was taken over untranslated. It bears witness to the fact that from the earliest days of the church, the One who had been exalted as Lord was expected to return as Lord.

Another key New Testament text that shows the sense in which Jesus was acknowledged as Lord is Philippians 2:5–11. In these verses Paul may be quoting an early confession of faith. If so, he endorsed it and made it his own. This passage tells how Jesus did not regard equality with God as something that He should exploit to His own advantage. Instead, He humbled Himself to become a man, displaying "the form of God" in "the form of a servant." He became "obedient to the point of death, even the death of the cross. Therefore God also has highly exalted Him and given Him the name which is above every name, that at the name of Jesus every knee should bow, ... and that every tongue should confess that Jesus Christ is Lord" (Phil. 2:8–11).

The "name which is above every name" is probably the title "Lord" in the highest sense that it can bear. The words echo Isaiah 45:23, where the God of Israel swears, "To Me every knee shall bow, every tongue shall take an oath [or, make confession]." In the Old Testament passage the God of Israel denies to any other being the right to receive the worship that belongs to Him alone. But in the passage from Philippians He readily shares that worship with the humiliated and exalted Jesus. More than that, He shares His own name with Him. When human beings honor Jesus as Lord, God is glorified.

God — If Jesus is called "Lord" in this supreme sense, it is not surprising that He occasionally is called "God" in the New Testament. Thomas, convinced that the risen Christ stood before him, abandoned his doubts with the confession, "My Lord and my God!" (John 20:28).

But the classic text is John 1:1. John declared that the Word existed not only "in the beginning," where He was "with God," but also actually "was God." This is the Word that became incarnate as real man in Jesus Christ, without ceasing to be what He had been from eternity. The Word was God in the sense that the Father shared with Him the fullness of His own nature. The Father remained, in a technical phrase of traditional theology, "the fountain of deity." But from that fountain the Son drew in unlimited measure.

The Bible thus presents Christ as altogether God and altogether man—the perfect mediator between God and mankind because He partakes fully of the nature of both.

The Work of Christ. The work of Christ has often been stated in relation to His threefold office of prophet, priest, and king. As prophet, He is the perfect spokesman of God to the world, fully revealing God's character and will. As priest, Jesus has offered to God by His death a sufficient sacrifice for the sins of the world. Now, on the basis of that sacrifice, He exercises a ministry of intercession on behalf of His people. As king, He is "the ruler over the kings of the earth" (Rev. 1:5)—the One to whose rule the whole world is subject.

The work of Jesus can be discussed in terms of past, present, and future.

The Finished Work of Christ — By the "finished" work of Christ is meant the work of atonement or redemption for the human race that He completed by His death on the cross. This work is so perfect in itself that it requires neither repetition nor addition. Because of this work, He is called "Savior of the world" (1 John 4:14) and "the Lamb of God who takes away the sin of the world" (John 1:29).

In the Bible sin is viewed in several ways: as an offense against God, which requires a pardon; as defilement, which requires cleansing; as slavery, which cries out for emancipation; as a debt, which must be canceled; as defeat, which must be reversed by victory; and as estrangement, which must be set right by reconciliation. However sin is viewed, it is through the work of Christ that the remedy is provided. He has procured the pardon, the cleansing, the emancipation, the cancellation, the victory, and the reconciliation. When sin is viewed as an offense against God, it is also interpreted as a breach of His law. The law of God, like law in general, involves penalties against the lawbreaker. So strict are these penalties that they appear to leave no avenue of escape for the lawbreaker. The apostle Paul, conducting his argument along these lines, quoted one uncompromising declaration from the Old Testament: "Cursed is everyone who does not continue in all things which are written in the book of the law, to do them" (Deut. 27:26; Gal. 3:10).

But Paul goes on to say that Christ, by enduring the form of death on which a divine curse was expressly pronounced in the law, absorbed in His own person the curse invoked on the lawbreaker: "Christ has redeemed us from the curse of the law, having become a curse for us (for it is written, 'Cursed is everyone who hangs on a tree')" (Deut. 21:23; Gal. 3:13).

Since Christ partakes of the nature of both God and humanity, He occupies a unique status with regard to them. He represents God to humanity, and He also represents humanity to God. God is both Lawgiver and Judge; Christ represents Him. The human family has put itself in the position of the lawbreaker; Christ has voluntarily undertaken to represent us. The Judge has made Himself one with the guilty in order to bear our guilt. It is ordinarily out of the question for one person to bear the guilt of others. But when the one person is the representative human being, Jesus Christ, bearing the guilt of those whom He represents, the case is different. In the hour of His death, Christ offered His life to God on behalf of mankind. The perfect life that He offered was acceptable to God. The salvation secured through the giving up of that life is God's free gift to mankind in Christ. When the situation is viewed in terms of a law court, one might speak of the accused party as being acquitted. But the term preferred in the New Testament, especially in the apostle Paul's writings, is the more positive word *justified*. Paul goes on to the limit of daring in speaking of God as "Him who justifies the ungodly" (Rom. 4:5). God can be so described because "Christ died for the ungodly" (Rom. 5:6). Those who are united by faith to Him are "justified" in Him. As Paul explained elsewhere, "He made Him who knew no sin to be sin for us, that we might become the righteousness of God in Him" (2 Cor. 5:21). The work of Christ, seen from this point of view, is to set humanity in a right relationship with God.

When sin is considered as defilement that requires cleansing, the most straightforward affirmation is that "the blood of Jesus Christ His Son cleanses us from all sin" (1 John 1:7). The effect of His death is to purify a conscience that has been polluted by sin. The same thought is expressed by the writer of the book of Hebrews. He speaks of various materials that were prescribed by Israel's ceremonial law to deal with forms of ritual pollution, which was an external matter. Then he asks, "How much more shall the blood of Christ, who through the eternal Spirit offered Himself without spot to God, purge your conscience from dead works to serve the living God?" (Heb. 9:14). Spiritual defilement calls for spiritual cleansing, and this is what the death of Christ has accomplished.

When sin is considered as slavery from which the slave must be set free, then the death of Christ is spoken of as a ransom or a means of redemption. Jesus Himself declared that He came "to give His life a ransom for many" (Mark 10:45). Paul not only spoke of sin as slavery; he also personified sin as a slaveowner who compels his slaves to obey his evil orders. When they are set free from his control by the death of Christ to enter the service of God, they find this service, by contrast, to be perfect freedom.

The idea of sin as a debt that must be canceled is based on the teaching of Jesus. In Jesus' parable of the creditor and the two debtors (Luke 7:40–43), the creditor forgave them both when they could make no repayment. But the debtor who owed the larger sum, and therefore had more cause to love the forgiving creditor, represented the woman whose "sins, which are many, are forgiven" (Luke 7:47). This is similar to Paul's reference to God as "having canceled the bond which stood against us with its legal demands" (Col. 2:14, NRSV).

Paul's words in Colossians 2:15 speak of the "principalities and powers" as a personification of the hostile forces in the world that have conquered men and women and held them as prisoners of war. There was no hope of successful resistance against them until Christ confronted them. It looked as if they had conquered Him too, but on the cross He conquered death itself, along with all other hostile forces. In His victory all who believe in Him have a share: "Thanks be to God, who gives us the victory through our Lord Jesus Christ" (1 Cor. 15:57).

Sin is also viewed as estrangement, or alienation, from God. In this case, the saving work of Christ includes the reconciliation of sinners to God. The initiative in this reconciling work is taken by God: "God was in Christ reconciling the world to Himself" (2 Cor. 5:19). God desires the well-being of sinners; so He sends Christ as the agent of His reconciling grace to them (Col. 1:20).

Those who are separated from God by sin are also estranged from one another. Accordingly, the work of Christ that reconciles sinners to God also brings them together as human beings. Hostile divisions of humanity have peace with one another through Him. Paul celebrated the way in which the work of Christ overcame the mutual estrangement of Jews and Gentiles: "For He Himself is our peace, who has made both one, and has broken down the middle wall of division between us" (Eph. 2:14).

When the work of Christ is pictured in terms of an atoning sacrifice, it is God who takes the initiative. The word *propitiation*, used in this connection in older English versions of the Bible (Rom. 3:25; 1 John 2:2; 4:10), does not mean that sinful men and women have to do something to appease God or turn away His anger; neither does it mean that Christ died on the cross to persuade God to be merciful to sinners. It is the nature of God to be a pardoning God. He has revealed His pardoning nature above all in the person and work of Christ. This saving initiative is equally and eagerly shared by Christ: He gladly cooperates with the Father's purpose for the redemption of the world.

JETHRO [JETH roe] (*his excellency*) — the father-in-law of Moses (Ex. 3:1), also called Reuel (Ex. 2:18), Hobab (Judg. 4:11), and Raguel (Num. 10:29; Reuel, NIV).

After Moses fled from Egypt into the region of the Sinai Peninsula, he married one of Jethro's daughters, Zipporah (Ex. 2:21). Then Moses tended Jethro's sheep for 40 years (Acts 7:30) before his experience at the burning bush (Exodus 3), when he was called to lead the Israelites from bondage in Egypt.

During the Exodus, Jethro and the rest of Moses' family joined Moses in the wilderness near Mount Sinai (Ex. 18:5). During this visit, Jethro taught Moses to delegate his responsibilities. He noted that Moses was doing all the work himself and advised Moses to decide the difficult cases and to secure able men to make decisions in lesser matters (Ex. 18:13–23). Following this meeting, Jethro departed from the Israelites.

JEZEBEL [JEZ uh bel] (*there is no prince*) — the name of two women in the Bible:

1. The wife of Ahab, king of Israel, and mother of Ahaziah, Jehoram, and Athaliah (1 Kin. 16:31). Jezebel was a tyrant who

corrupted her husband, as well as the nation, by promoting pagan worship.

She was reared in Sidon, a commercial city on the coast of the Mediterranean Sea, known for its idolatry and vice. When she married Ahab and moved to Jezreel, a city that served the Lord, she decided to turn it into a city that worshiped Baal, a Phoenician god.

The wicked, idolatrous queen soon became the power behind the throne. Obedient to her wishes, Ahab erected a sanctuary for Baal and supported hundreds of pagan prophets (1 Kin. 18:19).

When the prophets of the Lord opposed Jezebel, she had them "massacred" (1 Kin. 18:4, 13). After Elijah defeated her prophets on Mount Carmel, she swore revenge. She was such a fearsome figure that the great prophet was afraid and "ran for his life" (1 Kin. 19:3).

After her husband, Ahab, was killed in battle, Jezebel reigned for 10 years through her sons Ahaziah and Joram (or Jehoram). These sons were killed by Jehu, who also disposed of Jezebel by having her thrown from the palace window. In fulfillment of the prediction of the prophet Elijah, Jezebel was trampled by the horses and eaten by the dogs (1 Kin. 21:19). Only Jezebel's skull, feet, and the palms of her hands were left to bury when the dogs were finished (2 Kin. 9:30–37).

2. A prophetess of Thyatira who enticed the Christians in that church "to commit sexual immorality and to eat things sacrificed to idols" (Rev. 2:20). John probably called this woman "Jezebel" because of her similarity to Ahab's idolatrous wicked queen.

JEZREEL [JEZ reel] (*God scatters*) — the name of two people, two cities, and a valley or plain in the Old Testament:

1. A man of the tribe of Judah (1 Chr. 4:3).

2. A symbolic name given by the prophet Hosea to his oldest son (Hos. 1:4). The name Jezreel signified the great slaughter that God would bring on the house of Jehu because of the violent acts he had committed (2 Kings 9).

3. A city in the hill country of Judah, near Jokdeam and Zanoah (Josh. 15:56). Apparently David obtained one of his wives from this place (1 Sam. 25:43). The site is probably present-day Khirbet Terrama on the Plain of Dibleh.

4. A city in northern Israel, on the Plain of Jezreel about 90 kilometers (56 miles) north of Jerusalem. The city was in the territory of Issachar, but it belonged to the tribe of Manasseh (Josh. 19:18). It was between Megiddo and Beth Shean (1 Kin. 4:12) and between Mount Carmel and Mount Gilboa. The palace of King Ahab of Israel was situated in Jezreel. Here Jezebel and all the others associated with Ahab's reign were assassinated by the followers of Jehu (2 Kings 9–10). The city of Jezreel has been identified with modern Zer'in.

5. The Old Testament name of the entire valley that separates Samaria from Galilee (Josh. 17:16). Some authors now refer to the western part of this valley as Esdraelon (Greek for "Jezreel"), while the name Jezreel is restricted to the eastern part of the valley.

The entire valley is the major corridor through the rugged Palestinian hills. It was a crossroads of two major routes: one leading from the Mediterranean Sea on the west to the Jordan River valley on the east, the other leading from Syria, Phoenicia, and Galilee in the north to the hill country of Judah and to the land of Egypt on the south. Throughout history, the Valley of Jezreel has been a major battlefield of nations.

JOAB [JO ab] (*the Lord is father*) — the name of three men and one village in the Old Testament:

1. One of the three sons of Zeruiah (2 Sam. 2:13; 8:16; 14:1; 17:25; 23:18, 37; 1 Kin. 1:7; 2:5, 22; 1 Chr. 11:6, 39; 18:15; 26:28; 27:24) who

was David's sister (or half-sister). Joab was the "general" or commander-in-chief of David's army (2 Sam. 5:8; 1 Chr. 11:6; 27:34).

Joab's father is not mentioned by name, but his tomb was at Bethlehem (2 Sam. 2:32). Joab's two brothers were Abishai and Asahel. When Asahel was killed by Abner (2 Sam. 2:18–23), Joab got revenge by killing Abner (2 Sam. 3:22–27).

When David and his army went to Jerusalem, in an attempt to capture that city (then called Jebus), he said, "Whoever attacks the Jebusites first shall be chief and captain" (1 Chr. 11:6). Joab led the assault at the storming of the Jebusite stronghold on Mount Zion, apparently climbing up into the city by way of a water shaft. The city was captured and Joab was made the general of David's army (2 Sam. 5:8).

Other military exploits by Joab were achieved against the Edomites (2 Sam. 8:13–14; 1 Kin. 11:15) and the Ammonites (2 Sam. 10:6–14; 11:1–27; 1 Chr. 19:6–15; 20:1–3). His character was deeply stained, as was David's, by his participation in the death of Uriah the Hittite (2 Sam. 11:14–25). In putting Absalom to death (2 Sam. 18:1–14), he apparently acted from a sense of duty.

When Absalom revolted against David, Joab remained loyal to David. Soon afterward, however, David gave command of his army to Amasa, Joab's cousin (2 Sam. 19:13; 20:1–13). Overcome by jealous hate, Joab killed Amasa (2 Sam. 20:8–13).

Another of David's sons, Adonijah, aspired to the throne, refusing to accept the fact that Solomon was not only David's choice but also the Lord's choice as the new king. Joab joined the cause of Adonijah against Solomon. Joab was killed by Benaiah, in accordance with Solomon's command and David's wishes. Joab fled to the tabernacle of the Lord, where he grasped the horns of the altar. Benaiah then struck him down with a sword. Joab was buried "in his own house in the wilderness" (1 Kin. 2:34).

2. A village apparently situated in Judah near Bethlehem (1 Chr. 2:54). The KJV translation, "Ataroth, the house of Joab," is better rendered by the NKJV, "Atroth Beth Joab."

3. A son of Seraiah and grandson of Kenaz (1 Chr. 4:13–14). He was the "father of Ge-Harashim" (1 Chr. 4:14), or the founder of a place in Judah called the "Valley of Craftsmen."

4. A man of the house of Pahath-Moab, some of whose descendants returned from the Exile with Zerubbabel (Ezra 2:6; 8:9; Neh. 7:11).

JOASH, JEHOASH [JOE ash, juh HOE ash] (*the Lord supports*) — the name of eight men in the Old Testament:

1. The father of Gideon (Judg. 6:11). Apparently Joash was an idolater who built an altar to Baal on his land. Gideon pulled down his father's altar, and the men of the city of Ophrah demanded that Joash put his son to death. But Joash refused, saying, "If he [Baal] is a god, let him plead for himself" (Judg. 6:31). After this event, Joash called his son Jerubbaal, which means "Let Baal plead" (Judg. 6:32).

2. A man who was commanded by Ahab, king of Israel, to imprison the prophet Micaiah (1 Kin. 22:26).

3. The eighth king of Judah; he was a son of King Ahaziah (2 Kin. 11:2) by Zibiah of Beersheba (2 Kin. 12:1). Joash was seven years old when he became king, and he reigned 40 years in Jerusalem (2 Chr. 24:1), from about 835 B.C. until 796 B.C. He is also called Jehoash (2 Kin. 11:21).

After Ahaziah died, Athaliah killed all the royal heirs to the throne. But God spared Joash through his aunt, Jehosheba, who hid him for six years in the house of the Lord (2 Kin. 11:2–3). When Joash reached the age of seven, Jehoiada the priest arranged for his coronation as king (2 Kin. 11:4–16).

Early in his reign, Joash repaired the temple and restored true religion to Judah, destroying Baal worship (2 Kin. 11:18–21). But the king who began so well faltered upon the loss of his advisor, Jehoiada. After Jehoiada died, Joash allowed idolatry to grow (2 Chr. 24:18). He even went so far as to have Zechariah, the son of Jehoiada, stoned to death for rebuking him (2 Chr.

24:20–22). God's judgment came quickly in the form of a Syrian invasion, which resulted in the wounding of Joash (2 Chr. 24:23–24). He was then killed by his own servants.

4. The thirteenth king of Israel; he was the son and successor of Jehoahaz, king of Israel, and was the grandson of Jehu, king of Israel. He is also called Jehoash (2 Kin. 13:10, 25; 14:8–17). Joash reigned in Samaria for 16 years (2 Kin. 13:9–10), from about 798 B.C. to 782/81 B.C. Israel was revived during the reign of Joash (2 Kin. 13:7), following a long period of suffering at the hands of the Syrians. But while achieving political success, Joash suffered spiritual bankruptcy: "He did evil in the sight of the LORD; he did not depart from all the sins of Jeroboam the son of Nebat, who had made Israel sin; but he walked in them" (2 Kin. 13:11). He was succeeded by his son Jeroboam II.

5. A descendant of Shelah, of the family of Judah (1 Chr. 4:22).

6. A descendant of Becher, of the family of Benjamin (1 Chr. 7:8).

7. A commander of the warriors who left Saul and joined David's army at Ziklag (1 Chr. 12:3).

8. An officer in charge of David's olive oil supplies (1 Chr. 27:28).

JOB [jobe] — the name of two men in the Old Testament:
1. The third son of Issachar, and founder of a tribal family, the Jashubites (Gen. 46:13). He is also called Jashub (Num. 26:24; 1 Chr. 7:1).

2. The central personality of the book of Job. He was noted for his perseverance (James 5:11) and unwavering faith in God, in spite of his suffering and moments of frustration and doubt. All the facts known about Job are contained in the Old Testament book that bears his name. He is described as "a man in the land of Uz" (Job 1:1) and "the greatest of all the people of

the East" (Job 1:3). Uz is probably a name for a region in Edom (Jer. 25:20; Lam. 4:21).

A prosperous man, Job had 7,000 sheep, 3,000 camels, 500 yoke of oxen, 500 female donkeys, and a large household, consisting of seven sons and three daughters. He was also "blameless and upright, and one who feared God and shunned evil" (Job 1:1).

Satan suggested to God that Job would remain righteous as long as it was financially profitable for him to do so. Then the Lord permitted Satan to test Job's faith in God. Blow after blow fell upon Job: his children, his servants, and his livestock were taken from him and he was left penniless. Nevertheless, "In all this Job did not sin nor charge God with wrong" (Job 1:22).

Satan continued his assault by sneering, "Touch his bone and his flesh, and he will surely curse You to Your face!" (Job 2:5). The Lord allowed Satan to afflict Job with painful boils from the soles of his feet to the crown of his head, so that Job sat in the midst of ashes and scraped his sores with a piece of pottery. "Do you still hold fast to your integrity?" his wife asked him. "Curse God and die!" (Job 2:9). But Job refused to curse God. "Shall we indeed accept good from God," he replied, "and shall we not accept adversity?" (Job 2:10).

Job's faith eventually triumphed over all adversity, and he was finally restored to more than his former prosperity. He had 14,000 sheep, 6,000 camels, 1,000 yoke of oxen, and 1,000 female donkeys. He also had seven sons and three daughters. He died at a ripe old age (Job 42:12–13, 16–17).

Job is a model of spiritual integrity—a person who held fast to his faith, without understanding the reason behind his suffering. He serves as a continuing witness to the possibility of authentic faith in God in the most troubling of circumstances.

JOEL [JOE uhl] (*the Lord is God*) — the name of 14 men in the Old Testament:

1. The oldest son of Samuel the prophet (1 Sam. 8:2; 1 Chr. 6:28; Vashni, KJV) and the father of Heman the singer (1 Chr. 6:33).

2. A leader of the tribe of Simeon (1 Chr. 4:35).

3. The father of Shemaiah, of the tribe of Reuben (1 Chr. 5:4).

4. A man of the tribe of Gad and a chief in the land of Bashan (1 Chr. 5:12).

5. A Levite ancestor of Samuel the prophet (1 Chr. 6:36).

6. A chief of the tribe of Issachar (1 Chr. 7:3).

7. One of David's mighty men (1 Chr. 11:38).

8. A Levite who helped bring the ark of the covenant from the house of Obed-Edom to Jerusalem (1 Chr. 15:7).

9. A keeper of the temple treasuries in David's time (1 Chr. 26:22).

10. A son of Pedaiah who lived during the time of David (1 Chr. 27:20).

11. A Levite who helped cleanse the temple during the reign of King Hezekiah of Judah (2 Chr. 29:12).

12. A son of Nebo who divorced his pagan wife after the captivity (Ezra 10:43).

13. Overseer of the Benjamites in Jerusalem in Nehemiah's government (Neh. 11:9).

14. An Old Testament prophet and author of the book of Joel. A citizen of Jerusalem, he spoke often of the priests and their duties (Joel 1:9, 13–14, 16). For this reason, many scholars believe he may have been a temple prophet. He also had an ear for nature (Joel 1:4–7), and included imagery from agriculture and the natural world in his messages.

JOHN THE APOSTLE — one of Jesus' disciples, the son of Zebedee, and the brother of James. Before his call by Jesus, John was a fisherman, along with his father and brother (Matt. 4:18–22; Mark 1:16–20). His mother was probably Salome (Matt.

27:56; Mark 15:40), who may have been a sister of Mary (John 19:25), the mother of Jesus.

Although it is not certain that Salome and Mary were sisters, if it were so it would make James and John cousins of Jesus. This would help explain Salome's forward request of Jesus on behalf of her sons (Matt. 20:20–28). The Zebedee family apparently lived in Capernaum on the north shore of the Sea of Galilee (Mark 1:21). The family must have been prosperous, because the father owned a boat and hired servants (Mark 1:19–20). Salome the mother provided for Jesus out of her substance (Mark 15:40–41; Luke 8:3). John must have been the younger of the two brothers, for he is always mentioned second to James in the Gospels of Matthew, Mark, and Luke.

The brothers Zebedee were called by Jesus after His baptism (Mark 1:19–20). This happened immediately after the call of two other brothers, Simon Peter and Andrew (Mark 1:16–18), with whom they may have been in partnership (Luke 5:10). Three of the four—Peter, James, and John—eventually became Jesus' most intimate disciples. They were present when Jesus healed the daughter of Jairus (Mark 5:37; Luke 8:51). They witnessed His transfiguration (Matt. 17:1–2; Mark 9:2; Luke 9:28–29), as well as His agony in Gethsemane (Matt. 26:37; Mark 14:33). Along with Peter, John was entrusted by Jesus with preparations for the Passover supper (Luke 22:8).

James and John must have contributed a headstrong element to Jesus' band of followers, because Jesus nicknamed them "Sons of Thunder" (Mark 3:17). On one occasion (Luke 9:51–56), when a Samaritan village refused to accept Jesus, the two offered to call down fire in revenge, as the prophet Elijah had once done (2 Kin. 1:10, 12). On another occasion, they earned the anger of their fellow disciples by asking if they could sit on Jesus' right and left hands in glory (Mark 10:35–45).

Following the ascension of Jesus, John continued in a prominent position of leadership among the disciples (Acts 1:13). He was present when Peter healed the lame man in the temple. Together with Peter he bore witness before the Sanhedrin to his faith in Jesus Christ. The boldness of their testimony brought the hostility of the Sanhedrin (Acts 3–4). When the apostles in Jerusalem received word of the evangelization of Samaria, they sent Peter and John to investigate whether the conversions were genuine (Acts 8:14–25). This was a curious thing to do. The Samaritans had long been suspect in the eyes of the Jews (John 4:9). John himself had once favored the destruction of a Samaritan village (Luke 9:51–56). That he was present on this mission suggests he had experienced a remarkable change.

In these episodes Peter appears as the leader and spokesman for the pair, but John's presence on such errands indicates his esteem by the growing circle of disciples. After the execution of his brother James by Herod Agrippa I, between A.D. 42–44 (Acts 12:1–2), John is not heard of again in Acts. Paul's testimony to John as one of the "pillars," along with Peter and James (the Lord's brother, Gal. 2:9), however, reveals that John continued to hold a position of respect and leadership in the early church.

As might be expected of one of Jesus' three closest disciples, John became the subject of an active and varied church tradition. Tertullian (about A.D. 160–220) said that John ended up in Rome, where he was "plunged, unhurt, into boiling oil." A much later tradition believed that both James and John were martyred. The dominant tradition, however, was that the apostle John moved to Ephesus in Asia Minor, and that from there he was banished to the island of Patmos (during Domitian's reign, A.D. 81–96). Tradition also held that he returned later to Ephesus, where he died some time after Trajan became emperor in A.D. 98.

Stories that John reclaimed a juvenile delinquent, raised a dead man, and opposed the Gnostic heretic Cerinthus survive from this era in his life. It was also the general opinion of the time that from Ephesus John composed the five writings that bear his name in the New Testament (gospel of John; 1, 2, and 3 John; and Revelation).

Only the Revelation identifies its author as John (1:1, 9). The second and third epistles of John identify the author as "the elder" (2 John 1; 3 John 1). Although 1 John and the gospel of John do not name their author, he can be none other than "the elder," because style and content in these writings are unmistakably related. It may be, as tradition asserts, that the apostle John wrote all five documents. It appears more likely, however, that four of the five writings were actually penned not by John the apostle but by John the elder, a disciple and friend of John's who relied directly on the apostle's testimony as he wrote the documents. This would explain those passages in the gospel that speak about the beloved disciple (who presumably is John the apostle; John 19:35; 21:24), as well as the reference to "the elder" in 2 and 3 John. The Revelation, however, was probably written directly by the apostle John himself.

JOHN THE BAPTIST — forerunner of Jesus; a moral reformer and preacher of messianic hope. According to Luke 1:36, Elizabeth and Mary, the mothers of John and Jesus, were either blood relatives or close kinswomen. Luke adds that both John and Jesus were announced, set apart, and named by the angel Gabriel even before their birth.

As is true of Jesus, practically nothing is known of John's boyhood, except that he "grew and became strong in spirit" (Luke 1:80). The silence of his early years, however, was broken by his thundering call to repentance some time around A.D. 28–29, shortly before Jesus began His ministry. Matthew reports that the place where John preached was the wilderness of Judea (3:1). It is likely that he also preached in Perea, east of the Jordan River. Perea, like Galilee, lay within the jurisdiction of Herod Antipas, under whom John was later arrested.

The four Gospels are unanimous in their report that John lived "in the wilderness." There he was raised (Luke 1:80) and was called by God (Luke 3:2), and there he preached (Mark 1:4) until his execution. The wilderness—a vast badland of crags, wind, and heat—was the place where God had dwelled with His people after the Exodus. Ever since, it had been the place of religious hope for Israel. John called the people away from the comforts of their homes and cities and out into the wilderness, where they might meet God.

The conviction that God was about to begin a new work among this unprepared people broke upon John with the force of a desert storm. He was called to put on the prophet's hairy mantle with the resolve and urgency of Elijah himself. Not only did he dress like Elijah, in camel's hair and leather belt (2 Kin. 1:8; Mark 1:6), he understood his ministry to be one of reform and preparation, just as Elijah did (Luke 1:17). In the popular belief of the time, it was believed that Elijah would return from heaven to prepare the way for the Messiah (Mal. 4:5–6). John reminded the people of Elijah because of his dress and behavior (Matt. 11:14; Mark 9:12–13).

John was no doubt as rugged as the desert itself. Nevertheless, his commanding righteousness drew large crowds to hear him. What they encountered from this "voice ... crying in the wilderness" (Mark 1:3) was a call to moral renewal, baptism, and a messianic hope.

The bite of John's moral challenge is hard for us to appreciate today. His command to share clothing and food (Luke 3:11) was a painful jab at a society that was hungry to acquire material objects. When he warned the tax collectors not to take more money than they had coming to them (Luke 3:12–13), he exposed the greed that had drawn persons to such positions in the first place. And the soldiers, whom he told to be content with their wages, must have winced at the thought of not using their power to take advantage of the common people (Luke 3:14).

John's baptism was a washing, symbolizing moral regeneration, administered to each candidate only once. He criticized the people for presuming to be righteous and secure with God because they were children of Abraham (Matt. 3:9). John laid an ax to the root of this presumption. He warned that they, the Jews, would be purged and rejected unless they demonstrated fruits of repentance (Matt. 3:7–12).

John's effort at moral reform, symbolized by baptism, was his way of preparing Israel to meet God. He began his preaching with the words "Prepare the way of the Lord, make His paths straight" (Mark 1:3). He had a burning awareness of one who was to come after him who would baptize in fire and Spirit (Mark 1:7–8). John was a forerunner of this mightier one, a herald of the messianic hope that would dawn in Jesus.

John was a forerunner of Jesus not only in his ministry and message (Matt. 3:1; 4:17) but also in his death. Not until John's arrest did Jesus begin His ministry (Mark 1:14), and John's execution foreshadowed Jesus' similar fate. Imprisoned by Antipas in the fortress of Machaerus on the lonely hills east of the Dead Sea, John must have grown disillusioned by his own failure and the developing failure he sensed in Jesus' mission. He sent messengers to ask Jesus, "Are You the Coming One, or do we look for another?" (Matt. 11:3). John was eventually killed by a functionary of a puppet king who allowed himself to be swayed by a scheming wife, a loose daughter-in-law, and the people around him (Mark 6:14–29).

Josephus records that Herod arrested and executed John because he feared his popularity might lead to a revolt. The Gospels reveal it was because John spoke out against Herod's immoral marriage to Herodias, the wife of his brother Philip (Mark 6:17–19). The accounts are complementary, because

John's moral righteousness must have fanned many a smoldering political hope to life.

Jesus said of John, "Among those born of women there has not risen one greater than John the Baptist" (Matt. 11:11). He was the last and greatest of the prophets (Matt. 11:13–14). Nevertheless, he stood, like Moses, on the threshold of the promised land. He did not enter the kingdom of God proclaimed by Jesus; and consequently, "he who is least in the kingdom of heaven is greater than he" (Matt. 11:11).

John's influence continued to live on after his death. When Paul went to Ephesus nearly 30 years later, he found a group of John's disciples (Acts 19:1–7). Some of his disciples must have thought of John in messianic terms. This compelled the author of the gospel of John, writing also from Ephesus some 60 years after the Baptist's death, to emphasize Jesus' superiority (John 1:19–27; 3:30).

JONAH [JOE nuh] (*a dove*) — the prophet who was first swallowed by a great fish before he obeyed God's command to preach repentance to the Assyrian city of Nineveh. Jonah was not always a reluctant spokesman for the Lord. He is the same prophet who predicted the remarkable expansion of Israel's territory during the reign of Jeroboam II (ruled about 793–753 B.C.; 2 Kin. 14:25). This passage indicates that Jonah, the son of Amittai, was from Gath Hepher, a town in Zebulun in the northern kingdom of Israel.

While Jonah is described as a servant of the Lord in 2 Kings 14:25, he is a sad and somewhat tragic figure in the book bearing his name. It is a mark of the integrity and reliability of the Bible that a prophet like Jonah is described in such a candid manner. The natural tendency of human writers would be to obscure and hide such a character. But the Spirit of God presents valiant heroes along with petty people to illustrate truth, no matter how weak and unpleasant these characters may have been. We know nothing of Jonah after he returned to Israel from his preaching venture in Nineveh.

JONATHAN [JAHN uh thuhn] (*the Lord has given*) — the name of 14 men in the Old Testament:

1. A Levite from Bethlehem in Judah (Judg. 17:7–9) who was employed by Micah. Jonathan became the priest at Micah's idol shrine in the mountains of Ephraim. When the tribe of the Danites took Micah's graven image, ephod, household idols, and molded image (Judg. 18:18), Jonathan went with them. Jonathan and the Danites settled in the newly captured city of Dan (formerly Laish), and he became their priest (Judges 17–18).

2. The oldest son of King Saul and a close friend of David. The first time Jonathan is mentioned in Scripture he is described as a commander of 1,000 men (1 Sam. 13:2). When Jonathan attacked the Philistine garrison at Geba, his action brought swift retaliation by the Philistines, who subdued and humiliated the Israelites. But Jonathan and his armorbearer courageously attacked the Philistine garrison at Michmash and were successful. This action inspired the Israelites to overthrow their oppressors (1 Sam. 14:1–23).

Perhaps the best-known fact about Jonathan is his close friendship with David. He made a covenant with David (1 Sam. 18:3–4) and warned David of Saul's plot against his life (1 Sam. 19:1–2). When Saul sought David's life, Jonathan interceded on behalf of David, and Saul reinstated David to his good favor (1 Sam. 19:1–7). Jonathan's loyalty to David was proven time after time as he warned David of Saul's threats of vengeance (1 Samuel 20) and encouraged David in times of danger (1 Sam. 23:16, 18).

The tragic end for Jonathan came at Mount Gilboa when he, his father Saul, and two of his brothers were slain by the Philistines (1 Sam. 31:1–2; 1 Chr. 10:1–6). When David heard of this, he mourned and fasted (2 Sam. 1:12). He then composed a lamentation, the "Song of the Bow," in which he poured out his grief over the death of Saul and Jonathan (2 Sam. 1:17–27).

Because David loved Jonathan, he treated Jonathan's lame son, Mephibosheth, kindly (2 Sam. 9:1–13). As a final act of love and respect, David brought the bones of Saul and Jonathan from Jabesh Gilead and buried them "in the country of Benjamin in Zelah, in the tomb of Kish his father" (2 Sam. 21:12–14). In this way David honored God's anointed king, Saul, and recognized the loyal, unselfish love of his friend. The story of David and Jonathan is a good example of the unselfish nature of love.

3. A son of Abiathar, a high priest in David's time (2 Sam. 15:27, 36; 17:17, 20). During Absalom's rebellion, when David and his supporters were forced to flee from Jerusalem, Jonathan relayed messages to David about developments in Jerusalem.

4. A son of Shimeah (2 Sam. 21:21), or Shimea (1 Chr. 20:7), one of David's brothers.

5. One of David's mighty men (1 Chr. 11:34).

6. A son of Jada (1 Chr. 2:32).

7. An uncle of David. Jonathan was "a counselor, a wise man, and a scribe" (1 Chr. 27:32).

8. The father of Ebed (Ezra 8:6).

9. A son of Asahel who opposed Ezra's proposal that pagan wives should be divorced (Ezra 10:15).

10. A descendant of Jeshua the high priest (Neh. 12:10–11), also called Johanan (Neh. 12:22).

11. A priest descended from Melichu (Neh. 12:14).

12. A priest descended from Shemaiah (Neh. 12:35), also called Jehonathan (Neh. 12:18).

13. A scribe in whose house Jeremiah the prophet was imprisoned (Jer. 37:15; 38:26).

14. A son of Kareah who joined Gedaliah after the fall of Jerusalem (Jer. 40:8).

JOPPA [JAH puh] (*beautiful*) — an ancient seaport city on the Mediterranean Sea, about 56 kilometers (35 miles) northwest of Jerusalem.

A walled city, Joppa was built about 35 meters (116 feet) high on a rocky ledge overlooking the Mediterranean. It supposedly received its name "beautiful" from the sunlight that its buildings reflected. The first mention of Joppa in the Bible indicates it was part of the territory inherited by the tribe of Dan (Josh. 19:46; Japho, KJV). The only natural harbor on the Mediterranean between Egypt and Acco, it was the seaport for the city of Jerusalem and the site of significant shipping in both Old and New Testament times. Rafts of cedar logs from the forests of Lebanon were floated from Tyre and Sidon to Joppa and then transported overland to Jerusalem to be used in building Solomon's temple (2 Chr. 2:16).

In New Testament times Joppa was the home of a Christian disciple, Tabitha (or Dorcas), a woman "full of good works and charitable deeds" (Acts 9:36). After she became sick and died, she was raised to life by Simon Peter. As a result, many believed on the Lord (Acts 9:36–42).

Joppa was also the home of Simon the tanner (Acts 10:32). Simon Peter stayed many days in Joppa with Simon. On the roof of Simon's house, Peter received his vision of a great sheet descending from heaven (Acts 10:9–16)—a vision that indicated that all who believe in Christ, Gentiles as well as Jews, are accepted by God.

JOSEPH [JOE zeph] (*may he add*) — the name of several men in the Bible:

1. The eleventh son of Jacob (Gen. 30:24). Joseph was sold into slavery and later rose to an important position in the Egyptian government. The account of Joseph's life is found in Genesis 37–50.

Joseph was the first child of Rachel (30:24) and his father's favorite son (37:31). This is most clearly shown by the special coat that Jacob gave to Joseph. This favoritism eventually brought serious trouble for the whole family. Joseph's ten older brothers hated him because he was Jacob's favorite and because Joseph had dreams that he interpreted to his brothers in a conceited way. It is no surprise that Joseph's brothers hated him enough to kill him (37:4).

Joseph's brothers were shepherds in the land of Canaan. One day Jacob sent Joseph to search for his brothers, who were tending the flocks in the fields. When Joseph found them, they seized upon the chance to kill him. The only opposing voice was Reuben's, but they finally sold Joseph into slavery to passing merchants. To hide the deed from their father, Jacob, Joseph's brothers took his coat and dipped it in animal blood. When Jacob saw the coat, he was convinced that Joseph had been killed by a wild animal (37:34–35).

Joseph was taken to Egypt, where he was sold to Potiphar, an officer of the ruling pharaoh of the nation. His good conduct soon earned him the highest position in the household. Potiphar's wife became infatuated with Joseph and tempted him to commit adultery with her. When he refused, she accused him of the crime and Joseph was sent to prison.

While in prison, Joseph's behavior earned him a position of responsibility over the other prisoners. Among the prisoners Joseph met were the pharaoh's baker and his butler. When each of them had a dream, Joseph interpreted their dreams. When the butler left prison, he failed to intercede on Joseph's behalf, and Joseph spent two more years in prison. When the pharaoh had dreams that none of his counselors could interpret, the butler remembered Joseph and mentioned him to the pharaoh. Then Joseph was called to appear before the pharaoh. He interpreted the pharaoh's dreams, predicting seven years of plentiful food, followed by seven years of famine. He also advised the pharaoh to appoint a commissioner to store up supplies during the plentiful years. To Joseph's surprise, the pharaoh appointed him as food commissioner. This was a position of great prestige. Under Joseph's care, many supplies were stored and the land prospered (41:37–57). Joseph was given many comforts, including servants and a wife. He was called Zaphenath-Paneah. When the famine struck, Joseph was second only to the pharaoh in power. People from all surrounding lands came to buy food from him.

Many years passed between Joseph's arrival in Egypt as a slave and his rise to power in the nation during the famine. The famine also struck Canaan, and Joseph's brothers eventually came to Egypt to buy grain. When they met Joseph, they did not recognize him. He recognized them, however, and decided to test them to see if they had changed. He accused them of being spies. Then he sold them grain only on the condition that Simeon stay as a hostage until they brought Benjamin, the youngest brother, to Egypt with them. Upon returning to Canaan, the brothers told Jacob of their experiences. He vowed not to send Benjamin to Egypt. But the continuing famine forced him to change his mind. On the next trip Benjamin went with his brothers to Egypt. When they arrived, Joseph treated them royally, weeping openly at the sight of his youngest brother. Simeon was returned to them. After purchasing their grain, they started home. On their way home, however, they were stopped by one of Joseph's servants, who accused them of stealing Joseph's silver cup. The cup was found in Benjamin's bag, where Joseph had placed it. The brothers returned to face Joseph, who declared that Benjamin must stay in Egypt. At this point Judah pleaded with Joseph, saying that it would break their father Jacob's heart if Benjamin failed to return with them. Judah's offer to stay in Benjamin's place is one of the most moving passages in the Old Testament. Joseph was overcome with emotion. He revealed himself to them as their brother, whom they had sold into slavery years earlier. At first Joseph's brothers were afraid that Joseph would take revenge against them, but soon they were convinced that Joseph's forgiveness was genuine. Judah's plea on Benjamin's behalf was evidence of the change that Joseph had hoped to find in his brothers. He sent them back to Canaan with gifts for his father and invited the family to come live in Egypt. The grace of God working in the family of Jacob is evident in the way Joseph dealt with his brothers. Joseph did not want revenge against them. He realized that his personal suffering had preserved the family as an instrument of God's will. Joseph also was aware that his rise to power was for the good of his family, not for his own glory (45:7–8).

2. The father of one of the spies sent into Canaan (Num. 13:7).

3. A son of Asaph (1 Chr. 25:2, 9).

4. One who married a foreign wife during the Exile (Ezra 10:42).

5. A priest of the family of Shebaniah (Neh. 12:14).

6. The husband of Mary, mother of Jesus (Matt. 1:16–24; 2:13; Luke 1:27; 2:4).

7. A converted Jew of Arimathea in whose tomb Jesus was laid (Matt. 27:57, 59; Luke 23:50–53).

8.–10. Three different ancestors of Christ, about whom little is known (Luke 3:24, 26, 30).

11. A disciple (known also as Barsabas and Justus) considered to take the place of Judas Iscariot (Acts 1:23).

JOSHUA [JAHSH oo uh] (*the Lord is salvation*) — the successor to Moses and the man who led the nation of Israel to conquer and settle the promised land.

Joshua was born in Egypt. He went through the great events of the Passover and the Exodus with Moses and all the Hebrew people who escaped from slavery in Egypt at the hand of their Redeemer God. In the Wilderness of Sinai, Moses took his assistant Joshua with him when he went into the mountains to talk with God (Ex. 24:13). Moses also gave Joshua a prominent place at the Tabernacle. As Moses' servant, Joshua would remain at the tabernacle as his representative while the great leader left the camp to fellowship with the Lord (Ex. 33:11).

When Moses sent spies to scout out the land of Canaan, Joshua was selected as the representative of the tribe of Ephraim (Num. 13:8). Only Joshua and Caleb returned to the camp with a report that they could conquer the land with God's help. The other ten spies complained that they were "like grasshoppers" in comparison to the Canaanites (Num. 13:33). Because of their show of faith, Joshua and Caleb were allowed to enter the land at the end of their years of wandering in the wilderness. But all the other Israelites who lived at that time died before the nation entered the promised land (Num. 14:30).

At Moses' death, Joshua was chosen as his successor (Josh. 1:1–2). He led the Israelites to conquer the land (Joshua 1–2), supervised the division of the territory among the 12 tribes, and led the people to renew their covenant with God (Joshua 13–22).

When Joshua died at the age of 110, he was buried in the land of his inheritance at Timnath Serah (Josh. 24:30). As Moses' successor, Joshua completed the work that this great leader had begun. Moses led Israel out of Egypt; Joshua led Israel into Canaan. Joshua's name, an Old Testament form of Jesus, means "the Lord is salvation." By his name and by his life, he demonstrated the salvation that comes from God.

JOSIAH [joe SIGH uh] — the name of two men in the Old Testament:

1. The sixteenth king of Judah, the son of Amon, and the grandson of Manasseh (2 Kin. 21:23–23:30). The three decades of Josiah's reign were characterized by peace, prosperity, and reform. Hence, they were among the happiest years experienced by Judah. King Josiah devoted himself to pleasing God

and reinstituting Israel's observance of the Mosaic law. That a wicked king like Amon could have such a godly son and successor is a tribute to the grace of God. The Bible focuses almost exclusively on Josiah's spiritual reform, which climaxed in the 18th year of his reign with the discovery of the Book of the Law.

Josiah's reform actually occurred in three stages. Ascending to the throne at age eight, he apparently was blessed with God-fearing advisors who resisted the idolatrous influence of his father. More important, however, at the age of 16 (stage one), Josiah personally "began to seek the God of his father David" (2 Chr. 34:3).

At the age of 20 (stage two), Josiah began to cleanse Jerusalem and the land of Judah of idolatrous objects (2 Chr. 34:3–7). His reform was even more extensive than that of his predecessor, Hezekiah (2 Kin. 18:4; 2 Chr. 29:3–36). Josiah extended his cleansing of the land into the territory of fallen Israel; at the time Israel was nominally controlled by Assyria. Josiah personally supervised the destruction of the altars of the Baals, the incense altars, the wooden images, the carved images, and the molded images as far north as the cities of Naphtali. Josiah's efforts were aided by the death of the great Assyrian king, Ashurbanipal, which brought about a serious decline in Assyria's power and allowed Josiah freedom to pursue his reforms.

At the age of 26 (stage three), Josiah ordered that the temple be repaired under the supervision of Hilkiah, the high priest. In the process, a copy of the book of the Law was discovered (2 Chr. 34:14–15). When it was read to Josiah, he was horrified to learn how far Judah had departed from the law of God. This discovery provided a new momentum for the reformation that was already in progress.

In 609 B.C. Josiah attempted to block Pharaoh Necho II of Egypt as he marched north to assist Assyria in her fight with Babylon for world supremacy. Despite the pharaoh's assurance to the contrary, Josiah saw Necho's northern campaign as a threat to Judah's security. When he engaged Necho in battle at Megiddo, Josiah was seriously injured. He was returned to Jerusalem, where he died after reigning 31 years. His death was followed by widespread lamentation (2 Chr. 35:20–27). In the New Testament, Josiah is referred to as Josias (Matt. 1:10, KJV).

2. A captive who returned to Jerusalem from Babylon in Zechariah's day (Zech. 6:10), also called Hen (Zech. 6:14).

JUDAH [JOO duh] (*praise*) — the name of seven men and a place in the Old Testament:

1. The fourth son of Jacob and Leah and the founder of the family out of which the messianic line came (Gen. 29:35; Num. 26:19–21; Matt. 1:2).

Judah was one of the most prominent of the 12 sons of Jacob. He saved Joseph's life by suggesting that his brothers sell Joseph to Ishmaelite merchants rather than kill him (Gen. 37:26–28). In Egypt it was Judah who begged Joseph to detain him rather than Benjamin, Jacob's beloved son. In an eloquent speech Judah confessed what he and his brothers had done to Joseph; shortly thereafter, Joseph identified himself to his brothers (Gen. 44:14–45:1).

It appears that Judah was the leader of Jacob's sons who remained at home. Even though he was not the oldest son, Judah was sent by Jacob to precede him to Egypt (Gen. 46:28). Also Judah, rather than his older brothers, received Jacob's blessing (Gen. 49:3–10). In that blessing, Jacob foretold the rise of Judah: "Your father's children shall bow down before you.... The scepter shall not depart from Judah ... until Shiloh comes" (Gen. 49:8, 10).

Judah had three sons: Er, Onan, and Shelah (Gen. 38:3–5). Er and Onan were killed by divine judgment because of their sins (Gen. 38:7–10). Judah also fathered twin sons, Perez and Zerah, by Tamar, Er's widow (Gen. 38:29–30). The line of Judah ran through Perez to David and thus became the messianic line (Luke 3:30; Judas, KJV).

2. An ancestor of certain Israelites who helped rebuild the temple after the captivity (Ezra 3:9).

3. A Levite who divorced his pagan wife after returning from the captivity (Ezra 10:23).

4. A son of Senuah (Neh. 11:9).

5. A Levite who returned from the captivity with Zerubbabel (Neh. 12:8).

6. A leader of Judah who participated in the dedication of the Jerusalem wall (Neh. 12:34).

7. A musician and son of a priest (Neh. 12:36).

8. A place on the border of Naphtali (Josh. 19:34).

JUDAS [JOO duhs] (*praise*) — the name of five men in the New Testament:

1. One of the four brothers of Jesus (Matt. 13:55; Mark 6:3; Juda, KJV). Some scholars believe he was the author of the Epistle of Jude.

2. One of the twelve apostles of Jesus. John is careful to distinguish him from Judas Iscariot (John 14:22). He is called "Judas the son of James" (Luke 6:16; Acts 1:13). In the list of the Twelve given in Mark, instead of "Judas ... of James" a Thaddaeus is mentioned (Mark 3:18). Matthew has Lebbaeus, whose surname was Thaddaeus (Matt. 10:3). He was also called Judas the Zealot. Tradition says he preached in Assyria and Persia and died a martyr in Persia.

3. Judas of Galilee (Acts 5:37). In the days of the census (Luke 2:2), he led a revolt against Rome. He was killed, and his followers were scattered. According to the Jewish historian Josephus, Judas founded a sect whose main belief was that their only ruler and lord was God.

4. A man with whom the apostle Paul stayed in Damascus after his conversion (Acts 9:11).

5. A disciple surnamed Barsabas who belonged to the church in Jerusalem. The apostles and elders of that church chose Judas and Silas to accompany Paul and Barnabas to Antioch; together they conveyed to the church in that city the decree of the Jerusalem Council about circumcision.

JUDAS ISCARIOT [JOO duhs iss KAR ih uht] — the disciple who betrayed Jesus. Judas was the son of Simon (John 6:71), or of Simon Iscariot (NRSV). The term "Iscariot," which is used to distinguish Judas from the other disciple named Judas (Luke 6:16; John 14:22; Acts 1:13), refers to his hometown of Kerioth, in southern Judah (Josh. 15:25). Thus, Judas was a Judean, the only one of the Twelve who was not from Galilee.

The details of Judas's life are sketchy. Because of his betrayal of Jesus, Judas, however, is even more of a mystery. It must be assumed that Jesus saw promise in Judas, or He would not have called him to be a disciple. Judas's name appears in three of the lists of the disciples (Matt. 10:2–4; Mark 3:16–19; Luke 6:14–16), although it always appears last. His name is missing from the list of the 11 disciples in Acts 1:13; by that time Judas had already committed suicide. Judas must have been an important disciple, because he served as their treasurer (John 12:6; 13:29).

During the week of the Passover festival, Judas went to the chief priests and offered to betray Jesus for a reward (Matt. 26:14–16; Mark 14:10–11). At the Passover supper, Jesus announced that He would be betrayed and that He knew who His betrayer was—one who dipped his hand with him in the dish (Mark 14:20), the one to whom He would give the piece of bread used in eating (John 13:26–27). Jesus was saying that a friend, one who dipped out of the same dish as He, was His betrayer. These verses in John indicate that Judas probably was reclining beside Jesus, evidence that Judas was an important disciple.

Jesus said to Judas, "What you do, do quickly" (John 13:27). Judas left immediately after he ate (John 13:30). The first observance of the Lord's Supper was probably celebrated afterward, without Judas (Matt. 26:26–29).

Judas carried out his betrayal in the Garden of Gethsemane. By a prearranged sign, Judas singled out Jesus for the soldiers by kissing him. The Gospels do not tell us why Judas was needed to point out Jesus, who had become a well-known figure. It is possible that Judas disclosed where Jesus would be that night, so that He could be arrested secretly without the knowledge of His many supporters (Matt. 26:47–50).

Matthew reports that, realizing what he had done, Judas attempted to return the money to the priests. When the priests refused to take it, Judas threw the money on the temple floor, went out, and hanged himself. Unwilling to use "blood money" for the temple, the priests bought a potter's field, which became known as the "Field of Blood" (Matt. 27:3–10). This field is traditionally located at the point where the Kidron, Tyropoeon, and Hinnom valleys come together.

It is difficult to understand why Judas betrayed Jesus. Since he had access to the disciples' treasury, it seems unlikely that he did it for the money only; 30 pieces of silver is a relatively small amount. Some have suggested that Judas thought that his betrayal would force Jesus into asserting His true power and overthrowing the Romans. Others have suggested that Judas might have become convinced that Jesus was a false messiah, and that the true Messiah was yet to come, or that he was upset over Jesus' apparent indifference to the law and His association with sinners and his violation of the Sabbath. Whatever the reason, Judas's motive remains shrouded in mystery. Acts 1:20 quotes Psalm 109:8 as the basis for electing another person to fill the place vacated by Judas: "Let another take his office." When the 11 remaining apostles cast lots for Judas's replacement, "the lot fell on Matthias. And he was numbered with the eleven apostles" (Acts 1:26).

JUDE [jood] (*praise*) — the author of the Epistle of Jude, in which he is described as "a servant of Jesus Christ, and brother of James" (Jude 1). Jude is an English form of the name Judas. Many scholars believe that the James mentioned in this passage is James the brother of Jesus. In Matthew 13:55 the people said concerning Jesus, "Is this not the carpenter's son? Is not His mother called Mary? And His brothers James, Joses, Simon, and Judas?" (Mark 6:3).

If Jude (Judas) was the brother of James and of Jesus, Jude did not believe in Him (John 7:5) until after Jesus' resurrection (Acts 1:14).

KADESH, KADESH BARNEA [KAY desh bar NEE uh] *(consecrated)* — a wilderness region between Egypt and the land of Canaan where the Hebrew people camped after the Exodus. Kadesh Barnea (the modern oasis of Ain el-Qudeirat) was situated on the edge of Edom (Num. 20:16) about 114 kilometers (70 miles) from Hebron and 61 kilometers (50 miles) from Beersheba in the Wilderness of Zin. Kadesh Barnea is also said to be in the Wilderness of Paran (Num. 13:26). Paran was probably the general name for the larger wilderness area, while Zin may have been the specific name for a smaller portion of the wilderness territory.

The first mention of Kadesh Barnea occurred during the time of Abraham. Chedorlaomer, king of Elam, and his allied armies waged war against the Amalekites and Amorites from Kadesh (Gen. 14:7). When Hagar was forced by Sarah to flee from Abraham's home, she was protected by the angel of the Lord, who brought her to the well Beer Lahai Roi, between Kadesh and Bered (16:14). Later Abraham moved to Gerar, situated between Kadesh and Shur (20:1).

The most important contacts of the Israelites with Kadesh Barnea occurred during the years of the wilderness wanderings. During the second year after the Exodus from Egypt, the Israelites camped around Mount Horeb, or Sinai. God told them to leave Sinai and take an 11-day journey to Kadesh Barnea (Num. 10:11–12; Deut. 1:2). From here the people would have direct entry into the land of Canaan. Moses selected one man from each tribe as a spy and sent them to "spy out the land" (Num. 13:2). After 40 days they returned with grapes and other fruits, proving Canaan to be a fertile, plentiful land.

Ten of these spies reported giants in the land, implying that Israel was too weak to enter Canaan (Num. 13:33). But two of the spies, Joshua and Caleb, said, "Do not fear" (Num. 14:9). The people wanted to stone the two for their report (Num. 14:10), and they went so far as to ask for another leader to take them back to Egypt.

Because of their fear and rebellion at Kadesh (Deut. 9:23), the Israelites were forced to wander in the Wilderness of Paran for 38 years. Kadesh apparently was their headquarters while they moved about during these years. In the first month of the 40th year of the Exodus, the people again assembled at Kadesh for their final march to the promised land.

While they were still camped at Kadesh, a number of the leaders of the people rebelled against Moses and Aaron (Num. 16:1–3). They were killed in an earthquake (16:31, 32). Miriam, Moses' sister, also died and was buried (20:1). At Kadesh, Moses also disobeyed God by striking the rock to bring forth water (20:8–11). He had been told to speak, not strike the rock. Soon after Moses and the people began to move from Kadesh toward Canaan, Aaron died and was buried (20:23–29).

KETURAH [keh TUR uh] — a wife of Abraham (Gen. 25:1, 4), also called Abraham's concubine (1 Chr. 1:32–33). Some suggest that Keturah had been Abraham's "concubine-wife," before the death of Sarah. After Sarah died, Keturah was then elevated to the full status of Abraham's wife. Keturah bore to Abraham six sons: Zimran, Jokshan, Medan, Midian,

Ishbak, and Shuah (Gen. 25:1–4). These men were the founders or ancestors of six Arabian tribes in southern and eastern Palestine. Late Arabian genealogies mention a tribe by the name of Katura dwelling near Mecca.

Keturah's sons were not on the same level as Abraham's promised son, Isaac. Through Isaac God would carry out His promise to Abraham to make of his descendants a chosen people. While he was still alive, therefore, Abraham gave Keturah's sons gifts and sent them to "the country of the east" (Gen. 25:6).

Abraham was already advanced in years when he married Keturah. She brought him both companionship and children in his old age. Keturah apparently outlived Abraham (Gen. 25:7).

KIDRON [KIH drun] (*gloomy*) — a valley on the eastern slope of Jerusalem through which a seasonal brook of the same name runs. The meaning of the name is fitting, in view of the great strife that has surrounded the Kidron throughout Bible times. A torrent in the winter rains, it contains little water in the summer months.

The ravine of the Kidron valley begins north of Jerusalem, running past the temple, Calvary, the Garden of Gethsemane, and the Mount of Olives to form a well-defined limit to Jerusalem on its eastern side. From there the valley and the brook reach into the Judean wilderness, where the land is so dry that the brook takes the name of Wady en-Nar or "fire wady." Finally its dreary course brings it to the Dead Sea. Kidron was the brook crossed by David while fleeing from Absalom (2 Sam. 15:23, 30). While the brook is not large, the deep ravine is a significant geographical obstacle. When David crossed the Kidron and turned east to retreat from Absalom to the safety of Hebron, he signaled his abandonment of Jerusalem (2 Sam. 15:23).

On the west side of the Kidron is the spring of Gihon, which King Hezekiah tapped for city water before the Assyrians besieged Jerusalem. Hezekiah also blocked the Kidron and lesser springs in the valley to deny water to the besieging Assyrians.

Asa, Hezekiah, and Josiah, the great reforming kings of Judah, burned the idols and objects of worship of the pagan cults that they suppressed in the Kidron valley (1 Kin. 15:13). Beside the brook King Asa destroyed and burned his mother's idol of Asherah (1 Kin. 15:13). After this, the valley became the regular receptacle for the impurities and abominations of idol worship when they were removed from the temple and destroyed (2 Kin. 23:4, 6, 12; 2 Chr. 29:16; 30:14).

From the Kidron valley Nehemiah inspected the walls of Jerusalem at night, probably because the walls were clearly visible along that side (Neh. 2:15). In the time of Josiah, this valley was the common cemetery of Jerusalem (2 Kin. 23:6; Jer. 26:23). When Jesus left Jerusalem for the Garden of Gethsemane on the night of His arrest, He crossed the Kidron along the way.

KIR HARASETH [kir HAHR uh seth] — a fortified city of Moab (2 Kin. 3:25), also spelled Kir Hareseth (Is. 16:7), Kir Heres (Is. 16:11; Jer. 48:31, 36), and Kirharesh (Is. 16:11, KJV). Kir of Moab (Is. 15:1) is also thought to be identical with Kir Haraseth.

Mesha, king of Moab, fled to Kir Haraseth after he was defeated by Jehoram, king of Israel, and Jehoshaphat, king of Judah. Accompanied by the king of Edom, these two rulers crushed the rebellion Mesha had started (2 Kin. 3:4). Because Kir Haraseth was the only city of Moab that could not be overthrown, it was the last refuge of Mesha (2 Kin. 3:25).

The prophets foretold God's certain destruction of Kir Haraseth, a seemingly invincible city (Is. 16:7). Many commentators identify Kir Haraseth with present-day el-Kerak, about 80 kilometers (50 miles) southeast of Jerusalem.

KIRJATH JEARIM [KIR jath JEE uh rim] (*city of forests*) — a fortified city that originally belonged to the Gibeonites. Kirjath Jearim is first mentioned as a member of a Gibeonite confederation of four fortress cities, which also included Gibeon, Chephirah, and Beeroth (Josh. 9:17). Kirjath Jearim was also known as Baalah (Josh. 15:9), Baale Judah (2 Sam. 6:2), and Kirjath Baal (Josh. 15:60), and Kirjath (Josh. 18:28, NKJV, KJV). These names suggest that perhaps it was an old Canaanite "high place," a place of idolatrous worship.

Originally assigned to the tribe of Judah (Josh. 15:60), and later assigned to Benjamin (Josh. 18:14–15, 28), Kirjath Jearim was on the western part of the boundary line between Judah and Benjamin (Josh. 15:9). When the ark of the covenant was returned to the Israelites by the Philistines, it was brought from Beth Shemesh to Kirjath Jearim and entrusted to a man named Eleazar (1 Sam. 7:1–2). The ark remained in Kirjath Jearim, in the house of Abinadab, the father of Eleazar, for many years. It was from here that David transported the ark to Jerusalem (2 Sam. 6:2–3).

KISH [kish] — the name of four men in the Old Testament:
1. The father of King Saul (1 Chr. 12:1).

2. A Levite who lived in David's time (1 Chr. 23:21–22; 24:29). He was a son of Mahli and a grandson of Merari.

3. A Levite who helped cleanse the temple during the reign of King Hezekiah of Judah (2 Chr. 29:12).

4. A Benjamite ancestor of Mordecai (Esth. 2:5).

KISHON [KIGH shuhn] — a river in Palestine, which flows from sources on Mount Tabor and Mount Gilboa westward through the Plain of Esdraelon and the Valley of Jezreel, then empties into the Mediterranean Sea near the northern base of Mount Carmel. Because the Kishon falls slightly as it crosses the level plain, it often becomes swollen and floods much of the valley during the season of heavy rains.

At the river Kishon the Israelites won a celebrated victory over Sisera under the leadership of Deborah and Barak (Judg. 4:7). Fully armed with 900 chariots of iron (Judg. 4:13), the forces of Sisera became bogged down in the overflow of the Kishon (Judg. 5:21), and the Israelites defeated them. It was at the brook Kishon, also, that the prophets of Baal were executed following their contest with Elijah on Mount Carmel (1 Kin. 18:40).

L

LABAN [LAY bihn] (*white*) — father-in-law of Jacob. Laban lived in the city of Nahor in Padan Aram where Abraham sent his servant to find a wife for Isaac. Laban, brother of Rebekah, is introduced when he heard of the servant's presence, saw the golden jewelry given Rebekah, and eagerly invited Abraham's emissary into their home (Gen. 24:29–60). Laban played an important role in the marriage arrangements. His stubbornness and greed characterized his later dealings with Rebekah's son, Jacob.

Many years later, Jacob left home to escape Esau's wrath. At the well of Haran he met Rachel, Laban's daughter. Laban promised her to his nephew Jacob in return for seven years of labor from Jacob. Laban consequently dealt with Jacob with deception and greed; he gave him the wrong wife and then forced him to work seven more years for Rachel. Then he persuaded Jacob to stay longer, but the wages he promised were changed ten times in six years (Genesis 29–30).

When family situations became tense, Jacob quietly left with his wives, children, and possessions, only to be pursued by Laban (Genesis 31). Laban and Jacob eventually parted on peaceful terms, but they heaped up stones as a mutual testimony that they would have no further dealings with each other.

They called upon God as their witness that they would not impose upon each other again (Gen. 31:43–55).

LAODICEA [LAY ah duh SEE uh] — a city in the Lycus Valley of the province of Phrygia where one of the seven churches of Asia Minor was situated (Rev. 3:14). About 65 kilometers (40 miles) east of Ephesus and about 16 kilometers (10 miles) west of Colossae, Laodicea was built on the banks of the river Lycus, a tributary of the Maeander River.

The words of the risen Christ to Laodicea in Revelation 3:14–22 contain allusions to the economic prosperity and social prominence of the city. Founded by the Seleucids and named for Laodice, the wife of Antiochus II (261–247 B.C.), Laodicea became extremely wealthy during the Roman period. For example, in 62 B.C. Flaccus seized the annual contribution of the Jews of Laodicea for Jerusalem amounting to 20 pounds of gold. Moreover, when the city was destroyed by an earthquake in A.D. 60 (along with Colossae and Hierapolis), it alone refused aid from Rome for rebuilding (compare the self-sufficient attitude of the church of Laodicea in Revelation 3:17). Laodicea was known for its black wool industry; it manufactured garments from the raven-black wool produced by the sheep of the surrounding area.

The apostle Paul does not seem to have visited Laodicea at the time he wrote Colossians 2:1. Epaphras, Tychicus, Onesimus, and Mark seem to have been the early messengers of the gospel there (Col. 1:7; 4:7–15). A letter addressed to the Laodiceans by Paul (Col. 4:16) has apparently been lost; some consider it to be a copy of the Ephesian letter. A church council was supposedly held at Laodicea (A.D. 344–363), but all that has come down to us are statements from other councils.

The site of Laodicea is now a deserted heap of ruins that the Turks call Eski Hisar, or "old castle."

According to the comments about the church at Laodicea in the book of Revelation, this congregation consisted of lukewarm Christians (Rev. 3:14–22). The living Lord demands enthusiasm and total commitment from those who worship Him.

LAZARUS [LAZ ah russ] (*God has helped*) — the name of two men in the New Testament:

1. The beggar in Jesus' story about a rich man and a poor man (Luke 16:19–25). The wealthy man despised the beggar, paying no attention to his needs when he passed him each day. After the death of Lazarus, the poor man, he was carried by angels to Abraham's bosom, where he found comfort. But the rich man at death found himself in hades, in eternal torment.

This story was not intended to praise the poor and condemn the rich. It shows the dangers of turning away from the needs of others. It teaches that our attitude on earth will result in an eternal destiny that parallels our attitude. This note is sounded frequently in the teaching of Jesus (Matt. 7:24–27; Luke 16:9).

2. The brother of Martha and Mary of Bethany (John 11:1). One long account in the gospel of John tells about his death and resurrection at the command of Jesus (John 11). A second account in the same Gospel describes him as sitting with Jesus in the family home after the resurrection miracle (John 12:1–2). Because of the publicity surrounding this event, the chief priest plotted to kill Lazarus (John 12:9–11).

Twice John's Gospel records Jesus' love for Lazarus (John 11:3, 5). Yet, upon hearing of the sickness of his friend, Jesus delayed in returning to Bethany. When He finally arrived, both Martha and Mary rebuked Jesus for not coming sooner. Jesus showed His impatience at their unbelief (11:33) as well as His personal sorrow ("Jesus wept"). Then he brought Lazarus back to life (11:43).

Traditional tomb of Lazarus, who was raised from the dead by Jesus (John 11:1–44).

LEAH [LEE uh] — the older daughter of Laban, who deceitfully gave her in marriage to Jacob instead of her younger sister Rachel (Gen. 29:16–30). Although Rachel was the more beautiful of the two daughters of Laban and obviously was Jacob's favorite wife, the Lord blessed Leah and Jacob with six sons—Reuben, Simeon, Levi, Judah (Gen. 29:31–35), Issachar, and Zebulun (Gen. 30:17–20)—and a daughter, Dinah (Gen. 30:21). Leah's maid, Zilpah, added two more sons: Gad and Asher (Gen. 30:9–13).

Leah was the less favored of the two wives of Jacob, and she must have been painfully conscious of this during all the years of her marriage. But it was Leah rather than Rachel who gave birth to Judah, through whose line Jesus the Messiah was eventually born. Apparently Leah died in the land of Canaan before the migration to Egypt (Gen. 46:6). She was buried in the Cave of Machpelah in Hebron (Gen. 49:31).

LEVI [LEE vigh] (*joined*) — the name of four men and one tribe in the Bible:

1. The third son of Jacob and Leah (Gen. 29:34). His three sons were ancestors of the three main divisions of the Levitical priesthood: the Gershonites, the Kohathites, and the Merarites (Gen. 46:11). Levi participated in the plot against Joseph (Gen. 37:4) and later took his family to Egypt with Jacob. On his deathbed Jacob cursed Simeon and Levi because of their "cruelty" and "wrath," and foretold that their descendants would be divided and scattered (Gen. 49:5–7). Levi died in Egypt at the age of 137 (Ex. 6:16).

2. A tribe descended from Levi (Ex. 6:19).

3. Another name for Matthew, one of the twelve apostles (Mark 2:14). Levi was formerly a tax collector.

4. An ancestor of Jesus Christ (Luke 3:24). Levi was a son of Melchi and the father of Matthat.

5. Another ancestor of Jesus Christ (Luke 3:29). This Levi was a son of Simeon and the father of Matthat.

LOT [laht] — Abraham's nephew. Lot accompanied Abraham from Mesopotamia to Canaan and to and from Egypt (Gen. 11:27–31; 12:4–5; 13:1). Both Lot and Abraham had large herds of cattle, and their herdsmen quarreled over their pasturelands. At Abraham's suggestion, the two decided to separate.

Abraham gave Lot his choice of land; and Lot chose the more fertile, well-watered site—the Jordan River valley—as opposed to the rocky hill country. Failing to take into account the character of the inhabitants, Lot "pitched his tent toward Sodom" (Gen. 13:12, KJV).

When the Elamite king Chedorlaomer invaded Canaan with his allies, Lot was taken captive. Abraham attacked Chedorlaomer's forces by night and rescued his nephew (Gen. 13:1–14:16).

When two angels were sent to warn Lot that God intended to destroy Sodom, Lot could not control the Sodomites, who wished to abuse the two visitors carnally. The angels struck the Sodomites blind to save Lot (Gen. 19:1–11), and Lot and his family fled the doomed city. Lot's wife, however, did not follow the angels' orders and looked back at Sodom. Because of her disobedience she was turned into a "pillar of salt" (Gen. 19:26). Our Lord Jesus warned, "Remember Lot's wife" (Luke 17:32), as a reminder of the disastrous results of disobedience.

Following his escape from Sodom, Lot lived in a cave near Zoar (Gen. 19:30–38). His two daughters served their father wine and enticed him into incest. They did this because "there is no man on the earth to come in to us as is the custom of all the earth" (Gen. 19:31). Out of that union came two sons, Moab and Ben-Ammi, the ancestors of the Moabites and the Ammonites respectively.

LUKE — a "fellow laborer" of the apostle Paul (Philem. v. 24) and the author of the gospel of Luke and the Acts of the Apostles. By profession he was a physician (Col. 4:14). During one of Paul's imprisonments, probably in Rome, Luke's faithfulness was recorded by Paul when he declared, "Only Luke is with me" (2 Tim. 4:11). These three references are our only direct knowledge of Luke in the New Testament.

A bit more of Luke's life and personality can be pieced together with the aid of his writings (Luke and Acts) and some outside sources. Tradition records that he came from Antioch in Syria. This is possible, because Antioch played a significant role in the early Gentile mission that Luke described in Acts (Acts 11; 13; 14; 15; 18). Luke was a Gentile (Col. 4:10–17) and the only non-Jewish author of a New Testament book. A comparison of 2 Corinthians 8:18 and 12:18 has led some to suppose that Luke and Titus were brothers, but this is a guess.

Luke accompanied Paul on parts of his second, third, and final missionary journeys. At three places in Acts, the narrative changes to the first person ("we"). This probably indicates that Luke was personally present during those episodes. On the second journey (A.D. 49–53), Luke accompanied Paul on the short voyage from Troas to Philippi (Acts 16:10–17). On the third journey (A.D. 54–58), Luke was present on the voyage from Philippi to Jerusalem (Acts 20:5–21:18). Whether Luke had spent the intervening time in Philippi is uncertain, but his connection with Philippi has led some to favor it (rather than Antioch) as Luke's home.

Once in Palestine, Luke probably remained close by Paul during his two-year imprisonment in Caesarea. During this time, Luke probably drew together material, both oral and written, which he later used in the composition of his gospel (Luke 1:1–4). A third "we" passage describes in masterful suspense the shipwreck during Paul's voyage to Rome for his trial before Caesar. Each of the "we" passages involves Luke on a voyage, and the description of the journey from Jerusalem to Rome is full of observations and knowledge of nautical matters (Acts 27).

Luke apparently was a humble man, with no desire to sound his own horn. More than one-fourth of the New Testament comes from his pen, but not once does he mention himself by name. He had a greater command of the Greek language and was probably more broad-minded and urbane than any other New Testament writer. He was a careful historian, both by his own admission (Luke 1:1–4) and by the judgment of later history.

Luke's gospel reveals his concern for the poor, sick, and outcast, thus offering a clue to why Paul called him "the beloved physician" (Col. 4:14). He was faithful not only to Paul, but to the greater cause he served—the publication of "good tidings of great joy" (Luke 2:10).

M

MACHPELAH [mahk PEE luh] — a field, a cave, and the surrounding land purchased by Abraham as a burial place for his wife Sarah. The cave was to the east of Mamre, or Hebron (Gen. 23:19). At an earlier time, Abraham pitched his tent "and went and dwelt by the terebinth trees of Mamre, which are in Hebron, and built an altar there to the LORD" (Gen. 13:18). He also received three visitors who spoke of a child of promise to be born to Sarah (Gen. 18:1–15).

Abraham purchased the field of Machpelah from Ephron the Hittite. Abraham, Sarah, Isaac, Rebekah, Jacob, and Leah were all buried here (Gen. 49:31; 50:13).

Today the modern city of el-Khalil (Hebron) is built up around the site of Machpelah. The site of the cave was once protected by a Christian church but is now marked by a Muslim mosque. The Muslims held this site so sacred that for centuries Christians were forbidden to enter the ancient shrine. It is open to the public today.

MAGDALA [MAG duh luh] (*tower*) — a place on the Sea of Galilee, perhaps on the west shore, about 5 kilometers (3 miles) northwest of Tiberias. Jesus and His disciples withdrew to this place after the feeding of the 4,000 (Matt. 15:39;

Magadan, NIV, NASB, REB, NRSV). The parallel passage (Mark 8:10) has Dalmanutha. Magdala was either the birthplace or the home of Mary Magdalene.

MAGDALENE [mag de LEE nih] (*from Magdala*) — the designation given to a woman named Mary, one of Jesus' most prominent Galilean female disciples, to distinguish her from the other Marys. The first appearance of Mary Magdalene in the Gospels is in Luke 8:2, which mentions her among those who were ministering to Jesus. Mary Magdalene has sometimes mistakenly been described as a woman of bad character and loose morals, simply because Mark 16:9 states that Jesus had cast seven demons out of her. Nor is there any reason to conclude that she was the same person as the sinful woman whom Simon the Pharisee treated with such disdain and contempt (Luke 7:36–50).

Mary Magdalene was among the "many women who followed Jesus from Galilee, ministering to Him" (Matt. 27:55). She was one of the women at Calvary who were "looking on from afar" (Mark 15:40) when Jesus died on the cross (also John 19:25). She was at Joseph's tomb when the body of Jesus was wrapped in a fine linen cloth and a large stone was rolled against the door of the tomb (Matt. 27:61; Mark 15:47). And she was a witness of the risen Christ (Matt. 28:1; Mark 16:1; Luke 24:10; John 20:1). In fact, she was the first of any of Jesus' followers to see Him after His resurrection (Mark 16:9; John 20:11–18).

Apparently Mary is called "Magdalene" because she was a native or inhabitant of Magdala.

MAGOG [MAY gog] (*land of Gog*) — the name of a man and a people in the Bible:

1. The second son of Japheth and a grandson of Noah (Gen. 10:2).

2. The descendants of Magog (Ezek. 38:2), possibly a people who lived in northern Asia and Europe. The Jewish historian Josephus identified these people as the Scythians, known for their destructive warfare. Magog may be a comprehensive term meaning "northern barbarians." The people of Magog are described as skilled horsemen (Ezek. 38:15) and experts in the use of the bow and arrow (Ezek. 39:3, 9). The book of Revelation uses Ezekiel's prophetic imagery to portray the final, apocalyptic encounter between good and evil at the end of this age. "Gog and Magog" (Rev. 20:8–9) symbolize the anti-Christian forces of the world.

MAHANAIM [may huh NAY im] (two armies) — an ancient town in Gilead, east of the Jordan River in the vicinity of the river Jabbok. Located on the border between the tribes of Manasseh and Gad (Josh. 13:26, 30), Mahanaim was later assigned to the Merarite Levites (Josh. 21:38).

On his way home after an absence of 20 years, Jacob was met by angels of God at this site. "When Jacob saw them, he said, 'This is God's camp.' " He named the place Mahanaim, meaning "two armies." This was a significant moment for Jacob, who was about to meet his estranged brother Esau. The knowledge that he was being accompanied by an angelic band undoubtedly brought him the confidence and assurance he needed. Following the slaying of King Saul by the Philistines, his son Ishbosheth reigned for two years at Mahanaim (2 Sam. 2:8, 12, 29). Later, Mahanaim became the headquarters for David during the rebellion of his son, Absalom (2 Sam. 17:24). Solomon also made Mahanaim the capital of one of his 12 districts (1 Kin. 4:14).

MAHER-SHALAL-HASH-BAZ [MAY her SHAL al HASH baz] (hasten the booty, speed the plunder) — the symbolic name of the second son of the prophet Isaiah

(Is. 8:1, 3), signifying the doom of Damascus and Samaria and the destruction of Syria and Israel, who had formed a military alliance against Jerusalem (Is. 7:1).

MALACHI [MAL ah kie] (*my messenger*) — Old Testament prophet and author of the prophetic book that bears his name. Nothing is known about Malachi's life except the few facts that may be inferred from his prophecies. He apparently prophesied after the captivity, during the time when Nehemiah was leading the people to rebuild Jerusalem's wall and recommit themselves to following God's law. The people's negligence in paying tithes to God was condemned by both Nehemiah and Malachi (Neh. 13:10–14; Mal. 3:8–10).

MAMRE [MAM reh] — the name of a man and a place in the Old Testament:

1. An Amorite chief who formed an alliance with Abraham against Chedorlaomer (Gen. 14:13, 24).

2. A place in the district of Hebron, west of Machpelah, where Abraham lived. It was noted for its "terebinth trees" (Gen. 13:18; 18:1), or "oaks" (NRSV). Near Mamre was the cave of Machpelah, in which Abraham, Isaac, and Jacob—and their wives, Sarah, Rebekah, and Leah—were buried (Gen. 49:13). The site of ancient Mamre has been identified as Ramet el-Khalil, about 3 kilometers (2 miles) north of Hebron.

MANASSEH [muh NASS uh] (*causing to forget*) — the name of five men in the Old Testament:

1. Joseph's firstborn son who was born in Egypt to Asenath the daughter of Poti-Pherah, priest of On (Gen. 41:50–51). Like his younger brother, Ephraim, Manasseh was half Hebrew and half Egyptian. Manasseh's birth caused Joseph to forget the bitterness of his past experiences. Manasseh and Ephraim were

both adopted by Jacob and given status as sons just like Jacob's own sons Reuben and Simeon (Gen. 48:5).

2. The grandfather of the Jonathan who was one of the priests of the graven image erected by the tribe of Dan (Judg. 18:30).

3. The fourteenth king of Judah, the son of Hezekiah born to Hephzibah (2 Kin. 21:1–18). Manasseh reigned longer (55 years) than any other Israelite king and had the dubious distinction of being Judah's most wicked king. He came to the throne at the age of 12, although he probably co-reigned with Hezekiah for ten years. His father's godly influence appears to have affected Manasseh only negatively, and he reverted to the ways of his evil grandfather, Ahaz.

Committed to idolatry, Manasseh restored everything Hezekiah had abolished. Manasseh erected altars to Baal; he erected an image of Asherah in the temple; he worshiped the sun, moon, and stars; he recognized the Ammonite god Molech and sacrificed his son to him (2 Kin. 21:6); he approved divination; and he killed all who protested his evil actions. It is possible that he killed the prophet Isaiah; rabbinical tradition states that Manasseh gave the command that Isaiah be sawn in two (see also Heb. 11:37). Scripture summarizes Manasseh's reign by saying he "seduced them [Judah] to do more evil than the nations whom the Lord had destroyed before the children of Israel" (2 Kin. 21:9).

Manasseh was temporarily deported to Babylon where he humbled himself before God in repentance (2 Chr. 33:11–13). Upon Manasseh's return to Jerusalem, he tried to reverse the trends he had set; but his reforms were quickly reversed after his death by his wicked son Amon.

4. A descendant, or resident, of Pahath-Moab (Ezra 10:30). After the captivity he divorced his pagan wife.

5. An Israelite of the family of Hashum. Manasseh divorced his pagan wife after the captivity (Ezra 10:33).

MARK, JOHN — an occasional associate of Peter and Paul, and the probable author of the second gospel. Mark's lasting impact on the Christian church comes from his writing rather than his life. He was the first to develop the literary form known as the "gospel" and is rightly regarded as a creative literary artist.

John Mark appears in the New Testament only in association with more prominent personalities and events. His mother, Mary, was an influential woman of Jerusalem who possessed a large house with servants. The early church gathered in this house during Peter's imprisonment under Herod Agrippa I (Acts 12:12). Barnabas and Saul (Paul) took John Mark with them when they returned from Jerusalem to Antioch after their famine-relief visit (Acts 12:25). Shortly thereafter, Mark accompanied Paul and Barnabas on their first missionary journey as far as Perga. He served in the capacity of "assistant" (Acts 13:5), which probably involved making arrangements for travel, food, and lodging; he may have done some teaching, too.

At Perga John Mark gave up the journey for an undisclosed reason (Acts 13:13); this departure later caused a rift between Paul and Barnabas when they chose their companions for the second missionary journey (Acts 15:37–41). Paul was unwilling to take Mark again and chose Silas; they returned to Asia Minor and Greece. Barnabas persisted in his choice of Mark, who was his cousin (Col. 4:10), and returned with him to his homeland of Cyprus (Acts 15:39; also Acts 4:36).

This break occurred about A.D. 49–50, and John Mark is not heard from again until a decade later. He is first mentioned again, interestingly enough, by Paul—and in favorable terms. Paul asks the Colossians to receive Mark with a welcome (Col. 4:10), no longer as an assistant but as one of his "fellow laborers" (Philem. v. 24). And during his imprisonment in Rome, Paul tells Timothy to bring Mark with him to Rome, "for he is useful to me for ministry" (2 Tim. 4:11). One final reference to

Mark comes also from Peter in Rome; Peter affectionately refers to him as "my son" (1 Pet. 5:13). Thus, in the later references to Mark in the New Testament, he appears to be reconciled to Paul and laboring with the two great apostles in Rome.

Information about Mark's later life is dependent on early church tradition. Writing at an early date, Papias (A.D. 60–130), whose report is followed by Clement of Alexandria (A.D. 150–215), tells us that Mark served as Peter's interpreter in Rome and wrote his gospel from Peter's remembrances. Of his physical appearance we are only told, rather oddly, that Mark was "stumpy fingered." Writing at a later date (about A.D. 325), the church historian Eusebius says that Mark was the first evangelist to Egypt, the founder of the churches of Alexandria, and the first bishop of that city. So great were his converts, both in number and sincerity of commitment, says Eusebius, that the great Jewish philosopher, Philo, was amazed.

MARTHA [MAR thuh] (*lady, mistress*) — the sister of Mary and Lazarus of Bethany (Luke 10:38–41; John 11:1–44; 12:1–3). All three were sincere followers of Jesus, but Mary and Martha expressed their love for Him in different ways. The account of the two women given by Luke reveals a clash of temperaments between Mary and Martha. Martha "was distracted with much serving" (Luke 10:40); she was an activist busy with household chores. Her sister Mary "sat at Jesus' feet and heard His word" (Luke 10:39); her instinct was to sit still, meditate, and receive spiritual instruction.

While Martha busied herself making Jesus comfortable and cooking for Him in her home, Mary listened intently to His teaching. When Martha complained that Mary was not helping her, Jesus rebuked Martha. "You are worried and troubled about many things," He declared. "But one thing is needed, and Mary has chosen that good part, which will not be taken away from her" (Luke 10:41–42). He told her, in effect, that Mary was feeding her spiritual needs. This was more important than Martha's attempt to feed His body.

Jesus recognized that Martha was working for Him, but He reminded her that she was permitting her outward activities to hinder her spiritually. Because of her emphasis on work and her daily chores, her inner communion with her Lord was being hindered.

MARY [MAIR ee] — the name of six women in the New Testament:

1. Mary, the mother of Jesus (Luke 1–2). We know nothing of Mary's background other than that she was a peasant and a resident of Nazareth, a city of Galilee. She must have been of the tribe of Judah and thus in the line of David (Luke 1:32), although the genealogies in Matthew 1 and Luke 3 do not say so, because they trace Joseph's genealogy rather than Mary's. We do know that Mary's cousin, Elizabeth, was the mother of John the Baptist.

When Mary was pledged to be married to Joseph the carpenter, the angel Gabriel appeared to her. Calling her "highly favored one" and "blessed ... among women" (Luke 1:28), the angel announced the birth of the Messiah. After Gabriel explained how such a thing could be possible, Mary said, "Let it be to me according to your word" (Luke 1:38). That Mary "found favor with God" and was allowed to give birth to His child indicates she must have been of high character and faith.

When Jesus was born in Bethlehem of Judea, Mary "wrapped him in swaddling cloths, and laid Him in a manger" (Luke 2:7). She witnessed the visits of the shepherds and the wise men and "pondered them in her heart" (Luke 2:19) and heard Simeon's prophecy of a sword that would pierce through her own soul (Luke 2:35). Joseph and Mary fled to Egypt to escape Herod's murder of all males under two years old (Matt. 2:13–18). Neither Mary nor Joseph appear again until Jesus is 12 years old, at which time He stayed behind in the temple with the teachers (Luke 2:41–52). Both Mary and Joseph accepted Jesus' explanation, realizing He was Israel's Promised One.

Mary was present at Jesus' first miracle—the turning of water into wine at the wedding feast in Cana of Galilee (John 2:1–12). Mary seemed to be asking her Son to use His power to meet the crisis. Jesus warned her that His time had not yet come; nevertheless, He turned the water into wine. At another time Mary and Jesus' brothers wished to see Jesus while He was teaching the multitudes—perhaps to warn Him of impending danger. But again Jesus mildly rebuked her, declaring that the bond between Him and His disciples was stronger than any family ties (Luke 8:19–21).

The Scriptures do not mention Mary again until she stands at the foot of the cross (John 19:25–27). No mention is made of Joseph; he had likely been dead for some time. Jesus' brothers were not among His followers. Of His family, only His mother held fast to her belief in His messiahship—even though it appeared to be ending in tragedy. From the cross Jesus gave Mary over to the care of the beloved disciple, John. The last mention of Mary is in the Upper Room in Jerusalem, awaiting the coming of the Holy Spirit (Acts 1:14). We do not know how or when Mary died. The Tomb of the Virgin is in the Valley of Kidron in Jerusalem, southeast of the temple area; but there is no historical basis for this site.

According to Scripture, Jesus had four brothers—James, Joses, Judas, and Simon—and unnamed sisters (Matt. 13:55–56; Mark 6:3). The Roman Catholic Church, however, claims that Mary remained a virgin and that these "brothers" and "sisters" were either Joseph's children by an earlier marriage or were cousins of Jesus. Legends concerning Mary began circulating in written form as early as the fifth century, but there is no valid historical evidence for them.

In reaction to the Roman Catholic teachings about Mary, many Protestants almost totally neglect her and her contribution. What can be said of her that is consistent with Holy Scripture?

God was in her womb. In conceiving and bearing the Lord Jesus Christ, she gave earthly birth not to mere man but to the Son of God Himself. She conceived as a virgin through the mysterious power of the Holy Spirit. We are to bless and honor her, for as she herself said under the inspiration of the Holy Spirit, "Henceforth all generations will call me blessed" (Luke 1:48).

As the first member of the human race to accept Christ, she stands as the first of the redeemed and as the flagship of humanity itself. She is our enduring example for faith, service to God, and a life of righteousness.

2. Mary Magdalene, the woman from whom Jesus cast out seven demons. The name Magdalene indicates that she came from Magdala, a city on the southwest coast of the Sea of Galilee. After Jesus cast seven demons from her, she became one of His followers. The Scriptures do not describe her illness. Mary Magdalene has been associated with the "woman in the city who was a sinner" (Luke 7:37) who washed Jesus' feet, but there is no scriptural basis for this. According to the Talmud (the collection of rabbinic writings that make up the basis of religious authority for traditional Judaism), the city of Magdala had a reputation for prostitution. This information, coupled with the fact that Luke first mentions Mary Magdalene immediately following his account of the sinful woman (Luke 7:36–50), has led some to equate the two women.

Mary Magdalene is also often associated with the woman whom Jesus saved from stoning after she had been taken in adultery (John 8:1–11)—again an association with no evidence. We do know that Mary Magdalene was one of those women who, having "been healed of evil spirits and infirmities," provided for Jesus and His disciples "from their substance" (Luke 8:2–3).

Mary Magdalene witnessed most of the events surrounding the crucifixion. She was present at the mock trial of Jesus; she heard Pontius Pilate pronounce the death sentence; and she saw Jesus beaten and humiliated by the crowd. She was one of the women who stood near Jesus during the crucifixion to try to comfort Him. The earliest witness to the resurrection of Jesus, she was sent by Jesus to tell the others (John 20:11–18). Although this is the last mention of her in the Bible, she was probably among the women who gathered with the apostles to await the promised coming of the Holy Spirit (Acts 1:14).

3. Mary of Bethany, sister of Martha and Lazarus (Luke 10:38–42). As with Martha, we know nothing of Mary's family background. Martha was probably older than Mary since the house is referred to as Martha's, but she could have inherited it from an unmentioned husband. All we really know is that Mary, Martha, and Lazarus loved one another deeply. When Jesus visited their house in Bethany, Mary sat at Jesus' feet and listened to His teachings while Martha worked in the kitchen. When Martha complained that Mary was no help, Jesus gently rebuked Martha. When Lazarus died, Mary's grief was deep. John tells us that when Jesus came following Lazarus's death Mary stayed in the house. After she was summoned by Martha, she went to Jesus, fell at His feet weeping, and, like Martha, said, "Lord, if You had been here, my brother would not have died" (John 11:21, 32).

Following Lazarus's resurrection, Mary showed her gratitude by anointing Jesus' feet with "a pound of very costly oil of spikenard" (John 12:3) and wiping His feet with her hair. Judas called this anointing extravagant, but Jesus answered, "Let her alone; she has kept this for the day of My burial" (John 12:7).

Jesus called Mary's unselfish act "a memorial to her" (Mark 14:9).

4. Mary, the mother of the disciple James and Joses (Matt. 27:55–61). In light of her presence at Jesus' death and resurrection, it is likely that Mary was one of the women who followed Jesus and His disciples and provided food for them (Luke 8:2–3). Since Mark 15:40 tells us that this Mary, along with Mary Magdalene, observed Jesus' burial, the "other Mary" (Matt. 27:61) must refer to this mother of James and Joses. Mary was one of the women who went to the tomb on the third day to anoint Jesus' body with spices and discovered that Jesus was no longer among the dead (Mark 16:1–8).

5. Mary, the mother of John Mark (Acts 12:12). The mother of the author of the gospel of Mark opened her home to the disciples to pray for the release of Peter, who had been imprisoned by Herod Antipas. When Peter was miraculously released, the angel immediately delivered him to Mary's house. Tradition has it that Mary's house was a primary meeting place for the early Christians of Jerusalem. We know that Barnabas and Mark were related (Col. 4:10), but whether through Mark's mother or through his father (who is never mentioned), we do not know.

6. Mary of Rome (Rom. 16:6). All we know about this Christian woman of Rome is found in Paul's salutation: "Greet Mary, who labored much for us."

MASSAH [MASS uh] (*testing*) — a place in the Wilderness of Sin, near Mount Horeb. The Israelites murmured against Moses at Massah because of no water, indicating their lack of faith. At the command of God, Moses struck the rock with his rod to produce water. The place is also called Meribah, which means "rebellion, strife, contention" (Ex. 17:7).

MATTHEW [MA thue] (*gift of the Lord*) — a tax collector who became one of the twelve apostles of Jesus (Matt.

9:9). Matthew's name appears seventh in two lists of apostles (Mark 3:18; Luke 6:15), and eighth in two others (Matt. 10:3; Acts 1:13).

In Hebrew, Matthew's name means "gift of the Lord," but we know from his trade that he delighted in the gifts of others as well. He was a tax collector (Matt. 9:9–11) who worked in or around Capernaum under the authority of Herod Antipas. In Jesus' day, land and poll taxes were collected directly by Roman officials, but taxes on transported goods were contracted out to local collectors. Matthew was such a person, or else he was in the service of one. These middlemen paid an agreed-upon sum in advance to the Roman officials for the right to collect taxes in an area. Their profit came from the excess they could squeeze from the people.

The Jewish people hated these tax collectors not only for their corruption but also because they worked for and with the despised Romans. Tax collectors were ranked with murderers and robbers, and a Jew was permitted to lie to them if necessary. The attitude found in the Gospels is similar. Tax collectors are lumped together with harlots (Matt. 21:31), Gentiles (Matt. 18:17), and, most often, sinners (Matt. 9:10). They were as offensive to Jews for their economic and social practices as lepers were for their uncleanness; both were excluded from the people of God.

It is probable that the Matthew mentioned in Matthew 9:9–13 is identical with the Levi of Mark 2:13–17 and Luke 5:27–32; the stories obviously refer to the same person and event. The only problem in the identification is that Mark mentions Matthew rather than Levi in his list of apostles (Mark 3:18), thus leading one to assume two different persons. It is possible, however, that the same person was known by two names (compare "Simon" and "Peter"), or, less likely, that Levi and James the son of Alphaeus are the same person, since Mark calls Alphaeus the father of both (Mark 2:14; 3:18). Following his call by Jesus, Matthew is not mentioned again in the New Testament.

MATTHIAS [muh THIGH us] (*gift of the Lord*) — a disciple chosen to succeed Judas Iscariot as an apostle (Acts 1:23, 26). Matthias had been a follower of Jesus from the beginning of His ministry until the day of His ascension and had been a witness of His resurrection. In this way he fulfilled the requirements of apostleship (Acts 1:21–22). Probably he was one of the "seventy" (Luke 10:1, 17). The New Testament makes no further mention of him after his election. One tradition says that Matthias preached in Judea and was stoned to death by the Jews. Another tradition holds that he worked in Ethiopia and was martyred by crucifixion.

MEGIDDO [muh GID doe] — a walled city east of the Carmel Mountain range where many important battles were fought in Old Testament times. Megiddo was situated on the main road that linked Egypt and Syria. Overlooking the Valley of Jezreel (Plain of Esdraelon), Megiddo was one of the most strategic cities in Palestine. All major traffic through northern Palestine traveled past Megiddo, making it a strategic military stronghold.

Megiddo is first mentioned in the Old Testament in the account of the 31 kings conquered by Joshua (Josh. 12:21). In the division of the land of Canaan among the tribes of the Hebrew people, Megiddo was awarded to Manasseh. But the tribe was unable to drive out the native inhabitants of the city (Josh. 17:11; Judg. 1:27; 1 Chr. 7:29).

During the period of the judges, the forces of Deborah and Barak wiped out the army of Sisera "by the waters of Megiddo" (Judg. 5:19). During the period of the united kingdom under Solomon, the Israelites established their supremacy at Megiddo. The city was included in the fifth administrative district of

Solomon (1 Kin. 4:12). Along with Hazor, Gezer, Lower Beth Horon, Baalath, and Tadmor, Megiddo was fortified and established as a chariot city for the armies of King Solomon (1 Kin. 9:15–19).

The prophet Zechariah mentioned the great mourning that would one day take place "in the plain of Megiddo" (Zech. 12:11; Megiddon, KJV). The fulfillment of Zechariah's prophecy is the battle at the end of time known as the Battle of Armageddon. Armageddon is a compound word that means "mountain of Megiddo."

In the end times, God will destroy the armies of the Beast and the False Prophet in "the battle of that great day of God Almighty" (Rev. 16:14) when He shall gather them "together to the place called in Hebrew, Armageddon" (Rev. 16:16). Jesus Christ will ride out of heaven on a white horse (Rev. 19:11) as the "King of kings and Lord of lords" (Rev. 19:16).

MELCHIZEDEK [mel KIZ eh deck] (*king of righteousness*) — a king of Salem (Jerusalem) and priest of the Most High God (Gen. 14:18–20; Ps. 110:4; Heb. 5:6–11; 6:20–7:28). Melchizedek's appearance and disappearance in the book of Genesis are somewhat mysterious. Melchizedek and Abraham first met after Abraham's defeat of Chedorlaomer and his three allies. Melchizedek presented bread and wine to Abraham and his weary men, demonstrating friendship and religious kinship. He bestowed a blessing on Abraham in the name of El Elyon ("God Most High"), and praised God for giving Abraham a victory in battle (Gen. 14:18–20).

Abraham presented Melchizedek with a tithe (a tenth) of all the booty he had gathered. By this act Abraham indicated that he recognized Melchizedek as a fellow-worshiper of the one true God as well as a priest who ranked higher spiritually than himself. Melchizedek's existence shows that there were people other than Abraham and his family who served the true

God. In Psalm 110, a messianic psalm written by David (Matt. 22:43), Melchizedek is seen as a type of Christ. This theme is repeated in the book of Hebrews, where both Melchizedek and Christ are considered kings of righteousness and peace. By citing Melchizedek and his unique priesthood as a type, the writer shows that Christ's new priesthood is superior to the old Levitical order and the priesthood of Aaron (Heb. 7:1–10; Melchisedec, KJV).

Attempts have been made to identify Melchizedek as an imaginary character named Shem, an angel, the Holy Spirit, Christ, and others. All are products of speculation, not historical fact; and it is impossible to reconcile them with the theological argument of Hebrews. Melchizedek was a real, historical king-priest who served as a type for the greater King-Priest who was to come, Jesus Christ.

MENAHEM [MEN ah him] (*comforter*) — a son of Gadi and seventeenth king of Israel (2 Kin. 15:14–23). Some scholars believe Menahem probably was the military commander of King Zechariah. When Shallum took the throne from Zechariah by killing him in front of the people, Menahem determined that Shallum himself must be killed. After Shallum had reigned as king of Israel for a month in Samaria, Menahem "went up from Tirzah, came to Samaria, and struck Shallum ... and killed him; and he reigned in his place" (2 Kin. 15:14).

When the city of Tiphsah refused to recognize Menahem as the lawful ruler of Israel, Menahem attacked it and inflicted terrible cruelties upon its people (2 Kin. 15:16). This act apparently secured his position, because Menahem remained king for ten years (752–742 B.C.). His reign was evil, marked by cruelty, oppression, and idolatrous worship.

During his reign Menahem faced a threat from the advancing army of Pul (Tiglath-Pileser III), king of Assyria. To strengthen his own position as king and to forestall a war with

Assyria, he paid tribute to the Assyrian king by exacting "from each man fifty shekels of silver" (2 Kin. 15:20). After Menahem's death, his son Pekahiah became king of Israel (2 Kin. 15:22).

MEPHIBOSHETH [meh FIB oh shehth] (*from the mouth of* [the] *shame*[ful god Baal]) — the name of two men in the Old Testament:

1. A son of Jonathan and grandson of Saul. Mephibosheth was also called Merib-Baal (1 Chr. 8:34; 9:40), probably his original name, meaning "a striver against Baal." His name was changed because the word *Baal* was associated with idol worship.

Mephibosheth was only five years old when his father, Jonathan, and his grandfather, Saul, died on Mount Gilboa in the Battle of Jezreel (2 Sam. 4:4). When the child's nurse heard the outcome of the battle, she feared for Mephibosheth's life. As she fled for his protection, "he fell and became lame" (2 Sam. 4:4). For the rest of his life he was crippled.

After David consolidated his kingdom, he remembered his covenant with Jonathan to treat his family with kindness (1 Samuel 20). Through Ziba, a servant of the house of Saul, David found out about Mephibosheth. The lame prince had been staying "in the house of Machir the son of Ammiel, in Lo Debar" (2 Sam. 9:4). David then summoned Mephibosheth to his palace, restored to him the estates of Saul, appointed servants for him, and gave him a place at the royal table (2 Sam. 9:7–13).

When David's son Absalom rebelled, the servant Ziba falsely accused Mephibosheth of disloyalty to David (2 Sam. 16:1–4). David believed Ziba's story and took Saul's property from Mephibosheth. Upon David's return to Jerusalem, Mephibosheth cleared himself. David in turn offered Mephibosheth half of Saul's estates (2 Sam. 19:24–30), but he refused. David's return to Jerusalem as king was the only reward Mephibosheth desired.

2. A son of King Saul and Rizpah (2 Sam. 21:8).

MERARI [meh RAY eye] (*bitter*) — the third and youngest son of Levi and the founder of the Merarites, one of the three Levitical families. Merari was the father of Mahli and Mushi (Ex. 6:16–19), who, in turn, were the founders of the Mahlites and the Mushites (Num. 3:33; 26:58).

MERIBAH [MEHR ih bah] (*contention*) — the name of two different places where Moses struck a rock with his rod, and water gushed forth to satisfy the thirsty Israelites:

1. A place "in Rephidim" at the foot of Mount Horeb. The Israelites camped here near the beginning of their 40 years in the wilderness (Ex. 17:1–7).

2. A second place where Moses struck a rock. This camp was in Kadesh, in the Wilderness of Zin. The Israelites camped here near the end of their period of wilderness wandering (Num. 20:2–13). In Deuteronomy 32:51, this place is referred to as Meribath-Kadesh (Meribah Kadesh, NIV).

MESHACH [MEE shak] — the Chaldean name given to Mishael, one of Daniel's companions (Dan. 1:7). Along with Shadrach and Abed-Nego, Meshach would not bow down and worship the pagan image of gold set up by Nebuchadnezzar. They were cast into "the burning fiery furnace," but were preserved from harm by the power of God.

MICAH [MIE kuh] (*who is like the Lord?*) — the name of six men in the Old Testament:

1. A man from the mountains of Ephraim during the period of the judges in Israel's history. Micah's worship of false gods led the Danites into idolatry (Judges 17–18).

2. A descendant of Reuben (1 Chr. 5:5).

3. A son of Merib-Baal listed in the family tree of King Saul of Benjamin (1 Chr. 8:34–35; 9:40–41). Micah was the father of Pithon, Melech, Tarea (or Tahrea), and Ahaz. His father Merib-Baal (also called Mephibosheth, 2 Sam. 4:4) was a son of Jonathan and a grandson of Saul.

4. A son of Zichri and grandson of Asaph (1 Chr. 9:15). Micah is also called "Micha, the son of Zabdi" (Neh. 11:17; also Neh. 11:22) and "Michaiah, the son of Zaccur" (Neh. 12:35).

5. The father of Abdon (2 Chr. 34:20) or Achbor (2 Kin. 22:12). Abdon was one of five men whom King Josiah of Judah sent to inquire of Huldah the prophetess when Hilkiah the priest found the book of the Law. Micah is also called Michaiah (2 Kin. 22:12).

6. An Old Testament prophet and author of the book of Micah. A younger contemporary of the great prophet Isaiah, Micah was from Moresheth Gath (Mic. 1:1, 14), a town in southern Judah. His prophecy reveals his country origins; he uses many images from country life (Mic. 7:1).

Micah spoke out strongly against those who claimed to be prophets of the Lord but who used this position to lead the people of Judah into false hopes and further errors: "The sun shall go down on the prophets, and the day shall be dark for them" (Mic. 3:6). Micah's love for God would not allow him to offer false hopes to those who were under His sentence of judgment.

Little else is known about this courageous spokesman for the Lord. He tells us in his book that he prophesied during the reigns of three kings in Judah: Jotham, Ahaz, and Hezekiah (Mic. 1:1). This would place the time of his ministry from about 750 to 687 B.C.

MICAIAH [mie KAY yah] (*who is like the Lord?*) — the prophet who predicted the death of King Ahab of Israel in the battle against the Syrians at Ramoth Gilead (1 Kin. 22:8–28;

2 Chr. 18:7–27). Ahab gathered about 400 prophets, apparently all in his employment. They gave their unanimous approval to Ahab's proposed attack against the Syrian king, Ben-Hadad.

King Jehoshaphat of Judah was unconvinced by this display. He asked, "Is there not still a prophet of the LORD here, that we may inquire of Him?" (1 Kin. 22:7; 2 Chr. 18:6). Ahab replied, "There is still one man, Micaiah the son of Imlah, by whom we may inquire of the LORD but I hate him, because he does not prophesy good concerning me, but evil" (1 Kin. 22:8; 2 Chr. 18:7). The prophet Micaiah was then summoned.

When Ahab asked this prophet's advice, Micaiah answered, "Go and prosper, for the LORD will deliver it into the hand of the king!" (1 Kin. 22:15; 2 Chr. 18:14).

Micaiah's answer was heavy with sarcasm, irony, and contempt. Ahab realized he was being mocked; so he commanded him to speak nothing but the truth. Micaiah then said, "I saw all Israel scattered on the mountains as sheep that have no shepherd" (1 Kin. 22:17; 2 Chr. 18:16). Ahab turned to Jehoshaphat and said, "Did I not tell you that he would not prophesy good concerning me, but evil?" (1 Kin. 22:18; 2 Chr. 18:17).

Zedekiah then struck Micaiah on the cheek and accused him of being a liar. Ahab commanded that Micaiah be put in prison until the king's victorious return from Ramoth Gilead. Then Micaiah said, "If you ever return ... the LORD has not spoken by me" (1 Kin. 22:28; 2 Chr. 18:27).

Ahab did not return; he died at Ramoth Gilead, just as Micaiah had predicted.

MIDIAN [MID ee un] — the name of a man and a territory in the Old Testament:

1. A son of Abraham by his concubine Keturah (Gen. 25:1–6). Midian had four sons (1 Chr. 1:33).

2. The land inhabited by the descendants of Midian. Situated east of the Jordan River and the Dead Sea, the land stretched

southward through the Arabian desert as far as the southern and eastern parts of the peninsula of Sinai.

MIGDOL [MIG dahl] (*watchtower*) — the name of two Egyptian sites in the Old Testament:

1. An encampment of the Israelites while they were leaving Egypt in the Exodus led by Moses. "Speak to the children of Israel, that they turn and camp before Pi Hahiroth, between Migdol and the sea, opposite Baal Zephon" (Ex. 14:2). Migdol lay west of the Red Sea in the eastern region of the Nile Delta.

2. A site in northeastern Egypt (Jer. 44:1; 46:14). After the destruction of Jerusalem by the Babylonians under Nebuchadnezzar, some Israelites fled to Egypt and lived in Migdol.

MILCAH [MILL kuh] (*queen*) — the name of two women in the Old Testament:

1. A daughter of Haran and the wife of Nahor (Gen. 22:20–22).

2. One of the five daughters of Zelophehad, of the tribe of Manasseh. Zelophehad had no sons. When he died, his daughters asked Moses for permission to share their father's inheritance. Their request was granted, providing they married within their own tribe in order to keep the inheritance within Manasseh (Num. 36:11–12).

MILETUS [my LEE tuhs] — an ancient seaport in Asia Minor visited by the apostle Paul (Act 20:15, 17; 2 Tim. 4:20; Miletum, KJV). Situated on the shore of the Mediterranean Sea, Miletus was about 60 kilometers (37 miles) south of Ephesus and on the south side of the Bay of Latmus. Because of silting, the site is now more than 8 kilometers (5 miles) from the coast.

Colonized by Cretans and others, Miletus became a leading harbor during the Persian and Greek periods. It prospered economically and boasted a celebrated temple of Apollo. Although

Miletus was still an important trade center in Roman times, the river was already silting in the harbor. The apostle Paul visited Miletus on his journey from Greece to Jerusalem. In Miletus Paul delivered a farewell message to the elders of the church of Ephesus (Acts 10:18–35).

MISHAEL [MISH eh uhl] (*who is what God is?*) — the name of three men in the Old Testament:

1. A son of Uzziel and grandson of Kohath, of the tribe of Levi (Lev. 10:4).

2. An Israelite who helped Ezra read the book of the Law to the people (Neh. 8:4).

3. One of the three friends of Daniel who were cast into the fiery furnace. "Now from among those of the sons of Judah were Daniel, Hananiah, Mishael, and Azariah." The Babylonians changed his name to Meshach (Dan. 1:6–7).

MIZPAH [MIZ pah] (*watchtower*) — the name of six sites in the Old Testament:

1. One of three names given to a mound of stones erected as a memorial. Jacob set up this memorial in Gilead as a witness of the covenant between him and his father-in-law, Laban (Gen. 31:49). Both Jacob and Laban called this monument "heap of witness." The mound was also called Mizpah, meaning "watch[tower]." The stones were erected as a boundary marker between the two. God was the One who was to watch between them.

2. A district at the foot of Mount Hermon called "the land of Mizpah" and "the Valley of Mizpah" (Josh. 11:3, 8).

3. A city of Judah (Josh. 15:38) in the Shephelah, or lowland plain.

4. A city of Benjamin in the region of Geba and Ramah (1 Kin. 15:22). At Mizpah Samuel assembled the Israelites for prayer after the ark of the covenant was returned to Kirjath

Jearim (1 Sam. 7:5–6). Saul was first presented to Israel as king at this city (1 Sam. 10:17). Mizpah was also one of the places that Samuel visited on his annual circuit to judge Israel (1 Sam. 7:16–17). Mizpah was one of the sites fortified against the kings of the northern tribes of Israel by King Asa (1 Kin. 15:22). After the destruction of Jerusalem in 586 B.C., Gedaliah was appointed governor of the remaining people of Judah; his residence was at Mizpah (2 Kin. 25:23, 25). After the fall of Jerusalem Mizpah became the capital of the Babylonian province of Judah. Mizpah also was reinhabited by Israelites after the Babylonian captivity (Neh. 3:7, 15, 19). The site is modern Tell en-Nasbch.

5. A town or site in Gilead known as Mizpah of Gilead and the home of Jephthah the judge (Judg. 11:29, 34). This site was probably known as Ramath Mizpah (Josh. 13:26)—the Ramoth in Gilead listed as one of the six cities of refuge (Josh. 20:8).

6. A city in Moab to which David took his parents for safety when King Saul sought to kill him (1 Sam. 22:3). Some scholars believe Mizpah of Moab was another name for Kir of Moab (present-day Kerak), the capital of Moab.

MOAB [MOE abb] (*of my father*) — the name of a man and a nation in the Old Testament:

1. A son of Lot by an incestuous union with his older daughter (Gen. 19:37). Moab became an ancestor of the Moabites.

2. A neighboring nation whose history was closely linked to the fortunes of the Hebrew people. Moab was situated along the eastern border of the southern half of the Dead Sea, on the plateau between the Dead Sea and the Arabian desert. It was about 57 kilometers (35 miles) long and 40 kilometers (25 miles) wide. Throughout much of its history, the northern border of Moab was the Arnon River and the southern border was the Zered. Although it was primarily a high plateau, Moab also had mountainous areas and deep gorges. It was a fertile area for crops and herds. To the south and west of Moab was the nation of

Edom; to the north was Ammon. After the Israelites invaded the land, the tribe of Reuben displaced the Moabites from the northern part of their territory and the tribe of Gad pushed the Ammonites eastward into the desert.

MORDECAI [MAWR deh kie] (*related to Marduk*) — the name of two men in the Old Testament:

1. One of the Jewish captives who returned with Zerubbabel from Babylon (Ezra 2:2; Neh. 7:7).

2. The hero of the book of Esther. Mordecai was probably born in Babylonia during the years of the captivity of the Jewish people by this pagan nation. He was a resident of Susa (Shushan), the Persian capital during the reign of Ahasuerus (Xerxes I), the king of Persia (ruled 486–465 B.C.).

When Mordecai's uncle, Abihail, died (Esth. 2:5), Mordecai took his orphaned cousin, Hadassah (Esther), into his home as her adoptive father (Esth. 2:7). When two of the king's eunuchs, Bigthan and Teresh, conspired to assassinate King Ahasuerus, Mordecai discovered the plot and exposed it, saving the king's life (Esth. 2:21–22). Mordecai's good deed was recorded in the royal chronicles of Persia (Esth. 2:23).

Mordecai showed his loyalty to God by refusing to bow to Haman, the official second to the king (Esth. 3:2, 5). According to the Greek historian Herodotus, when the Persians bowed before their king, they paid homage as to a god. Mordecai, a Jew, would not condone such idolatry.

Haman's hatred for Mordecai sparked his plan to kill all the Jews in the Persian Empire (Esth. 3:6). Mordecai reminded his cousin, who had become Queen Esther, of her God-given opportunity to expose Haman to the king and to save her people (Esth. 3:1–4:17). The plot turned against Haman, who ironically was impaled on the same stake that he had prepared for Mordecai (Esth. 7:10).

Haman was succeeded by Mordecai, who now was second in command to the most powerful man in the kingdom. He used his new position to encourage his people to defend themselves against the scheduled massacre planned by Haman. Persian officials also assisted in protecting the Jews, an event celebrated by the annual Feast of Purim (Esth. 9:26–32).

MORESHETH GATH [MOH reh sheth gath] (*possession of Gath*) — the birthplace, hometown, or residence of the prophet Micah (Mic. 1:14). Micah is also called the Morasthite (Jer. 26:18, KJV; Mic. 1:1, KJV)—that is, a native or resident of Moresheth. The site of Moresheth Gath is identified with present-day Tell ej-Judeideh, in the lowland plain of Judah.

MORIAH [moh RYE uh] — the name of two sites in the Old Testament:

1. A land to which God commanded Abraham to take his son Isaac and to offer him as a burnt offering on one of the mountains. The mountains of this land were a three-day journey from Beersheba and were visible from a great distance (Gen. 22:2, 4).

2. The hill at Jerusalem where Solomon built "the house of the Lord," the temple. Originally this was the threshing floor of Ornan the Jebusite (2 Chr. 3:1), also called Araunah the Jebusite (2 Sam. 24:16–24), where God appeared to David. David purchased the threshing floor from Ornan (1 Chr. 21:15–22:1) and built an altar on the site. It was left to David's son (Solomon) to build the temple.

Some Jews believe the altar of burnt offering in the temple at Jerusalem was situated on the exact site of the altar on which Abraham intended to sacrifice Isaac. To them the two Mount Moriahs mentioned in the Bible are identical. The Muslim structure, the Dome of the Rock in Jerusalem, reputedly is situated on this site.

MOSES [MOE zez] — the Hebrew prophet who delivered the Israelites from Egyptian slavery and who was their leader and lawgiver during their years of wandering in the wilderness. He was from the family line of Amram and Jochebed (Ex. 6:18, 20; Num. 26:58–59), Kohath and Levi. He was also the brother of Aaron and Miriam.

Moses was a leader so inspired by God that he was able to build a united nation from a race of oppressed and weary slaves. In the covenant ceremony at Mount Sinai, where the Ten Commandments were given, he founded the religious community known as Israel. As the interpreter of these covenant laws, he was the organizer of the community's religious and civil traditions. His story is told in the Old Testament—in the books of Exodus, Leviticus, Numbers, and Deuteronomy.

Moses' life is divided into three major periods:

The Forty Years in Egypt. The Hebrew people had been in slavery in Egypt for some 400 years. This was in accord with God's words to Abraham that his seed, or descendants, would be in a foreign land in affliction for 400 years (Gen. 15:13). At the end of this time, God began to set His people free from their bondage by bringing Moses to birth. He was a child of the captive Hebrews, but one whom the Lord would use to deliver Israel from her oppressors.

Moses was born at a time when the pharaoh, the ruler of Egypt, had given orders that no more male Hebrew children should be allowed to live. The Hebrew slaves had been reproducing so fast that the king felt threatened by a potential revolt against his authority. To save the infant Moses, his mother made a little vessel of papyrus waterproofed with asphalt and pitch. She placed Moses in the vessel, floating among the reeds on the bank of the Nile River. By God's providence, Moses—the child of a Hebrew slave—was found and adopted by an Egyptian princess, the daughter of the pharaoh himself. He was reared in the royal court as a prince of the Egyptians: "And Moses was learned in all the wisdom of the Egyptians, and was mighty in words and deeds" (Acts 7:22). At the same time, the Lord determined that Moses should be taught in his earliest years by his own mother. This meant that he was founded in the faith of his fathers, although he was reared as an Egyptian (Ex. 2:1–10).

One day Moses became angry at an Egyptian taskmaster who was beating a Hebrew slave; he killed the Egyptian and buried him in the sand (Ex. 2:12). When this became known, however, he feared for his own life and fled from Egypt to the land of Midian. Moses was 40 years old when this occurred (Acts 7:23–29).

The Forty Years in the Land of Midian. Moses' exile of about 40 years was spent in the land of Midian (mostly in northwest Arabia), in the desert between Egypt and Canaan. In Midian Moses became a shepherd and eventually the son-in-law of Jethro, a Midianite priest. Jethro gave his daughter Zipporah to Moses in marriage (Ex. 2:21); and she bore him two sons, Gershom and Eliezer (Ex. 18:3–4; Acts 7:29). During his years as a shepherd, Moses became familiar with the wilderness of the Sinai Peninsula, learning much about survival in the desert. He also learned patience and much about leading sheep. All of these skills prepared him to be the shepherd of the Israelites in later years when he led them out of Egypt and through the Wilderness of Sinai.

Near the end of his 40-year sojourn in the land of Midian, Moses experienced a dramatic call to ministry. This call was given at the burning bush in the wilderness near Mount Sinai. The Lord revealed to Moses His intention to deliver Israel from Egyptian captivity into a "land flowing with milk and honey" that He had promised centuries before to Abraham, Isaac, and Jacob. The Lord assured Moses that He would be with him, and that by God's presence, he would be able to lead the people out.

God spoke to Moses from the midst of a burning bush, but Moses doubted that it was God who spoke. He asked for a sign.

Instantly his rod, which he cast on the ground, became a serpent (Ex. 4:3).

In spite of the assurance of this miraculous sign, Moses was still hesitant to take on this task. He pleaded that he was "slow of speech and slow of tongue" (Ex. 4:10), perhaps implying that he was a stutterer or a stammerer. God countered Moses' hesitation by appointing his brother, Aaron, to be his spokesman. Moses would be God's direct representative, and Aaron would be his mouthpiece and interpreter to the people of Israel. Finally Moses accepted this commission from God and returned to Egypt for a confrontation with pharaoh.

Soon after his return, Moses stirred the Hebrews to revolt and demanded of pharaoh, "Let My people go, that they may hold a feast to Me in the wilderness" (Ex. 5:1). But pharaoh rejected the demand of this unknown God of whom Moses and Aaron spoke: "Who is the LORD, that I should obey His voice to let Israel go? I do not know the LORD, nor will I let Israel go" (Ex. 5:2). He showed his contempt of this God of the Hebrews by increasing the oppression of the slaves (Ex. 5:5–14). As a result, the people grumbled against Moses (Ex. 5:20–21).

But Moses did not waver in his mission. He warned pharaoh of the consequences that would fall on his kingdom if he should refuse to let the people of Israel go. Then followed a stubborn battle of wills with pharaoh hardening his heart and stiffening his neck against God's commands. Ten terrible plagues were visited upon the land of Egypt (Ex. 7:14–12:30), the tenth plague being the climax of horrors.

The ultimate test of God's power to set the people free was the slaying of the firstborn of all Egypt, on the night of the Passover feast of Israel (Ex. 11:1–12:30). That night Moses began to lead the slaves to freedom, as God killed the firstborn of Egypt and spared the firstborn of Israel through the sprinkling of the blood of the Passover lamb. This pointed to the day when God's own Lamb would come into the world to deliver, by His own blood, all of those who put their trust in Him, setting them free from sin and death "but with the precious blood of Christ, as of a lamb without blemish and without spot" (1 Pet. 1:19).

After the Hebrews left, pharaoh's forces pursued them to the Red Sea (or Sea of Reeds), threatening to destroy them before they could cross. A pillar, however, stood between the Israelites and the Egyptians, protecting the Israelites until they could escape. When Moses stretched his hand over the sea, the waters were divided and the Israelites passed to the other side. When the Egyptians attempted to follow, Moses again stretched his hand over the sea, and the waters closed over the Egyptian army (Ex. 14:19–31).

The Forty Years in the Wilderness. Moses led the people toward Mount Sinai, in obedience to the word of God spoken to him at the burning bush (Ex. 3:1–12). During the long journey through the desert, the people began to murmur because of the trials of freedom, forgetting the terrible trials of Egyptian bondage. Through it all, Moses was patient, understanding both the harshness of the desert and the blessings of God's provision for them.

In the Wilderness of Shur the people murmured against Moses because the waters of Marah were bitter. The Lord showed Moses a tree. When Moses cast the tree into the waters, the waters were made sweet (Ex. 15:22–25). In answer to Moses' prayers, God sent bread from heaven—manna—and quail to eat (Exodus 16). In the Wilderness of Sin, when they again had no water, Moses performed a miracle by striking a rock, at a place called Massah (Testing) and Meribah (Contention), and water came out of the rock (Ex. 17:1–7). When they reached the land of Midian, Moses' father-in-law, Jethro, came to meet them. He gave Moses sound advice on how to exercise his leadership and authority more efficiently by delegating responsibility to subordinate rulers who would judge the people in small cases (Exodus 18).

When the Israelites arrived at Mount Sinai, Moses went up onto the mountain for 40 days (Ex. 24:18). The Lord appeared in a terrific storm—"thunderings and lightnings, and a thick cloud" (Ex. 19:16). Out of this momentous encounter came the covenant between the Lord and Israel, including the Ten Commandments (Ex. 20:1–17).

In giving the law to the Hebrew people, Moses taught the Israelites what the Lord expected of them—that they were to be a holy people separated from the pagan immorality and idolatry of their surroundings. Besides being the lawgiver, Moses was also the one through whom God presented the Tabernacle and instructions for the holy office of the priesthood. Under God's instructions, Moses issued ordinances to cover specific situations, instituted a system of judges and hearings in civil cases, and regulated the religious and ceremonial services of worship.

When Moses delayed in coming down from Mount Sinai, the faithless people became restless. They persuaded Aaron to take their golden earrings and other articles of jewelry and to fashion a golden calf for worship. When he came down from the mountain, Moses was horrified at the idolatry and rebellion of his people. The sons of Levi were loyal to Moses, however; and he ordered them to punish the rebels (Ex. 32:28). Because of his anger at the golden calf, Moses cast down the two tablets of stone with the Ten Commandments and broke them at the foot of the mountain (Ex. 32:19). After the rebellion had been put down, Moses went up onto Mount Sinai again and there received the Ten Commandments a second time (Ex. 34:1, 29).

After leaving Mount Sinai, the Israelites continued their journey toward the land of Canaan. They arrived at Kadesh Barnea, on the border of the promised land. From this site, Moses sent 12 spies, one from each of the 12 tribes of Israel, into Canaan to explore the land. The spies returned with glowing reports of the fruitfulness of the land. They brought back samples of its figs and pomegranates and a cluster of grapes so large that it had to be carried between two men on a pole (Num. 13:1–25). The majority of the spies, however, voted against the invasion of the land. Ten of them spoke fearfully of the huge inhabitants of Canaan (Num. 13:31–33).

The minority report, delivered by Caleb and Joshua, urged a bold and courageous policy. By trusting the Lord, they said, the Israelites would be able to attack and overcome the land (Num. 13:30). But the people lost heart and rebelled, refusing to enter Canaan and clamoring for a new leader who would take them back to Egypt (Num. 14:1–4). To punish them for their lack of faith, God condemned all of that generation, except Caleb and Joshua, to perish in the wilderness (Num. 14:26–38).

During these years of wandering in the wilderness, Moses' patience was continually tested by the murmurings, grumblings, and complaints of the people. At one point, Moses' patience reached its breaking point and he sinned against the Lord, in anger against the people. When the people again grumbled against Moses, saying they had no water, the Lord told Moses to speak to the rock and water would flow forth. Instead, Moses lifted his hand and struck the rock twice with his rod. Apparently because he disobeyed the Lord in this act, Moses was not permitted to enter the promised land (Num. 20:1–13). That privilege would belong to his successor, Joshua.

When Moses had led the Israelites to the borders of Canaan, his work was done. In "the Song of Moses" (Deut. 32:1–43), Moses renewed the Sinai Covenant with the survivors of the wanderings, praised God, and blessed the people, tribe by tribe (Deut. 33:1–29). Then he climbed Mount Nebo to the top of Pisgah and viewed the promised land from afar and died. The Hebrews never saw him again, and the circumstances of his death and burial remain shrouded in mystery (Num. 34:1–8).

After his death, Moses continued to be viewed by Israel as the servant of the Lord (Josh. 1:1–2) and as the one through whom God spoke to Israel (Josh. 1:3; 9:24; 14:2). For that reason, although it was truly the law of God, the law given at Mount Sinai was consistently called the law of Moses (Josh. 1:7; 4:10). Above all, Joshua's generation remembered Moses as the man of God (Josh. 14:6).

This high regard for Moses continued throughout Israelite history. Moses was held in high esteem by Samuel (1 Sam. 12:6, 8), the writer of 1 Kings (1 Kin. 2:3), and the Jewish people who survived in the times after the captivity (1 Chr. 6:49; 23:14).

The psalmist also remembered Moses as the man of God and as an example of a great man of prayer (Ps. 99:6). He recalled that God worked through Moses (Pss. 77:20; 103:7), realizing that the consequence of his faithfulness to God was to suffer much on behalf of God's people (Ps. 106:16, 32).

The prophets of the Old Testament also remembered Moses as the leader of God's people (Is. 63:12), as the one by whom God brought Israel out of Egypt (Mic. 6:4), and as one of the greatest of the interceders for God's people (Jer. 15:1). Malachi called the people to remember Moses' law and to continue to be guided by it, until the Lord Himself should come to redeem them (Mal. 4:4).

Jesus showed clearly, by what He taught and by how He lived, that He viewed Moses' law as authoritative for the people of God (Matt. 5:17–18). To the two disciples on the road to Emmaus, Jesus expounded the things concerning Himself written in the law of Moses, the Prophets, and the other writings of the Old Testament (Luke 24:27). At the transfiguration, Moses and Elijah appeared to Jesus and talked with Him (Matt. 17:1–4; Mark 9:2–5; Luke 9:28–33).

In his message before the Jewish Council, Stephen included a lengthy reference to how God delivered Israel by Moses and how Israel rebelled against God and against Moses' leadership (Acts 7:20–44).

The writer of the book of Hebrews spoke in glowing terms of the faith of Moses (Heb. 11:24–29). These and other passages demonstrate how highly Moses was esteemed by various writers of the Old and New Testaments.

The New Testament, however, shows that Moses' teaching was intended only to prepare humanity for the greater teaching and work of Jesus Christ (Rom. 1:16–3:31). What Moses promised, Jesus fulfilled: "For the law was given through Moses, but grace and truth came through Jesus Christ" (John 1:17).

MOUNT BAAL HERMON [BAY uhl HUR mun] — a mountain from which the Israelites were unable to expel the Hivites (Judg. 3:3). East of the Jordan River, the site marked the northern limit of the half-tribe of Manasseh. Some scholars believe the Hebrew text may originally have read "Baal Gad near Mount Hermon" (Josh. 13:5; 1 Chr. 5:23).

MOUNT HERES [HE reez] (*mountain of the sun*) — a mountain near Aijalon and Shaalbim on the border between Judah and Dan (Judg. 1:35; in Aijalon, and in Shaalbim, NRSV).

MOUNT OF CORRUPTION — a hill on the southern ridge of the Mount of Olives. On the Mount of Corruption King Solomon built high places for his wives' pagan gods. These hillshrines were destroyed in the religious reformation instituted by King Josiah (2 Kin. 23:13; Hill of Corruption, NIV; mount of destruction, NASB).

MOUNT OF OLIVES — a north-to-south ridge of hills east of Jerusalem where Jesus was betrayed on the night before His crucifixion. This prominent feature of Jerusalem's landscape is a gently rounded hill, rising to a height of about 830 meters (2,676 feet) and overlooking the temple.

The closeness of the Mount of Olives to Jerusalem's walls made this series of hills a grave strategic danger. The Roman commander Titus had his headquarters on the northern extension of the ridge during the siege of Jerusalem in A.D. 70. He named the place Mount Scopus, or "Lookout Hill," because of the view it offered over the city walls. The whole hill must have provided a platform for the Roman catapults that hurled heavy objects over the Jewish fortifications of the city.

In ancient times the whole mount must have been heavily wooded. As its name implies, it was covered with dense olive groves. It was from this woodland that the people, under Nehemiah's command, gathered their branches of olive, oil trees, myrtle, and palm to make booths when the Feast of Tabernacles was restored after their years of captivity in Babylon (Neh. 8:15).

The trees also grew on this mountain or hill in New Testament times. When Jesus entered the city, the people who acclaimed him king must have gathered the branches with which they greeted His entry from this same wooded area. Another summit of the Mount of Olives is the one on which the "men of Galilee" stood (Acts 1:11–12) as they watched the resurrected Christ ascend into heaven. Then there is the point to the south above the village of Silwan (or Siloam) on the slope above the spring. Defined by a sharp cleft, it faces west along the converging Valley of Hinnom. It is called the Mount of Offense, or the "Mount of Corruption" (2 Kin. 23:13), because here King Solomon built "high places" for pagan deities that were worshiped by the people during his time (1 Kin. 11:5–7).

Although the Mount of Olives is close to Jerusalem, there are surprisingly few references to this range of hills in the Old Testament. As David fled from Jerusalem during the rebellion by his son Absalom, he apparently crossed the shoulder of the hill: "So David went up by the ascent of the Mount of Olives" (2 Sam. 15:30). Support may be found in this account for the claim that the road from the Jordan Valley did not go around the ridge in Bible times but crossed over the ridge, allowing the city of Jerusalem to break spectacularly on the traveler's sight as he topped the hill.

The Mount of Olives is also mentioned in a reference by the prophet Zechariah to the future Day of the Lord: "In that day His feet will stand on the Mount of Olives, which faces Jerusalem on the east. And the Mount of Olives shall be split in two from east to west, making a very large valley; half of the mountain shall move toward the north and half of it toward the south" (Zech. 14:4). Christian tradition holds that when Christ returns to earth, His feet will touch first upon the Mount of Olives, the exact point from which He ascended into heaven (Acts 1:11–12).

In the New Testament the Mount of Olives played a prominent part in the last week of our Lord's ministry. Jesus approached Jerusalem from the east, by way of Bethphage and Bethany, at the Mount of Olives (Matt. 21:1; Mark 11:1). As He drew near the descent of the Mount of Olives (Luke 19:37), the crowd spread their garments on the road, and others cut branches from the trees and spread them before Him. They began to praise God and shout, "Hosanna to the Son of David!" (Matt. 21:9). When Jesus drew near Jerusalem, perhaps as He arrived at the top of the Mount of Olives, He saw the city and wept over it (Luke 19:41).

Jesus then went into Jerusalem and cleansed the temple of the moneychangers; He delivered parables to the crowd and silenced the scribes and Pharisees with His wisdom. Later, as He sat on the Mount of Olives, the disciples came to Him privately, and He delivered what is known as "the Olivet Discourse," a long sermon that speaks of the signs of the times and the end of the age, the Great Tribulation, and the coming of the Son of Man (Matt. 24:3–25:46; Mark 13:3–37).

After Jesus had instituted the Lord's Supper on the night of His betrayal, He and His disciples sang a hymn and went out to the Mount of Olives (Matt. 26:30; Mark 14:26), to the Garden of Gethsemane (Matt. 26:36; Mark 14:32). In this garden Jesus was betrayed by Judas and delivered into the hands of His enemies.

NAAMAN [NAY a man] (*pleasant*) — the name of three or four men in the Old Testament:

1. A son of Benjamin (Gen. 46:21).

2. A son of Bela and the founder of a family, the Naamites (Num. 26:40). He may be the same person as No. 1.

3. A commander of the Syrian army who was cured of leprosy by the Lord through the prophet Elisha. Naaman was a "great and honorable man in the eyes of his master [Ben-Hadad, king of Syria] ... but he was a leper" (2 Kin. 5:1–27). Although leprosy was a despised disease in Syria, as in Israel, those who suffered from the disease were not outcasts.

On one of Syria's frequent raids of Israel, a young Israelite girl was captured and became a servant to Naaman's wife. The girl told her mistress about the prophet Elisha, who could heal Naaman of his leprosy. Ben-Hadad sent a letter about Naaman to the king of Israel. Fearing a Syrian trick to start a war, the king of Israel had to be assured by Elisha that Naaman should indeed be sent to the prophet. To demonstrate to Naaman that it was God, not human beings, who healed, Elisha refused to appear to Naaman. Instead, he sent the commander a message, telling him to dip himself in the Jordan River seven times. Naaman considered such treatment an affront and angrily asked if the Syrian rivers, the Abana and the Pharpar, would not do just as well. His servants, however, persuaded him to follow Elisha's instructions. Naaman did so and was healed. In gratitude, Naaman became a worshiper of God and carried two mule-loads of Israelite earth back to Syria in order to worship the Lord "on Israelite soil," even though he lived in a heathen land. Before he departed for Damascus, however, Naaman asked Elisha's understanding and pardon for bowing down in the temple of Rimmon when he went there with Ben-Hadad (2 Kin. 5:18). Elisha said to him, "Go in peace" (v. 19), thus allowing Naaman to serve his master, the king.

4. A son of Ehud, of the tribe of Benjamin (1 Chr. 8:7).

NABOTH [NAY bahth] — an Israelite of Jezreel who owned a vineyard next to the summer palace of Ahab, king of Samaria (1 Kin. 21:1). Ahab coveted this property. He wanted to turn it into a vegetable garden to furnish delicacies for his table. He offered Naboth its worth in money or a better vineyard. But Naboth refused to part with his property, explaining that it was a family inheritance to be passed on to his descendants.

Jezebel obtained the property for Ahab by bribing two men to bear false witness against Naboth and testify that he blasphemed God and the king. Because of their lies, Naboth was found guilty; and both he and his sons (2 Kin. 9:26) were stoned to death. Elijah the prophet pronounced doom upon Ahab and his house for this disgusting act of false witness (1 Kin. 21:1–29; 2 Kin. 9:21–26).

NAHOR [NAY hor] — the name of two men and a city in the Old Testament:

1. Father of Terah, grandfather of Abraham (Gen. 11:22–25), and an ancestor of Jesus Christ (Luke 3:34; Nachor, KJV).

2. A son of Terah and a brother of Abraham and Haran (Gen. 11:26–29). Nahor had 12 children, 8 by his wife Milcah and 4 by

his concubine Reumah. One of his children was Bethuel, who became the father of Rebekah and Laban (Gen. 28:5).

3. A city mentioned in Genesis 24:10. Some confusion exists about the phrase "city of Nahor." This may refer either to the city called Nahor or to the city where Nahor lived. When Abraham and Lot migrated to Canaan, Nahor remained in Haran.

NAHUM [NAY hum] (*compassionate*) — the name of two men in the Bible:

1. An Old Testament prophet and author of the book of Nahum whose prophecy pronounced God's judgment against the mighty nation of Assyria. Very little is known about Nahum. His hometown, Elkosh in the nation of Israel (Nah. 1:1), has not been located. But he must have lived some time shortly before 612 B.C., the year when Assyria's capital city, Ninevch, was destroyed by the Babylonians. Nahum announced that the judgment of God would soon be visited upon this pagan city.

The book of Nahum is similar to the book of Obadiah, since both these prophecies were addressed against neighboring nations. Obadiah spoke the word of the Lord against Edom, while Nahum prophesied against Assyria. Both messages contained a word of hope for God's covenant people, since they announced that Israel's enemies would soon be overthrown. While little is known about Nahum the man, his prophetic writing is one of the most colorful in the Old Testament. The book of Nahum is marked by strong imagery, a sense of suspense, and vivid language, with biting puns and deadly satire. Nahum was a man who understood God's goodness, but he could also describe the terror of the Lord against His enemies.

2. An ancestor of Jesus (Luke 3:25).

NAOMI [nay OH mee] (*my joy*) — the mother-in-law of Ruth. After her husband and two sons died, Naomi returned to her home in Bethlehem, accompanied by Ruth.

Naomi advised Ruth to work for a near kinsman, Boaz (Ruth 2:1), and to seek his favor. When Boaz and Ruth eventually married, they had a son, whom they named Obed. This child became the father of Jesse, the grandfather of David, and an ancestor of Jesus Christ (Ruth 4:21–22; Matt. 1:5).

NAPHTALI [NAF tuh lie] (*my wrestling*) — the sixth son of Jacob (Gen. 35:25). Because Jacob's wife Rachel was barren and her sister Leah had borne four sons to Jacob, Rachel was distraught. She gave her maidservant Bilhah to Jacob. Any offspring of this union were regarded as Rachel's. When Bilhah gave birth to Dan and Naphtali, Rachel was joyous. "With great wrestlings I have wrestled with my sister," she said, "and indeed I have prevailed" (Gen. 30:8). So she called his name Naphtali, which means "my wrestling."

NATHAN [NAY thun] (*he gave*) — the name of several men in the Old Testament:

1. A son of David and Bathsheba and an older brother of Solomon. Nathan was David's third son born in Jerusalem (2 Sam. 5:14). Six sons had been born to David earlier, while he was at Hebron. Through Nathan the line of descent passed from David to Jesus Christ (Luke 3:31).

2. A prophet during the reign of David and Solomon. Nathan told David that he would not be the one to build the temple (1 Chr. 17:1–15). Using the parable of the "one little ewe lamb," Nathan confronted David ("You are the man!") with his double sin, the murder of Uriah the Hittite and his adultery with Bathsheba, Uriah's wife (2 Sam. 12:1–15). Nathan, as the Lord's official prophet, named Solomon Jedidiah, which means "Beloved of the Lord" (2 Sam. 12:25). Nathan was also involved in David's arrangement of the musical services of the sanctuary (2 Chr. 29:25).

When David was near death, Nathan advised Bathsheba to tell David of the plans of David's son Adonijah to take the throne. Bathsheba related the news to David, who ordered that Solomon be proclaimed king (1 Kin. 1:8–45). Nathan apparently wrote a history of David's reign (1 Chr. 29:29) and a history of Solomon's reign (2 Chr. 9:29).

3. A man from Zobah, an Aramean, or Syrian, kingdom between Damascus and the Euphrates River (2 Sam. 23:36).

4. Father of two of Solomon's officials (1 Kin. 4:5), perhaps the same person as No. 1 or No. 2.

5. A descendant of Jerahmeel, of the tribe of Judah (1 Chr. 2:36).

6. A brother of Joel (1 Chr. 11:38) and probably the same man as No. 3.

7. A leader sent by Ezra to find Levites for the temple (Ezra 8:15–16).

8. A son of Bani (Ezra 10:34) who divorced his pagan wife after returning from the captivity in Babylon (Ezra 10:39), probably the same person as No. 7.

NAZARETH [NAZ ah reth] (*watchtower*) — a town of lower Galilee where Jesus spent His boyhood years (Matt. 2:23). For centuries Nazareth has been a beautifully secluded town nestled in the southernmost hills of the Lebanon Mountain range. Situated in the territory belonging to Zebulun, the city must have been of late origin or of minor importance. It is never mentioned in the Old Testament.

Nazareth lay close to the important trade routes of Palestine. It overlooked the Plain of Esdraelon through which caravans passed as they traveled from Gilead to the south and west. North of the city was the main road from Ptolemais to the Decapolis, a road over which the Roman legions frequently traveled. This fact may account for the possible source of the name Nazareth in the Aramaic word meaning "watchtower." However, Nazareth itself was situated in something of a basin, a high valley about 366 meters (1,200 feet) above sea level overlooking the Esdraelon Valley. To the north and east were steep hills, while on the west the hills rose to an impressive 488 meters (1,600 feet). Nazareth, therefore, was somewhat secluded and isolated from nearby traffic. This apparent isolation of Nazareth as a frontier town on the southern border of Zebulun contributed to the reputation that Nazareth was not an important part of the national and religious life of Israel. This, coupled with a rather bad reputation in morals and religion and a certain crudeness in the Galilean dialect, prompted Nathanael, when he first learned of Jesus of Nazareth, to ask, "Can anything good come out of Nazareth?" (John 1:46).

Although it was not an important town before the New Testament era, Nazareth became immortal as the hometown of Jesus the Messiah. It was here that the angel appeared to Mary and informed her of the forthcoming birth of Christ (Luke 1:26–38). Jesus was born in Bethlehem (Luke 2). But after their sojourn in Egypt (Matt. 2:19–22) to escape the ruthless murders of Herod the Great (Matt. 2:13–18), Joseph and Mary brought the baby Jesus to Nazareth where they had lived (Matt. 2:23). Here Jesus was brought up as a boy (Luke 4:16) and spent the greater part of His life (Mark 1:9; Luke 3:23). Apparently Jesus was well received as a young man in Nazareth (Luke 2:42; 4:16). But this changed after He began His ministry. His own towns-people twice rejected Him (Mark 6:1–6; Luke 4:28–30).

Because of His close association with this city, Christ became known as "Jesus of Nazareth" (Luke 18:37; 24:19; John 1:45). There is prophetic significance as well to His being known as a "Nazarene." Matthew records that Joseph and Mary returned to their city during the reign of Herod Archelaus (ethnarch of Judea, Idumea, and Samaria, 4 B.C.–A.D. 6) "that it might be fulfilled which was spoken by the prophets, 'He shall be called a Nazarene' " (Matt. 2:23).

NEBO [NEE boe] — the name of two towns, a mountain, and a man in the Old Testament:

1. A town in Moab east of the Jordan River that was captured and rebuilt by the tribe of Reuben (Num. 32:3, 38). Nebo is also mentioned on the Moabite Stone as having been taken back by Mesha, king of Moab.

2. A mountain of the Abarim range in Moab opposite Jericho (Num. 33:47). From Nebo Moses was permitted to view the promised land. He was buried in a nearby valley (Deut. 32:49, 50; 34:6).

3. A town mentioned immediately after Bethel and Ai in the lists of Israelites who returned from the captivity (Ezra 2:29). Nehemiah calls it "the other Nebo," apparently to distinguish it from No. 1.

4. The ancestor of seven Israelites who divorced their pagan wives after the captivity (Ezra 10:43).

NEGEV, THE [NEG ev] (*dry, parched*) — a term used by some English translations of the Bible for the southern desert or wilderness area of Judah, including about 4,500 square miles. Abraham journeyed in the Negev (Gen. 12:9; 13:1, 3; the South, NKJV). When the 12 spies explored the land of Canaan, they went up by way of the Negev (Num. 13:17, 22) and saw the Amalekites who lived there (Num. 13:29). The Canaanite king of Arad also lived in the Negev (Num. 21:1).

The prophet Isaiah described the Negev as a land of trouble and anguish, hardship and distress—a badland populated by lions and poisonous snakes (Is. 30:6). Through its arid wastes donkey and camel caravans made their way to and from the land of Egypt. Negev is also spelled Negeb.

The Negev contained important copper deposits, and it connected Israel to trade centers in Arabia and Egypt. King Solomon built fortresses in the Negev to guard the trade routes. He also established at Ezion Geber, on the Gulf of Aqaba, a port from which he shipped goods to foreign lands. King Uzziah made great efforts to develop the region, building fortresses and expanding agriculture (2 Chr. 26:10).

In modern times, the desert is being made to "blossom as the rose" (Is. 35:1); the Israelis have built an impressive irrigation system that channels life-giving water from northern Galilee to the dry, parched region of the Negev.

NEHEMIAH [knee uh MY ah] (*the Lord is consolation*) — the name of three men:

1. A clan leader who returned with Zerubbabel from the captivity (Ezra 2:2; Neh. 7:7).

2. The governor of Jerusalem who helped rebuild the wall of the city (Neh. 1:1; 8:9; 10:1; 12:26, 47). Nehemiah was a descendant of the Jewish population that had been taken captive to Babylon in 586 B.C. In 539 B.C. Cyrus the Persian gained control over all of Mesopotamia. He permitted the Jewish exiles to return to the city of Jerusalem. Nearly a century later, in Nehemiah's time, the Persian ruler was Artaxerxes I Longimanus (ruled 465–424 B.C.). Nehemiah was his personal cupbearer (Neh. 1:11).

In 445 B.C. Nehemiah learned of the deplorable condition of the returned exiles in Jerusalem (Neh. 1:2–3). The wall of the city was broken down, the gates were burned, and the people were in distress. Upon hearing this, Nehemiah mourned for many days, fasting and praying to God. His prayer is one of the most moving in the Old Testament (Neh. 1:5–11).

Nehemiah then received permission from Artaxerxes to go to Judah to restore the fortunes of his people. He was appointed governor of the province with authority to rebuild the city walls. Once in Jerusalem, Nehemiah surveyed the walls at night (Neh. 2:12–15). He gave his assessment of the city's condition to the leaders and officials and then organized a labor force to begin the work.

Nehemiah and his work crew were harassed by three enemies: Sanballat the Horonite (a Samaritan), Tobiah the Ammonite official, and Geshem the Arab (Neh. 2:10, 19; 6:1–14). But neither their ridicule (Neh. 4:3) nor their conspiracy to harm Nehemiah (Neh. 6:2) could stop the project. The builders worked with construction tools in one hand and weapons in the other (Neh. 4:17). To the taunts of his enemies, Nehemiah replied: "I am doing a great work, so that I cannot come down" (Neh. 6:3). Jerusalem's wall was finished in 52 days (Neh. 6:14)—a marvelous accomplishment for such a great task. Nehemiah's success stems from the fact that he kept praying, "O God, strengthen my hands" (Neh. 6:9).

Nehemiah's activities did not stop with the completion of the wall. He also led many social and political reforms among the people, including a return to pure worship and a renewed emphasis on true religion.

3. A son of Azbuk and leader of half the district of Beth Zur (Neh. 3:16). After his return from the captivity, Nehemiah helped with the repair work on the wall of Jerusalem.

NEHUM [NEE hum] (*consoled* [by God]) — a leader of the Jews who returned from the captivity with Zerubbabel (Neh. 7:7), also called Rehum (Ezra 2:2).

NER [nur] (*light*) — father of Abner, Saul's commander-in-chief (1 Sam. 14:50–51).

NICODEMUS [nick oh DEE mus] (*conqueror of the people*) — a Pharisee and a member of the Sanhedrin who probably became a disciple of Jesus (John 3:1, 4, 9; 7:50). He was described by Jesus as "the teacher of Israel," implying he was well trained in Old Testament law and tradition.

Nicodemus was a wealthy, educated, and powerful man—well respected by his people and a descendant of the patriarch

Abraham. Yet Jesus said to him, "You must be born again" (John 3:7). The Greek adverb translated "again" can also mean "from the beginning" (suggesting a new creation) and "from above" (that is, from God). In other words, Jesus told Nicodemus that physical generation was not enough, nor could his descent from the line of Abraham enable him to be saved. Only as a person has a spiritual generation—a birth from above—will he be able to see the kingdom of God.

The next time Nicodemus appears in the gospel of John, he shows a cautious, guarded sympathy with Jesus. When the Sanhedrin began to denounce Jesus as a false prophet, Nicodemus counseled the court by saying, "Does our law judge a man before it hears him and knows what he is doing?" (John 7:51).

Nicodemus appears a third and final time in the gospel of John. Obviously a wealthy man, he purchased about a hundred pounds of spices to be placed between the folds of the cloth in which Jesus was buried (John 19:39). Nothing else is known of Nicodemus from the Bible. But there is reason to believe that he became a follower of Jesus.

Christian tradition has it that Nicodemus was baptized by Peter and John, suffered persecution from hostile Jews, lost his membership in the Sanhedrin, and was forced to leave Jerusalem because of his Christian faith. Further mention is made of him in The gospel of Nicodemus, an apocryphal narrative of the crucifixion and resurrection of Christ.

NIMROD [NIM rahd] — a son of Cush and grandson of Ham, the youngest son of Noah (Gen. 10:8–12; 1 Chr. 1:10). Nimrod was a "mighty one on the earth"—a skilled hunter-warrior who became a powerful king. He is the first mighty hero mentioned in the Bible.

The principal cities of Nimrod's Mesopotamian kingdom were "Babel, Erech, Accad, and Calneh, in the land of Shinar"

(Gen. 10:10). From the land of Babylon he went to Assyria, where he built Nineveh and other cities (Gen. 10:11). In Micah 5:6 Assyria is called "the land of Nimrod."

The origin and meaning of the name Nimrod is uncertain, but it is doubtful that it is Hebrew. It may be Mesopotamian, originating from the Akkadian (northern Babylonian) god of war and hunting, Ninurta, who was called "the Arrow, the mighty hero." Some scholars believe Nimrod was Sargon the Great, a powerful ruler over Accad who lived about 2400 B.C. Others think he was the Assyrian king Tukulti-Ninurta I (about 1246–1206 B.C.), who conquered Babylonia. However, if Nimrod was indeed a Cushite, he may have been the Egyptian monarch Amenophis III (1411–1375 B.C.).

Nimrod was more likely Assyrian. His fierce aggressiveness, seen in the combination of warlike prowess and the passion for the chase, makes him a perfect example of the warrior-kings of Assyria.

NOAH [NOE uh] (*rest, relief*) — the name of a man and a woman in the Bible:

1. A son of Lamech and the father of Shem, Ham, and Japheth. He was a hero of faith who obeyed God by building an ark (a giant boat), thus becoming God's instrument in saving mankind from total destruction by the Flood (Gen. 5:28–9:29). The line of descent from Adam to Noah was as follows: Adam, Seth, Enosh, Cainan, Mahalaleel, Jared, Enoch, Methuselah, Lamech, and Noah (Gen. 5:1–32). If this genealogy does not allow for any gaps, Noah was only nine generations removed from Adam; and his father, Lamech, was 56 years old at the time of Adam's death.

Noah lived at a time when the whole earth was filled with violence and corruption. Yet Noah did not allow the evil standards of his day to rob him of fellowship with God. He stood out as the only one who "walked with God" (Gen. 6:9), as was true of his great-grandfather Enoch (Gen. 5:22). Noah was a just or righteous man (Gen. 6:9). The Lord singled out Noah from among all his contemporaries and chose him as the man to accomplish a great work.

When God saw the wickedness that prevailed in the world (Gen. 6:5), He disclosed to Noah His intention to destroy the world by a flood. He instructed Noah to build an ark in which he and his family would survive the catastrophe. Noah believed God and obeyed Him and "according to all that God commanded him, so he did" (Gen. 6:22). He is therefore listed among the heroes of faith (Heb. 11:7).

With unswerving confidence in the word of God, Noah started building the ark. For 120 years the construction continued. During this time of grace, Noah continued to preach God's judgment and mercy, warning the ungodly of their approaching doom (2 Pet. 2:5). He preached for 120 years, however, without any converts (1 Pet. 3:20). People continued in their evil ways and turned deaf ears to his pleadings and warnings until they were overtaken by the Flood.

When the ark was ready, Noah entered in with all kinds of animals "and the Lord shut him in" (Gen. 7:16), cut off completely from the rest of mankind.

Noah was grateful to the Lord who had delivered him from the Flood. After the Flood he built an altar to God (Gen. 8:20) and made a sacrifice, which was accepted graciously (Gen. 8:21). The Lord promised Noah and his descendants that He would never destroy the world again with a flood (Gen. 9:15). The Lord made an everlasting covenant with Noah and his descendants, establishing the rainbow as the sign of His promise (Gen. 9:12–17). The Lord also blessed Noah and restored the creation command, "Be fruitful and multiply, and fill the earth" (Gen. 9:1). These were the same words He had spoken earlier to Adam (Gen. 1:28).

Noah became the first tiller of the soil and keeper of vineyards after the Flood. His drunkenness is a prelude to the curse that was soon to be invoked on Canaan and his descendants, the Canaanites (Gen. 9:18–27). The Bible is silent about the rest of Noah's life after the Flood, except to say that he died at the age of 950 years (Gen. 9:28–29).

In the Gospels of the New Testament, the account of Noah and the Flood is used as a symbol of the end times. Warning His hearers about the suddenness of His return, Jesus referred to the sudden catastrophe that fell upon unbelievers at the time of the Flood: "As the days of Noah were, so also will the coming of the Son of Man be" (Matt. 24:37).

2. A daughter of Zelophehad (Josh. 17:3).

NOD [nahd] (*wandering*) — an unidentified land east of the garden of Eden where Cain fled after he murdered his brother (Gen. 4:16).

NOPH [nohf] — the Hebrew name for Memphis, an ancient Egyptian city on the western bank of the Nile and south of modern Cairo (Is. 19:13).

OBADIAH [oh bah DIE ah] (*servant of the Lord*) — the name of 13 men in the Old Testament:

1. The governor of Ahab's palace (1 Kin. 18:3–7, 16).

2. A descendant of David and the head of a family (1 Chr. 3:21).

3. A son of Izrahiah, of the tribe of Issachar (1 Chr. 7:3).

4. A descendant of King Saul (1 Chr. 8:38).

5. A Levite, a son of Shemaiah (1 Chr. 9:16).

6. A Gadite captain who joined David at Ziklag (1 Chr. 12:9).

7. A leader of the tribe of Zebulun during the reign of David (1 Chr. 27:19).

8. A leader of Jehoshaphat commissioned to teach the book of the Law (2 Chr. 17:7).

9. A Levite who supervised workmen repairing the temple (2 Chr. 34:12).

10. A son of Jehiel, a descendant of Joab (Ezra 8:9).

11. A priest who sealed the covenant after the captivity (Neh. 10:5).

12. A gatekeeper in Judah after the return from captivity (Neh. 12:25).

13. A prophet of Judah (Obadiah 1). The fourth of the "minor" prophets, Obadiah's message was directed against

Edom. Some scholars believe Obadiah was a contemporary of Jehoram, during whose reign (about 844 B.C.) Jerusalem was invaded by Philistines and Arabians (2 Chr. 21:16–17). Other scholars suggest a date following 586 B.C., the time of the destruction of Jerusalem by the Babylonians. Still others suggest an earlier Babylonian assault on Jerusalem, in 605 B.C. Whatever date is assigned to Obadiah, he lived during a time of trouble for Jerusalem. His prophecy against Edom condemned the Edomites for taking sides against Jerusalem in its distress (Obadiah 15). The strongest mountain fortresses would be no defense for the Edomites against the day — the time when God would bring His final judgment upon the world.

OG [ahg] — a king of the Amorites of the land of Bashan, a territory east of the Jordan River and north of the river Jabbok (Num. 21:33; 32:33). Og was king over 60 fortified cities, including Ashtaroth and Edrei. He was defeated by Moses and the Israelites (Deut. 3:6). Then his kingdom was given to the tribes of Reuben, Gad, and the half-tribe of Manasseh.

Og was the last survivor of the race of giants (Deut. 3:11). His huge iron bedstead was kept on display in Rabbah long after his death (Deut. 3:11).

OHOLAH [oh HOH lah] (*her own tent*) — a symbolic name for Samaria, capital of the Northern Kingdom, and the ten tribes that made up this nation (Ezek. 23:4–5, 36, 44). The prophet Ezekiel used the allegorical figure of two harlot sisters, Oholah (Aholah, KJV) and Oholibah (Aholibah, KJV), to represent Jerusalem and the kingdom of Judah. Oholah and Oholibah are pictured as lusting after the Assyrians, Babylonians, and Egyptians.

OHOLIBAH [o HOLE ih bah] (*my tent is in her*) — a symbolic name given by the prophet Ezekiel to Jerusalem, the capital of Judah (Ezek. 23:4–44), to signify its unfaithfulness to God.

O MRI [UM rih] — the name of four men in the Old Testament:

1. The sixth king of the northern kingdom of Israel (885–874 B.C.). Omri is first mentioned as the commander of the army of Israel under King Elah. While Omri besieged the Philistine city of Gibbethon, another military figure, Zimri, conspired against Elah, killed him, and established himself as king. Zimri, however, had little support in Israel, and the army promptly made Omri its king. Omri returned to the capital with his army, besieged the city, and Zimri committed suicide. Tibni, the son of Ginath, continued to challenge Omri's reign, but after four years Tibni died and Omri became the sole ruler of Israel (1 Kin. 16:21–28).

Omri was a king of vision and wisdom. From Shemer he purchased a hill on which he built a new city, Samaria, making it the new capital of Israel. Samaria was more defensible than Tirzah had been. Because it was strategically located, Omri was able to control the north–south trade routes in the region. Archaeological excavations at Samaria revealed buildings of excellent workmanship—an indication of the prosperity the city enjoyed during his reign. The Moabite Stone tells of Omri's success against King Mesha of Moab (2 Kin. 3:4). But Omri's conflict with Syria proved to be less successful, and he was forced to grant a number of cities to the Syrians (1 Kin. 20:34).

2. A member of the tribe of Benjamin and a son of Becher (1 Chr. 7:8).

3. A member of the tribe of Judah and a son of Imri (1 Chr. 9:4).

4. The son of Michael and a prince of the tribe of Issachar during the time of David (1 Chr. 27:18).

ONAN [OH nan] — the second son of Judah by the daughter of Shua the Canaanite (Gen. 38:2, 4). He was a wicked man, and the Lord put him to death (Gen. 38:10).

ONESIMUS [oh NESS ih muss] (*useful*) — a slave of Philemon and an inhabitant of Colossae (Col. 4:9; Philem. v. 10). When Onesimus fled from his master to Rome, he met the apostle Paul. Paul witnessed to him, and Onesimus became a Christian. In his Letter to Philemon, Paul spoke of Onesimus as "my own heart" (Philem. v. 12), indicating that Onesimus had become like a son to him.

Paul convinced Onesimus to return to his master, Philemon. He also sent a letter with Onesimus, encouraging Philemon to treat Onesimus as a brother rather than a slave. Paul implied that freeing Onesimus was Philemon's Christian duty, but he stopped short of commanding him to do so. Onesimus accompanied Tychicus, who delivered the Epistle to the Colossians as well as the Epistle to Philemon. Some scholars believe this Onesimus is Onesimus the bishop, praised in a letter to the second-century church at Ephesus from Ignatius of Antioch.

ORPAH [AWR pah] — a Moabite woman who married Chilion, one of the two sons of Elimelech and Naomi (Ruth 1:4). When Elimelech and his sons died in Moab, Orpah accompanied Naomi, her mother-in-law, part of the way to Bethlehem and then returned "to her people and to her gods" (Ruth 1:14) in Moab.

OTHNIEL [OATH nih el] — the name of two men in the Old Testament:

1. The first judge of Israel (Judg. 1:13; 3:9, 11). Othniel was a son of Kenaz and probably was a nephew of Caleb. When the Israelites forgot the Lord and served the pagan gods of Canaan, the king of Mesopotamia oppressed them for eight years. When

the Israelites repented of their evil and cried out to the Lord for deliverance, Othniel was raised up by the Lord to deliver His people. Othniel was one of four judges (the other three were Gideon, Jephthah, and Samson) of whom the Scripture says, "The Spirit of the LORD came upon him" (Judg. 3:10).

2. An ancestor of Heldai (1 Chr. 27:15).

P

PADAN ARAM [PAD uhn AH rem] (*the plain of Aram*) — the area of Upper Mesopotamia around Haran and the home of Abraham after he moved from Ur of the Chaldeans (Gen. 25:20; Paddan Aran, NIV; Paddan-aram, NRSV). Abraham later sent his servant to Padan Aram to find a bride for his son Isaac (Gen. 25:20). Much later, Isaac's son Jacob fled to Padan Aram to avoid the wrath of his brother Esau and dwelled there with Laban (Gen. 28:2, 5–7). The region was also referred to as Padan (Gen. 48:7; Paddan, NIV, NRSV).

PAMPHYLIA [pam FIL ih uh] (*a region of every tribe*) — a Roman province on the southern coast of central Asia Minor. The province consisted mainly of a plain about 130 kilometers (80 miles) long and up to about 32 kilometers (20 miles) wide. The capital city of Pamphylia, its largest city, was Perga (Acts 13:13–14).

Pamphylia is first mentioned in the New Testament in Acts 2:10. People from Pamphylia were among those present in Jerusalem on the Day of Pentecost. In Pamphylia Paul first entered Asia Minor (Acts 13:13) during his first missionary journey. It was at Pamphylia that John Mark left Paul and Barnabas

(Acts 15:38). On his voyage to Rome, Paul sailed off the coast of Pamphylia (Acts 27:5).

PARAN [PAH ruhn] — a wilderness region in the central part of the Sinai Peninsula. Although the boundaries of this desert region are somewhat obscure, it probably bordered the Arabah and the Gulf of Aqaba on the east. The modern Wadi Feiran in central Sinai preserves the ancient name.

Paran is frequently mentioned in the Old Testament. Chedorlaomer, one of the four kings who attacked Sodom, conquered as far as "El Paran, which is by the wilderness" (Gen. 14:6). After Hagar was driven from Abraham's household (Gen. 21:21), she fled to this wilderness with her son, Ishmael. The Israelites crossed Paran during their Exodus from Egypt (Num. 10:12; 12:16), and Moses dispatched spies from Paran to explore the land of Canaan (Num. 13:3). After their mission, these spies returned "unto the wilderness of Paran, to Kadesh" (Num. 13:26).

Much later, after the death of Samuel, David fled to Paran (1 Sam. 25:1). After revolting from King Solomon, Hadad went through Paran on his flight to Egypt (1 Kin. 11:18).

PATMOS [PAT muhs] — a small rocky island to which the apostle John was banished and where he wrote the book of Revelation (Rev. 1:9). The island, about 16 kilometers (10 miles) long and 10 kilometers (6 miles) wide, lies off the southwest coast of Asia Minor (modern Turkey). Because of its desolate and barren nature, Patmos was used by the Romans as a place to banish criminals, who were forced to work at hard labor in the mines and quarries of the island. Because Christians were regarded as criminals by the Roman emperor Domitian (ruled A.D. 81–96), the apostle John probably suffered from harsh treatment during his exile on Patmos. An early Christian tradition said John was in exile for 18 months.

PAUL, THE APOSTLE — the earliest and most influential interpreter of Christ's message and teaching; an early Christian missionary; correspondent with several early Christian churches.

The Life of Paul. Paul was born at Tarsus, the chief city of Cilicia (southeast Asia Minor). He was a citizen of Tarsus, "no mean city," as he called it (Acts 21:39). He was also born a Roman citizen (Acts 22:28), a privilege that worked to his advantage on several occasions during his apostolic ministry. Since Paul was born a Roman citizen, his father must have been a Roman citizen before him. "Paul" was part of his Roman name. In addition to his Roman name, he was given a Jewish name, "Saul," perhaps in memory of Israel's first king, a member of the tribe of Benjamin, to which Paul's family belonged.

His Jewish heritage meant much more to Paul than Roman citizenship. Unlike many Jews who had been scattered throughout the world, he and his family did not become assimilated to the Gentile way of life that surrounded them. This is suggested when Paul describes himself as "a Hebrew of the Hebrews" (Phil. 3:5), and confirmed by Paul's statement in Acts 22:3 that, while he was born in Tarsus, he was brought up in Jerusalem "at the feet of Gamaliel," the most illustrious rabbi of his day (Acts 5:34). Paul's parents wanted their son to be well grounded in the best traditions of Jewish orthodoxy.

Paul proved an apt pupil. He outstripped many of his fellow students in his enthusiasm for ancestral traditions and in his zeal for the Jewish law. This zeal found a ready outlet in his assault on the infant church of Jerusalem. The church presented a threat to all that Paul held most dear. Its worst offense was its proclamation of one who had suffered a death cursed by the Jewish law as Lord and Messiah (Deut. 21:22–23). The survival of Israel demanded that the followers of Jesus be wiped out.

The first martyr of the Christian church was Stephen, one of the most outspoken leaders of the new movement. Luke told

how Paul publicly associated himself with Stephen's executioners and then embarked on a campaign designed to suppress the
church. Paul himself related how he "persecuted the church of
God beyond measure and tried to destroy it" (Gal. 1:13).

Conversion and Apostolic Commission — At the height of
Paul's campaign of repression, he was confronted on the road
to Damascus by the risen Christ. In an instant his life was
reoriented. The Jewish law was replaced as the central theme of
Paul's life by Jesus Christ. He became the leading champion of
the cause he had tried to overthrow.

The realization that Jesus, whom he had been persecuting,
was alive and exalted as the Son of God exposed the weakness of the Jewish law. Paul's zeal for the law had made him
an ardent persecutor. He now saw that his persecuting activity
had been sinful; yet the law, instead of showing him the sinfulness of such a course, had really led him into sin. The law
had lost its validity. Paul learned that it was no longer by keeping the law that a person was justified in God's sight, but by
faith in Christ. And if faith in Christ provided acceptance with
God, then Gentiles might enjoy that acceptance as readily as
Jews. This was one of the implications of the revelation of Jesus
Christ that gripped Paul's mind. He was assured that he himself
had received that revelation in order that he might proclaim
Christ and His salvation to the Gentile world. Paul began to
carry out this commission not only in Damascus but also in
the kingdom of the Nabatean Arabs, to the east and south. No
details are given of his activity in "Arabia" (Gal. 1:17), but he did
enough to attract the hostile attention of the authorities there,
as the representative of the Nabatean king in Damascus tried to
arrest him (2 Cor. 11:32–33).

After leaving Damascus, Paul paid a short visit to Jerusalem
to make the acquaintance of Peter. During his two weeks' stay
there, he also met James, the Lord's brother (Gal. 1:18–19). Paul
could not stay in Jerusalem because the animosity of his former

associates was too strong. He had to be taken down to Caesarea on the Mediterranean coast and put on a ship for Tarsus.

Paul spent the next ten years in and around Tarsus, actively engaged in the evangelizing of Gentiles. Very few details of those years have been preserved. At the end of that time Barnabas came to Tarsus from Antioch and invited Paul to join him in caring for a young church there. A spontaneous campaign of Gentile evangelization had recently occurred at Antioch, resulting in the formation of a vigorous church. Barnabas himself had been commissioned by the apostles in Jerusalem to lead the Gentile evangelization in the city of Antioch.

About a year after Paul joined Barnabas in Antioch, the two men visited Jerusalem and conferred with the three "pillars" of the church there—the apostles Peter and John, and James the Lord's brother (Gal. 2:1–10). The result of this conference was an agreement that the Jerusalem leaders would concentrate on the evangelization of their fellow Jews, while Barnabas and Paul would continue to take the gospel to Gentiles.

The Jerusalem leaders reminded Barnabas and Paul, in conducting their Gentile mission, not to forget the material needs of the impoverished believers in Jerusalem. Barnabas and Paul (especially Paul) readily agreed to bear those needs in mind. This may have been the occasion when they carried a gift of money from the Christians in Antioch to Jerusalem for the relief of their fellow believers who were suffering hardship in a time of famine (Acts 11:30).

Apostle to the Gentiles — The way was now open for a wider Gentile mission. Barnabas and Paul were released by the church of Antioch to pursue a missionary campaign that took them to Barnabas's native island of Cyprus and then into the highlands of central Asia Minor (modern Turkey), to the province of Galatia. There they preached the gospel and planted churches in the cities of Pisidian Antioch, Iconium, Lystra, and Derbe. The missionaries then returned to Antioch in Syria.

The great increase of Gentile converts caused alarm among many of the Jewish Christians in Judea. They feared that too many Gentiles would hurt the character of the church. Militant Jewish nationalists were already attacking them. A movement began that required Gentile converts to become circumcised and follow the Jewish law. The leaders of the Jerusalem church, with Paul and Barnabas in attendance, met in A.D. 48 to discuss the problem. It was finally decided that circumcision was not necessary, but that Gentile converts should conform to the Jewish code of laws in order to make fellowship between Jewish and Gentile Christians less strained (Acts 15:1–29).

After this meeting, Barnabas and Paul parted company. Paul chose Silas, a leading member of the Jerusalem church and a Roman citizen like himself, to be his new colleague. Together they visited the young churches of Galatia. At Lystra they were joined by Timothy, a young convert from Barnabas and Paul's visit some two years before. Paul in particular recognized qualities in Timothy that would make him a valuable helper in his missionary service. From that time to the end of Paul's life, Timothy was his most faithful attendant.

Paul and Silas probably planned to proceed west to Ephesus, but they felt the negative guidance of the Holy Spirit. They instead turned north and northwest, reaching the seaport of Troas. Here Paul was told in a vision to cross the north Aegean Sea and preach the gospel in Macedonia. This Paul and his companions did. By now their number had increased to four by the addition of Luke. The narrative reveals his presence at this point by using "we" instead of "they" (Acts 16:10).

Their first stop in Macedonia was the Roman colony of Philippi. Here, in spite of running into trouble with the magistrates and being imprisoned, Paul and his companions planted a strong church. They moved on to Thessalonica, the chief city of the province, and formed a church there, as well. But serious trouble broke out in Thessalonica. The missionaries were accused of rebelling against the Roman emperor by proclaiming Jesus as his rival. They were forced to leave the city quickly.

Paul moved south to Berea, where he was favorably received by the local synagogue, but his opponents from Thessalonica followed him, making it necessary for him to move on once more. Although churches of Macedonia would later give Paul much joy and satisfaction, he felt dejected at this time from being forced to flee city after city.

Paul, alone now, moved south into the province of Achaia. After a short stay in Athens, he came "in weakness, in fear, and in much trembling" (1 Cor. 2:3) to Corinth, the seat of provincial administration. Corinth had a reputation as a wicked city in the Greco-Roman world and it did not seem likely that the gospel would make much headway there. Surprisingly, however, Paul stayed there for 18 months and made many converts. While he was there, a new Roman proconsul, Gallio, arrived to take up residence in Corinth. The beginning of his administration can be accurately dated as July 1, A.D. 51. Paul was prosecuted before Gallio on the charge of preaching an illegal religion, but Gallio dismissed the charge. This provided other Roman magistrates with a precedent that helped the progress of the gospel over the next ten years.

The church of Corinth was large, lively, and talented but deficient in spiritual and moral stability. This deficiency caused Paul much anxiety over the next few years, as his letters to the Corinthians reveal. After his stay in Corinth, Paul paid a brief visit to Jerusalem and Antioch and then traveled to Ephesus, where he settled for the next three years. Paul's Ephesian ministry was perhaps the most active part of his apostolic career. A number of colleagues shared his activity and evangelized the city of Ephesus as well as the whole province of Asia (western Asia Minor). Ten years earlier there had been no churches in the great provinces of Galatia, Asia, Macedonia, or Achaia. Now Christianity had become so strong in them that Paul realized his work in that part of the world was finished. He began to think of a new area where he might repeat the same kind of missionary program. He wanted to evangelize territories where the gospel had never been heard before, having no desire to "build on another man's foundation" (Rom. 15:20). He decided to journey to Spain, and to set out as soon as he could. This journey would also give him a long-awaited opportunity to visit Rome on the way.

Before he could set out, however, an important task had to be completed. Paul had previously organized a relief fund among the Gentile churches to help poorer members of the Jerusalem church. Not only had he promised the leaders in Jerusalem to do such a thing, but he hoped it would strengthen the bond of fellowship among all the churches involved. Before leaving, Paul arranged for a member of each of the contributing churches to carry that church's donation. Paul himself would go to Jerusalem with them, giving the Jerusalem Christians an opportunity to see some of their Gentile brethren face-to-face in addition to receiving their gifts. Some of Paul's hopes and misgivings about the trip are expressed in Romans 15:25–32. His misgivings were well founded.

A few days after his arrival in Jerusalem, Paul was attacked by a mob in the area of the temple. He was rescued by a detachment of Roman soldiers and kept in custody at the Roman governor's headquarters in Caesarea for the next two years. At the end of that period he exercised his privilege as a Roman citizen and appealed to Caesar in order to have his case transferred from the provincial governor's court in Judea to the emperor's tribunal in Rome. He was sent to Rome in the fall of A.D. 59. The great apostle spent a further two years in Rome under house arrest, waiting for his case to come up for hearing before the supreme tribunal.

Paul, the Prisoner of Jesus Christ — The restrictions under which Paul lived in Rome should have held back his efforts to proclaim the gospel, but just the opposite actually happened. These restrictions, by his own testimony, "actually turned out for the furtherance of the gospel" (Phil. 1:12). Although he was confined to his lodgings, shackled to one of the soldiers who guarded him in four-hour shifts, he was free to receive visitors and talk to them about the gospel. The soldiers who guarded him and the officials in charge of presenting his case before the emperor were left in no doubt about the reason for his being in Rome. The gospel actually became a topic of discussion. This encouraged the Christians in Rome to bear more open witness to their faith, allowing the saving message to be proclaimed more fearlessly in Rome than ever before "and in this," said Paul, "I rejoice" (Phil. 1:18).

From Rome, Paul was able to correspond with friends in other parts of the Roman Empire. Visitors from those parts came to see him, bringing news of their churches. These visitors included Epaphroditus from Philippi and Epaphras from Colossae. From Colossae, too, Paul received an unexpected visitor, Onesimus, the slave of his friend Philemon. He sent Onesimus back to his master with a letter commending him "no longer as a slave but ... as a beloved brother" (Philem. v. 16).

The letters of Philippi and Colossae were sent in response to the news brought by Epaphroditus and Epaphras, respectively. At the same time as the letter to Colossae, Paul sent a letter to Laodicea and a more general letter that we now know as Ephesians. The Roman captivity became a very fruitful period for Paul and his ministry. We have very little information about the rest of Paul's career. We do not know the outcome of his trial before Caesar. He was probably discharged and enjoyed a further period of liberty. It is not known whether he ever preached the gospel in Spain. It is traditionally believed that Paul's condemnation and execution occurred during the persecution of Christians under the Roman Emperor Nero. The probable site of his execution may still be seen at Tre Fontane on the Ostian Road. There is no reason to doubt the place of his burial marked near the Basilica of St. Paul in Rome. There, beneath the high altar, is a stone inscription going back to at least the fourth century: "To Paul, Apostle and Martyr."

The Teaching of Paul. Paul is the most influential teacher of Christianity. More than any other disciple or apostle, Paul was given the opportunity to set forth and explain the revelations of Jesus Christ. Because Paul was called to teach Gentiles rather than Jews, he was in the unique position of confronting and answering problems that could only be presented by those completely unfamiliar with Jewish traditions. Several themes come through in his writings.

Christ, the Son of God — Paul knew that the one who appeared to him on the Damascus Road was the risen Christ. "Last of all He was seen by me also," he says (1 Cor. 15:8), counting this as the last of Christ's appearances.

Paul seems to have entertained no doubt of the validity of the appearance or of the words "I am Jesus" (Acts 9:5). Both the appearance and the words validated themselves in his later life. His whole Christian outlook on the world, like the gospel he preached, stemmed from that "revelation of Jesus Christ" (Gal. 1:12).

Christ was, in a unique sense, the Son of God. Other human beings became sons and daughters of God through their faith-union with Christ and their reception of the Spirit of Christ. From this point of view the Spirit was "the Spirit of adoption," enabling them to address God spontaneously as "Abba, Father" (Rom. 8:15).

Another token of the indwelling Spirit was giving Jesus the designation "Lord": "No one can say that Jesus is Lord except by the Holy Spirit" (1 Cor. 12:3). This designation is given by Paul to Jesus in the highest sense possible. It was bestowed on Jesus by God Himself when He rose to supremacy over the universe after His humiliation and death on the cross.

One striking designation that Paul gives to Christ—"the image of God" (2 Cor. 4:4) or "the image of the invisible God" (Col. 1:15)—appears to be closely associated with his conversion experience. Paul emphasizes the heavenly light that was such a memorable feature of that experience. Paul speaks of the minds of unbelievers being darkened to keep them from seeing "the light of the gospel of the glory of Christ, who is the image of God" (2 Cor. 4:4). This suggests that when "the glory of that light" (Acts 22:11) dispelled the darkness from Paul's own mind, he recognized the one who appeared to him as being the very image of God. ✳

Christ is presented by Paul as the one "through whom are all things, and through whom we live" (1 Cor. 8:6), and in whom, through whom, and for whom "all things were created" (Col. 1:16).

This landmark known as the tomb of Caecilia Metella (wife of a Roman official) stood on the Appian Way when Paul went to Rome to appear before Nero (Acts 28:15, 16).

Displacement of the Law — After his conversion Paul said, "To me, to live is Christ" (Phil. 1:21). Before his conversion he might well have said, "To me, to live is law." In his mind he had judged Christ according to the Jewish law, finding Him condemned by it. Since the law pronounced a curse on one who was impaled on a stake (Deut. 21:23; Gal. 3:13), Paul took the side of the law and agreed that both Christ and His people were accursed.

After his conversion, Paul recognized the continuing validity of the Scripture that declared the impaled man to be accursed by God, but now he understood it differently. If Christ, the Son of God, subjected Himself to the curse pronounced by the law, another look at the law was called for. The law could not provide anyone with righteous standing before God, however carefully he kept it. Paul knew that his life under the law stood condemned in the light of his Damascus Road experience. It was not the law in itself that was defective, because it was God's law. It was instead the people with whom the law had to work who were defective. The righteous standing that the law could not provide was conferred on believers through their faith in Christ. That righteous standing was followed by a righteous life. In one tightly packed sentence Paul declared that God has done what the law, weakened by the flesh, could not do, "sending His own Son in the likeness of sinful flesh, on account of sin: He condemned sin in the flesh, that the righteous requirement of the law might be fulfilled in us who do not walk according to the flesh but according to the Spirit" (Rom. 8:3–4).

The law could lead neither to a righteous standing before God nor to a righteous life. Paul, while faithfully keeping the law, was condemned before God rather than justified. His life was not righteous but was sinful because he "persecuted the church of God" (1 Cor. 15:9). This situation radically changed when Paul believed in Christ and knew himself to "be found in Him, not having my own righteousness, which is from the law, but that which is through faith in Christ, the righteousness which is from God by faith" (Phil. 3:9).

Christ, then, "is the end of the law for righteousness to everyone who believes" (Rom. 10:4). The word *end* is ambiguous: it may mean "goal" or "completion." As the law revealed the character and will of God, it pointed to Christ as the goal. He was the fulfillment of all the divine revelation that had preceded Him: "All the promises of God in Him are Yes" (2 Cor. 1:20). But when the law came to be regarded as the way of salvation or the rule of life, Christ put an end to it. The law pronounced a curse on those who failed to keep it; Christ redeemed His people from that curse by undergoing it Himself. He exhausted the curse in His own person through His death.

According to Paul, the law was a temporary provision introduced by God to bring latent sin into the open. When they broke its individual commands, men and women would realize their utter dependence on divine grace. Centuries before the law was given, God promised Abraham that through him and his offspring all nations would be blessed. This promise was granted in response to Abraham's faith in God. The later giving of the law did not affect the validity of the promise. Instead, the promise was fulfilled in Christ, who replaced the law. The law had been given to the nation of Israel only, providing a privilege that set it apart from other nations. God's original promise embraced all nations and justified Paul's presentation of the gospel to Gentiles as well as Jews. The promise had wide implications: "Christ has redeemed us from the curse of the law … that the blessing of Abraham might come upon the Gentiles in Christ Jesus, that we might receive the promise of the Spirit through faith" (Gal. 3:13–14).

The Age of the Spirit — Those who believe God as Abraham did are not only justified by faith but also receive the Holy Spirit. The blessing promised to Abraham, secured through the redemptive work of Christ, is identified with the gift of the Spirit. The age of the Spirit has replaced the age of law.

It is common teaching in the New Testament that the age of the Spirit followed the completion of Christ's work on earth. Paul presents this teaching with his own emphasis. His negative evaluation of the place of law in Christian life naturally caused others to ask how ethical and moral standards were to be maintained. Paul answered that the Spirit supplied a more effective power for holy living than the law could ever supply. The law imposed bondage, but "where the Spirit of the Lord is, there is liberty" (2 Cor. 3:17). The law told people what to do, but could provide neither the will nor the power to do it; the Spirit, operating within the believer's life, can provide both the will and the power.

The Spirit is called not only the Spirit of God but also the Spirit of Christ. He is the Spirit who dwelled within Christ during His earthly ministry, empowering Him to accomplish merciful works and to teach wisdom and grace. The qualities that characterized Christ are reproduced by His Spirit in His people: "love, joy, peace, longsuffering, kindness, goodness, faithfulness, gentleness, self-control" (Gal. 5:22–23).

John the Baptist predicted that Christ would baptize men and women with the Holy Spirit (Matt. 3:11; Mark 1:8; Luke 3:16). The New Testament teaches that this prediction was fulfilled with the coming of the Holy Spirit at Pentecost (Acts 2:2–12). Paul accepted this teaching about baptism with the Spirit, but linked it with his teaching about the church as the body of Christ. "For by one Spirit," he wrote to his converts in Corinth, "we were all baptized into one body—whether Jews or Greeks, whether slaves or free" (1 Cor. 12:13).

In various ways Paul views the present indwelling of the Spirit as an anticipation of the coming glory. The Spirit's work in the lives of Christ's people differs in degree, but not in kind, from their full sharing of Christ's glory at His advent. It is through the work of the Spirit that they, "beholding ... the glory of the Lord, are being transformed into the same image from glory to glory" (2 Cor. 3:18).

The Spirit is referred to by Paul as the one who identifies the people of God to secure them "for the day of redemption" (Eph. 4:30), as the "firstfruits" of the coming glory (Rom. 8:23), as the "deposit," "guarantee," or initial downpayment of the resurrection life that is their assured heritage (2 Cor. 1:22; 5:5).

The Body of Christ — Paul is the only New Testament writer who speaks of the church as a body. The members of the church, he suggests, are as interdependent as the various parts of the human body, each making its contribution in harmony with the others for the good of the whole. Just as a body functions best when all the parts follow the direction of the head, the church best fulfills its purpose on earth when all the members are subject to the direction of Christ. He is, by divine appointment, "head over all things to the church, which is His body"

(Eph. 1:22–23). The Spirit of Christ not only dwells within each member but also dwells within the church as a whole, continually giving His life to the entire body together. The body cannot be thought of without the Spirit. "There is one body and one Spirit," and when the members show one another the love of God they "keep the unity of the Spirit in the bond of peace" (Eph. 4:3–4).

The source of Paul's concept of the church as the body of Christ has been long debated. One source may have been the Old Testament principle of "corporate personality"—the principle of regarding a community, nation, or tribe as a person to the point where it is named and described as if it were an individual. God said to pharaoh through Moses, "Israel is My Son, My firstborn ... Let My son go that he may serve Me" (Ex. 4:22–23).

Perhaps the most satisfactory source of Paul's concept can be found in the words of the risen Christ who appeared to him on the Damascus Road: "Why are you persecuting me?" (Acts 9:4). Paul did not think he was persecuting Jesus, who was beyond his direct reach. But that is exactly what he was doing when he persecuted Jesus' followers. When any part of the body is hurt, it is the head that complains. Jesus' words may have sown the seed of that doctrine in Paul's mind. The Lord told Ananias of Damascus that He would show Paul "how many things he must suffer for My name's sake" (Acts 9:16). Paul later echoed this in his statement, "If one member suffers, all the members suffer with it" (1 Cor. 12:26).

The first time Paul wrote of this subject (1 Cor. 12:12–27), his purpose was to impress on his readers the fact that, as Christians, they have mutual duties and common interests that must not be neglected. When he next expounded on it (Rom. 12:4–8), he wrote of the variety of service rendered by the various members of the church. In accordance with their respective gifts, all members build up the one body to which they belong.

The health of the whole body depends on the harmonious cooperation of the parts.

In his later letters, Paul dealt with the relation that the church, as the body of Christ, bears to Christ as head of the body. The well-being of the body depends on its being completely under the control of the head. It is from Christ, as head of the church, that "all the body, nourished and knit together by joints and ligaments, grows with the increase which is from God" (Col. 2:19).

Paul's doctrine of the church as the body of Christ is closely bound up with his description of believers as being "in Christ" at the same time as Christ is in them. They are in Him as members of His body, having been "baptized into Christ" (Gal. 3:27). He is in them because it is His risen life that animates them. Jesus once used another organic analogy when He depicted Himself as "the true vine" and His disciples as the branches (John 15:1–6). The relationship is similar to that between the head and the body. The branches are in the vine and the vine at the same time is in the branches.

Eschatology — Eschatology is the teaching about things to come, especially things to come at the end times.

Paul originally held the views of eschatology taught in the Pharisaic schools. When Paul became a Christian, he found no need to abandon the eschatological teaching he had received at the feet of Gamaliel. But his experience of Christ did bring about some important modifications of his views. The distinction between the present age and the age to come was basic to this teaching. The present age was subject to evil influences that affected the lives and actions of men and women. The God of righteousness and truth, however, was in control of the situation. One day He would bring in a new age from which evil would be banished. The Pharisees taught that the end of the present age and beginning of the new age would be marked by the resurrection of the dead. Whether all the dead would be raised or only the righteous among them was a matter of debate. In Acts 24:15 Paul stated before the governor, Felix, that he shared the hope "that there will be a resurrection of the dead, both of the just and the unjust." In his letters he spoke only of the resurrection of believers in Christ, perhaps because it was to such people that his letters were written.

An important question was the relation of this framework to the messianic hope. When would the Messiah, the expected ruler of David's line, establish His kingdom? His kingdom might mark the closing phase of the present age; it might be set up with the inauguration of the age to come; or it might occupy a phase between the two ages. There was no general agreement on this question. Another question on which there was no general agreement concerned the extent to which the Messiah would revoke or replace the law of Moses. When Paul was confronted with the risen Christ on the Damascus Road, he realized that the Messiah had come and that in Him the resurrection had begun to take place. Having been raised from the dead, Christ had now entered upon His reign. The age of the Spirit for His people on earth coincided with the reign of Christ in His place of exaltation in the presence of God. There "He must reign till He has put all enemies under His feet" (1 Cor. 15:25). The present age had not yet come to an end, because men and women, and especially the people of Christ, still lived on earth in mortal bodies. But the resurrection age had already begun, because Christ had been raised.

The people of Christ, while living temporarily in the present age, belong spiritually to the new age that has been inaugurated. The benefits of this new age are already made good to them by the Spirit. The last of the enemies that will be subdued by Christ is death. The destruction of death will coincide with the resurrection of the people of Christ. Paul wrote, "Each one in his own order: Christ the firstfruits, afterward those who are

Christ's at His coming" (1 Cor. 15:23). The eternal kingdom of God will be consummated at that time.

The resurrection of the people of Christ, then, takes place at His coming again. In one of his earliest letters Paul said that, when Christ comes, "the dead in Christ will rise first. Then we who are alive and remain shall be caught up together with them in the clouds to meet the Lord in the air. And thus we shall always be with the Lord" (1 Thess. 4:16–17).

Further details are provided in 1 Corinthians 15:42–57. When the last trumpet announces the Second Coming of Christ, the dead will be raised in a "spiritual body," replacing the mortal body they wore on earth. Those believers who are still alive at the time will undergo a similar change to fit them for the new conditions. These new conditions, the eternal kingdom of God, are something that "flesh and blood cannot inherit"; they make up an imperishable realm that cannot accommodate the perishable bodies of this present life (1 Cor. 15:50).

The assurance that the faithful departed would be present at the Second Coming of Christ was a great comfort to Christians whose friends and relatives had died. But the question of their mode of existence between death and the Second Coming remained to be answered. Paul's clearest answer to this question was given shortly after a crisis in which he thought he faced certain death (2 Cor. 1:8–11).

Paul answered that to be "absent from the body" is to be "present with the Lord" (2 Cor. 5:8). Whatever provision is required for believers to enjoy the same communion with Christ after death as they enjoyed before death will certainly be supplied (2 Cor. 5:1–10). Or, as he put it when the outcome of his trial before Caesar was uncertain, "To live is Christ, and to die is gain," for to die would mean to "be with Christ, which is far better" (Phil. 1:21, 23).

The church as a whole and its members as individuals could look forward to a consummation of glory at the Second Coming of Christ. But the glory is not for them alone. In a vivid passage, Paul describes how "the creation eagerly waits for the revealing of the sons of God" (Rom. 8:19). This will liberate it from the change and decay to which it is subject at present and allow it to obtain "the glorious liberty of the children of God" (Rom. 8:21). In Genesis 3:17–19 man's first disobedience brought a curse on the earth. Paul looked forward to the removal of that curse and its replacement by the glory provided by the obedience of Christ, the "second Man" (1 Cor. 15:47).

This prospect is integrated into Paul's message, which is above all a message of reconciliation. It tells how God "reconciled us to Himself through Jesus Christ" (2 Cor. 5:18) and calls on people to "be reconciled to God" (2 Cor. 5:20). It proclaims God's purpose through Christ "to reconcile all things to Himself, … whether things on earth or things in heaven, having made peace through the blood of His cross" (Col. 1:20).

Paul and the Message of Jesus. Some critics charge that Paul corrupted the original "simple" message of Jesus by transforming it into a theological structure. But the truth is completely otherwise. No one in the apostolic age had a surer insight into Jesus' message than Paul.

A shift in perspective between the ministry of Jesus and the ministry of Paul must be recognized. During His own ministry Jesus was the preacher; in the ministry of Paul He was the one being preached. The Gospels record the works and words of the earthly Jesus; in Paul's preaching Jesus, once crucified, has been exalted as the heavenly Lord. Jesus' earthly ministry was confined almost entirely to the Jewish people; Paul was preeminently the apostle to the Gentiles. Paul's Gentile hearers required that the message be presented in a different vocabulary from that which Jesus used in Galilee and Judea. The gospel of Jesus and the gospel preached by Paul are not two gospels but one—a gospel specifically addressed to sinners. Paul, like Jesus, brought good news to outsiders. This was the assurance that in God's sight they were not outsiders, but men and women whom He lovingly accepted. In the ministry of Jesus, the outsiders were the social outcasts of Israel. In the ministry of Paul the outsiders were Gentiles. The principle was the same, although its application was different. Paul's achievement was to communicate to the Greco-Roman world, in terms it could understand, the good news that Jesus announced in His teaching, action, and death. Paul did not have before him the Gospels as we know them, but he knew the main lines of Jesus' teaching, especially parts of the Sermon on the Mount. This teaching was passed orally among the followers of Jesus before it circulated in written form. If Jesus summed up the law of God in the two great commandments of love toward God and love toward one's neighbor, Paul echoed Him: "All the law is fulfilled in one word, even in this: 'You shall love your neighbor as yourself' " (Gal. 5:14; also Rom. 13:9).

Paul's Legacy. Paul was a controversial figure in his lifetime, even within the Christian movement. He had many opponents who disagreed with his interpretation of the message of Jesus. In the closing years of his life, when imprisonment prevented him from moving about freely, Paul's opponents were able to make headway with their rival interpretations. Even though Asia had been Paul's most fruitful mission field, at the end of his life he wrote, "All those in Asia have turned away from me" (2 Tim. 1:15).

In the following generation, however, there was a resurgence of feeling in Paul's favor. His opponents were largely discredited and disabled by the dispersal of the church of that city shortly before the destruction of Jerusalem in A.D. 70. Throughout most of the church Paul became a venerated figure. His letters, together with the Gospels, became the foundation of the Christian movement.

Paul's liberating message has proved its vitality throughout the centuries. Repeatedly, when the Christian faith has been in danger of being shackled by legalism or tradition, Paul's message has allowed the gospel to set people free. The relevance of Paul's teaching for human life today may be brought out in a summary of four of his leading themes:

1. True religion is not a matter of rules and regulations. God does not deal with men and women like an accountant, but He accepts them freely when they respond to His love. He implants the Spirit of Christ in their hearts so they may extend His love to others.

2. In Christ men and women have come of age. God does not keep His people on puppet strings but liberates them to live as His responsible sons and daughters.

3. People matter more than things, principles, and causes. The highest of principles and the best of causes exist only for the sake of people. Personal liberty itself is abused if it is exercised against the personal well-being of others.

4. Discrimination on the grounds of race, religion, class, or sex is an offense against God and humanity alike.

PEKAH [PEE kuh] ([God] *has opened the eyes*) — the son of Remaliah and eighteenth king of Israel (2 Kin. 15:25–31; 2 Chr. 28:5–15). Pekah became king after he assassinated King Pekahiah. Pekah continued to lead Israel in the idolatrous ways of Jeroboam I (2 Kin. 15:28).

Pekah took the throne at the time when Tiglath-Pileser III, king of Assyria, was advancing toward Israel. To resist this threat, Pekah formed an alliance with Rezin, king of Syria. He also hoped to enlist the sister Israelite nation of Judah in the alliance. Under the counsel of the prophet Isaiah, however, Judah's kings, Jotham and later Ahaz, refused. Pekah and Rezin attempted to enlist Judah by force, marching first against Jerusalem. They were unsuccessful, and so they divided their armies. Rezin successfully captured Elath, and Pekah slew thousands in the districts near Jericho, taking many prisoners into

Samaria. Later, these prisoners were returned to Jericho upon the advice of the prophet Oded. Pekah probably was unaware that he was God's instrument to punish Judah (2 Chr. 28:5–6).

As Tiglath-Pileser III of Assyria advanced, King Ahaz of Judah met him to pay tribute and ask his help against Syria and Israel (2 Kin. 16:10). Assyria planned to march against Syria, and so Damascus was taken and Rezin was killed. The Assyrians also invaded northern Israel, with city after city taken and their inhabitants deported to Assyria. Through the Assyrian army God brought His judgment on Israel and Syria, even as the prophet Isaiah had warned (Is. 7:8–9).

Pekah was left with a stricken nation, over half of which had been plundered and stripped of its inhabitants. Soon Hoshea, son of Elah, conspired against Pekah and assassinated him. However, in his own writings Tiglath-Pileser III claimed that he was the power that placed Hoshea on the throne of Israel, possibly indicating he was a force behind the conspiracy. Pekah's dates as king of Israel are usually given as 740–732 B.C.

PEKAHIAH [pek uh HIGH uh] (*the Lord has opened the eyes*) — a son of Menahem and the seventeenth king of Israel (2 Kin. 15:22–26). Pekahiah assumed the throne after his father's death. He was an evil king who continued the idolatrous worship first introduced by King Jeroboam I. After reigning only two years (about 742–740 B.C.), Pekahiah was killed by his military captain, Pekah, and 50 Gileadites. Pekah then became king.

PELEG [PEE leg] (*division*) — a descendant of Noah through Shem and a son of Eber (Gen. 10:25). Peleg was an ancestor of Jesus (Luke 3:35; Phalec, KJV). He was named Peleg (meaning "division"), because "in his days the earth was divided" (Gen. 10:25; 1 Chr. 1:19), probably referring to the scattering of Noah's descendants as God's judgment following the attempt to build the tower of Babel (Gen. 11:8, 16–19).

PENUEL [pih NOO uhl] (*face of God*) — the name of a place and two men in the Old Testament:

1. A place north of the river Jabbok where Jacob wrestled with "a Man" until daybreak. Hosea 12:4 calls the "man" an "Angel." Jacob called the place Penuel, "For I have seen God face to face" (Gen. 32:30). A city was built there later, not far to the east of Succoth. When Gideon and his band of 300 men pursued the Midianites, the people of Succoth and Penuel insulted Gideon, refusing to give supplies to his army. Gideon later killed the men of the city (Judg. 8:17). Penuel is about 65 kilometers (40 miles) northeast of Jerusalem. It is also called Peniel (Gen. 32:30).

2. A son of Hur and grandson of Judah (1 Chr. 4:4).

3. A son of Shashak, of the tribe of Benjamin (1 Chr. 8:25).

PEOR [PEE ohr] — a mountain near Mount Nebo, northeast of the Dead Sea, in the land of Moab. Balak took Balaam to the summit of Peor (Num. 23:28) to encourage Balaam to curse the Israelites.

PERGA [PUR guh] — the capital city of Pamphylia, a province on the southern coast of Asia Minor, twice visited by the apostle Paul. During Paul's first missionary journey, he sailed to Perga from Paphos, on the island of Cyprus (Acts 13:13–14). Some time later, Paul and Barnabas stopped a second time at Perga (Acts 14:25).

Ruins of the walls and city gate at Perga, a city visited by Paul and Barnabas on their first missionary journey (Acts 13:13, 14).

PERGAMOS [PURR guh mos] — the chief city of Mysia, near the Caicus River in northwest Asia Minor (modern Turkey) and the site of one of the seven churches of Asia (Rev. 1:11; 2:12–17; Pergamum, NRSV, NIV, REB, NASB). The city, situated opposite the island of Lesbos, was about 24 kilometers (15 miles) from the Aegean Sea.

In its early history Pergamos became a city-state, then a powerful nation after Attalus I (241–197 B.C.) defeated the Gauls (Galatians). It stood as a symbol of Greek superiority over the barbarians. Great buildings were erected and a library containing over 200,000 items was established. The Egyptians, concerned with this library, which rivaled their own at Alexandria, refused to ship papyrus to Pergamos. As a result, a new form of writing material, Pergamena charta, or parchment, was developed.

In the days of Roman dominance throughout Asia Minor, Pergamos became the capital of the Roman province of Asia. In a gesture of friendship, Mark Antony gave Pergamos's library to Cleopatra; its volumes were moved to Alexandria. Not only was Pergamos a government center with three imperial temples but it was also the site of the temple of Asklepios (the Greco-Roman god of medicine and healing), and the medical center where the physician Galen worked (about A.D. 160). Here also was a temple to Athena and a temple to Zeus with an altar showing Zeus defeating snake-like giants. In the book of Revelation, John spoke of Pergamos as the place "where Satan's throne is" (Rev. 2:13). This could be a reference to the cult of emperor worship, because Pergamos was a center where this form of loyalty was pledged to the emperor of the Roman Empire.

PERIZZITES [PER uh zights] (*villagers*) — inhabitants of the "forest country" (Josh. 17:15) in the territory of the tribes of Ephraim, Manasseh, and Judah (Judg. 1:4–5). The Perizzites, who lived in Canaan as early as the time of Abraham and Lot (Gen. 13:7), were subdued by the Israelites. After the conquest of the land of Canaan under Joshua, the Perizzites were allowed to live. They entered into marriages with their conquerors and seduced the Israelites into idolatry (Judg. 3:5–6). In the time of the judges, Bezek was their stronghold and Adoni-Bezek was their leader (Judg. 1:4–5). In the days of King Solomon the Perizzites were recruited for the king's forced-labor force (1 Kin. 9:20).

PETER, SIMON — the most prominent of Jesus' twelve apostles. The New Testament gives a more complete picture of Peter than of any other disciple, with the exception of Paul. Peter is often considered to be a big, blundering fisherman. But this is a shallow portrayal. The picture of his personality portrayed in the New Testament is rich and many-sided. A more fitting appraisal of Peter is that he was a pioneer among the twelve apostles and the early church, breaking ground that the church would later follow.

The First Apostle to Be Called. Peter's given name was Simeon or Simon. His father's name was Jonah (Matt. 16:17; John 1:42). Simon's brother, Andrew, also joined Jesus as a disciple (Mark 1:16). The family probably lived at Capernaum on the north shore of the Sea of Galilee (Mark 1:21, 29), although it is possible they lived in Bethsaida (John 1:44).

Peter was married, because the Gospels mention that Jesus healed his mother-in-law (Matt. 8:14–15). The apostle Paul later mentioned that Peter took his wife on his missionary travels (1 Cor. 9:5). Peter and Andrew were fishermen on the Sea of Galilee, and perhaps in partnership with James and John, the sons of Zebedee (Luke 5:10). In the midst of his labor as a fisherman, Peter received a call from Jesus that changed his life (Luke 5:8).

The gospel of John reports that Andrew and Peter were disciples of John the Baptist before they joined Jesus. John also reports that Peter was introduced to Jesus by his brother Andrew, who had already recognized Jesus to be the Messiah (John 1:35–42). Whether Andrew and Peter knew Jesus because they were disciples of John is uncertain. But it is clear that they followed Jesus because of His distinctive authority.

The First Among the Apostles. Jesus apparently gathered His followers in two stages: first as disciples (learners or apprentices), and later as apostles (commissioned representatives). Peter was the first disciple to be called (Mark 1:16–18) and the first to be named an apostle (Mark 3:14–16). His name heads every list of the Twelve in the New Testament. He was apparently the strongest individual in the band. He frequently served as a spokesman for the disciples, and he was their recognized leader (Mark 1:36; Luke 22:32). Typical of Peter's dominant personality was his readiness to walk to Jesus on the water (Matt. 14:28), and to ask Jesus the awkward question of how often he should forgive a sinning fellow believer (Matt. 18:21).

An inner circle of three apostles existed among the Twelve. Peter was also the leader of this small group. The trio—Peter, James, and John—was present with Jesus on a number of occasions. They witnessed the raising of a young girl from the dead (Mark 5:37; Luke 8:51); they were present at Jesus' transfiguration (Matt. 17:1–2); and they were present during Jesus' agony in Gethsemane (Matt. 26:37; Mark 14:33). During Jesus' final week in Jerusalem, two of the three, Peter and John, were sent to make preparations for their last meal together (Luke 22:8).

The First Apostle to Recognize Jesus as Messiah. The purpose of Jesus' existence in the flesh was that people would come to a true picture of who God is and what He has done for our salvation. The first apostle to recognize that was Peter. He confessed Jesus as Lord in the region of Caesarea Philippi (Matt. 16:13–17).

Jesus began the process that would lead to Peter's awareness by asking a nonthreatening question, "Who do men say that I, the Son of Man, am?" (Matt. 16:13). After the disciples voiced various rumors, Jesus put a more personal question to them, "But who do you say that I am?" (Matt. 16:15). Peter confessed Jesus to be the Messiah, the Son of God. According to Matthew, it was because of this confession that Jesus renamed Simon Cephas (in Aramaic) or Peter (in Greek), both meaning "rock."

Why Jesus called Simon a "rock" is not altogether clear. Peter's character was not always rock-like, as his denial of Jesus indicates. His new name probably referred to something that, by God's grace, he would become—Peter, a rock.

The First Apostle to Witness the Resurrection. How ironic that the one who denied Jesus most vehemently in His hour of suffering should be the first person to witness His resurrection from the dead. Yet according to Luke (Luke 24:34) and Paul (1 Cor. 15:5), Peter was the first apostle to see the risen Lord. We can only marvel at the grace of God in granting such a blessing to one who did not seem to deserve it. Peter's witnessing of the resurrection was a sign of his personal restoration to fellowship with Christ. It also confirmed His appointment by God to serve as a leader in the emerging church.

The First Apostle to Proclaim Salvation to the Gentiles. The earliest information about the early church comes from the book of Acts. This shows clearly that Peter continued to exercise a key leadership role in the church for a number of years. Indeed, the first 11 chapters of Acts are built around the activity of the apostle Peter.

When the Holy Spirit visited the church in Samaria, the apostles sent Peter and John to verify its authenticity (Acts 8:14–25). But this event was only a prelude to the one event that concluded Peter's story in the New Testament: the preaching of the gospel to the Gentiles (Acts 10–11). The chain of events that happened before the bestowal of the Holy Spirit on Gentile believers—beginning with Peter's staying in the house of a man of "unclean" profession (Acts 9:43), continuing with his vision of "unclean" foods (Acts 10:9–16), and climaxing in his realization that no human being, Gentile included, ought to be considered "unclean" (Acts 10:34–48)—is a masterpiece of storytelling. It demonstrates the triumph of God's grace to bring about change in stubborn hearts and the hardened social customs of Jewish believers.

Following the death of James, the brother of John, and Peter's miraculous release from prison (Acts 12), Peter drops out of the narrative of Acts. Luke reports that he "went to another place" (Acts 12:17). We know, however, that Peter did not drop out of active service in the early church.

Peter probably broadened his ministry, once the mantle of leadership of the Jerusalem church fell from his shoulders to those of James. Peter played a key role at the Council of Jerusalem (Acts 15; Galatians 2), which decided in favor of granting church membership to Gentiles without first requiring them to become Jews. Paul mentioned a visit of Peter to Antioch of Syria (Gal. 2:11), and he may refer to a mission of Peter to Corinth (1 Cor. 1:12). Peter dropped into the background in the book of Acts not because his ministry ended. Luke simply began to trace the course of the gospel's spread to Gentile Rome through the ministry of Paul.

Peter in Rome: The First to Inspire the Writing of a Gospel. According to early Christian tradition, Peter went to Rome, where he died. Only once in the New Testament do we hear of Peter's being in Rome. Even in this case, Rome is referred to as "Babylon" (1 Pet. 5:13). Little is known of Peter's activities in Rome, although Papias, writing about A.D. 125, stated that Peter's preaching inspired the writing of the first gospel, drafted by Mark, who was Peter's interpreter in Rome. Peter was also the author of the two New Testament epistles that bear his name.

This early and generally reliable tradition supports the pioneer role played by Peter throughout his life and ministry. A number of other works—the Preaching of Peter, the gospel of Peter, the Apocalypse of Peter, the Acts of Peter, and the Epistle of Peter to James—are apocryphal in nature. They cannot be accepted as trustworthy sources of information for the life and thought of the apostle.

PHARAOH [PHAY row] — the title of the kings of Egypt until 323 B.C. In the Egyptian language the word *pharaoh* means "great house." This word was originally used to describe the palace of the king. Around 1500 B.C. this term was applied to the Egyptian kings. It meant something like "his honor, his majesty." In addition to this title, the kings also had a personal name (Amunhotep, Rameses) and other descriptive titles (King of Upper and Lower Egypt).

In several instances the Israelites came into contact with a pharaoh. Abram (Abraham) went to Egypt around 2000 B.C. because of a famine in the land of Canaan. Because Abram lied about Sarai (Sarah) being his sister, pharaoh wanted to take her into his harem, but God stopped him by sending a plague (Gen. 12:10–20). About 200 years later Joseph was thrown into prison in Egypt because the wife of Potiphar, the captain of pharaoh's guard, lied about Joseph's behavior (Genesis 39).

While in prison Joseph met two of pharaoh's servants, the butler and the baker, who had been put in prison because they displeased the powerful pharaoh (Genesis 40). Joseph correctly interpreted the dreams of the butler and baker and later was brought from prison to interpret the dream of the pharaoh (Genesis 41). The Egyptian priestly magicians could not interpret pharaoh's dream. But because God told Joseph the meaning of the dream, Joseph was appointed as second in command to collect one-fifth of the nation's crops during the seven years of plenty.

Because of the severity of the seven years of famine, the Egyptians had to sell their cattle, their property, and themselves to the pharaoh for grain; thus the pharaoh owned everything (Gen. 47:13–20). The pharaoh sent carts to bring Joseph's brothers to Egypt (Gen. 45:16–20) and settled them in the fertile land of Goshen (Gen. 47:1–6).

After about 300 more years in Egypt, a new dynasty came to power. Its kings did not acknowledge Joseph and his deeds to save Egypt (Ex. 1:8). Therefore all the Israelites but Moses were enslaved. He was raised in the pharaoh's own court (Ex. 1:11–2:10; Acts 7:21–22). At 80 years of age Moses returned to pharaoh to ask permission to lead the Israelites out of Egypt. Pharaoh did not know or accept the God of the Israelites and refused to obey Him (Ex. 5:1–2). On a second visit Moses functioned as God to pharaoh by delivering a divine message (Ex. 7:1), but the miracles and initial plagues only hardened pharaoh's heart (Ex. 7:8–13, 22; 8:15, 32). Each plague was carried out so the Israelites, the Egyptians, and the pharaoh would know that Israel's God was the only true God and that the Egyptian gods and their "divine pharaoh" were powerless before Him (Ex. 7:5, 17; 8:10, 22; 9:14, 29–30; 10:2).

Eventually pharaoh admitted his sin, but before long he again hardened his heart (Ex. 9:27, 34; 10:16, 20). When pharaoh's own "divine" first-born son was killed in the last plague, he finally submitted to God's power and let the people go (Ex. 12:29–33). Pharaoh later chased the Israelites to bring them back, but he and his army were drowned in the Red Sea (Ex. 14:5–31).

Solomon formed an alliance with an Egyptian pharaoh through marriage with his daughter (1 Kin. 3:1; 7:8; 9:24), thus demonstrating that Israel was a more powerful nation than Egypt. This pharaoh later gave the city of Gezer to his daughter (1 Kin. 9:16). The next pharaoh had less friendly relationships with Solomon and gave refuge to Solomon's enemy, Hadad the Edomite (1 Kin. 11:14–22). This may have been the pharaoh Shishak who protected Jeroboam (1 Kin. 11:40) and captured Jerusalem in the fifth year of Rehoboam (1 Kin. 14:25–28). Hoshea, the king of Israel, had a treaty with So, the king of

Egypt (2 Kin. 17:4). The pharaoh Tirhakah may have had a similar relationship with Hezekiah (2 Kin. 19:9).

In 609 B.C. the pharaoh Necho marched north through Palestine to save the Assyrians. King Josiah opposed this move, so Necho killed him (2 Kin. 23:29). Nebuchadnezzar later defeated Necho and took control of Judah (Jer. 46:2). It was possibly Pharaoh Hophra who challenged the Babylonians during the siege of Jerusalem in 587 B.C. (Jer. 37:5–10; 44:30; Ezek. 17:17).

The prophets Isaiah, Jeremiah, and Hosea condemned pharaoh and the Israelites who trusted in him and his army (Is. 30:1–5; 31:1; Jer. 42:18; Hos. 7:11). But the prophecies of Ezekiel are by far the most extensive (Ezekiel 29–32). Pharaoh is quoted as saying, "My River is my own; I have made it for myself" (Ezek. 29:3). Because pharaoh claimed the power and authority of God, Ezekiel declared, God will destroy pharaoh and Egypt (Ezek. 29:19; 30:21; 31:2; 32:2, 12).

PHILADELPHIA [fill ah DELL fih uh] (*brotherly love*) — a city of the province of Lydia in western Asia Minor (modern Turkey) and the site of one of the seven churches of Asia to which John wrote in the book of Revelation (Rev. 1:11).

Philadelphia was situated on the Cogamus River, a tributary of the Hermus (modern Gediz) and was about 45 kilometers (28 miles) southeast of Sardis. It was founded by Attalus II (Philadelphus), who reigned as king of Pergamos from 159 B.C. until 138 B.C. Philadelphia was a center of the wine industry. Its chief deity was Dionysus, in Greek mythology the god of wine (the Roman Bacchus).

In the book of Revelation, John describes the church in Philadelphia as the faithful church and the church that stood at the gateway of a great opportunity (Rev. 3:7–13). Christ said to this church, "See, I have set before you an open door and no one can shut it" (v. 8). The "open door" means primarily access to God, but it also refers to opportunity for spreading the gospel of Jesus Christ. Still a city of considerable size, Philadelphia is known today as Alashehir.

PHILEMON [fie LEE mun] — a wealthy Christian of Colossae who hosted a house church. Philemon was converted under the apostle Paul (Philem. v. 19), perhaps when Paul ministered in Ephesus (Acts 19:10). He is remembered because of his runaway slave, Onesimus, who, after damaging or stealing his master's property (Philem. vv. 11, 18), made his way to Rome, where he was converted under Paul's ministry (Philem. v. 10).

Accompanied by Tychicus (Col. 4:7), Onesimus later returned to his master, Philemon. He carried with him the Epistle to the Colossians, plus the shorter Epistle to Philemon. In the latter, Paul asked Philemon to receive Onesimus, not as a slave but as a "beloved brother" (Philem. v. 16).

PHILIP [FILL ihp] (*lover of horses*) — the name of two men in the New Testament:

1. One of the twelve apostles of Christ (Matt. 10:3; Mark 3:18; Luke 6:14) and a native of Bethsaida in Galilee (John 1:44; 12:21). According to the gospel of John, Philip met Jesus beyond the Jordan River during John the Baptist's ministry. Jesus called Philip to become His disciple. Philip responded and brought to Jesus another disciple, named Nathanael (John 1:43–51) or Bartholomew (Mark 3:18). Philip is usually mentioned with Nathanael.

Before Jesus fed the five thousand, He tested Philip by asking him how so many people could possibly be fed. Instead of responding in faith, Philip began to calculate the amount of food it would take to feed them and the cost (John 6:5–7).

When certain Greeks, who had come to Jerusalem to worship at the Feast of Passover, said to Philip, "Sir, we wish to see

Jesus" (John 12:21), Philip seemed unsure of what he should do. He first told Andrew, and then they told Jesus of the request. Philip was one of the apostles who was present in the Upper Room following the resurrection of Jesus (Acts 1:13).

2. Philip the evangelist, one of the seven men chosen to serve the early church because they were reported to be "full of faith and the Holy Spirit" (Acts 6:5). Their task was to look after the Greek-speaking widows and probably all of the poor in the Jerusalem church. Following the stoning of Stephen, the first Christian martyr, many Christians scattered from Jerusalem (Acts 8:1). Philip became an evangelist and, in Samaria, preached the gospel, worked miracles, and brought many to faith in Christ (Acts 8:5–8).

Probably the most noted conversion as a result of Philip's ministry was the Ethiopian eunuch, an official under Candace, the queen of the Ethiopians. Philip met the eunuch on the road from Jerusalem to Gaza. The eunuch was reading from Isaiah 53, the passage about the Suffering Servant. Philip used this great opportunity to preach Jesus to him. The eunuch said, "I believe that Jesus Christ is the Son of God" (Acts 8:37). Then Philip baptized him.

After this event, Philip preached in Azotus (the Old Testament Ashdod) and Caesarea (Acts 8:40). He was still in Caesarea many years later when the apostle Paul passed through the city on his last journey to Jerusalem (Acts 21:8). Luke adds that Philip had "four virgin daughters who prophesied" (Acts 21:9).

PHILIPPI [FIL uh pie] (*city of Philip*) — a city in eastern Macedonia (modern Greece) visited by the apostle Paul. Situated on a plain surrounded by mountains, Philippi lay about 16 kilometers (10 miles) inland from the Aegean Sea. The Egnatian Way, the main overland route between Asia and the West, ran through the city. Philippi was named for Philip II of

Macedonia, the father of Alexander the Great. In 356 B.C. Philip enlarged and renamed the city, which was formerly known as Krenides. Philip resettled people from the countryside in Philippi and built a wall around the city and an acropolis atop the surrounding mountain. Although they date from later periods, other points of interest in Philippi include a forum the size of a football field, an open-air theater, two large temples, public buildings, a library, and Roman baths.

In 42 B.C. Mark Antony and Octavian (later Augustus Caesar) combined forces to defeat the armies of Brutus and Cassius, assassins of Julius Caesar, at Philippi. In celebration of the victory, Philippi was made into a Roman colony; this entitled its inhabitants to the rights and privileges usually granted those who lived in cities in Italy. Eleven years later, Octavian defeated the forces of Antony and Cleopatra in a naval battle at Actium, on the west coast of Greece. Octavian punished the supporters of Antony by evicting them from Italy and resettling them in Philippi. The vacated sites in Italy were then granted to Octavian's own soldiers as a reward for their victory over Antony.

The apostle Paul visited Philippi on his second missionary journey in A.D. 49 (Acts 16:12; 20:6). Evidently the city did not have the necessary number of Jewish males (ten) to form a synagogue, because Paul met with a group of women for prayer outside the city gate (Acts 16:13).

French excavations at Philippi between 1914 and 1938 unearthed a Roman arch that lay about 1 mile west of the city. This arch may have served as a zoning marker to restrict undesirable religious sects from meeting in the city. One of the women of Philippi who befriended Paul, named Lydia, was a dealer in purple cloth (Acts 16:14). A Latin inscription uncovered in excavations mentions this trade, thus indicating its economic importance for Philippi. Philippi also is mentioned or implied in Acts 20:16; Philippians 1:1; and 1 Thessalonians 2:2.

PHILIPPIANS [fih LIP ih anz] — natives or inhabitants of Philippi (Phil. 4:15), a city of Macedonia situated about 113 kilometers (70 miles) northeast of Thessalonica (Acts 16:12; Phil. 1:1).

PHILISTINES [fih LIS teens] — an aggressive nation that occupied part of southwest Palestine from about 1200 to 600 B.C. The name Philistine was used first among the Egyptians to describe the sea people defeated by Rameses III in a naval battle about 1188 B.C. Among the Assyrians the group was known as Pilisti or Palastu. The Hebrew word *pelishti* is the basis of the name Palestine, a later name for Canaan, the country occupied by God's covenant people.

Little is known about the origins of the Philistines except what is contained in the Bible—that they came from Caphtor (Gen. 10:14), generally identified with the island of Crete in the Mediterranean Sea. Crete also was supposed to be the home of the Cherethites, who were sometimes associated with the Philistines (Ezek. 25:16). Philistine territory was considered Cherethite in 1 Samuel 30:14, suggesting that both peoples were part of the invading group defeated earlier by Rameses III of Egypt.

Liberal scholars have assumed that references to the Philistines during Abraham's time are incorrect historically and that the Philistine occupation actually occurred in the 12th century B.C. More careful examination indicates there were two Philistine settlements in Canaan, one early and another later. Both these settlements were marked by significant cultural differences.

The Philistines of Gerar, with whom Abraham dealt (Genesis 20–21), evidently were a colony of the early settlement located southeast of Gaza in southern Canaan. This colony was situated outside the area occupied by the five Philistine cities after 1188 B.C. Gerar was also a separate city-state governed by a king who bore the name or title of Abimelech.

That Abimelech's colony was the chief one in the area seems probable from his title, "king of the Philistines" (Gen. 26:1, 8). This is different from a later period when the Philistines were governed by five lords. Unlike the later Philistines who were Israel's chief foes in the settlement and monarchy periods, the Gerar Philistines were peaceful. They encouraged the friendship of Abraham and Isaac. Finally, Gerar was not included among the chief cities of Philistia (Josh. 13:3). It was not mentioned as one of the places conquered by the Israelites. It is best, therefore, to regard the Genesis traditions as genuine historical records.

The early Philistine settlements in Canaan took on a new appearance when five cities—Ashkelon, Ashdod, Ekron, Gath, and Gaza—and the areas around them were occupied by the Philistines in the 12th century B.C. Probably all of these except Ekron were already in existence when the sea peoples conquered them. These five Philistine cities formed a united political unit. Archaeological discoveries in the area have illustrated how they expanded to the south and east. Broken bits of Philistine pottery were found at archaeological sites in those areas.

The Philistines possessed superior weapons of iron when they began to attack the Israelites in the 11th century B.C. The tribe of Dan moved northward to escape these Philistine attacks, and Judah also came under increasing pressure (Judges 14–18). In Samuel's time the Philistines captured the ark of the covenant in battle. Although the ark was recovered later, the Philistines continued to occupy Israelite settlements (1 Sam. 10:5).

The threat of the Philistines prompted Israel's demands for a king. But even under Saul the united nation was still menaced by the Philistines—a threat that ultimately resulted in Saul's death (1 Samuel 31). David's slaying of Goliath, a giant from Gath, was a key factor in his rise to fame. By this time the Philistines had moved deep into Israelite territory. Archaeological evidence shows they had occupied Tell Beit Mirsim, Beth Zur, Gibeah, Megiddo, and Beth Shean. Yet by the end of David's reign their power had begun to decline significantly. By the time Jehoshaphat was made king of Judah (873–848 B.C.), the Philistines were paying tribute (2 Chr. 17:11), although they tried to become independent under Jehoshaphat's son, Jehoram (2 Chr. 21:16–17).

When the Assyrians began to raid Palestine in later years, the Philistines faced additional opposition. The Assyrian Adad-Nirari III (about 810–783 B.C.) placed the Philistine cities under heavy tribute early in his reign, while Uzziah of Judah (791–740 B.C.) demolished the defenses of several Philistine strongholds, including Gath. When he became king, Ahaz of Judah (732–715 B.C.) was attacked by Philistine forces, and cities in the Negev and the Judean lowlands were occupied. The Assyrian king Tiglath-Pileser III responded by conquering the chief Philistine cities.

In 713 B.C. Sargon II, king of Assyria, invaded Philistia and conquered Ashdod. The following year he launched another campaign against other Philistine cities. Hezekiah of Judah (716–686 B.C.) attacked Gaza (2 Kin. 18:8), supported by the people of Ekron and Ashkelon, but in 701 B.C. Sennacherib brought Philistine territory under his control to prevent any Egyptian interference. When Nebuchadnezzar came to power in Babylon, the Philistines formed an alliance with Egypt, but when the Jews were exiled to Babylonia between 597 and 586 B.C., the Philistines, too, were deported.

No Philistine literature has survived, making it difficult to reconstruct their religious beliefs or rituals. Old Testament records indicate they worshiped three gods, Ashtoreth, Dagon, and Baal-Zebub—each of which had shrines in various cities (Judg. 16:23; 1 Sam. 5:1–7; 2 Kin. 1:2). Philistine soldiers apparently carried images of their gods into battle, perhaps as standards (2 Sam. 5:21). Like other Near Eastern peoples, the Philistines were superstitious. They respected the power of Israel's ark of the covenant (1 Sam. 5:1–12).

As depicted on Egyptian reliefs, Philistine soldiers wore short tunics, were clean-shaven, had crested or decorated helmets, carried round shields, and fought with spears and swords. In the days before David's reign, the Philistine cities were governed by a representative from each city. These authorities exercised complete power in both peace and war. This centralized control made the Philistines strong, in contrast to the loosely organized Israelites. The Philistines were important culturally because they adopted the manufacture and distribution of iron implements and weapons from the Hittites. Goliath's equipment was obviously of Philistine manufacture. The golden objects that were offered to Israel's God (1 Sam. 6:4–5) show that the Philistines were skilled goldsmiths as well.

The remains of Philistine furnaces have been uncovered at Tell Jemmeh and Ashdod. The area around Ashdod has produced some examples of typical Philistine pottery. This pottery reflected Greek as well as Egyptian and Canaanite styles. The Philistines loved beer. Large beer mugs decorated with red and black geometric designs were some of their important pottery products, along with large cups, beakers, and bowls. Some Philistine burial places discovered at Tell Far'ah reveal bodies encased in clay coffins shaped to match the human body. The coffin lid was decorated with crude figures of the head and clasped arms of the deceased.

PHINEHAS [FIN ih uhs] (*the Nubian*) — the name of three men in the Old Testament:

1. A son of Eleazar and grandson of Aaron (Ex. 6:25). During the wilderness wandering, Phinehas killed Zimri, a man of Israel, and Cozri, a Midianite woman whom Zimri

had brought into the camp (Numbers 25). This action ended a plague by which God had judged Israel for allowing Midianite women to corrupt Israel with idolatry and harlotry. For such zeal Phinehas and his descendants were promised a permanent priesthood (Num. 25:11–13). Phinehas became the third high priest of Israel, serving for 19 years. His descendants held the high priesthood until the Romans destroyed the temple in A.D. 70, except for a short period when the house of Eli served as high priests.

2. The younger of the two sons of Eli the priest (1 Sam. 1:3). Phinehas and his brother, Hophni, were priests also, but they disgraced their priestly office by greed, irreverence, and immorality (1 Sam. 2:12–17, 22–25). The Lord told Eli his two sons would die (1 Sam. 2:34). They were killed in a battle with the Philistines. When Phinehas's wife heard the news, she went into premature labor and died in childbirth. The child was named Ichabod, which means "The glory has departed from Israel!" (1 Sam. 4:22). Because of the evil actions of Phinehas and Hophni, the high priesthood later passed from Eli's family.

3. The father of Eleazar (Ezra 8:33).

PHRYGIA [FRIJ ih uh] — a large province of the mountainous region of Asia Minor, visited by the apostle Paul (Acts 2:10; 16:6; 18:23). Because of its size, Phrygia was made a part of other provinces. In Roman times the region was split between two provinces. The cities of Colossae, Laodicea, and Hierapolis belonged to Asia, while Iconium and Antioch belonged to Galatia.

The apostle Paul visited Phrygia on two journeys (Acts 13:14–14:5, 21; 16:6). He apparently also passed through Phrygia on his third journey (Acts 18:22–24), although his letter to the Colossians suggests he did not found a church there (Col. 2:1). Jews who were at Jerusalem on the Day of Pentecost may have been the first Phrygian converts (Acts 2:10). Jews settled in Phrygia during the Seleucid period. Some of them apparently adopted non-Jewish practices. Consequently, strict Jews became hostile to new ideas (Acts 13:44–14:6).

PI HAHIROTH [**pie huh HIGH rahth**] — the site of the final Israelite encampment in Egypt before they crossed the Red Sea. Pi Hahiroth is described as being "between Migdol and the sea" and "opposite" Baal Zephon (Ex. 14:2). Numbers 33:8 has Hahiroth, a shortened form of Pi Hahiroth.

PILATE, PONTIUS [**PIE lat, PON chus**] — the fifth Roman prefect of Judea (ruled A.D. 26–36), who issued the official order sentencing Jesus to death by crucifixion (Matthew 27; Mark 15; Luke 23; John 18–19).

Pilate's Personal Life. The Jewish historian Josephus provides what little information is known about Pilate's life before A.D. 26, when Tiberius appointed him procurator of Judea. The sketchy data suggests that Pilate was probably an Italian-born Roman citizen whose family was wealthy enough for him to qualify for the middle class. Probably he held certain military posts before his appointment in Judea. He was married (Matt. 27:19), bringing his wife, Claudia Procula, to live with him at Caesarea, the headquarters of the province. Pilate governed the areas of Judea, Samaria, and the area south as far as the Dead Sea to Gaza. As prefect he had absolute authority over the non-Roman citizens of the province. He was responsible to the Roman governor who lived in Syria to the north (Luke 2:2).

Pilate never became popular with the Jews. He seemed to be insensitive to their religious convictions and stubborn in the pursuit of his policies. But when the Jews responded to his rule with enraged opposition, he often backed down, demonstrating his weakness. He greatly angered the Jews when he took funds from the temple treasury to build an aqueduct to supply water to Jerusalem. Many Jews reacted violently to this act, and

Pilate's soldiers killed many of them in this rebellion. It may be this or another incident to which Luke refers in Luke 13:1–2. In spite of this, Pilate continued in office for ten years, showing that Tiberius considered Pilate an effective administrator.

Pilate's later history is also shrouded in mystery. Josephus tells of a bloody encounter with the Samaritans, who filed a complaint with Pilate's superior, Vitellius, the governor of Syria. Vitellius deposed Pilate and ordered him to stand before the emperor in Rome and answer for his conduct. Legends are confused as to how Pilate died. Eusebius reports that he was exiled to the city of Vienne on the Rhone in Gaul (France) where he eventually committed suicide.

Pilate's Encounter with Jesus. Since the Jews could not execute a person without approval from the Roman authorities (John 18:31), the Jewish leaders brought Jesus to Pilate to pronounce the death sentence (Mark 14:64). Pilate seemed convinced that Jesus was not guilty of anything deserving death, and he sought to release Jesus (Matt. 27:24; Mark 15:9–11; Luke 23:14; John 18:38–40; 19:12). Neither did he want to antagonize the Jews and run the risk of damaging his own reputation and career. Thus, when they insisted on Jesus' crucifixion, Pilate turned Jesus over to be executed (Matt. 27:26; Mark 15:12–15; Luke 23:20–25; John 19:15–16).

Pilate's Character. Pilate is a good example of the unprincipled achiever who will sacrifice what is right to accomplish his own selfish goals. Although he recognized Jesus' innocence and had the authority to uphold justice and acquit Jesus, he gave in to the demands of the crowd rather than risk a personal setback in his career. This is a real temptation to all people who hold positions of power and authority.

PITHOM [PIE thuhm] — one of the supply cities, or store cities, in Lower Egypt built by the Israelites while they were slaves in Egypt (Ex. 1:11). Pithom was in the general area of Raamses. Some archaeologists suggest that the temple, fortress, and storage chambers discovered at Tell el-Maskhutah, in the valley connecting the Nile River and Lake Timsah, are the remains of biblical Pithom. Others believe that Pithom should be identified with Tell er-Ratabah, about 16 kilometers (10 miles) to the west and closer to the land of Goshen. The site of Pithom remains a subject of doubt and debate.

It is possible that Pithom and Raamses (Ex. 1:11) were built during the reign of Pharaoh Rameses II (who ruled from about 1292–1225 B.C.). Rameses II, however, often made claims to "build" a city, when actually he "rebuilt" it, or strengthened its fortifications. Pithom is supposed by some scholars to be identical with Succoth (Ex. 12:37)—Pithom being the sacred or religious name and Succoth being the secular or civil name.

POTIPHAR [PAHT uh fur] (*dedicated to Ra*) — the Egyptian to whom the Ishmaelites (Gen. 39:1) sold Joseph when he was brought to Egypt as a slave. Potiphar was a high officer of pharaoh and a wealthy man (Gen. 37:36). In time, he put Joseph in charge of his household. But Potiphar's wife became attracted to Joseph and attempted to seduce him. When he rejected her advances, she falsely accused him and had him imprisoned (Gen. 39:6–19).

PRISCILLA [prih SIL uh] — the wife of Aquila and a zealous advocate of the Christian cause (Rom. 16:3; 1 Cor. 16:19). Her name is also given as Prisca (2 Tim. 4:19). Aquila and Priscilla left their home in Rome for Corinth when the emperor Claudius commanded all Jews to depart from the city (Acts 18:2). Thus, they were fellow passengers of the apostle Paul from Corinth to Ephesus (Acts 18:18), where they met Apollos and instructed him further in the Christian faith (Acts 18:26).

PUAH [POO uh] — the name of two men and one woman in the Old Testament:

1. The second son of Issachar (1 Chr. 7:1), also called Puvah (Gen. 46:13, NRSV), Phuvah (KJV), and Pua (Num. 26:23, KJV).

2. One of two midwives whom pharaoh ordered to kill Hebrew males at their birth (Ex. 1:15). The midwives courageously disobeyed pharaoh's command.

3. The father of Tola, of the tribe of Issachar (Judg. 10:1).

PUT [put] — the name of a man and a land or people mentioned in the Old Testament:

1. One of the sons of Ham (Gen. 10:6; Phut, KJV; 1 Chr. 1:8). Put was a grandson of Noah.

2. The land where Put's descendants lived. This nation is mentioned in the Bible in connection with Egypt and Ethiopia (Cush). Some scholars identify this land with Punt, an area on the eastern shore of Africa (possibly Somaliland), famous for its incense. Since Put and Punt are not identical in spelling and because Put was known for its warriors rather than its incense, other scholars believe Put refers to certain Libyan tribes west of Egypt.

Men from Put and Lubim (Libya) were used as mercenary soldiers by the king of Tyre (Ezek. 27:10) and Magog (Ezek. 38:5). But most references in the Bible picture them as allies with Egypt (Jer. 46:9; Ezek. 30:5; Nah. 3:9). Although the warriors of Put were hired to help these different nations secure their borders and win their wars, the prophets point to the futility of such forces in the face of God's mighty power and judgment.

RACHEL [RAY chuhl] (*lamb*) — the younger daughter of Laban; the second wife of Jacob; and the mother of Joseph and Benjamin.

Jacob met Rachel, the beautiful younger daughter of his uncle Laban, at a well near Haran in Mesopotamia as he fled from his brother, Esau (Gen. 29:6, 11). Jacob soon asked Laban for Rachel as his wife (Gen. 29:15–18). However, it was customary in those days for the groom or his family to pay the bride's family a price for their daughter. Having no property of his own, Jacob served Laban seven years for Rachel, only to be tricked on the wedding day into marrying Rachel's older sister, Leah (Gen. 29:21–25). Jacob then had to serve another seven years for Rachel (Gen. 29:26–30).

Although Rachel was Jacob's favorite wife, she envied Leah, who had given birth to four sons—Reuben, Simeon, Levi, and Judah—while she herself had remained childless (Gen. 29:31–35). Her response was to give her handmaid Bilhah to Jacob. According to this ancient custom, the child of Bilhah and Jacob would have been regarded as Rachel's. Bilhah bore Dan and Naphtali (Gen. 30:1–8), but Rachel named them, indicating they were her children. Rachel's desperate desire to become fruitful is illustrated by her asking for Reuben's mandrakes, which she believed would bring fertility (Gen. 30:14–16). Mandrakes were considered love potions or magic charms by people of the ancient world.

Only after Zilpah, Leah's handmaid, produced two sons—Gad and Asher (Gen. 30:9–13)—and after Leah had borne two more sons and a daughter—Issachar, Zebulun, and Dinah (Gen. 30:17–21)—did Rachel finally conceive. She bore to Jacob a son named Joseph (Gen. 30:22–24), who became his father's favorite and who was sold into Egypt by his jealous brothers. Rachel died following the birth of her second son, whom she named Ben-Oni (son of my sorrow). But Jacob later renamed him Benjamin (son of the right hand). Jacob buried Rachel near Ephrath (or Bethlehem) and set a pillar on her grave (Gen. 35:16–20). Jews still regard Rachel's tomb with great respect. The traditional site is about 1 mile north of Bethlehem and about 4 miles south of Jerusalem.

Although Rachel was Jacob's favorite wife, the line of David and ultimately the messianic line passed through Leah and her son Judah, not Rachel. "Rachel weeping for her children" (Jer. 31:15; Rahel, KJV; Matt. 2:18) became symbolic of the sorrow and tragedy suffered by the Israelites. Matthew points out that the murder of all the male children in Bethlehem, from two years old and under, by Herod the Great, was the fulfillment of Jeremiah's prophecy (Matt. 2:16–18).

RAHAB [RAY hab] — a harlot of Jericho who hid two Hebrew spies, helping them to escape, and who became an ancestor of David and Jesus (Josh. 2:1–21; 6:17–25; Matt. 1:5). Rahab's house was on the city wall of Jericho. Rahab, who manufactured and dyed linen, secretly housed the two spies whom Joshua sent to explore Jericho and helped them escape by hiding them in stalks of flax on her roof (Josh. 2:6).

Rahab sent the king's messengers on a false trail, and then let the two spies down the outside wall by a rope through the window of her house (Josh. 2:15). When the Israelites captured Jericho, they spared the house with the scarlet cord in the window—a sign that a friend of God's people lived within. Rahab, therefore, along with her father, her mother, her brothers, and all her father's household, was spared. Apparently she and her family were later brought into the nation of Israel.

Matthew refers to Rahab as the wife of Salmon (Ruth 4:20–21; Matt. 1:4–5; Luke 3:32; Salma, 1 Chr. 2:11). Their son Boaz married Ruth and became the father of Obed, the grandfather of Jesse, and the great-grandfather of David. Thus, a Canaanite harlot became part of the lineage of King David out of which the Messiah came (Matt. 1:5; Rachab, KJV)—perhaps an early sign that God's grace and forgiveness is extended to all, that it is not limited by nationality or the nature of a person's sins.

The Scriptures do not tell us how Rahab, who came out of a culture where harlotry and idolatry were acceptable, recognized the Lord as the one true God. But her insights recorded in Joshua 2:9–11 leave no doubt that she did so. This Canaanite woman's declaration of faith led the writer of the Epistle to the Hebrews to cite Rahab as one of the heroes of faith (Heb. 11:31), while James commended her as an example of one who has been justified by works (James 2:25).

According to rabbinic tradition, Rahab was one of the four most beautiful women in the world and was the ancestor of eight prophets, including Jeremiah and the prophetess Huldah.

RAMAH [RAY mah] (*height*) — the name of six cities in the Old Testament:

1. Ramah of Benjamin, one of the cities allotted to the tribe of Benjamin (Josh. 18:25) in the vicinity of Bethel (Judg. 4:5) and Gibeah (Judg. 19:13). According to Judges 4:5, Deborah lived between Ramah and Bethel.

Shortly after the division of the nation of Israel into two kingdoms, King Baasha of Israel fortified Ramah against King

Asa of Judah (1 Kin. 15:16–17). Ramah lay on the border between the two kingdoms. The fortification was done to guard the road to Jerusalem so no one from the Northern Kingdom would attempt to go to Jerusalem to worship. Baasha was also afraid these people would want to live in the Southern Kingdom.

When Asa learned that Baasha was fortifying the city, he bribed the Syrians to invade the north (1 Kin. 15:18–21) so Baasha's attention would be turned away from Ramah. Meanwhile, Asa dismantled Ramah and used the stones to build two forts of his own nearby at Geba and Mizpah (1 Kin. 15:22; 2 Chr. 16:6).

When Nebuchadnezzar invaded Judah, he detained the Jewish captives, including Jeremiah, at Ramah (Jer. 40:1). The captives who were too old or weak to make the trip to Babylonia were slaughtered here. This was the primary fulfillment of the prophecy, "A voice was heard in Ramah, lamentation and bitter weeping, Rachel weeping for her children" (Jer. 31:15), although Matthew also applies it to Herod's slaughter of children after the birth of Christ (Matt. 2:18). This city also figures in the prophecies of Isaiah (10:29) and Hosea (5:8).

2. Ramah of Ephraim, the birthplace, home, and burial place of the prophet Samuel (1 Sam. 7:17; 19:18–23; 28:3). It is elsewhere referred to as Ramathaim Zophim (1 Sam. 1:1). The exact location of this Ramah is unknown.

It was at Ramah that the elders of Israel demanded a king (1 Sam. 8:4) and Saul first met Samuel (1 Sam. 9:6, 10). David sought refuge from Saul in Ramah as well (1 Sam. 19:18; 20:1). In New Testament times the name of this town was Arimathea.

3. Ramah of Naphtali, one of the fortified cities of Naphtali (Josh. 19:36). Ramah appears to have been in the mountainous country northwest of the Sea of Galilee. It is identified with Khirbet Zeitun er-Rama, about 3 kilometers (2 miles) southwest of the modern village of er-Rama.

4. Ramah of Asher, a town on the border of Asher (Josh. 19:29). Ramah is mentioned only once in the Bible and was

apparently near the seacoast. It has been identified both with er-Ramia, about 21 kilometers (13 miles) south of Tyre, and with an unknown site north of Tyre but south of Sidon.

5. Ramah of the South, a town of Simeon in the Negev (South country) of Judah (Josh. 19:8; Ramah in the Negev, NIV; Ramah of the Negeb, NRSV; Ramah of the Negev, NASB; Ramath-negeb, NEB; Ramath of the south, KJV). Joshua 19:8 identifies this town as Baalath Beer.

6. Ramah of Gilead (2 Kin. 8:29; 2 Chr. 22:6), elsewhere known as Ramoth Gilead. This was an important town on the Syrian border, about 40 kilometers (25 miles) east of the Jordan River. King Ahab was killed in a battle for this site after failing to heed the prophet Micaiah's warning (1 Kin. 22:1–40). Ahab's son Joram was wounded in a battle at Ramah (2 Kin. 8:28). Here too Jehu was anointed to succeed Joram as king of Israel (2 Kin. 9:1–13).

RAMOTH GILEAD [RAY muhth GIL ee uhd] (*heights of Gilead*) — an important fortified city in the territory of Gad near the border of Israel and Syria. It was approximately 40 kilometers (25 miles) east of the Jordan River. Ramoth Gilead was designated by Moses as one of the cities of refuge (Deut. 4:43; Josh. 20:8). In the time of Solomon, one of the king's 12 district officers was stationed at Ramoth Gilead to secure food for the king's household, since it was a commercial center.

Because of its strategic location near the border of Israel and Syria, Ramoth Gilead was frequently the scene of battles between the two nations. The Jewish historian Josephus says that the city was captured by King Omri from Ben-Hadad I. It then changed hands several times. King Ahab enlisted the aid of King Jehoshaphat to retake the city, but he was mortally wounded in the attempt (2 Chronicles 28–34). Ahab's son Joram was likewise wounded while attacking Ramoth Gilead (2 Kin. 8:28). While Jehu was maintaining possession of

Ramoth Gilead, Elisha sent his servant to anoint Jehu king of Israel (2 Kin. 9:1–13).

REBEKAH [ruh BEK uh] — the wife of Isaac and the mother of Esau and Jacob. The story of Rebekah (Genesis 24) begins when Abraham, advanced in age, instructs his chief servant to go to Mesopotamia and seek a bride for Isaac. Abraham insisted that Isaac marry a young woman from his own country and kindred, not a Canaanite.

When Abraham's servant arrived at Padan Aram, he brought his caravan to a well outside the city. At the well he asked the Lord for a sign that would let him know which young woman was to be Isaac's bride. When Rebekah came to the well carrying her water pitcher, she not only gave the servant a drink of water from her pitcher but she also offered to draw water for his camels. These actions were the signs for which the servant had prayed, and he knew that Rebekah was the young woman whom the Lord God had chosen for Isaac. When the servant asked Rebekah her name and the name of her family, he learned that she was the granddaughter of Nahor (Abraham's brother) and, therefore, was the grand-niece of Abraham. The servant then told Rebekah and her father the nature of his mission, and she chose to go to Canaan and become Isaac's wife. When a famine struck the land of Canaan, Isaac took Rebekah to Gerar, a city of the Philistines (Gen. 26:1–11). Fearful that Rebekah's beauty would lead the Philistines to kill him and seize his wife, he told them she was his sister. Abimelech, king of the Philistines, criticized Isaac for this deception. A similar story is told of Abraham and Sarah, who were scolded for their deception by Abimelech, king of Gerar (Gen. 20:1–18).

Nor was Rebekah above deception. When the time came for Isaac to give his birthright to Esau, she conspired with Jacob and tricked Isaac into giving it to Jacob instead. Jacob was forced to flee to Padan Aram to escape Esau's wrath. As a result of her scheming, Rebekah never again saw her son. Apparently she died while Jacob was in Mesopotamia. She was buried in the cave of Machpelah (Gen. 49:30–31), where Abraham, Isaac, Jacob, Sarah, and Leah were also buried.

Rebekah's name is spelled Rebecca in the New Testament (Rom. 9:10).

REHOB [REE hahb] (*open space*) — the name of three cities and two men in the Old Testament:

1. A city in northern Canaan in the upper Jordan River Valley (Num. 13:21). Rehob is the same place as Beth Rehob (Judg. 18:28; 2 Sam. 10:6).

2. A city in the territory of Asher, near Sidon (Josh. 19:28).

3. Another city in the territory of Asher (Josh. 19:30). The Israelites did not drive the Canaanites out of one of these Rehobs; the other Rehob was occupied by the Gershonite Levites.

4. The father of Hadadezer (2 Sam. 8:3–12), king of Zobah.

5. A Levite who sealed Nehemiah's covenant (Neh. 10:11).

REHOBOAM [ree uh BOE uhm] (*the people is enlarged*) — the son and successor of Solomon and the last king of the united monarchy and first king of the Southern Kingdom, Judah (reigned about 931–913 B.C.). His mother was Naamah, a woman of Ammon (1 Kin. 14:31).

Rehoboam became king at age 41 (1 Kin. 14:21) at a time when the northern tribes were discontented with the monarchy. They were weary of Solomon's heavy taxation and labor conscription. To promote unity, Rehoboam went to Shechem— center of much of the discontent among the northern tribes—to be made king officially and to meet with their leaders. They in turn demanded relief from the taxes and conscription.

Rehoboam first sought advice from older men who were of mature judgment and who had lived through Solomon's harsh years. They assured him that if he would be the people's servant, he would enjoy popular support. When he also sought the counsel of younger men, his arrogant contemporaries, he received foolish advice that he should rule by sternness rather than kindness. Misjudging the situation, he followed the foolish advice. The northern tribes immediately seceded from the kingdom and made Jeroboam king.

When Rehoboam attempted to continue his control over the northern tribes by sending Adoram to collect a tax from the people (1 Kin. 12:18), Adoram was stoned to death. Rehoboam fled in his chariot to Jerusalem. The prophet Shemaiah prevented Rehoboam from retaliating and engaging in civil war (1 Kin. 12:22–24).

To strengthen Judah, Rehoboam fortified 15 cities (2 Chr. 11:5–12) to the west and south of Jerusalem, undoubtedly as a defensive measure against Egypt. The spiritual life of Judah was strengthened, too, by the immigration of northern priests and Levites to Judah and Jerusalem because of the idolatrous worship instituted at Bethel and Dan by Jeroboam (2 Chr. 11:13–17).

Rehoboam's military encounters were primarily with Jeroboam and Egypt. No specific battles with Jeroboam are described in the Bible, but "there was war between Rehoboam and Jeroboam all their days" (1 Kin. 14:30). This warring probably involved border disputes over the territory of Benjamin, the buffer zone between the two kingdoms.

In Rehoboam's fifth year Judah was invaded by Shishak (Sheshonk I), king of Egypt, who came against Jerusalem and carried away treasures from the temple and from Solomon's house. When Shemaiah told him that this invasion was God's judgment for Judah's sin, Rehoboam humbled himself before God and was granted deliverance from further troubles (2 Chr. 12:1–12).

Rehoboam did not follow the pattern of David. Instead, he was an evil king (2 Chr. 12:14). During his 17-year reign, the people of Judah built "high places, sacred pillars, and wooden images" (1 Kin. 1:23) and permitted "perverted persons" to prosper in the land (1 Kin. 14:24). When he died, he was buried in the City of David (1 Kin. 14:31).

REHOBOTH [rih HOE buhth] (*broad places*) — a well dug by Isaac in the Valley of Gerar (Gen. 26:22). Rehoboth is probably present-day Wadi Ruheibeh, about 31 kilometers (19 miles) southwest of Beersheba.

REPHAIM [REF ih yuhm] — the name of a race of giants and a valley in the Old Testament:

1. A race of giants who lived in Palestine before the time of Abraham (Gen. 14:5; 15:20). The last survivor of the Rephaim was Og, king of Bashan (Deut. 3:11). The kingdom of Og—Gilead, Bashan, and Argob—was called "the land of the giants [Rephaim]" (Deut. 3:13).

2. A valley in Judah where David defeated the Philistines (2 Sam. 5:17–22). Rephaim lies between Jerusalem and Bethlehem (2 Sam. 23:13).

REPHIDIM [REF uh dim] — an Israelite encampment in the wilderness (Ex. 17:1–7). The Amalekites attacked the Israelites at Rephidim (Ex. 17:8–16). During the battle Moses stood on a hill and held the rod of God aloft. Aaron and Hur supported his arms until sundown, and the Israelites won the battle. Rephidim is probably the modern Wadi Feiran in south-central Sinai.

REUBEN [ROO ben] (*behold a son*) — the firstborn son of Jacob, born to Leah in Padan Aram (Gen. 29:31–32; 35:23). Leah named her first son Reuben because the Lord had looked upon her sorrow at being unloved by her husband. By presenting a son to Jacob, she hoped he would respond to her in love.

The only reference to Reuben's early childhood is his gathering of mandrakes for his mother (Gen. 30:14). Years later, as the hatred of Jacob's sons for Joseph grew, it was Reuben who advised his brothers not to kill their younger brother. He suggested that they merely bind him, which would have allowed him to return later to release Joseph to his father (Gen. 37:20–22). It also was Reuben who reminded his brothers that all their troubles and fears in Egypt were their just reward for mistreating Joseph (Gen. 42:22).

When Jacob's sons returned from Egypt, Reuben offered his own two sons as a guarantee that he would personally tend to the safety of Benjamin on the next trip to Egypt (Gen. 42:37). In view of these admirable qualities, it is tragic that he became involved in incest with Bilhah, his father's concubine (Gen. 35:22).

As the firstborn, Reuben should have been a leader to his brothers and should have received the birthright—the double portion of the inheritance (Deut. 21:17). His act of incest, however, cost him dearly. He never lost his legal standing as firstborn, but he forfeited his right to the birthright. When Reuben made his descent into Egypt with Israel, he was father of four sons who had been born to him in Canaan (Gen. 46:9).

REUEL [ROO uhl] (*friend of God*) — the name of four men in the Old Testament:

1. A son of Esau and Basemath, the daughter of Ishmael (Gen. 36:4, 10; 1 Chr. 1:35).

2. A priest of Midian who became Moses' father-in-law (Num. 10:29; Raguel, KJV). Reuel is also called Jethro (Ex. 3:1).

3. The father of Eliasaph (Num. 2:14), also called Deuel (Num. 10:20).

4. A son of Ibnijah (1 Chr. 9:8).

R HODES [roedz] (*a rose*) — a large island in the Aegean Sea off the southwest coast of Asia Minor visited by the apostle Paul (Acts 21:1). The island is about 68 kilometers (42 miles) long and about 24 kilometers (15 miles) wide; it lies about 19 kilometers (12 miles) off the coast of the province of Caria.

On the northeast corner of the island was the city of Rhodes, an important commercial, cultural, and tourist center for the Greeks as well as the Romans. At the entrance to the harbor of Rhodes stood the famous Colossus of Rhodes, a huge bronze statue of the sun-god Apollo built by the Greek sculptor Chares between 292 and 280 B.C. This towering statue was one of the seven wonders of the ancient world.

Because the island of Rhodes was on the natural shipping route from Greece to Syria and Palestine, the ship on which Paul traveled during his third missionary journey stopped at Rhodes (Acts 21:1). There is no evidence that Paul conducted any missionary activity on the island during his brief visit; he was in a hurry to get to Jerusalem for the Day of Pentecost. "For Paul had decided to sail past Ephesus" (Acts 20:16).

R UHAMAH [roo HAH muh] (*mercy is shown*) — a symbolic name given to Israel by the prophet Hosea to indicate the return of God's mercy (Hos. 2:1, KJV, NASB; mercy is shown, NKJV).

R UTH [rooth] (*friendship*) — the mother of Obed and great-grandmother of David. A woman of the country of Moab, Ruth married Mahlon, one of the two sons of Elimelech and Naomi. With his wife and sons, Elimelech had migrated to Moab to escape a famine in the land of Israel. When Elimelech and both of his sons died, they left three widows: Naomi, Ruth, and Orpah (Ruth's sister-in-law). When Naomi decided to return home to Bethlehem, Ruth chose to accompany her, saying, "Wherever you go, I will go" (Ruth 1:16).

In Bethlehem, Ruth was permitted to glean in the field of Boaz, a wealthy kinsman of Elimelech (Ruth 2:1). At Naomi's urging, Ruth asked protection of Boaz as next of kin—a reflection of the Hebrew law of Levirate marriage (Deut. 25:5–10). After a nearer kinsman waived his right to buy the family property and provide Elimelech an heir, Boaz married Ruth. Their son, Obed, was considered one of Naomi's family, according to the custom of the day.

Ruth's firm decision—"Your people shall be my people, and your God, my God" (Ruth 1:16)—brought a rich reward. She became an ancestor of David and Jesus (Matt. 1:5).

S

SALOME [suh LOE mee] (*peace*) — the name of two women in the New Testament:

1. The daughter of Herodias by her first husband, Herod Philip, a son of Herod the Great. The New Testament identifies her only as Herodias' daughter (Matt. 14:6–11; Mark 6:22–28). At the birthday celebration of Herod Antipas, who was now living with Herodias, Salome danced before the king and pleased him greatly. He offered to give her anything she wanted. At her mother's urging, Salome asked for John the Baptist's head on a platter. Salome later married her uncle Philip, tetrarch of Trachonitis (Luke 3:1), and then her cousin Aristobulus.

2. One of the women who witnessed the crucifixion of Jesus and who later brought spices to the tomb to anoint His body (Mark 15:40; 16:1). Salome apparently was the mother of James and John, two of the disciples of Jesus. She is pictured in the gospel of Matthew as asking special favors for her sons (Matt. 20:20–24). Jesus replied that Salome did not understand what kind of sacrifice would be required of her sons.

SALT, CITY OF — a city near the Dead Sea allotted to the tribe of Judah (Josh. 15:62; Irmelach, REB). Many scholars identify this city with Khirbet Qumran, about 13 kilometers

(8 miles) south of modern Jericho—a site made famous by the discovery of the Dead Sea Scrolls.

SALT SEA — an Old Testament name for the body of water at the southern end of the Jordan Valley (Gen. 14:3). It contains no marine life because of its heavy mineral content. The Salt Sea is also called the Sea of the Arabah (Deut. 3:17). Its modern name is the Dead Sea.

SALT, VALLEY OF — a barren valley, probably south of the Dead Sea, where the nation of Israel won two important victories over the Edomites. The army of King David killed 18,000 Edomites (2 Sam. 8:13; Syrians, KJV, NKJV; Arameans, NASB) in the Valley of Salt. Two centuries later the army of King Amaziah of Judah killed another 10,000 Edomites in this valley (2 Kin. 14:7).

SAMARIA, CITY OF [suh MAR ih uh] (*lookout*) — the capital city of the northern kingdom of Israel.
    Built about 880 B.C. by Omri, the sixth king of Israel (1 Kin. 16:24), Samaria occupied a 91-meter (300-foot) high hill about 68 kilometers (42 miles) north of Jerusalem and 40 kilometers (25 miles) east of the Mediterranean Sea. This hill was situated on the major north–south road through Palestine. It also commanded the east–west route to the Plain of Sharon and the Mediterranean Sea. Because of its hilltop location, Samaria could be defended easily. Its only weakness was that the nearest spring was a mile distant, but this difficulty was overcome by the use of cisterns.
    Samaria withstood an attack by Ben-Hadad, king of Syria (2 Kin. 6:24–25), but it finally fell to the Assyrians, in 722 B.C., and its inhabitants were carried into captivity. The city was repopulated by "people from Babylon, Cuthah, Ava, Hamath, and from Sepharvaim" (2 Kin. 17:24), all bringing their pagan

idolatries with them. Intermarriage of native Jews with these foreigners led to the mixed race of Samaritans so despised by full-blooded Jews during the time of Jesus (John 4:1–10).

In excavations of Samaria, archaeologists have uncovered several different levels of occupation by the Israelites. The first two levels, from the reigns of Omri and Ahab, show careful construction, apparently by Phoenician craftsmen. At this time, the city may have been 20 acres in extent, enclosed by an outer wall 6 to 8 meters (20 to 30 feet) thick, with a more narrow inner stone wall about 2 meters (5 feet) thick. A two-story palace was constructed at the higher western end of the hill around some courtyards. In one of these courtyards a pool about 5 by 9 meters (17 by 33 feet) was discovered. This may have been the pool where the blood of Ahab was washed from his chariot after he was killed in a battle against the Syrians (1 Kin. 22:38).

The palace was described as an "ivory house" (1 Kin. 22:39; Amos 3:15). Excavations near the pool uncovered a storeroom housing 500 plaques or fragments of ivory used for inlay work in walls and furniture.

The third level of the city, from the period of Jehu (about 841–813 B.C.), gave evidence of additions and reconstruction. Levels four to six covered the period of Jereboam II and showed that repairs had been made to Samaria before the Assyrians captured it in 722 B.C. From this period came several pieces of pottery inscribed with administrative records describing shipments of wine and oil to Samaria. One potsherd recorded the name of the treasury official who received the shipment, the place of origin, and the names of the peasants who had paid their taxes. Structures from the Greek period can still be seen in ruined form. A round tower is a magnificent monument of the Hellenistic age in Palestine. Roman remains include a colonnaded street leading from the west gate, an aqueduct, a stadium, and an impressive theater.

The small village of Sebastiyeh—an Arabic corruption of the Greco-Roman name Sebaste—now occupies part of the ancient site of this historic city. Even after the Israelite residents of Samaria were deported, the city continued to be inhabited by several different groups under the successive authority of Assyria, Babylonia, Persia, Greece, and Rome. Herod the Great, ruler in Palestine (ruled 37 B.C.–A.D. 4) when Jesus was born, made many improvements to Samaria and renamed it Sebaste— the Greek term for Augustus—in honor of the emperor of Rome. This Herodian city is probably the "city of Samaria" mentioned in the book of Acts (8:5).

SAMSON [SAM suhn] (*sunny*) — a hero of Israel known for his great physical strength as well as his moral weakness. The last of the "judges," or military leaders, mentioned in the book of Judges, Samson led his country in this capacity for about 20 years.

Samson lived in a dark period of Israelite history. After the generation of Joshua died out, the people of Israel fell into a lawless and faithless life. The author of the book of Judges summarized these times by declaring, "There was no king in Israel; everyone did what was right in his own eyes" (Judg. 17:6; 21:25). The standard of God's Word, His Law as handed down by Moses, was ignored.

Samson was a product of that age, but his parents gave evidence of faith in the Lord. During a time when the Philistines were oppressing the Israelites (Judg. 13:1), the Lord announced to Manoah and his wife that they would bear a son who would be raised as a Nazirite (Judg. 13:5, 7). This meant that Samson should serve as an example to Israel of commitment to God. Through most of his life, however, Samson fell far short of this mark.

Samson's mighty physical feats are well known. With his bare hands he killed a young lion that attacked him (Judg. 14:5–6).

He gathered 300 foxes (jackals; Judg. 15:4, REB) and tied them together, then sent them through the grain fields with torches in their tails to destroy the crops of the Philistines.

On one occasion, he broke the ropes with which the enemy had bound him (Judg. 15:14). He killed a thousand Philistine soldiers with the jawbone of a donkey (Judg. 15:15). And, finally, he carried away the massive gate of Gaza, a city of the Philistines, when they thought they had him trapped behind the city walls (Judg. 16:3).

But in spite of his great physical strength Samson was a foolish man. He took vengeance on those who used devious means to discover the answer to one of his riddles (Judg. 14). When deceived by his enemies, his only thought was for revenge, as when his father-in-law gave away his wife to another man (Judg. 15:6–7). He had not learned the word of the Lord, "Vengeance is mine" (Deut. 32:35).

Samson's life was marred by his weakness for pagan women. As soon as he became of age, he fell in love with one of the daughters of the Philistines. He insisted on marrying her, in spite of his parents' objection (Judg. 14:1–4).

This was against God's law, which forbade intermarriage of the Israelites among the women of Canaan. On another occasion he was almost captured by the Philistines while he was visiting a prostitute in the city of Gaza. Samson eventually became involved with Delilah, a woman from the Valley of Sorek (Judg. 16:4), who proved to be his undoing (Judges 16). The Philistines bribed her to find out the key to his strength. She teased him until he finally revealed that the secret was his uncut hair, allowed to grow long in accord with the Nazirite law. While Samson slept, she called the Philistines to cut his hair and turned him over to his enemies. Samson became weak, not only because his hair had been cut but also because the Lord had departed from him (Judg. 16:20).

After his enslavement by the Philistines, Samson was blinded and forced to work at grinding grain. Eventually he came to his senses and realized that God had given him his great strength to serve the Lord and his people. After a prayer to God for strength, he killed thousands of the enemy by pulling down the pillars of the temple of Dagon (Judg. 16:28–31). That one great act of faith cost Samson his life, but it won for him a place among the heroes of faith (Heb. 11:32). Out of weakness he was made strong by the power of the Lord (Heb. 11:34).

Samson was a person with great potential who fell short because of his sin and disobedience. Mighty in physical strength, he was weak in resisting temptation. His life is a clear warning against the dangers of self-indulgence and lack of discipline.

SAMUEL [SAM yoo uhl] (*name of God*) — the earliest of the great Hebrew prophets (after Moses) and the last judge of Israel. Samuel led his people against their Philistine oppressors. When he was an old man, Samuel anointed Saul as the first king of Israel and later anointed David as Saul's successor. Samuel is recognized as one of the greatest leaders of Israel (Jer. 15:1; Heb. 11:32).

Samuel's birth reveals the great faith of his mother, Hannah (1 Sam. 1:2–22; 2:1). Unable to bear children, she prayed earnestly for the Lord to give her a child. She vowed that if the Lord would give her a son she would raise him as a Nazirite (1 Sam. 1:11) and dedicate him to the Lord's service. Eventually, Samuel was born as an answer to Hannah's prayer.

Hannah made good on her promise to dedicate her son to the Lord's service. At a very early age, Samuel went to live with Eli the priest, who taught the boy the various duties of the priesthood. Here Samuel heard the voice of God, calling him to special service as a priest and prophet in Israel (1 Sam. 3:1–20). After Eli's death, Samuel became the judge of Israel in a ceremony at Mizpah (1 Samuel 7). This event was almost turned to disaster by an attack from the Philistines, but the Lord intervened with a storm that routed the enemies and established Samuel as God's man. The godly Samuel erected a memorial stone, which he called "Ebenezer," meaning "Stone of Help." "Thus far the LORD has helped us," he declared (1 Sam. 7:12).

In the early part of his ministry, Samuel served as a traveling judge. With his home in Ramah, he made a yearly circuit to Bethel, Gilgal, and Mizpah. In the person of Samuel, judges became more than military leaders called upon for dramatic leadership in times of national crises. Samuel became a judge with a permanent leadership office, an office approaching that of a king. When the people clamored for a king like those of the surrounding nations (1 Sam. 8:5), Samuel was reluctant to grant their request. He took this as a rejection of his long years of godly service on behalf of the people. He also was aware of the evils that went along with the establishment of a royal house. But the Lord helped Samuel to see the real issue: "Heed the voice of the people in all that they say to you; for they have not rejected you, but they have rejected Me, that I should not reign over them" (1 Sam. 8:7).

The person whom Samuel anointed as first king of Israel turned out to be a poor choice. Saul was handsome, likable, and tall. But he had a tragic flaw that led ultimately to his own ruin. He disobeyed God by taking spoils in a battle rather than wiping out all living things, as God had commanded (1 Sam. 15:18–26). Saul's false pride and extreme jealousy toward David also led him into some serious errors of judgment.

When God rejected Saul as king, He used Samuel to announce the prophetic words (1 Sam. 15:10–35). Samuel was faithful in presenting the stern words of rejection. Although he had no further dealings with Saul, Samuel mourned for him and for the death of the dream (1 Sam. 15:35). Samuel was then sent by the Lord to Bethlehem, to the house of Jesse, where he anointed the young man David as the rightful king over His people (1 Sam. 16:1–13).

In addition to his work as judge, prophet, and priest, Samuel is also known as the traditional author of the books of First and Second Samuel. He may have written much of the material contained in 1 Samuel during the early years of Saul's reign. After Samuel's death (1 Sam. 25:1), these books were completed by an unknown writer, perhaps Abiathar, the priest who served during David's administration.

When Samuel died, he was buried in his hometown of Ramah and was mourned by the nation (1 Sam. 25:1; 28:3). But he had one more message to give. After Samuel's death, Saul visited a fortune teller at En dor (1 Samuel 28). This fortune teller gave Saul a message that came from the spirit of Samuel: "The LORD has departed from you and has become your enemy" (1 Sam. 28:16). Even from the grave Samuel still spoke the word of God!

In many ways Samuel points forward to the person of the Savior, the Lord Jesus Christ. In the story of Samuel's birth, the direct hand of the Lord can be seen. In his ministry as judge, prophet, and priest, Samuel anticipates the ministry of the Lord as well as the work of his forerunner, John the Baptist. As Samuel marked out David as God's man, so John the Baptist pointed out Jesus as the Savior.

SARAH, SARAI [SAR uh, SAR eye] (*noble lady*) — the name of two women in the Bible:

1. The wife of Abraham, and the mother of Isaac. Sarah's name was originally Sarai, but it was changed to Sarah by God, much as her husband's name was changed from Abram to Abraham. Ten years younger than Abraham, Sarah was his half-sister; they had the same father but different mothers (Gen. 20:12).

Sarah was about 65 years old when she and Abraham left Haran (Gen. 12:5; 17:7). Passing through Egypt, Abraham introduced Sarah as his sister, apparently to keep himself from being killed by those who would be attracted by Sarah's beauty (Gen. 12:10–20; also see 20:1–18).

In spite of God's promise to Abraham that he would become the father of a chosen nation, Sarah remained barren. When she was 75, she decided that the only way to realize God's promise was to present to Abraham her Egyptian maidservant, Hagar, by whom he could father a child. Hagar bore a son named Ishmael (Gen. 16:1–16).

When Sarah was 90 years old, far beyond her childbearing years, she gave birth to a son, Isaac—the child of promise (Gen. 21:1–7). After Isaac was born, Sarah caught Ishmael mocking the young child and, with God's approval, sent both Ishmael and Hagar into the wilderness.

At the age of 127, Sarah died at Kirjath Arba (Hebron) and was buried by Abraham in the cave of Machpelah (Gen. 23:1–20). Sarah is the only woman in the Bible whose age was recorded at death—a sign of her great importance to the early Hebrews. The prophet Isaiah declared Abraham and Sarah as the father and mother of the Hebrew people: "Look to Abraham your father, and to Sarah who bore you" (Is. 51:2).

In the New Testament the apostle Paul pointed out that "the deadness of Sarah's womb" (Rom. 4:19) did not cause Abraham to waver in his faith; he believed the promise of God (Rom. 9:9). The apostle Peter cited Sarah as an example of the holy women who trusted in God, possessed inward spiritual beauty, and were submissive to their husbands (1 Pet. 3:5–6). The writer of the Epistle to the Hebrews also includes Sarah as one of the spiritual heroines in his roll call of the faithful (Heb. 11:11).

2. A daughter of Asher (Num. 26:46, KJV; Serah, NKJV, NIV).

SAUL [sawl] (*asked* [of God]) — the name of three men in the Bible:

1. The sixth of the ancient kings of Edom (Gen. 36:36–38; 1 Chr. 1:48–49).

2. The first king of Israel (1 Sam. 9:2–31:12; 1 Chr. 5:10–26:28). Saul lived in turbulent times. For many years, Israel had consisted of a loose organization of tribes without a single leader. In times of crisis, leaders had arisen; but there was no formal government. Samuel was Saul's predecessor as Israel's leader; but he was a religious leader, not a king. Threatened by the warlike Philistines, the people of Israel pressured Samuel to appoint a king to lead them in their battles against the enemy. Samuel gave in to their demands and anointed Saul as the first king of the nation of Israel.

Saul's Qualifications. Saul had several admirable qualities that made him fit to be king of Israel during this period in its history. He was a large man of attractive appearance, which led to his quick acceptance by the people. In addition, he was from the tribe of Benjamin, situated on the border between Ephraim and Judah. Thus, he appealed to both the northern and southern sections of Israel. Furthermore, he was a capable military leader, as shown by his victories early in his career.

One of the most important episodes of Saul's career was his first encounter with the Philistines. Saul took charge of 2,000 men at Michmash, leaving his son Jonathan with 1,000 men at Gibeah. After Jonathan made a successful, but unplanned, attack on a company of Philistines at Geba, the reaction of the Philistine forces drove the Israelites back to Gilgal. The Philistines gained control of central Canaan, and Saul's defeat seemed imminent. But Jonathan burst in unexpectedly upon the Philistines at Michmash, succeeding in starting a panic in their camp. Saul took advantage of this and routed the Philistines. This victory strengthened Saul's position as king.

Saul's Mistakes. Saul's first sin was his failure to wait for Samuel at Gilgal (1 Sam. 13:8–9). There he assumed the role of a priest by making a sacrifice to ask for God's blessing. His second sin followed soon afterward. After defeating Moab, Ammon, and Edom, Saul was told by Samuel to go to war against the Amalekites and to "kill both man and woman, infant and nursing child, ox and sheep, camel and donkey" (1 Sam. 15:3). Saul carried out his instructions well except that he spared the life of Agag, the king, and saved the best of the animals. When he returned, he lied and told Samuel that he had followed the instructions exactly.

Saul's disobedience in this case showed that he could not be trusted as an instrument of God's will. He desired to assert his own will instead. Although he was allowed to remain king for the rest of his life, the Spirit of the Lord departed from Saul. He was troubled by an evil spirit that brought bouts of madness. Meanwhile, Samuel went to Bethlehem to anoint David as the new king.

Saul and David. Saul's last years were tragic, clouded by periods of depression and gloom. David was brought into Saul's court to play soothing music to restore him to sanity. Saul was friendly toward David at first, but this changed as David's leadership abilities emerged. Enraged by jealousy, Saul tried to kill David several times. But David succeeded in eluding these attempts on his life for many years, often with the aid of Saul's son Jonathan and his daughter Michal.

Saul's Death. The closing years of Saul's life brought a decline in his service to his people and in his personal fortunes. Rather than consolidating his gains after his early victories, Saul wasted his time trying to kill David. Meanwhile, the Philistines sensed Israel's plight and came with a large army to attack the Hebrew nation. Saul's army was crushed, and three of his sons, including Jonathan, were killed. Wounded in the battle, Saul committed suicide by falling on his own sword.

An Appraisal of Saul. Saul is one of the most tragic figures in the Old Testament. He began his reign with great promise but ended it in shame. As Israel's first king, he had the opportunity to set the pattern for all future leaders. His weakness was his rebellious nature and his inability to adapt to the necessity of sharing power and popularity.

Saul also used his power to pursue unworthy purposes and wasted much time and energy in fruitless attempts on David's life. Commercial enterprises were not encouraged during his reign. As a result, the economic condition of the nation was not good. Saul also failed to unite the various tribes into one nation. Saul allowed the religious life of his people to deteriorate as well. However, he did provide distinct services to his people through his military actions. His victories paved the way for the brilliant career of his successor David.

3. The original name of Paul, a persecutor of the church, who became an apostle of Christ and a missionary of the early church (Acts 7:58–9:26; 11:25–13:9).

SEA, THE GREAT — another name for the Mediterranean Sea, a major body of water along the western coast of the land of Palestine (Josh. 15:47).

SECOND QUARTER, THE — a district of Jerusalem in which Huldah the prophetess lived (2 Kin. 22:14; Second District, NIV). This district lay in the angle formed by the west wall of the temple and the ancient wall of the city. It was later included within the wall restored by Nehemiah.

SEIR [SEE ur] (*hairy, rough*) — the name of two places and one person in the Old Testament:

1. The mountainous country stretching from the Dead Sea to the Red Sea, east of the gorge called the Arabah (Gen. 14:6).

The elevations of Seir range from 183 meters (600 feet) to 1,830 meters (6,000 feet).

Two of Seir's outstanding features are Mount Hor, where Aaron died (Num. 20:27–28), and the ancient city of rock, Petra or Sela (Is. 16:1). The region was named after a Horite (Hurrian) patriarch whose descendants settled in this area.

God gave this land to Esau and his descendants, who drove out the Horites, or Hurrians (Deut. 2:12). Esau and his descendants, the Edomites, lived in Seir (Deut. 2:29). This explains why God directed the people of Israel not to invade this territory when they moved from Egypt toward the promised land (Deut. 2:4–5).

Although Seir was originally the name of the mountain range in Edom, the name came to signify the entire territory of Edom south of the Dead Sea (2 Chr. 20:10). King David made these people his servants (2 Sam. 8:14).

Later, in the days of King Jehoshaphat of Judah, the people of Mount Seir (the Edomites) joined the Ammonites and the Moabites in an invasion against Judah (2 Chr. 20:10, 22–23). Later, the prophet Ezekiel predicted God's destruction of "Mount Seir" because of their strong hatred of Israel and their desire to possess the lands of Israel and Judah (Ezek. 35:1–15).

2. The grandfather of Hori, ancestor of the Horites (1 Chr. 1:39).

3. A mountain on the northern border of the territory of Judah (Josh. 15:10). Some have identified Seir with the rocky point near Chesalon on which the present-day village of Saris stands, about 19 kilometers (12 miles) west of Jerusalem.

SELA [SEE luh] (*rock, cliff*) — the name of three places in the Old Testament:

1. A fortress city, the capital of Edom, situated on the Wadi Musa ("the Valley of Moses") between the Dead Sea and the Gulf of Aqaba (2 Kin. 14:7; Selah, KJV). A rock formation about

1,160 meters (3,800 feet) above sea level, now known as Umm el-Bayyarah, the great acropolis of the Nabatean city of Petra dominates the site.

Sela was near Mount Hor, close to the Wilderness of Zin. Its name was changed to Joktheel by Amaziah, king of Judah, after he captured it (2 Kin. 14:7). Amaziah's men took 10,000 of the people of Seir (Edomites), "brought them to the top of the rock, and cast them down ... so that they all were dashed in pieces" (2 Chr. 25:12).

2. A place apparently in the territory of Judah near the boundary of the Amorites (Judg. 1:36; the rock, KJV). Some scholars believe the site was in Amorite territory.

3. An unidentified site in Moab mentioned by Isaiah in a prophecy of doom (Is. 16:1).

SELEUCIA [sih LOO shuh] — a seaport near Antioch of Syria from which Paul and Barnabas began their first missionary journey. Apparently they also landed at Seleucia when they returned to Antioch (Acts 14:26). Seleucia was an important Roman city because of its strategic location on the trade routes of the Mediterranean Sea.

SERGIUS PAULUS [SUR jee uhs PAW luhs] — the Roman proconsul, or governor, of Cyprus who was converted to Christianity when the apostle Paul visited that island on his first missionary journey, about A.D. 46 (Acts 13:7). Luke describes Sergius Paulus as an intelligent man. This Sergius Paulus may have been the same man as L. Sergius Paulus, a Roman official in charge of the Tiber during the reign of the emperor Claudius (ruled A.D. 41–54).

SETH [seth] (*appoint, compensate*) — the third son of Adam and Eve, born after Cain murdered Abel (Gen. 4:25–26;

5:3–8; Sheth, KJV). The father of Enosh (or Enos) and an ancestor of Jesus Christ (Luke 3:38), Seth died at the age of 912.

SHADRACH [SHAD rak] (*command of* [the god] *Aku*) — the name that Ashpenaz, the chief of Nebuchadnezzar's eunuchs, gave to Hananiah, one of the Jewish princes who was carried away to Babylon in 605 B.C. (Dan. 1:7; 3:12–30).

Shadrach was one of the three faithful Jews who refused to worship the golden image that King Nebuchadnezzar of Babylon set up (Dan. 3:1). Along with his two companions, Meshach and Abed-Nego, Shadrach was "cast into the midst of a burning fiery furnace" (Dan. 3:11, 21). But they were protected by a fourth "man" in the fire (Dan. 3:25), and they emerged without even the smell of fire upon them (Dan. 3:27).

SHAMGAR [SHAM gahr] — the third judge of Israel (Judg. 3:31) who delivered the nation from oppression by the Philistines. Using an ox goad as a weapon, Shamgar killed 600 Philistines who were terrorizing the main travel routes. Shamgar was a "son of Anath"—which may mean he was a resident of Beth Anath (Judg. 1:33), a fortified city in the territory of Naphtali.

SHARON [SHAR uhn] — the name of a plain and a district in the Old Testament:

1. The chief coastal plain of Palestine, running approximately 80 kilometers (50 miles) from south of the Carmel Mountain range to the vicinity of Joppa (1 Chr. 27:29). This lowland region was extremely fertile and was known for its agriculture (Is. 33:9).

In ancient times, an important caravan route ran along the Plain of Sharon, connecting Egypt, Mesopotamia, and Asia Minor. The flowers of Sharon (Is. 35:2), particularly the rose of Sharon (Song 2:1), were beautiful. Sharon is also called Lasharon (Josh. 12:18).

2. A district in Transjordan, the area east of the Jordan River, occupied by the tribe of Gad (1 Chr. 5:16).

SHEAR-JASHUB [shee ur JAY shuhb] (*a remnant shall return*) — a symbolic name given to a son of the prophet Isaiah in the days of King Ahaz of Judah (Is. 7:3). The name emphasized Isaiah's prophecy that a remnant of the nation would return to the land after their years of captivity in a foreign country (Is. 10:21–22).

SHEBA, QUEEN OF — a queen who came to visit King Solomon. She tested him with "hard questions" and found that Solomon's wisdom and prosperity exceeded his fame (1 Kin. 10:1–13). Some scholars believe she represented the region of Ethiopia, south of Egypt. But others insist she ruled among the tribes of southwestern Arabia. In the New Testament, Jesus referred to her as "the queen of the South," who "came from the ends of the earth to hear the wisdom of Solomon" (Matt. 12:42).

SHECHEM [SHEK uhm] (*shoulder*) — the name of a city and three men in the Bible:

1. An ancient fortified city in central Canaan and the first capital of the northern kingdom of Israel. Its name means "shoulder," probably because the city was built mainly on the slope, or shoulder, of Mount Ebal. Situated where main highways and ancient trade routes converged, Shechem was an important city long before the Israelites occupied Canaan. The city has been destroyed and rebuilt several times through the centuries.

Shechem is first mentioned in connection with Abraham's journey into the land of Canaan. When Abraham eventually came to Shechem, the Lord appeared to him and announced that this was the land He would give to Abraham's descendants (Gen. 12:6; Sichem, KJV). This fulfilled God's promise to Abraham at the time of his call (Gen. 12:1–3). In response, Abraham built his first altar to the Lord in Canaan at Shechem (Gen. 12:7). Because of this incident, Shechem is an important place in the religious history of the Hebrew people.

Upon his return from Padan Aram, Jacob, a grandson of Abraham, also built an altar to the Lord at Shechem (Gen. 33:18–20). This marked Jacob's safe return to the promised land from the land of self-imposed exile. According to Jewish tradition, Jacob dug a deep well here (John 4:12). Jacob's Well is one of the few sites visited by Jesus that is identifiable today.

After the Israelites conquered Canaan under the leadership of Joshua, an altar was built at Shechem. Its building was accompanied by a covenant ceremony in which offerings were given and the blessings and curses of the law were recited (Josh. 8:30–35). This was done in obedience to the command of Moses, given earlier in Deuteronomy 27:12–13. Because Shechem was situated between Mount Ebal and Mount Gerizim, this covenant ceremony took on a symbolic meaning. To this day Mount Gerizim is forested while Mount Ebal is barren. Thus the blessings of faithfully keeping the covenant were proclaimed from Mount Gerizim, while the curses of breaking the covenant were proclaimed from Mount Ebal.

At the close of his life, Joshua gathered the tribes of Israel at Shechem. Here he reviewed God's gracious dealings with Israel and performed a covenant-renewing ceremony on behalf of the nation. He closed his speech with his famous statement, "Choose for yourselves this day whom you will serve ... but as for me and my house, we will serve the Lord" (Josh. 24:15).

The significance of Shechem in Israel's history continued into the period of the Divided Kingdom. Rehoboam, successor to King Solomon, went to Shechem to be crowned king over all Israel (1 Kin. 12:1). Later, when the nation divided into two kingdoms, Shechem became the first capital of the northern kingdom of Israel (1 Kin. 12:25). Samaria eventually became the permanent political capital of the Northern Kingdom, but Shechem retained its religious importance. It apparently was a sanctuary for worship of God in Hosea's time in the eighth century B.C. (Hos. 6:9).

At Shechem (sometimes identified with Sychar) Jesus visited with the Samaritan woman at Jacob's Well (John 4). The Samaritans had built their temple on Mount Gerizim, where they practiced their form of religion. To this outcast woman of a despised sect Jesus offered salvation. This is a vivid example of the truth that the gospel of Christ is meant for all people.

2. A son of Hamor, a Hivite prince (Gen. 33:19; 34:1–31). Shechem raped Dinah, the daughter of Jacob. When Shechem later wanted to marry her, Dinah's half-brothers, Simeon and Levi, agreed to give Shechem permission only if "every male of you is circumcised" (Gen. 34:15). When Hamor, Shechem, and their followers agreed to the procedure, Simeon and Levi killed them before the circumcision operations had healed.

3. A son of Gilead and grandson of Manasseh (Num. 26:31; Josh. 17:2).

4. A son of Shemida, of the tribe of Manasseh (1 Chr. 7:19).

SHEM [shem] (*renown*) — the son of Noah and brother of Ham and Japheth. Shem was born after Noah became 500 years old (Gen. 5:32). He was one of eight people who entered Noah's ark and survived the Flood (Gen. 7:7, 13). Shem was married at the time of the Flood but had no children. After the Flood he became the father of Elam, Asshur, Arphaxad, Lud, and Aram (usually identified by scholars as Persia, Assyria, Chaldea, Lydia, and Syria, respectively). Thus Shem was the ancestor of the people of the ancient Near East generally, and the Hebrews specifically.

Shem died at the age of 600 (Gen. 11:10–11). He is listed by Luke as an ancestor of Jesus Christ (Luke 3:36; Sem, KJV).

SHESHACH [SHEE shak] — a code word for Babel, or Babylonia. The code operates according to the ancient Hebrew system known as atbash (the first letter of the Hebrew alphabet stands for the last, the second stands for the next to last, etc.). This code word was used by the prophet Jeremiah when he predicted the downfall of the Babylonian Empire (Jer. 25:26; 51:41).

SHILOH [SHIGH loe] — a city in the territory of Ephraim that served an Israelite religious center during the days before the establishment of the united kingdom. Shiloh was "north of Bethel, on the east side of the highway that goes up from Bethel to Shechem, and south of Lebonah" (Judg. 21:19). This pinpoints Khirbet Seilun, about 16 kilometers (10 miles) northeast of Bethel.

At Shiloh the tabernacle received its first permanent home, soon after the initial conquest of Canaan by the children of Israel (Josh. 18:1). This established Shiloh as the main sanctuary of worship for the Israelites during the period of the judges (Judg. 18:31). Here the last seven tribes received their allotments of land (Josh. 18:8–10).

Hannah prayed for a son at Shiloh (1 Sam. 1:3, 11). God granted her request by giving her Samuel. The tabernacle, with the ark of the covenant, was still located in Shiloh during Samuel's early years as priest and prophet (1 Sam. 1:9; 4:3–4). However the ark was captured by the Philistines because God had forsaken Shiloh as the center of worship (Ps. 78:60).

When the ark was returned to the Israelites by the Philistines, it was not returned to Shiloh (2 Sam. 6:2–17). Archaeologists have determined that Khirbet Seilun (Shiloh) was destroyed about 1050 B.C. After the ark was moved to another city, Shiloh gradually lost its importance. This loss was made complete when Jerusalem was established as capital of the kingdom. After the division of the kingdom, Jeroboam established worship centers at Dan and Bethel; but Ahijah, the prophet of the Lord, still remained at Shiloh (1 Kin. 14:2, 4). From here, Ahijah pronounced the doom of Jeroboam's rule (1 Kin. 14:7–16).

In the days of the prophet Jeremiah, Shiloh was in ruins (Jer. 7:12, 14), although some people continued to live on the site of this former city (Jer. 41:5). Shiloh became an inhabited town again in the days of the Greeks and Romans several centuries later.

SHULAMITE [SHOO lum ite] — a young woman mentioned in Song of Solomon 6:13 (Shulammite, NRSV, NIV, REB, NASB). Many scholars interpret Shulamite as Shunammite—a woman from the city of Shunem (1 Sam. 28:4).

Others believe this woman was Abishag, the lovely young Shunammite brought to David in his old age (1 Kin. 1:1–4, 15) and who later apparently was a part of Solomon's harem (1 Kin. 2:17–22).

SIHON [SIGH hun] — a king of the Amorites defeated by the Israelites during their journey toward the land of Canaan. Moses asked Sihon to let the Israelites pass peacefully through his kingdom, located east of the Jordan River. Sihon refused and later attacked the Israelites at Jahaz. In the battle that followed Sihon and his army were killed (Num. 21:21–32), and his territory was given to the tribes of Gad and Reuben (Num. 32:33). Sihon's defeat is mentioned often in the Old Testament (Deut. 1:4; Josh. 2:10; Ps. 135:11; Jer. 48:45).

SIMEON [SIM ih un] ([God] *hears*) — the name of four men in the Bible:

1. The second son of Jacob and Leah (Gen. 29:33). Simeon's descendants became one of the twelve tribes of Israel. He and his brother Levi tricked the Hivites of Shechem and massacred all the males because one of them had raped Dinah, their sister (Gen. 34:2, 25, 30). Simeon was the brother whom Joseph kept as security when he allowed his brothers to leave Egypt and return to their father, Jacob, in the land of Canaan (Gen. 42:24).

2. A devout Jew who blessed the infant Jesus in the temple (Luke 2:25, 34). The Holy Spirit had promised Simeon that he would not die until he had seen the long-awaited Messiah. Simeon recognized the child as the Messiah when Mary and Joseph brought him to the temple to present Him to the Lord.

3. An ancestor of Joseph listed in the genealogy of Jesus Christ (Luke 3:30).

4. A Christian prophet or teacher in the church at Antioch of Syria (Acts 13:1). Some scholars believe Simeon was the same person as Simon of Cyrene, who bore Jesus' cross (Luke 23:26).

SIMON [SIME un] ([God] *hears*) — the name of nine men in the New Testament:

1. Simon Peter, the Galilean fisherman who became an apostle of Christ (Matt. 4:18; 10:2). Simon was the son of Jonah (Matt. 16:17; John 21:15) and a brother of the apostle Andrew (John 1:40).

2. Another of the Twelve, called the Canaanite to distinguish him from Simon Peter. The name may also indicate he was a member of a fanatical Jewish sect, the Zealots (Matt. 10:4; Mark 3:18; Luke 6:15; Acts 1:13). Members of this group were fanatical opponents of Roman rule in Palestine. As a Zealot, Simon would have hated any foreign domination or interference.

3. One of Jesus' brothers (Matt. 13:55).

4. A former leper in whose house Mary, the sister of Lazarus, anointed Jesus' feet with a precious ointment (Matt. 26:6–13; Mark 14:3–9; John 12:1–8). Mary, Martha, and Lazarus were

present when this happened, and Martha took an active part in serving the dinner. This has led to speculation that Simon was a member of the family or at least was a very close friend.

5. A man of Cyrene who was forced to carry Jesus' cross (Matt. 27:32; Mark 15:21; Luke 23:26). Simon was the father of Alexander and Rufus, men who were known to the early Christians in Rome (Rom. 16:13).

6. A Pharisee in whose house Jesus ate (Luke 7:36–50). On that occasion a woman who was a sinner anointed Jesus' feet. Simon felt that Jesus should not have allowed her to come near Him. But Jesus explained that sinners like her were the very ones who needed forgiveness.

7. The father of Judas Iscariot (John 13:2). Both father and son are called Iscariot. The NRSV has "Judas the son of Simon Iscariot" (John 6:71; 13:26).

8. A sorcerer known as Simon Magus, or Simon the magician, who tried to buy spiritual powers from the apostle Peter (Acts 8:9–24). Simon's feats were so impressive that the people of Samaria declared, "This man is the great power of God" (Acts 8:10), and followed him. But when Philip the evangelist preached, the Samaritans believed and were baptized. Simon also believed and was baptized.

Later the apostles Peter and John visited Samaria to make sure these believers received the power of the Holy Spirit. When Simon saw that the Holy Spirit was bestowed by the laying on of hands, he attempted to buy this power. Peter rebuked him, "Your money perish with you, because you thought that the gift of God could be purchased with money! You have neither part nor portion in this matter, for your heart is not right in the sight of God" (Acts 8:20–21).

9. A tanner of Joppa and friend of the apostle Peter (Acts 9:43; 10:6, 17, 32).

SINAI [SIGH nih eye] — the name of a peninsula, a wilderness, and a mountain in the Bible. All three of these played a prominent role in the life of God's covenant people as they searched for the Land of Promise following their miraculous deliverance from enslavement in Egypt.

The Peninsula. Shaped like a triangle, the peninsula of Sinai is an area of great contrasts. It appears to hang from the southeast corner of the Mediterranean Sea with its base serving as the land bridge between Egypt and Israel. The peninsula is bounded on the west by the Gulf of Suez and on the east by the Gulf of Aqaba.

The Sinai peninsula is about 240 kilometers (150 miles) wide at the northern end and about 400 kilometers (250 miles) long. Its land area is desert and a tableland rising to about 762 meters (2,500 feet). On the north the Sinai plateau slopes away to the Mediterranean Sea. Near the south end of the peninsula a series of granite mountains rise 1,209 to 2,743 meters (4,000 to 9,000 feet) high, in striking contrast to the surrounding wastelands.

The Wilderness. Exodus 19:1 indicates that "in the third month after the children of Israel had gone out of the land of Egypt, on the same day, they came to the Wilderness of Sinai." This phrase may refer only to the particular desert that lies at the foot of Mount Sinai and in which the Israelites pitched their camp. But the phrase may also refer in a broader sense to the entire desert area of the Sinai Peninsula. If this is the case, it would include the Wilderness of Sin, through which the Israelites passed between Elim and Mount Sinai (Ex. 16:1); the Wilderness of Paran, in the central Sinaitic Peninsula (Num. 10:12); the Wilderness of Shur, east of Egypt in the northern Sinai (Gen. 16:7); and the Wilderness of Zin, close to the border of Canaan (Num. 13:21).

The Mountain. Perhaps the most frequent use of the word *Sinai* is in connection with the mountain. This was the mountain where God met Moses and gave him the law (Ex. 19:3, 20). This mountain is to be identified with Mount Horeb (Ex. 3:1), or perhaps Horeb refers to a mountain range or ridge and Sinai to an individual summit on that ridge. The name Sinai is used at the time when the Israelites were actually at the foot of the mountain (Ex. 19:11), whereas Horeb is used upon reflection about the events that happened here.

Although several mountains have been identified as possibilities, there are only two serious contenders for the title—Jebel Serbal (2,070 meters; 6,791 feet) in central Sinai and Jebel Musa (2,286 meters; about 7,500 feet) in southern Sinai. One of a cluster of three peaks, Jebel Musa, Arabic for "Mount Moses," has a broad plain at its base, where the Israelites may have camped.

Biblical References. After the Israelites left Egypt, they camped first in the Wilderness of Sin, then at Rephidim, and finally at Sinai. Moses climbed the mountain and received the tablets of the law from God. A stirring atmospheric disturbance accompanied God's meeting with the people (Ex. 19:18–19; 20:18).

During their years of wandering in the Sinai wilderness, the census was taken (Num. 1:1–46), the firstborn were redeemed (Num. 3:40–51), the office and duties of the Levites were established (Num. 4:1–49), and the first tabernacle was built (Num. 9:15).

SISERA [SIS uh rah] — the name of two men in the Old Testament:

1. The commander of the army of Jabin, king of Canaan. Deborah and Barak defeated Jabin's army under Sisera's command at the river Kishon. Sisera was later killed by a Kenite woman who drove a tent peg into his temple (Judg. 4:1–22).

2. One of the Nethinim who returned from the captivity with Zerubbabel (Neh. 7:55).

SODOM [SOD um] — a city at the southern end of the Dead Sea destroyed because of its wickedness (Gen. 10:19; Rom. 9:29). Together with her sister cities—Gomorrah, Admah, Zeboiim, and Zoar—Sodom formed the famous pentapolis of the plain or circle of the Jordan (Gen. 10:19; 13:10; 14:2) in the valley that surrounded the Dead Sea (Gen. 14:3).

Although Sodom was a notoriously wicked city, when Lot separated himself and his herdsmen from Abraham, he chose to pitch his tent toward Sodom (Gen. 13:5–13). This was because the fertile plain that surrounded the city "was well watered everywhere" (Gen. 13:10).

When Sodom was plundered by Chedorlaomer, the goods and captives he carried away had to be rescued by Abraham (Gen. 14:11, 21–24). However, the wickedness of the people of the city continued, and God finally had to destroy Sodom.

Fire and brimstone fell from heaven and consumed Sodom and Gomorrah and the other cities of the plain. When Lot's wife looked back at Sodom, she was instantly changed into a pillar of salt (Gen. 19:26).

Early tradition held that the northern end of the Dead Sea was the Valley of Sodom. But the geological conditions of the southern end of the Dead Sea matched those of the area around Sodom. Salt formations, asphalt, and sulfur are found in large quantities here. Many scholars believe the cities of the plain may be located beneath the shallow end of the Dead Sea. The basin surrounding the shallow southern end of the Dead Sea is fed by five streams, including the Wadi Zered (Num. 21:12), which would have provided for a fertile, well-watered plain. In addition, Zoar, one of the cities of the plain (Gen. 13:10), is reported by the Jewish historian Josephus to have been visible during his time at the southern end of the sea. Other scholars have recently claimed that the most likely site for the cities of the plain is on the eastern shore of the Dead Sea opposite Masada.

The sin, vice, and infamy of Sodom and the judgment of God on this city are referred to often throughout the Bible (Is. 1:9–10; Ezek. 16:46–49; Amos 4:11; Rom. 9:29).

SOLOMON [SAHL uh mun] (*peaceful*) — the builder of the temple in Jerusalem and the first king of Israel to trade commercial goods profitably to other nations; author of much of the book of Proverbs and perhaps also the author of the Song of Solomon and Ecclesiastes.

Solomon succeeded David, his father, as king of Israel. Solomon's rise met with widespread approval from the people, but David's officials were slow to accept the new king. They did warm up considerably, however, when they realized David was determined to anoint Solomon as his heir. Solomon became Israel's king because God had told David that Saul's heirs would not follow him to the throne. Thus, Solomon became king although there was no clear precedent for his succession. According to the chronology in 1 Kings 11:42, Solomon was about 20 years old when he was crowned. He assumed leadership of Israel at a time of great material and spiritual prosperity. During his 40-year reign (970–931 B.C.), he expanded his kingdom until it covered about 50,000 square miles—from Egypt in the south to Syria in the north to the borders of Mesopotamia in the east.

Great Beginnings. One of the first things Solomon did as king was to go to Gibeon to offer sacrifices to the Lord. God appeared to the new king at night and asked him, "What shall I give thee?" Solomon asked for an understanding heart to judge the people of Israel and the ability to tell good from evil. God not only granted Solomon's request but He also promised him riches and honor if he would walk in the steps of his father (1 Kin. 3:4–15).

Solomon organized Israel much as David had done, but he enlarged and expanded its government. He divided the country into 12 districts, each of which was responsible for providing the court with regular supplies one month out of the year, with a supply officer in charge of each district. As the years passed, Solomon's court reached a standard of luxury that had never existed in Israel's history.

Wisdom. Solomon is usually remembered as a wise man. His Proverbs and his Song of Songs demonstrate his deep knowledge of the natural world (plants, animals, etc.). He also had a profound knowledge of human nature, as demonstrated by the two women who claimed the same child. His suggestion that the child be physically divided between the two was a masterful strategy for finding out who was the real mother (1 Kin. 3:16–28). Solomon's concern with the ethics of everyday life is evident in his Proverbs. They show that Solomon loved wisdom and was always trying to teach it to others. They also indicate he was a keen observer who could learn from the mistakes of others.

Solomon's sayings in these Proverbs are so true that they sound almost trite today. Their clarity sometimes hides their depth. During his lifetime, Solomon's fame as a man of wisdom spread to surrounding lands, and leaders came from afar to hear him speak. When the queen of Sheba came to test his wisdom, he answered all her questions with ease. After she saw the extent of his empire and the vastness of his knowledge, she confessed that she had underestimated him (2 Chr. 9:1–12).

Solomon's Temple. One of Solomon's first major feats was the construction of the temple in Jerusalem as a place for worship of the God of Israel. The task was enormous, involving much planning and many workers. A work force of 30,000 was employed in cutting timber from the cedars of Lebanon. Also working on this massive project were 80,000 cutters of stone in the quarries of Jerusalem, 70,000 ordinary workers, and many superintendents. Gold, silver, and other precious metals were imported from other lands. Hiram, king of Tyre, sent architects and other craftsmen to assist with the project. The building was completed after seven years. The temple was famous not for its size—since it was relatively small—but for the quality of its elaborate workmanship (1 Kings 6–7).

After the temple was completed, Solomon planned an elaborate program of dedication. He invited the leaders of all twelve tribes to attend as he presided over the ceremony. The ark of the covenant was brought into the most sacred place in the temple as a cloud filled the room to hide God's presence. King Solomon then blessed the crowd, recounted the history of the building of the temple, and offered long prayers of dedication while standing at the altar. This reveals the admirable spirit of devotion in Solomon's heart. The dedication ceremony lasting seven days was followed by observance of the Feast of Tabernacles (1 Kings 8–9).

Immediately after the dedication, the Lord appeared to Solomon once again. He assured the king that his prayers had been heard and that the temple had been blessed. He also warned Solomon that the divine favor and protection that had been bestowed upon Israel would continue only if their faith remained uncorrupted by other beliefs. If idolatry should be introduced, Israel would be punished and the temple would be destroyed (1 Kin. 9:1–9).

Other Buildings. After completing the temple, Solomon built the palace complex, a series of five structures that took 13 years to complete. He also built many cities to assist the development of his trade empire. Among these were Tadmor (also called Palmyra) and Baalath (also called Baalbek) in Syria. To protect his kingdom, he built fortresses and lodgings for his army. These fortifications, especially the ones at Jerusalem, Gezer, Megiddo, and Hazor, had strong double walls and massive gateways.

Commercial Enterprises. Trade with other nations was another of Solomon's contributions to the nation of Israel.

The international situation was favorable for a strong leader to emerge in Israel; traditional centers of strength in Egypt and Syria were at an all-time low. Solomon entered into trade agreements with a number of nations, increasing Israel's wealth and prestige.

Although Solomon had a strong army, he relied upon a system of treaties with his neighbors to keep the peace. Egypt was allied with Israel through the marriage of Solomon to the daughter of the pharaoh. The seafaring cities of Tyre and Sidon were also united to Israel by trade agreements. Some of Israel's trade was conducted overland by way of camel caravans. But the most significant trade was by sea across the Mediterranean Sea through an alliance with Tyre. Solomon's ships apparently went as far west as Spain to bring back silver. Soon Solomon became the ruler of a huge commercial empire. Archaeologists believe that Solomon's trading may have brought him into conflict with the queen of Sheba. One purpose of her famous visit to Solomon may have been to establish trade agreements between Solomon's kingdom and her own nation (1 Kin. 10:1–13).

Solomon's Sins. Solomon's reign brought changes not only to Israel but also to his own life. Near the end of his life, the king lost the ideals of his youth, becoming restless and unsatisfied. The book of Ecclesiastes, proclaiming that "all is vanity" ("meaningless," NIV), supports the view that the world's wisest man had become a pathetic figure in his old age.

Solomon's greatest sin was his loss of devotion to the God of the Hebrew people. In this, he fell victim to his own trade agreements. By custom, beautiful women were awarded to the most powerful member of a treaty to seal the covenant. The constant influx of wives and concubines in Solomon's court led eventually to his downfall. Thus, Solomon broke the Mosaic law and violated the warning not to stray from the path of his father, David. The large number of foreign women in Solomon's court made many demands upon the king. He allowed these "outsiders" to practice their pagan religions. The result was that Jerusalem, and even its holy temple, was the scene of pagan practices and idol worship (1 Kin. 11:1–13).

Solomon's own faith was weakened. Eventually he approved of, and even participated in, these idolatrous acts. The example he set for the rest of the nation must have been demoralizing. This unfortunate error was a severe blow to the security of Solomon's throne and to the nation he had built.

The End of Solomon's Throne. Years before Solomon's death, his heavy taxation of the people brought unrest and rebellion. Surrounding nations began to marshal their forces to free themselves of Israel's tyranny, but the most serious uprising came from within the nation itself. When Solomon's son Rehoboam ascended the throne after his father, Jeroboam, a young leader who had been exiled to Egypt, returned to lead a successful civil war against him. The result was a division of Solomon's united kingdom into two separate nations—the southern kingdom of Judah and the northern kingdom of Israel.

Solomon's Character. In many ways, Solomon's 40-year reign as king of the Hebrew people is a puzzle. In his early years he was both noble and humble—undoubtedly one of the best rulers of his day. Although he was surrounded by wealth and luxury as a young man, he seemed to be a person of honor and integrity. He was the first king in Israel who was the son of a king. The glory of his empire was a reflection of his own royal tastes, which he satisfied through a shrewd and successful foreign policy.

Unfortunately, Solomon was not strong enough to withstand the temptations that go along with a long life of luxury. His contribution to the nation of Israel is figured largely in material terms. He made Jerusalem one of the most beautiful cities of the ancient world, and he will always be remembered as a great builder. The tragedy is that after the building of the temple, Solomon did very little to promote the religious life of his people.

SOSTHENES [SOS thuh knees] — the ruler of the synagogue at Corinth during the apostle Paul's first visit to this city (Acts 18:17). When the Roman ruler of the area refused to deal with the angry mob's charges against Paul, they beat Sosthenes. This may be the same Sosthenes as the one greeted by Paul in one of his Corinthian letters (1 Cor. 1:1). If so, he must have become a Christian some time after the mob scene in his city.

STEPHEN — one of the first seven deacons of the early church and the first Christian martyr. The story of Stephen is found in Acts 6:7–7:60.

In the period following Pentecost, the number of Christians in the New Testament church grew steadily. Followers were eventually recruited not only from among the Jews in Palestine but also from among the Jews in Greek settlements. The church had to appoint several men to handle the work of providing aid to these needy Christians.

Stephen was one of the first seven "good and worthy men" chosen to provide relief to these needy Christians from Greek backgrounds. Since Stephen is mentioned first in the list of the seven administrators, he was probably the most important leader in this group. Although they are not specifically named as deacons, these seven men are considered to be the forerunners of the office of deacon that developed later in the early church. Stephen assumed a place of prominence among these seven leaders as the church grew (Acts 6:7).

Stephen was probably critical of the system of Old Testament laws, claiming they had already lost their effectiveness because they had reached fulfillment in Christ. This viewpoint, which Stephen argued very skillfully, brought him into conflict with powerful leaders among the Jewish people. Stephen became well known as a preacher and a miracle-worker (Acts 6:8). His work was so effective that renewed persecution of the Christians broke out.

Members of certain Jewish synagogues felt that Stephen had blasphemed Moses and God. They accused him of being disloyal to the temple and rejecting Moses. He was also accused of hostility toward Judaism—a charge that had never been made before against other disciples. In debates the Jews were no match for Stephen; even Saul was outwitted by him. Thus, they resorted to force. Stephen was arrested and brought before the Sanhedrin, the Jewish council, where charges were placed against him. False witnesses testified against him. The high priest then asked Stephen if these things were true. Stephen was not dismayed. When he stood before them his face was "as the face of an angel" (Acts 6:15).

The lengthy speech Stephen made in his own defense is reported in detail in Acts 7:2–53. Stephen summarized Old Testament teachings, showing how God had guided Israel toward a specific goal. He reviewed Israel's history in such a way that he replied to all the charges made against him without actually denying anything. This amounted to a criticism of the Sanhedrin itself. Stephen denounced the council as "stiff-necked and uncircumcised in heart and ears" and accused them of resisting the Holy Spirit. Then he charged that they had killed Christ, just as their ancestors had killed the prophets. He accused them of failing to keep their own law (Acts 7:51–53).

Stephen's speech enraged the Sanhedrin so that they were "cut to the heart, and they gnashed at him with their teeth" (Acts 7:54). At this moment Stephen had a vision of God in heaven, with Jesus on His right hand. Stephen's fate was sealed when he reported this vision to his enemies. The crowd rushed upon him, dragged him out of the city, and stoned him to death (Acts 7:55–58).

Among the people consenting to Stephen's death that day was Saul, who later became the apostle Paul—great Christian missionary to the Gentiles. As he was being stoned, Stephen asked God not to charge his executioners with the sin of his death (Acts 7:59–60).

Stephen's martyrdom was followed by a general persecution that forced the disciples to flee from Jerusalem into the outlying areas. This scattering led to the preaching of the gospel first to the Samaritans and then to the Gentiles in the nations surrounding Palestine.

SYRO-PHOENICIAN [sigh row feh KNEE shun] — a Gentile woman whose daughter was healed by Jesus (Mark 7:26). She was from Phoenicia, a nation northeast of Palestine that had been incorporated into the Roman province of Syria— thus the term Syro-Phoenician. Although she was not a citizen of the Jewish nation, she believed Jesus could heal her daughter. Jesus commended her because of her great faith.

T

TAANACH [TAY uh nak] — an ancient royal city of the Canaanites whose king was conquered and slain by Joshua, but whose inhabitants were not driven out of the land (Josh. 12:21; Judg. 1:27). Tanaach was occupied by the tribe of Manasseh and was assigned to the Levites of the family of Kohath (Josh. 17:11–13; 21:25, Tanach, KJV). According to the Song of Deborah, the kings of Canaan fought against Deborah and Barak at Taanach, but they were defeated (Judg. 5:19).

The ruins of Taanach, Tell Taannek, are on the southwestern edge of the Valley of Jezreel about 8 kilometers (5 miles) southeast of Megiddo.

TAMAR [TAY mur] (*palm*) — the name of three women and a city in the Bible:

1. The widow of Er and Onan, sons of Judah (Gen. 38:6–30; Matt. 1:3; Thamar, KJV). According to the law of Levirate marriage, Judah's third son, Shelah, should have married Tamar; their first child would have been regarded as his brother's and would have carried on his name. However, Judah withheld his third son from marrying Tamar. Undaunted, Tamar disguised herself as a harlot and offered herself to Judah. Twin sons, Perez

and Zerah, were born of their union. Judah and Tamar became ancestors of Jesus through Perez (Matt. 1:3).

2. The lovely daughter of David by Maacah and sister of Absalom (2 Sam. 13:1–22, 32; 1 Chr. 3:9). Tamar was raped by her half-brother Amnon. She fled to Absalom, who plotted revenge. Two years later Absalom got his revenge for Tamar by arranging Amnon's murder.

3. Absalom's only surviving daughter, possibly named after his sister Tamar (2 Sam. 14:27).

4. A place southwest of the Dead Sea (Ezek. 47:19; 48:28).

TARSHISH [TAR shish] (*jasper*) — the name of a type of ship, a city or territory, a man, and a precious stone in the Old Testament:

1. The Hebrew name for a type of cargo ship fitted for long sea voyages (1 Kin. 10:22; Tharshish, KJV).

2. A city or territory in the western portion of the Mediterranean Sea with which the Phoenicians traded (2 Chr. 9:21; Ps. 72:10). Tarshish is believed by some to be Tartessus, in southern Spain, near Gibraltar. When Jonah fled from God's instruction to go to Nineveh, he boarded a ship bound for Tarshish, in the opposite direction from Nineveh (Jon. 1:3; 4:2). Tarshish was famous for its ships (Ps. 48:7; Is. 2:16), which carried gold, silver, iron, tin, lead, ivory, apes, and monkeys (1 Kin. 10:22; Jer. 10:9).

Because the ships of Tarshish carried such great riches, they became symbols of wealth, power, and pride. When God judged the nations for their sinful ways, He destroyed their "ships of Tarshish" to humble them and to demonstrate His great power (2 Chr. 20:35–37; Is. 2:16–17).

3. A high official at Shushan (Susa). He was one of seven princes of Persia and Media "who had access to the king's presence" (Esth. 1:14). Tarshish was one of those present at the royal

banquet of King Ahasuerus that Vashti, the queen, refused to attend.

4. The Hebrew name of a precious stone (Ex. 28:20; Ezek. 28:13). Its brilliant color is associated with the glorious appearance of God Himself (Ezek. 1:16; Dan. 10:6).

TARSUS [TAHR suss] — the birthplace of the apostle Paul (Acts 21:39; 22:3), formerly known as Saul of Tarsus (Acts 9:11). Tarsus was the chief city of Cilicia, a province of southeast Asia Minor. This important city was situated on the banks of the Cydnus River about 16 kilometers (10 miles) north of the shore of the Mediterranean Sea.

Because of its strategic location, protected on the north by the Taurus Mountains and open to navigation from the Mediterranean, the city of Tarsus was a prize location for the Hittites, Mycenean Greeks, Assyrians, Persians, Seleucids, and Romans. In the post-Roman period it dwindled to a small city in the wake of battles between various Christian and Muslim powers.

St. Paul's Gate at Tarsus. The chief city of Cilicia in eastern Asia Minor, Tarsus was the birthplace of the apostle Paul (Acts 21:39).

During the Seleucid period, however, Tarsus became a free city (about 170 B.C.), and was open to Greek culture and education. By the time of the Romans, Tarsus competed with Athens and Alexandria as the learning center of the world. "I am a Jew from Tarsus, in Cilicia," wrote the apostle Paul, "a citizen of no mean city" (Acts 21:39).

North of Tarsus were the famous Cilician Gates, a narrow gorge in the Taurus Mountains through which ran the only good trade route between Asia Minor and Syria. The location of Tarsus in a fertile valley brought great wealth to the city. The apostle Paul spent his early years at Tarsus (Acts 9:11; 21:39; 22:3) and revisited it after his conversion to Christianity (Acts 9:30; 11:25).

TEKOA [tuh KOE uh] (*trumpet blast*) — the birthplace of the prophet Amos. Situated in Judah (1 Chr. 2:24; 4:5), Tekoa is identified today with Khirbet Taqu'a, about 10 kilometers (6 miles) southeast of Bethlehem and about 16 kilometers (10 miles) south of Jerusalem. It was built on a hill in the wilderness of Tekoa toward En Gedi (2 Chr. 11:6; 20:20).

Tekoa is first mentioned in the Bible in connection with Joab employing a "wise woman" (2 Sam. 14:2) to bring reconciliation between David and Absalom (2 Sam. 14:2, 4, 9; Tekoah, KJV). Later Rehoboam, king of Judah (ruled 931–913 B.C.), fortified the site in order to prevent an invasion of Jerusalem from the south (2 Chr. 11:6).

Because of its elevation—about 850 meters (2,790 feet) above sea level—Tekoa became a station for warning Jerusalem of the approach of its enemies (Jer. 6:1). From Tekoa a person can see the Mount of Olives in Jerusalem and Mount Nebo beyond the Dead Sea. About 2 miles from Tekoa, Herod the Great (ruled 37–4 B.C.) built a fortress, the Herodium, in the Judean wilderness.

TERAH [TEE ruh] — the name of a man and a place in the Bible:

1. The father of Abraham and an ancestor of Christ (Gen. 11:26–27; Luke 3:34; Thara, KJV). Descended from Shem, Terah also was the father of Nahor and Haran. He lived at Ur of the Chaldeans most of his life; at Ur he worshiped the moon-god (Josh. 24:2). From Ur, Terah migrated with his son Abraham, his grandson Lot (Haran's son), and his daughter-in-law Sarah (Abraham's wife) to Haran, a city about 800 kilometers (500 miles) north of Ur and about 445 kilometers (275 miles)

northeast of Damascus. Terah died in Haran, another city where the moon-god was worshiped, at the age of 205 (Gen. 11:24–32).

2. An encampment of the Israelites in the wilderness (Num. 33:27–28; Tarah, KJV).

THADDAEUS [tha DEE uhs] — one of the twelve apostles of Jesus (Matt. 10:3; Mark 3:18; Thaddeus, KJV), also called Lebbaeus (Matt. 10:3) and Judas the son of James (Luke 6:16; Acts 1:13). He is carefully distinguished from Judas Iscariot (John 14:22). Nothing else is known about this most obscure of the apostles, but some scholars attribute the Epistle of Jude to him.

THEOPHILUS [thih AHF uh luhs] (*lover of God*) — a Christian to whom Luke dedicated the gospel of Luke and the book of Acts (Luke 1:3; Acts 1:1). The fact that Luke spoke of Theophilus as "most excellent" indicates that he was a prominent man of high rank and possibly a Roman. He may have chosen the name when he was converted to Christianity. According to tradition, both Luke and Theophilus were natives of Antioch in Syria. Much speculation surrounds Theophilus, but little is known for certain about him.

THESSALONICA [thes uh luh NIGH kuh] — a city in Macedonia visited by the apostle Paul (Acts 17:1, 11, 13; 27:2; Phil. 4:16). Situated on the Thermaic Gulf, Thessalonica was the chief seaport of Macedonia. The city was founded in about 315 B.C. by Cassander, who resettled the site with inhabitants from 26 villages that he had destroyed. He named the city after his wife, the sister of Alexander the Great and daughter of Philip II of Macedonia. The Egnatian Way, the main overland route from Rome to the East, ran directly through the city and can still be traced today.

Under Roman rule, Thessalonica achieved prominence. In 167 B.C. the Romans divided Macedonia into four districts, Thessalonica becoming capital of the second district. Some 20 years later Macedonia became a Roman province with Thessalonica as its capital. After the battle of Philippi in 42 B.C., when Octavian and Mark Antony defeated Brutus and Cassius, the assassins of Julius Caesar, Thessalonica became a free city. It was the most populous city of Macedonia.

In the third century A.D. Thessalonica was selected to oversee a Roman temple, and under Decius (ruled A.D. 249–251), infamous for his persecution of Christians, the city achieved the status of a Roman colony, which entitled it to the rights and privileges of the Roman Empire. The city was surrounded by a wall, stretches of which still stand. Archaeologists have uncovered a paved Roman forum some 63 by 99 meters (70 by 110 yards) in size, dating from the first or second centuries A.D. The apostle Paul visited Thessalonica in A.D. 49 or 50 during his second missionary journey (Acts 17:1–9). Paul's evangelistic efforts met with success. Within a short time a vigorous Christian congregation had blossomed, consisting of some members of the Jewish synagogue as well as former pagans.

The book of Acts leads some to assume that Paul stayed in Thessalonica only a few weeks before being forced to leave because of Jewish opposition. But in reality he probably stayed at least two or three months. A shorter stay would scarcely account for Paul's receiving two gifts of aid from the Philippians (Phil. 4:16), or for the depth of affection that developed between Paul and the Thessalonians (1 Thess. 2:1–12). Thessalonica was also the home of two of Paul's coworkers, Aristarchus and Secundus (Acts 20:4; 27:2).

THOMAS [TAHM uhs] (*twin*) — one of the twelve apostles of Jesus; also called *Didymus,* the Greek word for "twin" (Matt. 10:3; Mark 3:18; Luke 6:15). Thomas is probably best known for his inability to believe that Jesus had indeed risen from the dead. For that inability to believe, he forever earned the name "doubting Thomas."

Thomas was not present when Jesus first appeared to His disciples after His resurrection. Upon hearing of the appearance, Thomas said, "Unless I see in His hands the print of the nails, and put my finger into the print of the nails, and put my hand into His side, I will not believe" (John 20:25). Eight days later, Jesus appeared again to the disciples, including Thomas. When Jesus invited him to touch the nail prints and put his hand into His side, Thomas's response was, "My Lord and my God!" (John 20:28). Of that incident the great church father Augustine remarked, "He doubted so that we might believe."

Thomas appears three other times in the gospel of John. (Except for the listing of the disciples, Thomas does not appear in the other three Gospels.) When Jesus made known his intention to go into Judea, Thomas urged his fellow disciples, "Let us also go, that we may die with Him" (John 11:16). Knowing that His earthly life would soon end, Jesus said He was going to prepare a place for His followers and that they knew the way. Thomas asked, "Lord, we do not know where You are going, and how can we know the way?" (John 14:5). To that Jesus gave his well-known answer: "I am the way, the truth, and the life" (John 14:6).

After the resurrection, Thomas was on the Sea of Galilee with six other disciples when Jesus signaled to them from the shore and told them where to cast their net (John 21:2). Thomas was also with the other disciples in the Jerusalem Upper Room after the ascension of Jesus.

According to tradition, Thomas spread the gospel in Parthia and Persia, where he died. Later tradition places Thomas in India, where he was martyred. The Mar Thoma Church in India traces its origins to Thomas.

TIGRIS [TIE gris] — a major river of southwest Asia. Flowing about 1,850 kilometers (1,150 miles) from the Taurus Mountains of eastern Turkey, the Tigris joins the Euphrates River north of Basra. The Tigris and Euphrates flow roughly parallel to each other for hundreds of miles in the "Land of the Two Rivers," or Mesopotamia. The Tigris is identical with Hiddekel (Gen. 2:14, KJV, NKJV), one of the four branches of the river that flowed from the garden of Eden.

TIMOTHY [TIM uh thih] (*honored by God*) — Paul's friend and chief associate, who is mentioned as joint sender in six of Paul's epistles (2 Cor. 1:1; Phil. 1:1; Col. 1:1; 1 Thess. 1:1; 2 Thess. 1:1; Philem. 1).

Timothy first appears in the second missionary journey when Paul revisited Lystra (Acts 16:1–3). Timothy was the son of a Gentile father and a Jewish-Christian mother named Eunice, and the grandson of Lois (Acts 16:1; 2 Tim. 1:5). Timothy may have been converted under Paul's ministry, because the apostle refers to him as his "beloved and faithful son in the Lord" (1 Cor. 4:17) and as his "true son in the faith" (1 Tim. 1:2). Timothy was held in high regard in Lystra and Iconium, and Paul desired to take him along as a traveling companion (Acts 16:3).

Timothy played a prominent role in the remainder of the second missionary journey. When Paul was forced to leave Berea because of an uproar started by Jews from Thessalonica, Silas and Timothy were left behind to strengthen the work in Macedonia (Acts 17:14). After they rejoined Paul in Athens (Acts 18:5), Paul sent Timothy back to the believers in Thessalonica to establish them and to encourage them to maintain the faith (1 Thess. 3:1–9). Timothy's report of the faith and love of the Thessalonians greatly encouraged Paul.

During Paul's third missionary journey, Timothy was active in the evangelizing of Corinth, although he had little success. When news of disturbances at Corinth reached Paul at Ephesus, he sent Timothy, perhaps along with Erastus (Acts 19:22), to resolve the difficulties. The mission failed, perhaps because of fear on Timothy's part (1 Cor. 16:10–11). Paul then sent the more forceful Titus, who was able to calm the situation at Corinth (2 Cor. 7). Later in the third journey, Timothy is listed as one of the group that accompanied Paul along the coast of Asia Minor on his way to Jerusalem (Acts 20:4–5).

Timothy also appears as a companion of Paul during his imprisonment in Rome (Phil. 1:1; Col. 1:1; Philem. v. 1). From Rome, Paul sent Timothy to Philippi to bring back word of the congregation that had supported the apostle so faithfully over the years.

Timothy's strongest traits were his sensitivity, affection, and loyalty. Paul commends him to the Philippians, for example, as one of proven character, faithful to Paul like a son to a father, and without rival in his concern for the Philippians (Phil. 2:19–23; also 2 Tim. 1:4; 3:10). Paul's warnings, however, to "be strong" (2 Tim. 2:1) suggest that Timothy suffered from fearfulness (1 Cor. 16:10–11; 2 Tim. 1:7) and perhaps youthful lusts (2 Tim. 2:22). But in spite of his weaknesses, Paul was closer to Timothy than to any other associate.

Writing about A.D. 325, Eusebius reported that Timothy was the first bishop of Ephesus. In 356 Constantius transferred what was thought to be Timothy's remains from Ephesus to Constantinople (modern Istanbul) and buried them in the Church of the Apostles, which had been built by his father, Constantine.

TIRZAH [TUR zuh] — the name of a woman and a city in the Old Testament:

1. The youngest of the five daughters of Zelophehad (Num. 26:33; Josh. 17:3).

2. One of 31 ancient Canaanite cities west of the Jordan River conquered by Joshua (Josh. 12:24). Tirzah was the capital of the

northern kingdom of Israel from the time of Jeroboam I until the time of Omri (reigned 885–874 B.C.), who moved the capital to Samaria after reigning in Tirzah six years (1 Kin. 16:23).

TITUS [TIGH tuhs] — a "partner and fellow worker" (2 Cor. 8:23) of the apostle Paul. Although Titus is not mentioned in the book of Acts, Paul's letters reveal that he was the man of the hour at a number of key points in Paul's life.

Paul first mentions Titus in Galatians 2:1–3. As an uncircumcised Gentile, Titus accompanied Paul and Barnabas to Jerusalem as a living example of a great theological truth: Gentiles need not be circumcised in order to be saved.

Titus next appears in connection with Paul's mission to Corinth. While Paul was in Ephesus during his third missionary journey, he received disturbing news from the church at Corinth. After writing two letters and paying one visit to Corinth, Paul sent Titus to Corinth with a third letter (2 Cor. 7:6–9). When Titus failed to return with news of the situation, Paul left Ephesus and, with a troubled spirit (2 Cor. 7:5), traveled north to Troas (2 Cor. 2:12–13).

Finally, in Macedonia, Titus met the anxious apostle with the good news that the church at Corinth had repented. In relief and joy, Paul wrote yet another letter to Corinth (2 Corinthians), perhaps from Philippi, sending it again through Titus (2 Cor. 7:5–16). In addition, Titus was given responsibility for completing the collection for the poor of Jerusalem (2 Cor. 8:6, 16–24; 12:18).

Titus appears in another important role on the island of Crete (Titus 1:4). Beset by a rise in false teaching and declining morality, Titus was told by Paul to strengthen the churches by teaching sound doctrine and good works, and by appointing elders in every city (Titus 1:5). Paul then urged Titus to join him in Nicopolis (on the west coast of Greece) for winter (Titus

3:12). Not surprisingly, Titus was remembered in church tradition as the first bishop of Crete.

A final reference to Titus comes from 2 Timothy 4:10, where Paul remarks in passing that Titus has departed for mission work in Dalmatia (modern Croatia).

Titus was a man for the tough tasks. According to Paul, he was dependable (2 Cor. 8:17), reliable (2 Cor. 7:6), and diligent (2 Cor. 8:17); and he had a great capacity for human affection (2 Cor. 7:13–15). Possessing both strength and tact, Titus calmed a desperate situation on more than one occasion. He is a good model for Christians who are called to live out their witness in trying circumstances.

TOB [tahb] (*good*) — a land east of the Jordan River between Gilead and the Syrian desert. Jephthah fled to Tob from his half-brothers, who did not want him to share in their inheritance. And it was from Tob that Jephthah was called to lead the eastern tribes of Israel against the Ammonites (Judg. 11:3, 5).

TOPHET [TOE fet] — a place southeast of Jerusalem, in the Valley of Hinnom, where child sacrifices were offered and the dead bodies were buried or consumed (Is. 30:33; Jer. 7:31–32; 19:6, 11–14; Topheth, 2 Kin. 23:10). Chemosh, a Moabite god (1 Kin. 11:7, 33; 2 Kin. 23:13), and Molech, an Ammonite god (1 Kin. 11:7; 2 Kin. 23:10), were worshiped at Tophet through a practice despised by God—infant sacrifice (2 Kin. 16:3; Jer. 7:31; 19:5; 32:35).

Two kings of Judah—Ahaz, or Jehoahaz (2 Kin. 16:3), and Manasseh (2 Kin. 21:6)—made their own sons "pass through the fire." Godly King Josiah stopped this horrible practice (2 Kin. 23:10), possibly by dumping the garbage of Jerusalem at Tophet.

The prophet Isaiah used Tophet as a symbol of the death and destruction God would use as judgment against the king of Assyria (Is. 30:33). Jeremiah proclaimed that God's judgment would fall upon the people of Judah for sacrificing their infants to Baal (Jer. 19:5–6). The burial of slaughtered Judahites at this place would be so great, said Jeremiah, that the name Tophet would be changed to "Valley of Slaughter" (Jer. 7:31–32; 19:6). Jeremiah also announced that God would make Jerusalem itself a defiled place like Tophet because of the idolatry of the city (Jer. 19:6, 11–14).

TUBAL-CAIN [**too buhl KANE**] (*Tubal the smith*) — a son of Lamech and Zillah. Tubal-Cain was the "father" of all metalworkers (Gen. 4:22).

TYRE [**tire**] (*rock*) — an ancient seaport city of the Phoenicians situated north of Israel. Tyre was the principal seaport of the Phoenician coast, about 40 kilometers (25 miles) south of Sidon and 56 kilometers (35 miles) north of Carmel. It consisted of two cities: a rocky coastal city on the mainland and a small island city. The island city was just off the shore. The mainland city was on a coastal plain, a strip only 24 kilometers (15 miles) long and 3 kilometers (2 miles) wide.

Behind the plain of Tyre stood the rocky mountains of Lebanon. Tyre was easily defended because it had the sea on the west, the mountains on the east, and several other rocky cliffs (one the famous "Ladder of Tyre") around it, making it difficult to invade.

URIAH [you RYE uh] (*the Lord is my light*) — the name of three men in the Old Testament:

1. A Hittite married to Bathsheba. Uriah was one of David's mighty men (2 Sam. 11:3–26; 12:9–10, 15; 1 Kin. 15:5; Matt. 1:6; Urias, KJV).

Judging from the usual interpretation of his name and good conduct, Uriah was a worshiper of God. David's adultery with Uriah's wife, Bathsheba, occurred while Uriah was engaged in war at Rabbah, the Ammonite capital. Uriah was immediately recalled to Jerusalem to hide what had happened, but his sense of duty and loyalty only frustrated the king. Failing to use Uriah as a shield to cover his sin with Bathsheba, David ordered this valiant soldier to the front line of battle, where he was killed.

2. A priest, the son of Koz and father of Meremoth. Uriah helped rebuild the wall of Jerusalem under Nehemiah. He stood with Ezra the scribe as Ezra read the law and addressed the people (Ezra 8:33). The NKJV spells his name Urijah in Nehemiah 3:4, 21; 8:4.

3. A priest, one of two faithful witnesses to a scroll written by the prophet Isaiah (Is. 8:2).

UZZA, UZZAH [UHZ uh] (*strength*) — the name of five men in the Old Testament:

1. A man who was struck dead by God because he touched the ark of the covenant (2 Sam. 6:3–8; 1 Chr. 13:7–11).

2. A person in whose garden Manasseh, king of Judah, and Amon (Manasseh's son), also king of Judah, were buried (2 Kin. 21:18, 26).

3. A Levite of the family of Merari (1 Chr. 6:29).

4. A descendant of Ehud mentioned in the family tree of King Saul (1 Chr. 8:7).

5. An ancestor of a family of Nethinim (temple servants) who returned with Zerubbabel from the captivity (Ezra 2:49; Neh. 7:51).

UZZIAH [you ZIE uh] (*the Lord is my strength*) — the name of five men in the Old Testament:

1. The son of Amaziah and Jecholiah; ninth king of Judah and father of Jotham (2 Kin. 15:1–7; 2 Chr. 26). Uzziah is also called Azariah (2 Kin. 14:21; 15:1–7).

Uzziah ascended the throne at age 16 and reigned longer than any previous king of Judah or Israel—52 years. He probably co-reigned with his father and had his son Jotham as his co-regent during his final years as a leper. A wise, pious, and powerful king, he extended Judah's territory and brought the nation to a time of great prosperity. In the south he maintained control over Edom and rebuilt port facilities at Elath on the Gulf of Aqaba. To the west he warred against the Philistines, seizing several cities. He also apparently defeated and subdued the Ammonites. The foolishness of Uzziah's father, Amaziah, in fighting Joash, the king of Israel, had left the city of Jerusalem in a vulnerable position (2 Chr. 25:23). So Uzziah focused his attention on securing the defenses of both his capital and his country. He reinforced the towers of the city gates. On these towers and walls he placed huge catapults capable of shooting arrows and hurling stones at the enemy (2 Chr. 26:15). He also maintained a well-equipped army and fortified strategic places in the desert. His successes were directly related to his spiritual sensitivity, because he sought the Lord through a prophet who encouraged him to honor and obey God (2 Chr. 26:5).

However, Uzziah's heart was lifted up in pride. No longer satisfied to be a mortal king, he desired to be like some of his contemporaries—a divine king. He entered the temple to burn incense. When Azariah the high priest and 80 associates confronted him, he responded in anger instead of repentance. God judged him by striking him with leprosy. Uzziah was forced to live the rest of his life in a separate place, with his son Jotham probably acting as king. At Uzziah's death the prophet Isaiah had a transforming vision of the Lord, high and lifted up on a throne (Is. 1:1; 6:1–13; 7:1).

2. A Levite of the family of Kohath, Uzziah was the son of Uriel and the father of Shaul (1 Chr. 6:24).

3. The father of Jehonathan (1 Chr. 27:25). Jehonathan was an officer of David over the storehouses.

4. A priest commanded by Ezra to divorce his pagan wife (Ezra 10:21).

5. The father of Athaiah (Neh. 11:4).

VASHTI [VASH tie] — the beautiful queen of King Ahasuerus (Xerxes I, reigned 486–465 B.C.) who was banished from court for refusing the king's command to exhibit herself during a period of drunken feasting (Esth. 1:11). Her departure allowed Esther to become Ahasuerus's new queen and to be used as God's instrument in saving the Jewish people from destruction.

Z

ZACCHAEUS [zack KEY us] (*pure*) — a chief tax collector of Jericho who had grown rich by overtaxing the people. When Jesus visited Jericho, Zacchaeus climbed a tree in order to see Jesus (Luke 19:3). Jesus asked him to come down and then went to visit Zacchaeus as a guest. As a result of Jesus' visit, Zacchaeus became a follower of the Lord, repented of his sins, and made restitution for his wrongdoing. He gave half of his goods to the poor and restored fourfold those whom he had cheated. In associating with people like Zacchaeus, Jesus showed that He came to call sinners to repentance.

The mound of New Testament Jericho, the home of Zacchaeus the tax collector who became a disciple of Jesus (Luke 19:1–10).

ZACHARIAS [zack ah RYE us] (*the Lord has remembered*) — the name of two men in the New Testament:

1. The prophet whom the Jews "murdered between the temple and the altar" (Matt. 23:35, KJV) because he rebuked them for breaking God's commandments (Luke 11:51, KJV). This may be a reference to Zechariah, who was stoned to death in the court of the house of the Lord (2 Chr. 24:20–22).

2. The father of John the Baptist (Luke 1:13; 3:2). Zacharias was a priest of the division of Abijah. His wife, Elizabeth, was one "of the daughters of Aaron" (Luke 1:5), meaning she also was of priestly descent.

ZADOK [ZAY dock] (*just, righteous*) — the name of several men in the Bible:

1. A high priest in the time of David. Zadok was a son of Ahitub (2 Sam. 8:17) and a descendant of Aaron through Eleazar (1 Chr. 24:3). During David's reign he served jointly as high priest with Abiathar (2 Sam. 8:17).

Both Zadok and Abiathar fled from Jerusalem with David when the King's son Absalom attempted to take over the throne. They brought the ark of the covenant out with them. After Absalom had been killed, David asked Zadok and Abiathar to urge the people to recall David to the throne (2 Sam. 19:11).

When David was dying, another of his sons, Adonijah, tried to take the throne. This time only Zadok remained faithful to the king. When David heard of the plot, he ordered Zadok and the prophet Nathan to anoint Solomon king (1 Kin. 1:7–8, 32–45).

Consequently, Abiathar was deposed and Zadok held the high priesthood alone (1 Kin. 2:26–27). In this way the high priesthood was restored to the line of Eleazar, son of Aaron.

2. The grandfather of Jotham, king of Judah (2 Kin. 15:33; 2 Chr. 27:1).

3. A high priest in Solomon's temple (1 Chr. 6:12; 9:11).

4. A valiant warrior who joined David's army at Hebron (1 Chr. 12:28).

5. A son of Baana who helped repair part of the Jerusalem wall after the captivity (Neh. 3:4). He may be the same person as No. 7.

6. A son of Immer who helped repair Jerusalem's wall (Neh. 3:29). He may be the same person as No. 9.

7. An Israelite who sealed the covenant with Nehemiah (Neh. 10:21). He may be the same person as No. 5.

8. A son of Meraioth (Neh. 11:11).

9. A scribe in the time of Nehemiah (Neh. 13:13). Zadok was appointed a treasurer over the storehouse.

10. An ancestor of Jesus (Matt. 1:14; Sadoc, KJV).

ZEBADIAH [zebb ah DIE ah] (*the Lord has given*) — the name of nine men in the Old Testament:

1. A Benjamite, one of the sons of Beriah (1 Chr. 8:15).

2. A Benjamite, one of the sons of Elpaal (1 Chr. 8:17).

3. A son of Jeroham of Gedor (1 Chr. 12:7). With his brother, Zebadiah joined David at Ziklag.

4. A gatekeeper of the sanctuary in David's time (1 Chr. 26:2).

5. A captain of the fourth division of David's army (1 Chr. 27:7). Zebadiah took command of this division after Asahel was killed by Abner.

6. A leader sent by King Jehoshaphat to teach the law in the cities of Judah (2 Chr. 17:7–8).

7. A son of Ishmael in the time of King Jehoshaphat (2 Chr. 19:11).

8. A son of Michael who returned with Ezra from the captivity (Ezra 8:8).

9. A priest of the house of Immer (Ezra 10:20) who divorced his foreign wife.

ZEBEDEE [ZEBB uh dee] (*gift* [of the Lord]) — the father of James and John (Matt. 4:21–22; Mark 1:19–20). Apparently Zebedee's wife was named Salome (Matt. 20:20; Mark 15:40). He was a fisherman on the Sea of Galilee, perhaps living in Capernaum or Bethsaida. Zebedee was probably wealthy since he had "hired servants" (Mark 1:20). In later references to

Zebedee, he appears in the phrase "sons [or son] of Zebedee" (Matt. 10:2; Mark 10:35; Luke 5:10; John 21:2).

ZEBOIIM [zeh BOY yim] — one of the five cities of the plain in the Valley of Siddim destroyed along with Sodom and Gomorrah (Gen. 10:19; 14:2). The prophet Hosea used Admah and Zeboiim (Hos. 11:8; Zeboim, KJV) as examples of God's judgment on wicked cities. Many scholars believe Zeboiim was situated near the southern end of the Dead Sea in an area presently covered by water. Others believe it was located near the eastern shore of the Dead Sea.

ZEBULUN [ZEBB you lun] — the name of a man and a territory in the Old Testament:

1. The tenth of Jacob's 12 sons; the sixth and last son of Leah (Gen. 30:19–20; 35:23; 1 Chr. 2:1). Zebulun had three sons: Sered, Elon, and Jahleel (Gen. 46:14; Num. 26:26–27). These are the only details about Zebulun that appear in the Bible.

2. The territory in which the tribe of Zebulun lived. The land allotted to Zebulun after the conquest of Canaan was bounded by Issachar and Manasseh on the south, by Asher on the west, and by Naphtali on the north and east (Josh. 19:10–16, 27, 34). Zebulun was fertile. It included part of the mountainous area of lower Galilee and the northwest corner of the fertile Plain of Esdraelon (Valley of Jezreel).

ZECHARIAH [zeck ah RIE a] (*the Lord remembers*) — the name of about 31 men in the Bible:

1. The fifteenth king of Israel (2 Kin. 14:29; 15:8, 11; Zachariah, KJV), the last of the house of Jehu. The son of Jeroboam II, Zechariah became king when his father died. He reigned only six months (about 753/52 B.C.) before being assassinated by Shallum.

2. The father of Abi or Abijah, mother of Hezekiah (2 Kin. 18:2; Zachariah, KJV; 2 Chr. 29:1).

3. A chief of the tribe of Reuben (1 Chr. 5:7).

4. A son of Meshelemiah (1 Chr. 9:21; 26:2, 14) and a Levite doorkeeper in the days of David.

5. A son of Jeiel, of the tribe of Benjamin (1 Chr. 9:37), also called Zecher (1 Chr. 8:31).

6. A Levite musician in the days of David (1 Chr. 15:18).

7. A priest and musician in the days of David (1 Chr. 15:24).

8. A descendant of Levi through Kohath (1 Chr. 24:25).

9. A descendant of Levi through Merari (1 Chr. 26:11).

10. A Manassite of Gilead and the father of Iddo (1 Chr. 27:21).

11. A leader sent by King Jehoshaphat to teach the people of Judah (2 Chr. 17:7).

12. The father of Jahaziel, a Levite who encouraged Jehoshaphat against Moab (2 Chr. 20:14).

13. A son of King Jehoshaphat (2 Chr. 21:2).

14. A son of Jehoiada (2 Chr. 24:20). This Zechariah was stoned to death at the command of Joash, king of Judah (v. 21).

15. A prophet in the days of Uzziah, king of Judah (2 Chr. 26:5).

16. A Levite who helped cleanse the temple during the reign of King Hezekiah of Judah (2 Chr. 29:13).

17. A Levite who supervised temple repairs during Josiah's reign (2 Chr. 34:12).

18. A prince of Judah in the days of Josiah (2 Chr. 35:8).

19. A prophet in the days of Ezra (Ezra 5:1; 6:14; Zech. 1:1, 7; 7:1, 8) and author of the book of Zechariah. A leader in the restoration of the nation of Israel following the captivity, Zechariah was a contemporary of the prophet Haggai, the governor Zerubbabel, and the high priest Joshua. Zechariah himself was an important person during the period of the restoration of the community of Israel in the land of Palestine after the captivity.

The book of Zechariah begins with a note concerning the prophet. He is named as a grandson of Iddo, one of the heads of the priestly families who returned with Zerubbabel from Babylon (Zech. 1:1, 7; also Ezra 5:1; 6:14). This means that Zechariah himself was probably a priest and that his prophetic activity was in close association with the religious center of the nation. His vision of Joshua the high priest (Zech. 3:1–5) takes on added importance, since he served as a priest in association with Joshua. Zechariah began his ministry while still a young man (Zech. 2:4) in 520 B.C., two months after Haggai completed the prophecies that are recorded in the book of Haggai.

20. A leader of the Jews who returned to Palestine with Ezra after the captivity (Ezra 8:3).

21. A son of Bebai who returned with Ezra from the captivity (Ezra 8:11).

22. A leader of Israel after the captivity (Ezra 8:16). He may be the same person as No. 20 or No. 21.

23. An Israelite who divorced his pagan wife after the return from the captivity (Ezra 10:26).

24. A man who stood with Ezra at the public reading of the law (Neh. 8:4).

25. A descendant of Perez, of the tribe of Judah (Neh. 11:4).

26. A person whose descendants lived in Jerusalem after the captivity (Neh. 11:5).

27. A priest descended from Pashhur (Neh. 11:12).

28. A Levite who led a group of musicians at the dedication of the rebuilt wall of Jerusalem (Neh. 12:35–36).

29. A priest who took part in the dedication ceremony for the rebuilt wall of Jerusalem (Neh. 12:41).

30. A son of Jeberechiah (Is. 8:2) and a witness who recorded a prophecy given to Isaiah.

31. A prophet whom the Jews stoned (Matt. 23:35; Luke 11:51). He may be the same as No. 14.

ZEDEKIAH [zedd eh KIE ah] (*the Lord my righteousness*) — the name of five men in the Old Testament:

1. A false prophet, son of Chenaanah, who advised King Ahab of Israel to attack the Syrian army at Ramoth Gilead (1 Kin. 22:11). Zedekiah's flattery and unfounded optimism proved to be lies; the king was mortally wounded in the battle.

2. The last king of Judah (597–586 B.C.). The son of Josiah, Zedekiah was successor to Jehoiachin as king (2 Kin. 24:17–20; 25:1–7; 2 Chr. 36:10–13). After Jehoiachin had reigned only three months, he was deposed and carried off to Babylonia. Nebuchadnezzar installed Zedekiah on the throne as a puppet king and made him swear an oath that he would remain loyal (2 Chr. 36:13; Ezek. 17:13). Zedekiah's original name was Mattaniah, but Nebuchadnezzar renamed him to demonstrate his authority over him and his ownership of him (2 Kin. 24:17). Although Zedekiah reigned in Jerusalem for 11 years, he was never fully accepted as their king by the people of Judah.

Because Zedekiah was a weak and indecisive ruler, he faced constant political unrest. Almost from the first he appeared restless about his oath of loyalty to Babylon, although he reaffirmed that commitment in the fourth year of this reign (Jer. 51:59). However, he was under constant pressure from his advisors to revolt and look to Egypt for help. A new coalition composed of Edom, Moab, Ammon, and Phoenicia was forming against Babylonia and they urged Judah to join (Jer. 27:3). Adding to the general unrest was the message of false prophets who declared that the yoke of Babylon had been broken (Jeremiah 28).

In his ninth year Zedekiah revolted against Babylonia. King Nebuchadnezzar invaded Judah and besieged Jerusalem. While Jerusalem was under siege, other Judean cities were falling to the Babylonians (Jer. 34:7).

The final months of the siege were desperate times for Zedekiah and the inhabitants of Jerusalem. The king made frequent calls on the prophet Jeremiah, seeking an encouraging word from the Lord. Jeremiah's message consistently offered only one alternative: Surrender to Nebuchadnezzar in order to live in peace and save Jerusalem. To his credit, Zedekiah was not arrogant and heartless (Jer. 36:22–23). But he regarded God's prophetic word superstitiously and "did not humble himself before Jeremiah the prophet, who spoke from the mouth of the Lord" (2 Chr. 36:12).

In 586 B.C. the wall of Jerusalem was breached, and Zedekiah fled the city. The army of the Babylonians pursued the king, overtaking him in the plains of Jericho. He was brought before Nebuchadnezzar and forced to watch the slaying of his sons. Then his own eyes were put out and he was led away to Babylonia (2 Kin. 25:6–7). Zedekiah died during the years of the captivity of the Jewish people in Babylon. His reign marked the end of the nation of Judah as an independent, self-governing country.

3. A prominent Jewish official who sealed the covenant with Nehemiah after returning from the captivity (Neh. 10:1; Zidkijah, KJV).

4. A false prophet denounced by the prophet Jeremiah (Jer. 29:21).

5. A prince of Judah, son of Hananiah, in the days of the prophet Jeremiah and Jehoiakim, king of Judah (Jer. 36:12).

ZERUBBABEL [zeh RUB uh buhl] (*offspring of Babylon*) — head of the tribe of Judah at the time of the return from the Babylonian captivity; prime builder of the second temple.

Zerubbabel is a shadowy figure who emerges as the political and spiritual head of the tribe of Judah at the time of the Babylonian captivity. Zerubbabel led the first group of captives back to Jerusalem and set about rebuilding the temple on the old site. For some 20 years he was closely associated with prophets, priests, and kings until the new temple was dedicated and the Jewish sacrificial system was reestablished. As a child of the captivity, Zerubbabel's name literally means "offspring of Babylon." He was the son of Shealtiel or Salathiel (Ezra 3:2, 8; Hag. 1:1; Matt. 1:12) and the grandson of Jehoiachin, the captive king of Judah (1 Chr. 3:17). Zerubbabel was probably Shealtiel's adopted or Levirate son (1 Chr. 3:19). Whatever his blood relationship to King Jehoiachin, Zerubbabel was Jehoiachin's legal successor and heir.

A descendant of David, Zerubbabel was in the direct line of the ancestry of Jesus (Matt. 1:12; Luke 3:27). Zerubbabel apparently attained considerable status with his captors while living in Babylon. During the early reign of Darius, he was recognized as a "prince of Judah" (Ezra 1:8). Zerubbabel was probably in the king's service since he had been appointed by the Persians as governor of Judah (Hag. 1:1).

With the blessings of Cyrus (Ezra 1:1–2), Zerubbabel and Jeshua the high priest led the first band of captives back to Jerusalem (Ezra 2:2). They also returned the gold and silver vessels that Nebuchadnezzar had removed from the ill-fated temple (Ezra 1:11). Almost immediately they set up an altar for burnt offerings, kept the Feast of Tabernacles, and took steps to rebuild the temple (Ezra 3:2–3, 8).

After rebuilding the temple foundation the first two years, construction came to a standstill for 17 years. This delay came principally because of opposition from settlers in Samaria who wanted to help with the building (Ezra 4:1–2). When the offer was refused because of the Samaritans' association with heathen worship, the Samaritans disrupted the building project (Ezra 4:4). Counselors were hired who misrepresented the captives in court (Ezra 4:5), causing the Persian king to withdraw his support (Ezra 4:21). The delay in building also was due to the preoccupation of Zerubbabel and other captives with building houses for themselves (Hag. 1:2–4).

Urged by the prophets Haggai and Zechariah (Ezra 5:1–2), Zerubbabel diligently resumed work on the temple in the second year of the reign of Darius Hystaspes of Persia (Hag. 1:14). This renewed effort to build the temple was a model of cooperation involving the captives, the prophets, and Persian kings (Ezra 6:14). Zerubbabel received considerable grants of money and materials from Persia (Ezra 6:5) and continuing encouragement from the prophets Haggai and Zechariah (Ezra 5:2).

The temple was finished in four years (516/515 B.C.) and dedicated with great pomp and rejoicing (Ezra 6:16). The celebration was climaxed with the observance of the Passover (Ezra 6:19). If there was a discordant note, it likely came from older Jews who had earlier wept because the new temple lacked the splendor of Solomon's temple (Ezra 3:12).

For some mysterious reason, Zerubbabel is not mentioned in connection with the temple dedication. Neither is he mentioned after this time. Perhaps he died or retired from public life upon completion of the temple. His influence was so great, however, that historians designate the second temple as "Zerubbabel's Temple."

God was apparently pleased with Zerubbabel's role in bringing the captives home and reestablishing temple worship (Ezra 3:10). On God's instructions, Haggai promised Zerubbabel a special blessing: "I will take you, Zerubbabel My servant, the son of Shealtiel, says the Lord, and will make you as a signet ring; for I have chosen you" (Hag. 2:23).

ZILPAH [ZILL pah] — the mother of Gad and Asher (Gen. 30:9–13; 35:26). Zilpah was one of the female slaves of Laban, the father of Leah and Rachel. When Leah married Jacob, Laban gave her Zilpah to serve as her maid (Gen. 29:24; 46:18). Later, Leah gave Zilpah to Jacob as a concubine (Gen. 30:9).

ZIMRI [ZIMM rye] ([God is] *my protection*) — the name of four men and a tribe or district in the Old Testament:

1. A son of Salu, a Simeonite prince (Num. 25:14). In an outrageous move, Zimri brought a Midianite woman, Cozbi, into the camp while Israel was repenting for having worshiped Baal. When Phinehas, the son of Eleazar, saw Zimri take her to his tent, he was enraged, took a javelin in his hand, went into Zimri's tent, and thrust both of them through.

2. The fifth king of Israel (1 Kin. 16:8–20). Before he became king, Zimri was a servant of King Elah and commander of half of his chariots. One day, Zimri killed the drunken Elah and proclaimed himself king. When Omri, the commander of Elah's army, heard about the assassination, he abandoned the siege of Gibbethon and besieged Tirzah, the capital city. When Zimri saw that the city was taken, he "burned the king's house down upon himself" (1 Kin. 16:18). Zimri's reign lasted only seven days (1 Kin. 16:15).

3. The oldest of the five sons of Zerah (1 Chr. 2:6).

4. A Benjamite, son of Jehoaddah (1 Chr. 8:36) or Jarah (1 Chr. 9:42). Zimri was a descendant of King Saul and of King Saul's son, Jonathan.

5. An unknown place or people (Jer. 25:25).

ZIN [zihn] — a wilderness through which the Israelites passed on their journey to Canaan (Num. 13:21; 20:1). The Wilderness of Zin stretched along the extreme southern limits of the promised land (Num. 13:21).

ZION [ZIE un] — the city of David and the city of God. The designation of Zion underwent a distinct progression in its usage throughout the Bible.

The first mention of Zion in the Bible is in 2 Samuel 5:7: "David took the stronghold of Zion (that is, the City of David)." Zion, therefore, was the name of the ancient Jebusite fortress situated on the southeast hill of Jerusalem at the junction of the Kidron Valley and the Tyropoeon Valley. The name came to stand not only for the fortress but also for the hill on which the fortress stood. After David captured "the stronghold of Zion" by defeating the Jebusites, he called Zion "the City of David" (1 Kin. 8:1; 1 Chr. 11:5; 2 Chr. 5:2).

When Solomon built the temple on Mount Moriah (a hill distinct and separate from Mount Zion), and moved the ark of the covenant there, the word *Zion* expanded in meaning to include also the temple and the temple area (Pss. 2:6; 48:2, 11–12; 132:13). It was only a short step until Zion was used as a name for the city of Jerusalem, the land of Judah, and the people of Israel as a whole (Is. 40:9; Jer. 31:12). The prophet Zechariah spoke of the sons of Zion (Zech. 9:13). By this time the word *Zion* had come to mean the entire nation of Israel.

The most important use of the word *Zion* is in a religious or theological sense. Zion is used figuratively of Israel as the people of God (Is. 60:14). The spiritual meaning of Zion is continued in the New Testament, where it is given the Christian meaning of God's spiritual kingdom, the church of God, the heavenly Jerusalem (Heb. 12:22; Rev. 14:1; Sion, KJV).

ZIPPOR [ZIP or] (*bird, sparrow*) — the father of Balak (Num. 22:2; Josh. 24:9). Balak was the king of Moab who hired Balaam the soothsayer (Josh. 13:22) to curse Israel.

ZIPPORAH [zip POE rah] (*female bird*) — a daughter of Jethro, priest of Midian, and wife of Moses (Ex. 2:21–22; 4:25; 18:2–4). Their sons were Gershom and Eliezer. When the Lord sought to kill Moses because Eliezer had not been circumcised, Zipporah grabbed a sharp stone and immediately circumcised the child. She and the two sons must have returned to Jethro rather than continuing on to Egypt with Moses, because she is not mentioned again until after the Exodus. Along with Jethro, she and her two sons visited Moses in the wilderness after the Hebrew people left Egypt (Ex. 18:1–5).

ZIZ, ASCENT OF [zihz] — a steep ascent in a pass that runs from the western shore of the Dead Sea, at a point slightly north of En Gedi, into the Wilderness of Judah, toward Tekoa. Through the ascent of Ziz (2 Chr. 20:16) the allied forces of Ammon, Moab, and Mount Seir made their journey from En Gedi to attack the army of Jehoshaphat, king of Judah.

ZOAN [ZOE ann] — an ancient city in Egypt that dates back to the time of Abraham. Built seven years after Hebron (Num. 13:22), Zoan has often been identified with one of the royal cities in northern Egypt. The Greek translation of the Old Testament identified Zoan with Tanis, a city that is sometimes associated with an ancient capital of Egypt, Ramses (Ex. 1:11). Now many scholars identify Ramses with Qantir, while Zoan is probably the nearby San el-Hagar.

ZOAR [ZOE ahr] (*little*) — an ancient city apparently situated on the eastern shore of the Dead Sea (Gen. 13:10), and also known as Bela (Gen. 14:2, 8). It was one of five city-states in the area, each with its own king.

Zoar figures prominently in the story of Lot and the destruction of the wicked "cities of the plain" (Gen. 13:12; 19:29). Warned to flee to the mountains, Lot sought further mercy by asking to go instead to Zoar. His reasoning was that Zoar is only a "little" city (hence its name). His request was granted and Zoar was spared, while the four other cities (Sodom, Gomorrah, Admah, and Zeboiim) were destroyed (Gen. 19:22–23, 30).

Many scholars believe the site of Zoar to be es-Safi, at the foot of the mountains of Moab, about 7 kilometers (4.5 miles) up the river Zered from where it empties into the Dead Sea.

ZOPHAR [ZOE fer] — the third of the "friends" of Job to speak. He is called a Naamathite (Job 2:11; 11:1; 20:1; 42:9), indicating he was from Naamah, in northern Arabia. Zophar's two discourses are found in Job 11:1–20 and 20:1–29. He accused Job of wickedness and hypocrisy, urged Job to turn from his rebellion, and charged that God was punishing Job far less than his sins deserved (Job 11:6).